MITCHELL BEAZLEY
WINE GUIDES

WINES OF
ITALY

MICHÈLE SHAH

Wines of Italy
by Michèle Shah

Edited and designed by Mitchell Beazley, an imprint of Octopus Publishing
Group Ltd, 2–4 Heron Quays, London E14 4JP

First published in 1983 as *The Mitchell Beazley Pocket Guide to Italian Wines*.
Revised, expanded and updated editions 1988, 1992, 1998, 2000, 2002, 2004

This edition first published in 2006 as *Mitchell Beazley Wine Guides: Wines of
Italy* by Michèle Shah

A CIP catalogue record of this book is available from the British Library.

ISBN 13: 978 184533 215 0
ISBN 10: 1 84533 215 6

The author and publishers will be grateful for any information which will
assist them in keeping future editions up to date. Although all reasonable
care has been taken in the preparation of this book, neither the publishers
nor the author can accept responsibility for any consequences arising from
the use thereof or from the information contained therein.

Commissioning Editors: Hilary Lumsden, Susanna Forbes
Senior Editor: Julie Sheppard
Editors: Sylvia and David Tombesi-Walton
Editorial assistance: Philippa Bell
Cover Design: Gaelle Lochner
Index: Hilary Bird
Production: Faizah Malik

Printed and bound in China

Contents

Introduction

In wine terms, Italy is a champion of diversity. A person could spend a lifetime exploring its vineyards and still not taste everything. The aim of this compact volume is to single out the wines and winemakers that really count, along with promising emerging estates.

Over the past two decades, the world of Italian wine has become filled with optimism: new estates have been created, new wines have been produced, and money has been invested in emerging areas, as well as in the improvement of existing products. This has created a buoyant scene, light years away from the image of the prolific supplier of light-hearted, bargain-priced wines that typified the country until the early 1980s. Various factors have contributed to this remarkable improvement in quality. The new generation of winemakers have combined know-how with technical innovation, clonal research, and vineyard management. The most striking developments have been seen in the Asti and Roero zones in Piedmont, long tired of playing second fiddle to the renowned production of nearby Alba. In the Maremma in southern Tuscany, large amounts of potential vineyard land has been bought by producers from the region's more famous zones and elsewhere. Southern Italian regions, such as Sicily and Puglia, are today considered dynamic, forward regions, able to relate quality to quantity and maintain low prices and produce delicious, fruit-forward wines.

Yet this surge of enthusiasm calls for restraint. International varieties such as Chardonnay, Cabernet Sauvignon, Merlot, Syrah, and Sauvignon Blanc have staked an important place in Italian vineyards, and even more significant achievements have come from the many native varieties that yield wines of distinct taste, personality, and style. Blends of the two have created some fascinating wines of great class, but the sheer number of international plus indigenous combinations seems endless. While no one can blame Italy's winemakers for wanting to exploit such possibilities to the full, the country may simply be producing too many wines.

Italy's weather, despite common preconceptions, is anything but stable, and there are often significant variations from vintage to vintage (which this guide indicates). However, producers are now well equipped to coax their grapes to ripeness and are far bolder at eliminating imperfect grapes. It is therefore becoming ever more the case that a "poor" vintage will result in a reduction in the quantity of wines produced rather than lower quality.

Italy's classified wines are designated DOC (*denominazione di origine controllata*) or DOCG (*denominazione di origine controllata e garantita*). This might refer to the wine-growing hectares of an entire region or to only a few selected vineyards. The number of DOC(G) wines continues to rise, but only a minority of Italy's total production is classed in these (mostly) cream-of-the-crop categories. Today, ever more producers of high-quality wine in Italy prefer to market some, or all, of their range under the more liberal "lesser" IGT (*indicazione geografica tipica*) designation, which allows a number of grape varieties grown within the area of production.

This volume may serve as a tour guide providing outline maps of key regions, travel tips, and suggested hotels, country lodgings, restaurants and *trattorias* to help visitors discover the intricacies and delights of Italian wine and its wine country at first hand. For consumers abroad, it is designed to be used as a buyer's guide, compact enough to take along to a shop or restaurant, or as a quick reference in determining a top vintage.

How to Read an Entry

Key to Symbols

r	red
p	rosé
w	white
mc	*metodo classico* (for bottle-fermented sparkling wine)
sw	sweet
fz	*frizzante*
sp	sparkling
m	Moscato, which is sweet and *pétillant*
liq	*liquoroso*
pas	*passito*
ris	*riserva*
sup	*superiore*
cl	*classico*
nov	*novello*
vs	*vin santo*
vt	*vendemmia tardiva (late-harvest)*

☆	everyday wine
☆☆	above average
☆☆☆	superior in its category
☆☆☆☆	outstanding

* An asterisk indicates that the estate produces good-value wine in its class

IGT	wine typical of its geographical indication
DOC	name and origin controlled
DOCG	name and origin controlled and guaranteed
Age: 1 year etc.	ageing required under DOCG
96, 99, etc.	recommended vintages

Prices in the restaurant sections are given with a € symbol:
€ = up to €30; €€ = €30–€50; €€€ = €50–€100
Prices in the hotel sections are also given with a € symbol:
€ = up to €100; €€ = €100–€200; €€€ = €200–€300

Entries

The main wines and producers are dealt with in separate chapters that cover all twenty regions in a geographical sequence moving from north to south. Each chapter begins with a listing and a brief description of the region's classified wines designated under the DOCG appellation zones or sub-zones. Where relevant, the ageing required under DOCG is also noted. For DOC appellations, we have listed the relevant grape varieties, as well as special designations such as *riserva, superiore, classico*, or *novello*, along with the basic *rosso, rosato*, and *bianco*. Additional information is given if the DOC allows for sparkling, *frizzante, dolce*, or *vendemmia tardiva*. Vintage dates (97, 98, etc.) emphasize the good to exceptional vintages. Vintage information for some regions is, as pertinent, more detailed than for other regions and is assessed on the ageing potential of the wine.

Under Producers, the estates are listed alphabetically, giving locations by town and province. The symbols that follow relate to the types of wine produced (white, red, sparkling, etc.); a star system (one to four stars) rates the quality of the range; and an asterisk symbolizes that the estate also produces good-value wines. The presence of vintage years (90, 95, etc.) indicates the top vintages for the top wines. These normally refer to important reds that show good to excellent ageing potential, such as Brunello di Montalcino, Chianti Classico Riserva, and Nobile Riserva for Tuscany; Barolo and Barbaresco for Piedmont; Amarone for Valpolicella; Sagrantino for Umbria; and Aglianico for Basilicata and Campania. Vintage recommendations for wines that require long ageing may include recent harvests that won't be released until later – for example, Barolo 2004 may not be sold before 2008. A brief description of the estate follows, outlining the number of hectares under vine and the number of bottles produced.

The selected estates and wines, as well as the ratings, are personal assessments weighed against the opinions of other experts. Vintage assessments are always somewhat arbitrary. Wines from some vintages age better than wines from others, and some producers make good wines even in off years. Irrespective of what the charts say, personal taste is the best determinant of when a wine is at its prime.

Italy has thousands of registered wine-bottlers (currently 810,000), including many emerging estates and winemakers, so inevitably some worthy names will not have been included. Some Italian wines sold abroad are labelled with the bottler's, shipper's, or importer's brand name – names that are used only in the countries where the wines are sold. Most such wines, however qualified, are not considered here. The focus is on wines with origins that are verifiable in Italy.

The information under Wine & Food at the end of each chapter is meant to aid travellers in Italy, with a brief description of typical regional foods. The accommodation options include impressive historic buildings as well as simple bed-and-breakfast lodgings. The same philosophy goes for the selection of eateries – from renowned restaurants offering eclectic Italian cuisine with well-stocked wine cellars, to simple, characteristic *trattorias* where the traveller can taste regional recipes accompanied by local wines.

Anatomy of Italian Wine

Over the past quarter of a century, Italy's wine industry has undergone a radical transformation, with the rise of a new class of premium wines, both red and white, as well as the development of highly attractive light and bubbly styles for popular consumption. The main changes have come from the best class of Italy's traditional wines – the classic reds of Piedmont and Tuscany, and the elegant whites of Friuli – and from the expansion of quality wines on the Tuscan coast, the southern regions, and the islands of Sicily and Sardinia. With almost 350 indigenous vines in cultivation, Italy is in a position to offer the consumer something different and exciting, as well as having the potential to reverse the growing trend of wine globalization. The other side of the coin is that such a variety of wines does not assist effective marketing and can be confusing to the consumer.

In the 1990s, Italy produced an average of some fifty-eight million hectolitres a year – about a fifth of the world's wine. Yet, after the record crops of the early 1980s that contributed to what was known as Europe's "wine lake", production has diminished to an average of forty-five to fifty million hectolitres per year. In order to drain the "wine lake", the European Union (EU) required distillation of wine into alcohol, banned the planting of new vineyards, and paid premiums to growers to uproot old vines. As a result, the wine-growing area of Italy has fallen from more than 1.2 million hectares (1980s) to less than 800,000 hectares. In the 1980s the total DOC/G production amounted to twelve per cent and *Vino da Tavola* amounted to eighty-eight per cent. Today DOC/G production averages twenty-nine per cent, IGT twenty-seven per cent, and *Vino da Tavola* forty-four per cent.

Much of Italy's land mass is intrinsically suited to grape-growing. Four-fifths of it is hilly or mountainous. The Alps shield the northern regions from the cold of northern Europe, and the Apennines temper the hot climates of the centre and south. All twenty regions have favourable conditions for vine growth, but some have exploited them better than others. The eight northern regions, set in the vast arc formed by the Alps and Apennines, and bordered by the broad Po Valley, make more than half of the country's DOC(G) wine. The Veneto, with Soave and Valpolicella, produces more delimited wine than any other region; neighbouring Trentino-Alto Adige and Friuli-Venezia Giulia have built up enviable status for their varietals, especially the whites; and Piedmont's reds, led by Barolo and Barbaresco, have justified renown.

Change has also reverberated through central Italy. Tuscany has surged to the forefront with dramatically improved Chianti, Brunello di Montalcino, Vino Nobile di Montepulciano as well as the vaunted "Super Tuscans". White wines are also revealing ever more their intrinsic character, most notably Verdicchio from the Marche, Orvieto from Umbria, and Frascati from Lazio. The revolution in the south has been possibly even more sweeping, with the focus moving from bulk wine to good-quality bottled wine in less than a decade. In particular, wines from Puglia, Sicily, and Campania have increased markedly in both quantity and quality. Excellent, fruity-style Montepulciano from Abruzzo is also showing its muscle, along with more long-lived Aglianico reds from Campania and Basilicata.

Italy continues to vie with France as the world's leading wine producer and as the world's largest wine exporter, although much of this volume comes via blending wine sold mainly to France and Germany. With the higher-quality wines, new markets in the Pacific Basin have helped to offset the general decline in wine drinking in Europe. Meanwhile, wine consumption in Italy remains the second-highest worldwide, even though it has halved in the past thirty years to a little over fifty litres per head.

Grape Varieties

The vine varieties that thrive in a wine-producing country depend not only on soil, climate, and the lie of the land, but also on people, eating styles, and fashion. The latter, in particular, led to the diffusion of the so-called international varieties (most notably Cabernet Sauvignon, Merlot, Syrah, Chardonnay, and Sauvignon Blanc) throughout Italy in the 1990s. This trend is now on the wane, with a marked return to the use of indigenous varieties, thereby assisting the specificity and individuality of Italian wine styles.

There are more than 1,000 grape vines recorded in Italy, of which around 350 are recommended or approved in one or more regions. These include varieties that are either indigenous or have become so well-adjusted that they may be considered as such, carrying a local name. There is also an almost complete array of Europe's major vines. Listed are the more common varieties as well as local varieties that are of more-than-passing interest.

Abbuoto Outcrops of this rare red are scattered around southern Lazio and north Campania, where it is used in Cecubo, the modern version of the ancient Caecubum.

Aglianico An aristocrat of Greek origin, epitomised in Campania's Taurasi and Basilicata's Aglianico del Vulture. Together with the Piedmontese Nebbiolo, Aglianico is one of the best grape varieties in Italy, producing firm, tannic, long-lasting reds of power and refinement.

Albana Native to Romagna's hills, where it makes both dry and semi-sweet wines, still or bubbly.

Aleatico Makes perfumed, richly sweet, strongly fruited, red dessert wines in Elba, Lazio, Puglia, Tuscany, and Umbria.

Ansonica *See* Inzolia.

Arneis Elegant, delicate white found mostly in Piedmont's Roero hills.

Asprinio Campanian white making light, refreshing, uncomplicated but fairly acidic wines, often with a slight fizz.

Barbera Native of Piedmont, of outstanding class. Italy's most widely planted red after Sangiovese, it also produces everyday wines, sometimes lightly sparkling or semi-sweet. Excellent blended with Nebbiolo.

Biancolella White Campanian vine prominent on Ischia both as a varietal and blended with Forastera.

Bombino Bianco High-quality white grape grown predominantly in Abruzzo, Molise, and northern Puglia. Main grape of Puglia's San Severo Bianco.

Bombino Nero Red grape grown mainly in northern Puglia, where it is prized for Castel del Monte Rosato.

Bonarda Prominent in the Oltrepò Pavese (Lombardy) and Colli Piacentini (Emilia), where it makes supple, lively reds. Also known as Croatina. Bonarda Piemontese is a different variety and of lesser importance.

Bosco Prime ingredient of Cinqueterre in Liguria.

Brachetto Makes bubbly, usually sweet, red wines with strawberry-like flavours in Piedmont.

Cabernet Franc *See* Carmenère.

Cabernet Sauvignon Bordeaux native initially prominent in the northeast but now common throughout Italy. Produced as a varietal and in blends, both of high quality, although interest in the variety is on the wane.

Cagnina *See* Terrano.

Calabrese *See* Nero d'Avola.

Canaiolo Nero Mostly found in Tuscany and used with Sangiovese in Vino Nobile di Montepulciano and some Chianti. Opinions on its qualities vary.

Cannonau Sardinia's main red variety used for dry and, sometimes, sweet wines. The same vine as Spain's Garnacha and France's Grenache, it is found in Liguria as Granaccia, in the south as Guarnaccia and Alicante, and in the Veneto as Tocai Rosso.

Carignano The Carignan of France and Cariñena of Spain, grown in Sardinia, where it can make reds of real interest.

Carmenère It now appears that nearly all the Cabernet Franc of northern Italy is, in fact, the ancient variety Carmenère.

Carricante Chief grape of Etna Bianco in Sicily, making firm, lean whites with ageing potential.

Catarratto Widespread in Sicily, where it figures in many whites as well as marsala. Gives freshness and body, but little aroma unless grown at altitude.

Cesanese Native of Lazio producing tannic and slightly rustic reds. Best when blended.

Chardonnay A Burgundian grape with high stature in Italy, but its popularity has peaked. Used for still and sparkling wines, especially in the northeast.

Ciliegiolo This variety, once prominent in central Italy, has been revived in blended and varietal reds.

Cortese Piedmont's more structured whites, most notably Gavi, are made from this variety, which is also native to Oltrepò Pavese.

Corvina Leading grape variety in Valpolicella and Bardolino, along with Rondinella, Molinara, Negrara, and Rossignola; grown throughout Verona and around Lake Garda.

Croatina *See* Bonarda.

Dolcetto Much admired in the winelands of southern Piedmont, where it makes supple, mouth-filling, succulent red wines, usually drunk youngish. Also found in Valle d'Aosta and Liguria, where it is called Ormeasco.

Erbaluce Firm but perfumed white found in northern Piedmont. Makes dry wines and sweet Caluso Passito.

Falanghina Increasingly popular variety of Greek origin, making both stylish and simple whites in Campania and elsewhere in the south.

Favorita Lightweight but attractive white grown mainly in Piedmont's Roero.

Fiano Known as Apianum to the ancient Romans. Grown mainly in central Campania, it makes fine whites that can develop nutty characteristics.

Freisa Makes original, light but firm, often sparkling reds in Piedmont.

Gaglioppo Worthy source of most Calabrian reds, including Cirò. Its potential is not yet fully exploited.

Gamay This Beaujolais grape grows mostly in Valle d'Aosta, and sparsely elsewhere.

Garganega Fine mainstay of white Soave and Gambellara, in the Veneto.

Gewürztraminer Also known as Traminer Aromatico. Developed in Alsace, it is cultivated to great effect in Alto Adige, where it makes spicily aromatic wines of real character.

Grechetto Respected source of Umbrian whites, it may be of Greek origin; also known as Pignoletto.

Greco Of Greek origin, middle-ranking vine family, with red and white versions, although whites are more common. Grown quite widely but mainly in Campania and Calabria.

Grignolino Once-prominent Piedmontese variety, centred around Asti. Needs careful handling for its lightish red wines to develop style.

Grillo The grape giving class and style to marsala. Also used in Sicilian white wines, often with Catarratto.

Groppello Makes straightforward reds chiefly around Lake Garda.

Inzolia A native of Sicily, where it makes elegant, respected whites. Known as Ansonica in coastal Tuscany, it is showing its versatility in ever-improving rich, powerful wines in that region.

Lagrein Used in Alto Adige to make punchy, characterful red wines and gentle rosés.

Lambrusco Prolific, much sniffed-at variety abounding in the plains of Emilia, with several sub-varieties making light reds, often sweetish and bubbly. Turned into pink and white wines, too.

Magliocco Recently rediscovered variety now making highly lauded reds in Cirò in Calabria.

Malvasia Name applied to a vast range of southern European vines, also known as Malvoisie and malmsey, making wines of all types but frequently dry. White sub-varieties are grown throughout Italy, especially in Lazio, Friuli, and Sicily. Reds are concentrated in Puglia (where it is prominent), Piedmont, Alto Adige, and the centre.

Marzemino Produces easy-drinking reds in Trentino and Lombardy.

Merlot One of Italy's most heavily planted vines, this Bordeaux native is popular and makes impressive reds, particularly in the northeast

Monica Of Spanish origin, this varietal produces both dry and sweet wines in Sardinia.

Montepulciano Dominant dark variety of Abruzzo – versatile and richly fruited. Favoured in other regions, too, for varietals and blends.

Moscato Muscat vines are grown throughout Italy. White versions are most common, often with some sweetness and a grapey aroma. Most frequent styles are light, sparkling, or *frizzante*, as in Piedmont's Asti Spumante and Moscato d'Asti (from Moscato Bianco); or richly sweet, as in Sicily's Moscato d'Alessandria (also called Zibibbo). Moscato Rosa makes fragrant rosé in the Veneto; Moscato Nero is rare but makes sweet reds in Piedmont.

Müller-Thurgau A cross from Switzerland; produces elegant, aromatic wines in Trentino-Alto Adige and Friuli.

Nebbiolo Very high-quality variety. In southern Piedmont (Barbaresco, Barolo) it makes long-lived, powerful reds of supreme stature. In northern Piedmont (Gattinara, Ghemme), Lombardy (Valtellina), and Aosta, its wines are less intense. Sometimes blended, when mixed with Barbera it is particularly effective. Spanna, Chiavennasca, and Picutener are synonyms.

Negroamaro This variety's full, strapping, yet approachable reds and fresh, fruity rosés dominate Puglia's Salento peninsula.

Nerello Mascalese Worthy Sicilian grape giving lightish-coloured, firm, fruited wines, especially on Mount Etna. Usually blended.

Nero d'Avola Sicily's most esteemed source of red wines, with intense berry fruit, power, and attack. Also known as Calabrese.

Nosiola Curious Trentino native used for dry whites and *vin santo*.

Nuragus Ancient Sardinian vine making uncomplicated whites around Cagliari and Oristano.

Ormeasco *See* Dolcetto.

Ortrugo Full-bodied, lean reds come from this rare Emilian (Colli Piacentini) variety.

Perricone or **Pignatello** Sicilian variety that lends vigour to red blends.

Petit Rouge Used in some of Valle d'Aosta's finer reds.

Picolit Difficult to ripen but produces a highly prized, delicate, honeyed dessert wine in Friuli's Colli Orientali.

Piedirosso or **Per'e Palummo** Prominent in Campanian reds, notably those of Ischia.

Pigato Grown only in southwest Liguria. Produces fine dry whites.

Pinot Bianco (Pinot Blanc in France; Weissburgunder in Alto Adige) Grows primarily in northeastern Italy and makes elegant, creamy whites. Often drunk young it nonetheless has good ageing potential.

Pinot Grigio (Pinot Gris in France; Ruländer in Alto Adige) Very popular, grows widely in Friuli, Trentino-Alto Adige, the Veneto, and Lombardy. Quality of this white ranges from ordinary to rather good.

Pinot Nero (Pinot Noir in France; Blauburgunder in Alto Adige) Remains the holy grail for many northern and central Italian winemakers. Fine examples are now more numerous but not yet common. Best results overall are in Alto Adige. It also makes successful white and rosé sparklers.

Primitivo Puglian source of powerful, ripe, rich red wines, sometimes sweet, often quite alcoholic. This is the same variety as California's Zinfandel.

Prosecco Grown mainly in Veneto's Colli Trevigiani, it makes sparkling, semi-sparkling, still, dry, semi-dry, and sweet wines. The best (lightly sparkling and off-dry) are being overtaken by fully sparkling versions.

Prugnolo Gentile Clone of Sangiovese, also found in northern Italy.

Raboso Makes chunky reds in its native Veneto.

Rebo Idiosyncratic Trentino red, derived from a Merlot-Teroldego cross.

Refosco Friulian variety, fully titled Refosco dal Peduncolo Rosso, making sturdy reds. Refosco del Carso, also known as Terrano, is a different variety.

Ribolla Gialla Underrated vine from Friuli; makes lively, buttery whites. Also often used in blends.

Riesling Italico (Welschriesling in Alto Adige) Not a true Riesling, nor native to Italy. Produces undistinguished wines in the central north.

Riesling Renano (Rheinriesling in Alto Adige) The Johannisberg or White Riesling of Germany and Alsace shows its steely, incisive class in northern Italy only when from particular terrains and in skilled hands; otherwise the style is still fragrant but lighter.

Rossese Produces softish red wines in Liguria.

Sagrantino Gives pep to Sangiovese and makes vibrant varietals, some very powerful in Umbria's Montefalco. Strong, sweet (*passito*) versions are also made.

Sangiovese Italy's most widely planted variety is most at home in Tuscany, where it sets the stamp of Chianti, Brunello di Montalcino, Vino Nobile di Montepulciano, Morellino di Scansano (all Sangiovese clones), and others. Plummy but assertive wines range from simple and refreshing to intense, long-lived star performers.

Sauvignon Blanc The grassy, gooseberry character of Sauvignon Blanc is commonly realized in northern Italy and sometimes further south, too, although many producers opt for a more muted yet still distinctive style.

Schiava (Vernatsch in Alto Adige) Comprising a widespread family of vines in Trentino-Alto Adige, producing light, raspberryish reds, most notably from Santa Maddalena and Caldaro. It is now in decline.

Schioppettino Also known as Ribolla Nera. Grows only sporadically in eastern Friuli, making incisive, dense, powerful reds of great personality.

Semidano Attention in Sardinia is now returning to this intriguing white.

Sussumaniello Indigenous to Salento in Puglia, showing aromas of fleshy wild berries, leather, and graphite, with silky tannins.

Sylvaner Northern Alto Adige sees good, firm, perfumed whites from this Germanic variety.

Syrah This vine, prominent in France's Rhône Valley and Australia, makes impressive reds in much of Italy. It is diffusing rapidly throughout regions such as Sicily and Tuscany.

Tazzelenghe Rare, high-acidity red from Friuli.

Teroldego Grown almost exclusively on Trentino's Rotaliano plain, giving occasionally distinguished reds of high potential.

Tocai Friulano Friuli is under EU orders to change Tocai's name to avoid confusion with the Hungarian region of Tokaj. The vine, actually Sauvignonasse or Sauvignon Vert of French origin, is Friuli's pride with its appley, nut-cream character. Not the same as France's Tokay, which is in fact Pinot Gris.

Tocai Italico Considered the same variety as Tocai Friulano, but grown in parts of Veneto and Lombardy where it makes less compelling wines.

Tocai Rosso *See* Cannonau.

Torbato This Spanish native grape produces fine white wines in Sardinia's northern Alghero area.

Traminer Native of Asia but developed at Tramin in Alto Adige, this significantly toned-down, more productive relative of Gewürztraminer appeals to those who find the latter too intensely perfumed and spicy.

Trebbiano di Lugana *See* Verdicchio.

Trebbiano di Romagna A distinct Trebbiano clone grown throughout Romagna that often lacks character.

Trebbiano Toscano Widely diffused – Italy's most widespread white – but often unprepossessing variety. Known as Ugni Blanc in France.

Uva di Troia Respected red variety from northern Puglia.

Uva Rara Often confused with Bonarda, but a distinct red variety grown mainly in northern Piedmont. Mostly used in blends.

Verdeca Important Puglian grape used with Bianco d'Alessano in Locorotondo, Martina Franca, and other north Puglian whites.

Verdicchio Predominant variety of the Marche, where it produces a wealth of crisp yet deep wines of growing stature. Also grown on the south shores of Lake Garda, where it is called Trebbiano di Lugana.

Verduzzo Grape from Friuli that is used for stylish dry whites and dessert wines. Also found in the Veneto.

Vermentino Likely to be of Spanish origin, arriving in Sardinia, Liguria, and Tuscany from Corsica. Makes firm whites of increasing renown.

Vernaccia di Oristano Grown exclusively around the central Sardinian region of Oristano, where it gives a sherry-like dessert wine.

Vernaccia di San Gimignano Ancient vine used for the rapidly improving, fleshy white of Tuscany's famous towered town.

Vernaccia di Serrapetrona This results in a red wine, often sweet or sparkling, in the Marche.

Vespaiola Makes both dry whites and rich dessert wines in the Veneto.

Vespolina A red variety usually blended with Nebbiolo and others in
Piedmont's Novara and Vercelli hills.
Viognier A white variety from France's Rhône, with many admirers in Italy.
Zibibbo *See* Moscato.

Laws & Labels

The ancient Romans may have been the first people to formulate wine laws,
setting production codes for sixteen appellations on the Italian peninsula
and Sicily. In 1716, the Grand Duchy of Tuscany set a precedent by
delimiting the production zones for some important wines. Yet it wasn't
until the mid-1960s that Italy introduced the laws of controlled origin that
brought much-needed discipline and a new sense of dignity to modern
wine production. The laws cover the main classifications of *denominazione
di origine controllata* (DOC) *e garantita* (DOCG), as well as the category of
indicazione geografica tipica (IGT), which classifies wines from larger
geographical areas and vine varieties not covered under DOC/DOCG.
There are 307 approved DOC zones in Italy, thirty DOCGs, and 117 IGTs.

DOCs, which always indicate a delimited zone on the label, apply to
wines from specified vine varieties (alone or blended) produced with
limited yields which are vinified and aged to meet prescribed standards of
colour, odour, flavour, alcohol content, and acidity. DOC wines may be
defined by colour, type (still, *frizzante*, or sparkling; dry, semi-sweet, or
sweet; natural or fortified), or grape variety. Some DOCs apply to multiple
types (there are nineteen kinds in Friuli-Venezia Giulia's Collio, for
example, including seventeen varietals). Wines may be defined further by
age (young as *novello*, or aged as *vecchio*, *stravecchio*, or *riserva*), or by a
special sub-zone (as *classico*). The term *superiore* may apply to wine with a
higher degree of alcohol than the norm, or a longer period of ageing.

Details of each DOC region are determined by producers in the zone, who
sometimes join together in a consortium (*consorzio*) that acts as a monitoring
and promoting body. The *consorzio* passes on suggestions for changes in
production regulations to the national DOC committee in Rome, which may
either sanction them or turn them down. Despite a few dubious choices, DOC
has been a major factor in the improved status of Italian wine worldwide.

DOCG, which guarantees the authenticity of wines of "particular
esteem", has expanded from the original four (Barbaresco, Barolo,
Brunello di Montalcino, Vino Nobile di Montepulciano) to cover many
more. Although some question the use of the term "guaranteed", DOCG
has improved quality and made counterfeiting more difficult by imposing
more stringent quality specifications on producers, such as strict control
of the amounts produced and obligatory tasting checks by expert tasters.
DOCG wines must have the official strip seal at the top of each bottle.

The IGT category classifies wines from specific regions, provinces, or
general areas by colour, grape variety, or typology. There are more than
one hundred, with many sub-divided into numerous varietal versions. Some
of Italy's top modern wines are made by producers who choose to work
outside the DOC/DOCG norms and fall into the IGT category. This choice
gives the producer more scope, especially in the selection and quantities
of varieties used in a blend. *Vino da Tavola* applies to anonymous wine
that, if bottled, may not specify grape variety, vintage, or place of origin.

Labelling of all wines is restricted to pertinent data in which the wording, and in some cases even the type size, is controlled. Required on all labels are the wine name and category (DOC, IGT, etc.); the producer's or bottler's name and commune of bottling; the quantity of wine contained; and the alcohol percentage by volume. Labels may also carry a vintage (obligatory for most DOCG and many DOC wines), its sweetness category, and colour, plus a trademark, coat of arms, and consortium seal. Other details may be given on back labels or scrolls, but this should be verifiable and cannot include such terms as *riserva*, *speciale*, or *superiore* unless the wine qualifies for them.

Glossary

abboccato lightly sweet, literally "mouth-filling"

acidità acidity

amabile semi-sweet, literally "amiable"; a shade sweeter than *abboccato*

amaro bitter

amarognolo the almond-like, lightly bitter undertone detectable in certain wines, usually on the aftertaste

ambrato amber hue noted in many dessert or apéritif wines

annata year of vintage

asciutto bone-dry

assemblaggio wine made from two or more grapes, blended after fermentation

azienda agricola/agraria/viticola estate producing wine from its own grapes

azienda vinicola estate producing wine from bought-in grapes

barrique small barrel, usually of new French oak

bianco white

blanc de blancs white wine made only from white grapes; refers usually to sparkling wines

botte cask

bottiglia bottle

brut dry when referring to sparkling wine

cantina wine cellar or winery

cantina sociale or **cooperativa** co-op winery (abbreviated to "CS" in listings)

cascina farm or estate, usually in northern Italy

cerasuolo cherry-red, used to describe certain deepish-coloured rosés

Charmat method whereby wine is made sparkling by refermenting in sealed, pressure-resistant vats

chiaretto term referring to certain lightish-coloured rosé wines

classico classic, used to define heartland zones of tradition and particular quality within a DOC(G) – for example, Chianti Classico, Orvieto Classico

coltivatore grower

consorzio voluntary consortium of growers and producers set up to oversee production and/or promote the wines of an area

degustazione wine tasting

denominazione di origine controllata/e garantita (DOC/DOCG) *See* Laws & Labels

dolce sweet

enologia oenology, the study of winemaking

enologo oenologist, winemaker with a degree

enoteca literally wine library, but also wine shop and wine bar

enotecnico winemaking technician with a further-education diploma

etichetta label
ettaro hectare (2.471 acres); the standard European measure of land area
ettolitro hectolitre (100 litres), the standard European measure of wine volume
extra term to describe certain fortified wines of very high alcohol
extra dry term used to describe sparkling wine that is dry, but less so than brut
fattoria farm or estate, usually in central Italy
fermentazione naturale wine made lightly bubbly without a second fermentation
frizzante lightly bubbly, *pétillant*, but not fully sparkling
frizzantino refers to wine with a barely noticeable prickle
fusto cask, barrel
gradazione alcoolica alcohol percentages by volume
gusto flavour (not in the English sense of "gusto", however)
imbottigliato da bottled by
indicazione geografica tipica (IGT) *See* Laws & Labels
invecchiato aged
liquoroso high alcohol, fortified wine
litro litre, equivalent to 1.056 US quarts
marchio depositato registered brand name or trademark
marsalato or **maderizzato** refers to wines that through oxidation take on flavours reminiscent of marsala or madeira
metodo classico term for sparkling wine made by the classic Champagne method with a refermentation in bottle (abbreviated to mc in text)
millesimato sparkling wine from a stated vintage year
passito/a partially dried grapes and the wines – usually sweet, sometimes strong – made from them
pastoso full, round, mouth-filling
podere small farm or estate
produttore producer
profumo odour or scent
quintale quintal (100 kilograms)
riserva reserve, applied only to DOC or DOCG wines that have undergone specified ageing
rosato rosé
rosso red
rubino ruby colour
sapore flavour
secco dry (but medium-dry when referring to sparkling wine)
semi-secco medium-sweet, demi-sec, usually used to describe sparkling wine
spumante sparkling wine, whether bone-dry or fully sweet
stravecchio very old, applies to the longest-aged marsala and to some spirits
superiore term for DOC wine usually indicating higher alcohol
tappo di sughero cork top
tenuta farm or estate
uva grape
uvaggio wine made from two or more grapes blended before fermentation
vecchio old, describing certain aged wines
vendemmia the grape harvest, often also in the sense of vintage
vendemmia tardiva late-harvest; wines from overripe grapes
vigna, vigneto vineyard

vignaiolo grape-grower
vino da meditazione wine, often strong, sweet, or particularly concentrated, for sipping meditatively
vino da taglio strong wine used for blending
vino da tavola table wine. *See* Laws & Labels
vino novello new wine, usually red, in the Beaujolais Nouveau style. By law, *novello* wines are sold from 6 November in the year of harvest
vite vine
viticoltore grape-grower
vitigno vine or grape variety
vivace lively, as in lightly bubbly wines

Temperature

Wine expresses its best when it is served at the right temperature, although there is always considerable leeway for personal preference. The chart below indicates the suggested serving temperature for each type of wine.

	°F • °C	
	66 • 19	Big, aged reds: Barolo, Brunello, Amarone, Taurasi, Torgiano
Chianti Classico, Cabernet, Montepulciano d'Abruzzo, Teroldego	64 • 18	Riserva
	63 • 17	Barbera, Merlot, Valpolicella, Sangiovese di Romagna
	61 • 16	
Bardolino *rosso*, Dolcetto, Grignolino, Santa Maddalena, Marsala Vergine	59 • 15	Lambrusco, *vin santo*, Marsala Superiore,
	57 • 14	Recioto della Valpolicella
Most rosés and new wines: Bardolino Chiaretto, Ramandolo	55 • 13	
	54 • 12	
	52 • 11	Delicate, fruity whites: Fiano, oaked Chardonnay, Picolit, Moscato d'Asti,
	50 • 10	Recioto di Soave
Most dry whites: Soave, Gavi, Frascati, Pinot Grigio; best sparkling wines	48 • 9	
	46 • 8	Most dry and semi-sweet sparkling wines: Asti
	45 • 7	Room temp
Fortified dessert wines: Moscato Passito di Pantelleria	43 • 6	Ideal cellar
		Domestic refrigerator

Valle d'Aosta *Valle d'Aosta*

Italy's smallest region, tucked into the country's northwestern corner, has little space for vineyards amid its massive Alps. Most vines grow over pergolas on terraces hewn out of stone on south-facing slopes along the Dora Baltea River, which flows from the Mont Blanc through the capital Aosta and on into Piedmont. A wine production of less than three million litres a year (Italy's lowest) isn't nearly enough to supply the region's 114,000 citizens.

Wine here is made by plucky and persevering *vignerons*, including those who work Europe's highest-altitude classified vineyards at Morgex. They take in a little galaxy of *crus*, drawing some lustre from Piedmontese and French varieties, but making the most intriguing wines from indigenous grapes: Blanc de Valdigne, Petit Rouge, the mutation of Pinot Gris known locally as Malvoisie, and Vien de Nus.

A comprehensive DOC, Valle d'Aosta/Vallée d'Aoste (the region is officially Italian/French bilingual), includes twenty-five types of wine. An ambitious programme to upgrade winemaking techniques has improved quality, and wines are increasingly recognized for their excellence across Italy. The region's well-marked Route des Vins follows the Dora Baltea from Piedmont to Morgex. Aosta's Cave Valdôtaine and Enoteca Coio-Bertiglia in Courmayeur are great places to shop for wine.

Recent Vintages

Recommended vintages appear next to appellation wines capable of ageing.

Appellations

DOC
VALLE D'AOSTA/VALLÉE D'AOSTE *w r p*

Comprehensive appellation taking in most of the region's vineyards, and accounting for nearly 85% of its wine in 25 types and variations. Grape varieties include Fumin, Gamay, Mayolet, Merlot, Müller-Thurgau, Nebbiolo, Petite Arvine, Petit Rouge, Pinot Gris, Pinot Noir, Premetta, Syrah.

Sub-zones:

Arnad Montjovet *r 98 99 00 01 03 04*
Nebbiolo, Dolcetto, Pinot Noir, and other varieties.

Blanc de Morgex et de La Salle *w*
Blanc de Valdigne.

Chambave *w r m*
Chambave Moscato Passito/Muscat

Flétri Passito – from semi-dried Moscato *95 97 98 99 00 01 03 04*
Chambave Rosso/Rouge – from Petit Rouge with other varieties. *99 00 01 03 04*

Donnaz/Donnas *r 98 99 00 01 04*
Nebbiolo and other local red varieties.

Enfer d'Arvier *r 99 00 01 03 04*
Petit Rouge and other local red varieties.

Nus *w r pas*
Malvoisie
Nus Malvoisie Passito *95 96 97 98 00 01 04*
Nus Rosso/Rouge *99 00 01 03 04*

Torrette *r 97 98 99 00 01 03 04*
Petit Rouge, with other varieties.

Vin de la Sabla *r 97 98 99 00 01 03 04*
Petit Rouge, Fumin, and other varieties.

Producers

Anselmet, Villeneuve *w r sw* ☆☆☆ *
Fine Chardonnay, aromatic Traminer
and Müller-Thurgau, and excellent
sweet Arline Flétri from Pinot Grigio
and Traminer. In the reds, good Petit
Rouge- (Le Prisonnier) and some
Syrah-based (Henri Elevé) wines.

**Cave du Vin Blanc de Morgex et de La
Salle,** Morgex *w sw* ☆☆→☆☆☆ *
20ha, 160,000 bottles. A co-op of 100
members producing Chaudelune
Vin de Glace, a type of Icewine
made from 60-year-old Prié Blanc
pergolas. Also good extra-dry
Blanc Fripon, Valle d'Aosta Blanc
de Morgex et de la Salle, Rayon.

Caves Coopératives de Donnaz,
Donnaz *w p r sw* ☆→☆☆ 25ha,
150,000 bottles. A 90-member co-op.
Highlights: Valle d'Aosta Pinot Gris
– citrus, complex; and Nebbiolo-
based Donnas Napoleone – fruity,
gamey; and Barmet – cherry, spicy.

Caves des Onze Communes, Aymavilles
w p r ☆☆ * 60ha, 350,000 bottles.
A co-op with 220 members. Very
good Fumin – round, charming;
Petite Arvine – rich mineral notes;
Torrette – dark and juicy; and Rouge
Bouquetin – vivacious, savoury.

Costantino Charrère, Aymavilles *p r*
☆☆→☆☆☆ * 4 ha, 39,000 bottles.
Also owner of Les Cretes. Good
Valle d'Aosta Mayolet – full-bodied,
tannic; Torrette – fresh, mineral,
balsamic; and Premetta – floral,
elegant. Also fine Vin de la Sabla and
Grenache-based Vin Les Fourches.

Les Cretes, Aymavilles *w r* ☆☆☆→
☆☆☆☆ * 18ha, 180,000 bottles.
One of the largest privately owned
estates with biodynamically farmed
vines. An impressive range topped
by fine whites: Valle d'Aosta
Chardonnay Frissonnière Cuvée
Bois – elegant, floral; Coteau La
Tour Syrah – fine, spicy nose;
Petite Arvine Vigne Champorette –

good balance and length.

La Crotta di Vegneron, Chambave *w r
sw sp* ☆☆→☆☆☆ * 33ha, 320,000
bottles. Co-op producing
outstanding Chambave Moscato
Passito – complex, with rose petals,
peach, honey, and vanilla, very
persistent. Elegant Müller-Thurgau
Vendemmia Tardiva Boton d'Or, and
an interesting Chambave Supérieur
Quatre Vignobles – Petit Rouge
with Pinot Noir, Gamay, and Fumin.

Di Barrò, Villeneuve *w r sw* ☆☆ 10,000
bottles. Small estate renowned
for excellent Torrette Superiore –
structured, fruity, and vibrant. Also
good Moscato and Mayolet Cos de
Château Feullet and Petit Rouge.

Fratelli Grosjean, Quart *w r* ☆☆ 80,000
bottles. Second-largest private
estate in the region, owned by
Vincent Grosjean and his brothers.
Fine Torrette – dark, delicious, with
cherry and cassis; Fumin – ripe,
smoky, balsamic notes; Petite Arvine
– white peaches, apples, and pears.

Institut Agricole Régional, Aosta *w r*
☆☆→☆☆☆ * Agricultural school
run by monks, making unoaked
and oaked wines. Pinot *crus* lead
the former, Chardonnay the latter.
Highlights: Chardonnay Elevé en
Futs de Chene – delicate, citrus,
crisp; Pinot Grigio – extracted,
crisp, persistent; and Petite Arvine
– oily, sweet, with citrus notes.

La Kiuva, Arnad *w r* ☆☆ Emerging co-
op. Good Chardonnay La Perla, from
partly sweet, late-harvest grapes –
complex, well-integrated oak; and
predominantly Nebbiolo-based
Arnad-Montjovet Superiore.

Lo Triolet, Introd *w r* ☆☆→☆☆☆ 2ha,
25,000 bottles. Marco Martin's top
labels include a barrique-fermented
Pinot Gris – fruity and floral, and
full-bodied, with elegant vanilla
finish. Also good Syrah- and
excellent Fumin-based Rouge
Coteau Barrage – smoky, ripe fruit.

Albert Vevey, Morgex *w* ☆☆ 5,000 bottles. Local pioneer and producer of the fragrant, elegant Blanc de Morgex et de La Salle from Prié Blanc planted at 1,000m (3,280ft) to traditional pergolas. Few bottles are made, but they are of high quality.

Food & Wine

Aostans thrive on rustic fare – polenta, thick soups, fontina and toma cheeses, ideal for fondue – and meat plays a major part: salame, sausages, mountain prosciutto, *mocetta* (air-dried chamois meat), and tasty stews and game dishes cooked with wine. Meals often end with *grolla* (a spouted pot filled with coffee and grappa).

Boudins Blood sausages.

Capriolo alla valdostana Venison stew with vegetables, wine, grappa, and cream.

Carbonade Salted beef cooked with wine in a rich stew.

Cotoletta alla valdostana Breaded veal cutlets with fontina, and possibly truffles.

Polenta alla rascard Polenta baked with layers of fontina and a ragout of beef and sausage.

Zuppa valpellinentze Soup of fontina, ham, bread, cabbage, herbs, and spices.

Hotels

Antica Locanda La Clusaz, Gignot € A 14-room lodge with mountain views. Tasting menus allow a local gastronomic tour.

Hotel Bellevue, Cogne €€ Relais & Châteaux chalet with an alpine atmosphere and warm hospitality.

Agriturismo Les Ecureuils, St-Pierre € A country home off the beaten track, with five rooms and a library. Optional half-pension and excellent local specialties.

Locanda La Grolla, Località Pendeint, Courmayeur € Rooms and apartments available in the summer months.

Locanda della Vecchia Miniera, Ollomont € A 17th-century family-run home with five bedrooms and great food.

Restaurants

Baita Ermitage, Ermitage, Courmayeur € Mountain chalet with views of Mont Blanc and terrace for alfresco dining. Great *zuppa Ermitage*, with black bread, spinach and fontina, venison, hams, apple cake, and much more.

Nuovo Batezar da Renato, St-Vincent €€ Traditional Aostan ambience, rustic elegance. Typical fare: saffron and truffle *tajarin*, mountain meats, and mushrooms.

Les Pertzes, Cogne € Hospitable dining rooms with a fireplace, serving genuine fare: trout, potato and leek with fondue, and polenta with game sauce. Convivial ambience and a wonderful cellar.

Trattoria degli Amici, St-Vincent € Traditional Aostan cooking. The menu changes several times a week: trout marinade, vol-au-vent with fondue, *polenta concia* (made with wholewheat), garden vegetable gnocchi, braised beef.

Vecchio Ristoro, Aosta €€ Old mill in the historic centre of Aosta. The restaurant is built around the mill wheel. Rustic elegance offering typical tasting menu or local specialties.

Piedmont *Piemonte*

In terms of craftsmanship, sense of tradition, and respect for native vines in their traditional habitat, Piedmont has no equal outside of the most venerated wine zones of France, or so it would seem. There is something reminiscent of Burgundy in the Langhe hills near Alba, where Barolo and Barbaresco are grown: manicured vineyards fragmented into single-owner plots on every south-facing slope, trim villages where the lusty odour of fermenting grapes perfumes the autumn air, and the self-assured way in which the *vignaiolo* hands you a glass of his best. In the Langhe, as in the Côte d'Or, wine is a way of life. And yet, below the surface, there is as much, if not more, frenzy and uncertainty as in most other parts of the country.

Piedmontese wines are so distinctive that they are often hard for people to comprehend at a first encounter. Most of the region's classified wines derive from native vines, and single varietals predominate, though not all carry variety names. Nebbiolo – the source of Barolo and Barbaresco, not to mention of Gattinara, Ghemme, Carema, Lessona, Nebbiolo d'Alba, and

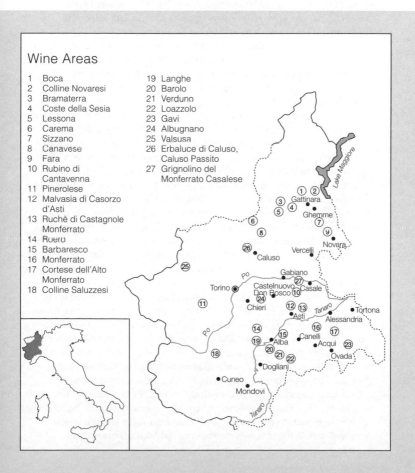

Wine Areas

1. Boca
2. Colline Novaresi
3. Bramaterra
4. Coste della Sesia
5. Lessona
6. Carema
7. Sizzano
8. Canavese
9. Fara
10. Rubino di Cantavenna
11. Pinerolese
12. Malvasia di Casorzo d'Asti
13. Ruchè di Castagnole Monferrato
14. Roero
15. Barbaresco
16. Monferrato
17. Cortese dell'Alto Monferrato
18. Colline Saluzzesi
19. Langhe
20. Barolo
21. Verduno
22. Loazzolo
23. Gavi
24. Albugnano
25. Valsusa
26. Erbaluce di Caluso, Caluso Passito
27. Grignolino del Monferrato Casalese

other eminent reds – is by far the noblest vine. But it is wine made from the once-derided Barbera variety that is now setting the pace.

Piedmont ranks only seventh among Italy's twenty regions in volume of production, but its fifty-two DOC(G) zones, including the comprehensive Piemonte denomination, are the most of any region. There are eight DOCG wines: Barbaresco, Barolo, Gattinara, Asti, Brachetto d'Acqui, Ghemme, Gavi, and Roero. DOC wines form eighty per cent of production and are the mainstay of the respected producers; even new wines, whether from indigenous or foreign grape varieties, usually come under DOC – mostly Piemonte DOC, Langhe DOC, or Monferrato DOC – because the region has chosen to avoid the introduction of IGTs.

Barolo and Barbaresco have undergone changes in style that have divided progressive winemakers, who have opted for short, hot macerations and brief spells in small new oak, and traditionalists, who macerate for weeks and then allow the wine to slumber for years in inert Slavonian barrels. The best modern interpretations of Barolo and Barbaresco maintain their ample dimensions, while being better-balanced and more approachable than before. But even the traditional styles have responded to modern know-how and are more impressive. A few Barolo producers make a Barolo Chinato tonic wine by steeping *china* (quinine, the bark of the cinchona tree) in the wine to give an exotic bitter taste.

The lively, fruity, uncomplicated – but not simplistic – nature of Dolcetto, a perfect accompaniment to a wide range of dishes, remains as popular as ever. The Piedmontese drink more red wine than white, and about half of that red is Barbera. This grape gives wines fruit and acidity but not tannin, a combination that provides wonderful vibrancy and lift when made from good-quality grapes. Yet many producers seek to make wines with added balance and complexity through ageing in small, new oak casks. This can give a classy but indistinct style. Others use oak less liberally, probably to better effect. Grignolino, Freisa, and Pelaverga are so unusual that they remain little more than local curiosities, but deserving of greater attention.

Among the whites, Asti, from the Moscato Bianco grape, is the world's most popular sweet sparkling wine, though it is often, unjustifiably, looked down on by connoisseurs who prefer the gently bubbly Moscato d'Asti. The native varieties Arneis, from the Roero hills near Alba, and Cortese, at its best in Gavi, are being used to make increasingly stylish dry whites.

Viticulture is most intense in the Langhe and Monferrato hills around Alba, Asti, and Alessandria, where thousands of growers work vineyards that are often little larger than a hectare. Many sell grapes to wineries producing vermouth, Asti, and other sparkling wines and centred around Canelli, Alba, and Turin; but more and more the urge to make one's own wine is taking over, and there has been an explosion of new estates and labels. Piedmont's other outstanding wine district lies at the Alpine foothills between Valle d'Aosta and Lake Maggiore, in the provinces of Vercelli and Novara. Cultivation is much more spasmodic here, but Nebbiolo still prevails, with Gattinara, Ghemme, and Lessona the leading wines.

Piedmont is among Italy's best-organized regions for wine tourism, with well-marked wine roads covering a score of production zones. Focal points for travellers include the Langhe and Monferrato hills and the towns of Alba and Asti. Wine shops in the region of particular note are the following: Del Santo and Il Vinaio in Turin, La Mia Crota in Biella, Ferrando in Ivrea, Vivian in Novara, Bava and Conca d'Oro in Cannobio, Al Nido della Cinciallegra in Neive, and I Piaceri del Gusto in Alba.

Recent Vintages

ALBA: BAROLO, BARBARESCO, BARBERA, DOLCETTO

As a rule, Barbaresco from an average-to-good harvest becomes more approachable at four to six years, and Barolo at five to eight, after which they hold well for several more years. From the best vintages, a couple of years more are needed. Among Alba's other DOC reds, Dolcetto is often best within a year or two of harvest, as is Nebbiolo from Roero, but the finest Barbera can improve for five to six years or more. Barbera from the neighbouring Asti province and the Monferrato hills can equal Alba's in class and durability.

2004 A later harvest with higher yield but with a long, balanced ripening period. It should yield a classic-quality vintage.

2003 A very hot, arid summer with some hail damaging the vineyards. Early harvest, with some rain in September helping the later ripening grapes to reach ripeness. Many wines lack acidity for ageing.

2002 A poor summer and occasional hailstorms made this a difficult vintage, with most producers harvesting selectively to achieve quality at the expense of quantity. The late-ripening Nebbiolo fared better than most.

2001 A remarkably fine vintage across the board, with perfectly ripened grapes.

2000 Another excellent harvest.

1999 The fifth of an uninterrupted series of perfect vintages.

1998 An outstanding vintage; many winemakers lean toward 1998 as the best of all for Nebbiolo and Barbera wines. Also excellent for Dolcetto and whites.

1997 Superb, rich, balanced Barolo, Barbaresco, and Barbera for ageing. Fine weather also benefited Dolcetto and white wines.

1996 This good vintage could have been even better if rains hadn't marred the late stages of the Nebbiolo harvest. Barolo, Barbaresco, and Barbera have full structure and good balance, and should age well.

1995 A small crop of generally good quality, except in spots where torrential rains and hail damaged the vineyards. Wines from Nebbiolo and Barbera show excellent structure and good ageing potential.

1990 A great vintage for Barolo and Barbaresco, similar to 1989, with extraordinary depth and harmony; equally favourable for Barbera.

1989 A hot, dry summer made southern Piedmont one of the few places in Italy where reds showed power and durability. An outstanding vintage is rated about even with 1990 and a shade superior to 1988. First-rate Barbera.

Notes on earlier vintages: 1988 Good wines from a limited crop. **1985** Great year. **1982** A fine year. **1979** Should be drunk now. **1978** This "miracle vintage" seems overrated. Only **1974** stood out between 1978 and the extraordinary **1971** vintage, the latter overshadowing the excellent **1970** crop. Other fine harvests were 1967, 1965 (especially Barolo), 1964 (especially Barbaresco), 1962, and 1961. Even wines that should already have been drunk can prove quite unforgettable.

NOVARA-VERCELLI HILLS AND CAREMA

Although Nebbiolo is often mixed with Bonarda and Vespaiola in these Alpine foothills, there are some wines able to equal Barolo in longevity. Gattinara, Carema, Lessona, Ghemme, and choice Spanna (the local name for Nebbiolo) need four to six years or more to reach their prime. Wines containing less Nebbiolo (Boca, Fara, Sizzano, Bramaterra) usually mature sooner. A series of good vintages since 1995 has breathed new life into the whole of Piedmont's wine-growing industry, which had experienced difficulties because of the supremacy of Barolo and a series of bad vintages. The result of this was, at one point, that their wines risked falling into oblivion.

2004 Classic-quality vintage.

2003 A very hot, arid summer. Wines lack acidity for ageing.

2002 The rainy summer compromised quality, but a sunny spell in September benefited the later-ripening Nebbiolo.

2001 Excellent year, giving a good crop of wines with fine ageing potential.

2000 Very good year. Smaller yields than usual because a spell of bad weather in the middle of October that interrupted harvest.

1999 Great year, better than 1998: a rainy summer and beautiful autumn led to intense colour and mature tannins, thus well-balanced, concentrated wines.

1998 A very good year. Wines do not have enormous concentration, but there are plenty of well-balanced, harmonious examples.

1997 An exceptional vintage for Nebbiolo wines, with almost perfect conditions through the season.

1996 A very good-to-excellent vintage for Nebbiolo-based wines of full structure and good balance.

1995 Very small yields because of late frosts, but a very good year. Nebbiolo ripened well thanks to a warm, sunny autumn.

1994 A challenging harvest in the autumn due to a period of rain; average year.

1993 Because of rain during the harvest, there were few outstanding wines.

1992 Mediocre.

1991 A disappointment after the great 1990 vintage. Few wines are capable of ageing.

1990 The best of recent vintages for reds of outstanding structure, balance, and ageing potential.

1989 Good to very good Nebbiolo wines of better-than-average life expectancy.

1988 Excellent quality from a small crop.

Appellations

DOCG
ASTI/ASTI SPUMANTE/
MOSCATO D'ASTI *w r fz sp sw*

Covers two types: aromatically sweet Asti Spumante and Moscato d'Asti, from Moscato Bianco.

BARBARESCO *r ris 82 85 86 88 89 90 93 94 95 96 97 98 99 00 01 04*

Made from Nebbiolo. One of Italy's great red wines – robust, austere, elegant. Not as powerful as Barolo: it requires less maturing in barrel and bottle to develop bouquet (4 to 8 years); it often has greater finesse and more consistent quality. Age: 2 years (1 in wood); *riserva* 4 years.

BAROLO *r ris 82 85 86 88 89 90 93 94 95 96 97 98 99 00 01 02 04*

"King of wine and wine of kings", as the Piedmontese defined it in the 19th century, Barolo is historically the most honoured red of Italy. Made from Nebbiolo grown in the Langhe southeast of Alba, it takes its name from the eponymous village. Traditional Barolo needed years to lose its initial tannic hardness; yet its austere robustness and intense concentration of fruit and extract could remain largely intact for well over a decade as colour evolved from deep ruby and garnet toward brick red, and bouquet became increasingly refined. Now a new breed of winemaker uses studied techniques to achieve a more approachable style, and the wine has gained fresh converts. Modern Barolo is often identified with single vineyards, although the zone has recognized the value of terrains for well over a century. Production is centred on the villages of Castiglione Falletto, Monforte d'Alba, and Serralunga d'Alba (where the firmest wines are made), and Barolo and La Morra (producing more graceful wines), as well as Novello, Verduno, and Grinzane Cavour. Age: 3 years (2 in wood); *riserva* 5 years.

BRACHETTO D'ACQUI *r sw fz sp*

A sweet, bubbly red with a delicate Muscat-like fragrance and moderate strawberry-like sweetness.

GATTINARA *r ris 85 86 88 89 90 93 95 96 97 98 99 00 01 02 04*

Nebbiolo (here called Spanna), grown around Gattinara, in the hills north of Vercelli, can reach notable heights of grandeur. With 10% Uva Rara permitted by the authorities in Nebbiolo, it develops distinct nuances. The Nebbiolo here is characterized by a hint of violets and tar on the nose, and a softer texture and flavours of bitter almond on the finish. Age: 3 years (2 in barrel); *riserva* 4 years.

GAVI OR CORTESE DI GAVI *w fz sp 00 01 02 04*

The most prestigious wines from Cortese grapes come from the hills around Gavi, in southeast Piedmont. Noted for acute dryness and fresh, flinty acidity when young, as the wines mature they take on greater depth, roundness, and fleshiness.

GHEMME *r ris 85 86 88 89 90 93 95 96 97 98 99 00 01 04*

Among the Nebbiolo-based wines of northern Piedmont, Ghemme ranks second to Gattinara in status but can certainly equal it in class. Made from 75–100% Nebbiolo with the addition of Vespolina and Uva Rara. Ghemme's sturdy, robust qualities smooth out with age as it develops an elegant bouquet. Age: 4 years (3 in wood).

ROERO/ROERO ARNEIS
w r sp

Rose to DOCG status in 2004. Roero is made from 95% Nebbiolo and 5% Arneis, aged 20 months, while the Roero *riserva* is aged 32 months. Both show the nobility of more vaunted Nebbiolo wines, with the advantage of being softer, easier, and less expensive. Prime is often reached at 3 to 6 years, but some vintages can last a decade.

DOC
ALBUGNANO *p r sup*
Barbera, Bonarda, Freisa, Nebbiolo.

ALTA LANGA *w p r sp*
Pinot Nero, Chardonnay, and other local non-aromatic varieties.

BARBERA D'ALBA *r sup*
Barbera.

BARBERA D'ASTI *r sup fz*
Barbera, Dolcetto, Freisa, Grignolino.

BARBERA DEL MONFERRATO
r sup
Barbera, Dolcetto, Freisa, Grignolino.

BOCA *r*
Nebbiolo, Uva Rara, Vespolina.

BRAMATERRA *r ris*
Croatina, Nebbiolo, Uva Rara, Vespolina.

CANAVESE *r p nov*
Erbaluce, Nebbiolo, Uva Rara, Neretto, Barbera, Bonarda, Freisa.

CAREMA *r ris*
Nebbiolo and other local non-aromatic red varieties.

CISTERNA D'ASTI *r sup fz*
Croatina and other local non-aromatic red varieties.

COLLI DI LUNI
See Liguria.

COLLI TORTONESI *w p r sup fz nov sw sp*
Barbera, Cortese, Dolcetto, and local non-aromatic whites and reds.

COLLINA TORINESE *r sw nov*
Barbera, Freisa, Bonarda, Malvasia Nera, Pelaverga.

COLLINE NOVARESI *w r nov*
Croatina, Erbaluce, Barbera, Nebbiolo, Uva Rara, Vespolina.

COLLINE SALUZZESI *r sp sw*
Pelaverga, Quagliano, Nebbiolo, Barbera.

CORTESE DELL'ALTO MONFERRATO *w fz sp*
Cortese and other local white varieties.

COSTE DELLA SESIA *w p r nov*
Pelaverga, Nebbiolo, Barbera, Erbaluce, Uva Rara, Croatina, Nebbiolo, Vespolina, and other local non-aromatic red varieties.

DOLCETTO D'ACQUI *r sup*
Dolcetto.

DOLCETTO D'ALBA *r sup*
Dolcetto.

DOLCETTO D'ASTI *r sup*
Dolcetto.

DOLCETTO DELLE LANGHE MONREGALESI *r sup*
Dolcetto.

DOLCETTO DI DIANO D'ALBA/ DIANO D'ALBA *r sup*
Dolcetto.

DOLCETTO DI DOGLIANI *r sup*
Dolcetto.

DOLCETTO DI OVADA *r sup*
Dolcetto.

ERBALUCE DI CALUSO *w sw pas liq sp*
Erbaluce.

FARA *r*
Nebbiolo, Vespolina, Bonarda, Novarese.

FREISA D'ASTI *r sw fz sup sp*
Freisa.

FREISA DI CHIERI *r sw fz sup sp*
Freisa.

GABIANO *r ris*
Barbera, Freisa, Grignolino.

GRIGNOLINO D'ASTI *r*
Grignolino, Freisa.

GRIGNOLINO DEL MONFERRATO CASALESE *r*
Grignolino, Freisa.

LANGHE *w r fz*
Nebbiolo, Dolcetto, Freisa, Arneis, Favorita, Chardonnay, Barbera.

LESSONA *r*
Nebbiolo, Vespolina, Bonarda.

LOAZZOLO *w m sw*
Moscato.

MALVASIA DI CASORZO D'ASTI *r p sw pas fz sp*
Malvasia Nera di Casorzo, Freisa, Grignolino, Barbera, and other local, aromatic varieties.

MALVASIA DI CASTELNUOVO DON BOSCO r sw fz sp
Malvasia di Schierano, Freisa.

MONFERRATO w p r fz nov sw
Barbera, Grignolino, Cortese, Bonarda, Cabernet Franc, Cabernet Sauvignon, Dolcetto, Freisa, Pinot Nero, Nebbiolo.

NEBBIOLO D'ALBA r fz sw sp
Nebbiolo.

PIEMONTE r nov fz w sp m pas
Barbera, Uva Rara, Grignolino, Brachetto, Chardonnay, Cortese, Pinot Bianco, Pinot Grigio, Pinot Nero, Moscato.

PINEROLESE r p sw fz
Barbera, Bonarda, Nebbiolo, Neretto, Uva Rara, Dolcetto, Freisa,

Doux d'Henry, Ramiè, Avarengo, and other local, non-aromatic reds.

RUBINO DI CANTAVENNA r
Barbera, Grignolino, Freisa.

RUCHÈ DI CASTAGNOLE MONFERRATO r
Ruchè, Barbera, Brachetto.

SIZZANO r nov ris
Nebbiolo, Vespolina, Bonarda, Sangiovese.

VALSUSA r
Avanà, Barbera, Dolcetto, Beretta Cuneese, and other local, non-aromatic red varieties.

VERDUNO/ VERDUNO PELAVERGA r
Pelaverga, and other local, non-aromatic red varieties.

Producers

The key provinces have been abbreviated as follows: AL = Alessandria; AT = Asti; CN = Cuneo; NO = Novara; TO = Torino.

Anna Maria Abbona, Farigliano (CN) r ☆→☆☆ * 8.5ha, 40,000 bottles. The production concentrates mainly on Dolcetto coming from one of the more traditional areas. Anna Maria, winemaker/graphic artist, has transferred her energy into promoting Dolcetto, and her creativity into producing some fine-quality labels that express personality and character: Dolcetto di Dogliani Sorì di But, Dolcetto di Dogliani Maioli, Langhe Dolcetto.

Accornero, Vignale Monferrato (AL) r sw ris ☆☆→☆☆☆ * 98 99 00 01 20ha, 80,000 bottles. A well-established estate founded in 1897 and managed by Ermanno and Giulio Accornero. It produces good Monferrato, Barbera, Grignolino, and Malvasia Passito. Highlights: Barbera del Monferrato

Superiore Cima Riserva, Grignolino del Monferrato Casalese Bricco del Bosco, Monferrato Rosso Centenario, and an excellent Casorzo Passito Pico.

Alario, Diano d'Alba (CN) r ☆☆ 10ha, 40,000 bottles. Passionate Dolcetto and Barolo producer focusing on quality with individual character. Top labels include: Nebbiolo D'Alba Cascinotto fruity, clean, with concentrated black cherry and blueberries; Barolo Riva good complexity, with hints of marasca cherry and coffee aromas, depth and persistence; and Dolcetto di Diano d'Alba Montagrillo – fruity, spicy character, long and slightly bitter, youthful, fine finish.

Gianfranco Alessandria, Monforte d'Alba (CN) r ☆☆→☆☆☆ * 96 97 98 99 00 01 04 5.5ha, 25,000 bottles. Excellent Barolo, Barbera, and Dolcetto. Alessandria is a man of few words, but he takes good care of his vineyards. Look out for Barolo San Giovanni, a dark dense, compact, modern-style Barolo. His entry-level Barolo, Barbera d'Alba, Langhe Nebbiolo, and Dolcetto d'Alba are all highly rated for their richness, good, ripe fruit, freshness, and length, as well as being well-priced for the quality.

Famiglia Anselma, Barolo (CN) *r* ☆☆ *96 97 98 99 00 01 04* 30ha, 38,000 bottles. A rapidly rising estate led by young, dynamic Maurizio Anselma, with Barolo vines in Barolo, Monforte, Serralunga, and Novello. The style is traditional, leading to austere wines that are characterized by leather and tobacco with spices and coffee. As they age, the wines show character and some refinement.

Antica Casa Vinicola Scarpa, Nizza Monferrato (AT) *r sw* ☆☆→☆☆☆ 10ha, plus 50ha of rented vines, 120,000 bottles. Founded in 1854, this is one of Asti's historic estates. The wines are noted for their fruity, aromatic freshness from Ruchè, Freisa, and Brachetto grapes. Highlights: Monferrato Rosso Rouchet Briccorosa and La Selva di Moirano Brachetto Secco, with a raspberry, peach, and rose-petal bouquet. Other labels include Monferrato Rosso Rossoscarpa, Barbaresco Tettineive, and a Rouchet Passito.

Elio Altare, La Morra (CN) *r* ☆☆☆→☆☆☆☆ *90 96 98 99 00 01 03 04* Altare is a passionate *vignaiolo* considered one of Piedmont's most eclectic winemakers. His outstanding Barolo Vigneto Arborina is characterized by power and complexity, with subtle notes of ripe marasca cherry, tobacco, and spice, balanced by fresh acidity and fine tannins, depth and elegant style. Altare's normal Barolo, Dolcetto d'Alba La Pria, as well as Langhe Vigna Larigi and Barbera d'Alba, are also praiseworthy.

Antichi Vigneti di Cantalupo, Ghemme (NO) *w r* ☆→☆☆☆ *

90 95 96 97 99 00 03 35ha, 180,000 bottles. The Arlunno family's vineyards lead the way in Ghemme for excellent, well-priced reds: Ghemme Collis Carellae, Signore di Bayard, and Collis Breclemae are produced by Alberto Arlunno and consultant oenologist Donato Landi. The wines have a fine, delicate floral essence, ripe fruit, and spice, and they are balanced by fresh acidity and length.

Giacomo Ascheri, Bra (CN) *w r* ☆☆ Nebbiolo *90 96 99 01 04* Barbera *90 97 00 03* Revitalized family firm with a huge range and good reliability across the board – from top Barolo Ascheri Coste & Bricco, Vigna dei Pola, and Nebbiolo d'Alba San Giacomo to experimental Montelupa white Viognier and Roero Arneis.

Azelia, Castiglione Falletto (CN) *r* ☆☆→☆☆☆☆ *90 96 97 98 99 00 01 04* 11ha, 55,000 bottles. Luigi Scavino is one of the rising stars of Piedmont. His two top Barolo labels, San Rocco and Bricco Fiasco, are of excellent stature, character, and elegance, both lively, intense, and balanced, with a classy finish. Also particularly noteworthy is his Dolcetto d'Alba Bricco dell'Oriolo.

Fratelli Barale, Barolo (CN) *w r ris* ☆☆→☆☆☆ * *95 98 01 03* 20ha, 100,000 bottles. Historic 1870 estate managed by Sergio Barale. It produces classic, slightly austere Barolo, characterized by leather, tar, tobacco, pepper, and marasca cherry, balanced by lively acidity, with a persistent finish. Aged 36 months in traditional Slavonian barrels, these Barolos are a pleasure to drink. Top labels include Barolo Vigna Bussia, Vigna Castellero, Langhe Nebbiolo Bussia, Barbaresco Riserva, and Dolcetto d'Alba Bussia.

Luigi Baudana, Serralunga d'Alba (CN) *w r* ☆☆→☆☆☆ 5ha, 25,000 bottles. Baudana is not as well known as he deserves to be, but his reputation is slowly rising. Baudana's vineyards produce excellent Barolos, true to the character of Serralunga Barolo – focused, with solid structure and fine, evident tannins, and well balanced, with lively acidity and tremendous ageing potential. Top labels: Barolo Baudana, Ceretta Piani, and a remarkable Dolcetto d'Alba Baudana. The Langhe Chardonnay is made in steel vats and has fine, mineral flavours, with good balance and structure.

Bava–Cocchi, Cocconato d'Asti (AT) *w r sw sp* ☆☆☆ * Cocchi *90 93 97 99 00 01 03* Bava *90 91 96 97 98 99 00 01 03 04* Family estate with a range of quality and *individualità*. Top labels: Barbera d'Asti Arbest, Libera, Piano Alto, Stradivario, Piemonte Chardonnay Thou Bianc, Monferrato Bianco (Alteserre), Ruchè di Castagnole Monferrato, and Malvasia di Castelnuovo Don Bosco. Also owners of the historic Giulio Cocchi estate (30km/18.5 miles from Bava), producers and inventors of the original Barolo Chinato recipe. Also known for Piemontese Spumante Classico Alta Langa DOC; Alta Langa Metodo Classico Blanc de Blanc Cocchi, and a sparkling Toto Corde Cocchi from Chardonnay and Pinot Noir, as well as Brachetto d'Acqui.

Alfiero Boffa Vigne Uniche San Marzano Oliveto (AT) *r sp* ☆☆ 25ha, 100,000 bottles. Established in 1878 and known for its Barbera d'Asti. Highlights: Barbera d'Asti Superiore Collina della Vedova, Barbera d'Asti Superiore Nizza La Riva, and Barbera d'Asti Vigna Muntrivè, as well as Monferrato Claret Gran Buchet, a fine rosé from 100% Pinot Noir with a floral bouquet, plenty of balance, and some structure.

Enzo Boglietti, La Morra (CN) *r* ☆☆→☆☆☆☆ 20ha, 70,000 bottles. Passionate winemaker and rising Langhe star well known for Barolo Brunate, Barolo Fossati, and Barolo Case Nere, characterized by full aromatic profile – intensely rich and concentrated, with hints of blackberry, raspberry, mint, prunes, and cassis, fleshy and balsamic, with a long finish. Boglietti also produces some fine Barbera d'Alba Vigna dei Romani, aged 18 months in barrique – very structured, with vibrant acidity; as well as a softer Langhe Buio.

Giacomo Borgogno & Figli, Barolo (CN) *r* ☆☆→☆☆☆ *90 96 98 03* 20ha, 150,000 bottles. One of Piedmont's historic estates, owned by the Boschis family. It was established in the small hamlet of Barolo in 1761. The production focuses on traditional, long-lived Barolo, from excellent sites and single vineyards.

Borgo Maragliano, Loazzolo (AT) *w sp sw* ☆☆ * 15ha, 150,000 bottles. Carlo Galliano's property produces attractive Loazzolo whites. His vineyards are based high up at 450m (1,476ft), and the ageing cellar is dug into the rock once used for the preservation of wine and food. Highlights: Loazzolo *vendemmia tardiva* made from 100% Moscato, and Moscato d'Asti La Caliera, both delightfully aromatic. The Giuseppe Galliano Chardonnay Brut made from 100% Chardonnay is excellent value, showing an elegant floral bouquet with good persistence.

E Pira & Figli – Chiara Boschis, Barolo (CN) *r* ☆☆ *90 95 96 97 98 99 00 01 03 04* 2.5ha, 17,000 bottles. Rising star Chiara Boschis recently took over this small estate in the heart of Barolo. She produces excellent, age-worthy Barolos: Cannubi and Via Nuova – tight, compact, with ripe berry fruit, minerality, and persistence. The wines are aged 25 months in new barriques. Also good Dolcetto and Barbera.

Francesco Boschis, Dogliani (CN) *w r* ☆☆☆ * *90 95 96 97 98 99 00 01 03 04* 11ha, 40,000 bottles. Mario Boschis's vines are tended to by Giuseppe Caviola and Paolo Boschis. This winery focuses mainly on Dolcetto di Dogliani under two distinct labels: Vigna Sorì San Martino, a fresh, juicy, ripe cherry wine, and Vigna dei Prey, a decisive, lively, elegant fruity wine. Langhe Bianco Vigna dei Garisin is limited to a small but excellent production.

Braida, Rochetta Tanaro (AT) *r m* ☆→☆☆☆☆ *90 91 95 96 97 98 99 00 01 03 04* 43ha, 500,000 bottles. The Bologna family are among Piedmont's pioneering winemakers of barrique-aged Barbera, and one of their best examples of this type is Bricco dell'Uccellone. Also worthwhile Barbera d'Asti Bricco della Bigotta, Ai Suma, and Barbera d'Asti Montebruna, the latter more traditional in style, aged in Slavonian barrel, plus a light, zesty, bubbly Barbera La Monella, Moscato, and Brachetto d'Acqui.

Brezza Giacomo & Figli, Barolo (CN) *r* ☆☆→☆☆☆☆ *90 96 97 98 99 00 01 03 04* 18ha, 90,000 bottles. Giacomo Brezza founded this estate in 1885; today the family-produced wines can also be enjoyed at their famous *trattoria* in the village of Barolo. Top labels include a fine traditional Barolo Bricco Sarmassa – rich in texture with a delicate floral bouquet and a fruity, spicy, savoury and round palate; Another wine,

Barolo Cannubi is aged 30 months in Slavonian oak and has hints of red cherries with a balsamic note. They also produce a very fruity Langhe Freisa Santa Rosalia, which is fresh, savoury, and delicious.

Bricco Maiolica, Diano d'Alba (CN) *r* ☆☆→☆☆☆☆ * 21ha, 90,000 bottles. The Accomo family produce truly first-rate Dolcetto. Highlights include Diano d'Alba Sorì Bricco Maiolica – powerful, juicy, ripe, with vibrant acidity and balsamic notes; Langhe Rosso Loriè, a 100% Pinot Noir – complex, evolved raspberry, and minty, balsamic notes; and Langhe Rosso Filius, a 100% Merlot – berry notes, with balanced freshness and a soft, round, fleshy texture.

Bricco Mondalino, Vignale Monferrato (AL) *r sw* ☆☆→☆☆☆☆ * *90 91 97 98 99 00 01 03 04* 18ha, 90,000 bottles. Mauro Gaudio's production, overseen by consultant oenologist Donato Lanati, includes fine Grignolino del Monferrato, as well as Barbera Monferrato, Barbera d'Asti, Monferrato Freisa, and Malvasia di Casorzo. Among the top labels are the structured, barrique-aged Barbera d'Asti Il Bergantino and the exemplary Grignolino del Monforte Casalese Bricco Mondalino, showing terroir character and drinkability. Also very good Malvasia di Casorzo Molignano, from an ancient variety giving a lively, fresh, slightly tannic dessert wine characterized by hints of pomegranate and peaches.

Gian Piero Broglia, Gavi (AL) *w r sp* ☆☆→☆☆☆☆ 49ha. A medium-sized property overseen by consultant winemaker Donato Lanati, producing some stylish Gavi. Top labels: Gavi di Gavi Bruno Broglia, La Meirana, Villa Broglia. The Bruno Broglia label is produced from 50-year-old vines vinified in steel, which allows the minerality of the terrain, as well as some fruit to prevail. The wines have a balanced, persistent finish.

Brovia, Castiglione Falletto (CN) *w r* ☆☆☆ *90 96 99 01* 15ha, 60,000 bottles. Established in 1863, this property is known for its firm, classic Barolo. Among the top labels is Barolo Ca'Mia, a fine example of Serralunga Barolo, characterized by a tight, tannic structure and vibrant acidity, making it an ageworthy wine. Ca'Mia needs considerable time to open and show its true potential. Barolo Rocche dei Brovia is similar in character, with elegant, mineral notes and a long finish; while Barolo Villero is intense, savoury, and dynamic, with firm tannins. The three Barolos are aged for about 34 months in traditional Slavonian oak.

Comm. G.B. Burlotto, Verduno (CN) *w p r* ☆☆→☆☆☆☆ *90 95 96 97 98 99 00 01 04* 12ha, 60,000 bottles. Historic estate established in 1850 and suppliers of Barolo to the Italian royal household of Savoia. Today the vines and production are managed by winemaker Fabio Alessandria. The wines are traditional and elegant and include two superb Barolos: Vigneto Cannubi, characterized by fresh floral and balsamic notes, with silky, seductive tannins; and Barolo Acclivi, a very elegant, balanced expression of Barolo, balsamic, ripe, and full-bodied, with good persistence. Also noteworthy is the unusual Verduno Pelaverga made from 100% Pelaverga – light in colour, fruity-spicy on the nose, with pepper, cherry, and red wooded fruit, and a clean finish.

Piero Busso, Neive (CN) *w r* ☆☆→☆☆☆☆ *90 96 98 99 01 03 04* 8ha, 35,000 bottles. One of Piedmont's most accomplished modern Barbaresco producers. Top labels: Barbaresco Gallina – deep, austere, with good complexity; and Barbaresco Vigna Borghese, a full and concentrated wine, with ripe fruit, floral notes, hints of tobacco, while also elegant and persistent. Barbaresco Mondino and San Stefanetto are reliable labels too. Their Barbera d'Alba San Stefanetto is a wine of great personality, drawing on classic notes of sour cherry with fresh vibrant acidity and complexity given in part by the ageing in barrique. Also, fine Dolcetto and Langhe Chardonnay.

Cascina Ballarin, La Morra (CN) *r ris* ☆☆ 7ha, 35,000 bottles. Luigi Viberti produces a firm Barolo Bussia characterized by dark berry fruit, liquorice, bitter chocolate, mint, and cassis, of rich extraction. Well balanced and persistent. Also good Barolo I Tre Ciabot and Langhe Rosso Cino.

Cascina Ca' Rossa, Canale (CN) *w r* ☆☆☆ 15ha, 60,000 bottles. Angelo Ferrio produces some outstanding Roero wines, including Arneis Merica – fresh, aromatic, and mineral in character; Good Roero Mompissano from 100% Nebbiolo – powerful, savoury, tannic, warm, and soft on the palate, with balanced acidity; and Barbera d'Alba – vinous, with notes of cherry, blackberry, and liquorice.

Cascina Castlèt, Costigliole d'Asti (AT) *r m* ☆☆ 18ha, 170,000 bottles. Maria Borio's vineyard delivers joyous Barbera d'Asti, running from the lively Goj to barrique Policalpo and Passum, a fine Moscato made from semi-dried grapes. Other highlights include Barbera d'Asti Superiore Litina, a ripe balsamic Barbera balanced by vibrant acidity, with an intense savoury finish. Also very good Moscato Passito Aviè.

Cascina Luisin, Barbaresco (CN) *r* ☆☆ * 7ha, 30,000 bottles. Luigi Minuto's production includes excellent Barbera d'Alba Asili and Barbera D'Alba Maggiur, characterized by berry fruit and aged in traditional Slavonian barrels. Traditional-style single-vineyard Barbarescos Rabajà and Sorì Paolin, aged 30 months in traditional barrels, show structure, balance, and persistence.

Castellari Bergaglio, Roverelo di Gavi (AL) *w* ☆☆→☆☆☆ * 12ha, 60,000 bottles. Vanda Castellari's Gavi di Gavi from 100% Cortese is full and round, with distinctive citrus and mineral notes. This is the fourth generation to cultivate the Cortese vineyards that stand at 300 metres (984ft) altitude, thriving on rich clay and iron soil. Highlights include Gavi Pilìn, Gavi di Gavi Rolona, and Gavi di Gavi Roverelo.

Castello di Neive, Neive (CN) *w r ris sp m* ☆☆→☆☆☆ * *90 98 99 01 03 04* 25ha, 120,000 bottles. Italo Stupino and winemaker Claudio Roggero make some of Neive's leading Barbarescos. Top label Barbaresco Santo Stefano Riserva, aged 24 months in traditional casks, shows elegance and balance, with fruity balsamic notes and is savoury and long. Also very good Barbera Santo Stefano, Dolcetto d'Alba Basarin, and Messoirano, as well as Langhe Arneis, Moscato d'Asti, and Spumante Castello di Neive, from 100% Pinot Noir.

Caudrina Dogliotti, Castiglione Tinella (CN) *m* ☆☆☆ * 35ha, 180,000 bottles. Romano Dogliotti's excellently made bottle-fermented Moscato d'Asti: La Caudrina and La Galeisa are characterized by a fine persistent perlage, and wonderful, floral, peachy notes. Also good-value Spumante Asti La Selvatica

and Moscato Passito Redento.

Ca' Viola, Dogliani (CN) *r* ☆☆→☆☆☆ * 6ha, 40,000 bottles. Giuseppe Caviola's fairly recent estate (established in 1991) has already produced some impressive really Dolcetto and Barbera. Top labels: Dolcetto d'Alba Barturot – intense, fleshy, with ripe fruit and a slightly balsamic, fine finish; and Barbera d'Alba Brichet – black cherries and prunes, slightly balsamic and spicy. L'Insieme is a Barbera/Nebbiolo/Pinot Noir/Cabernet blend, made into a modern, chewy wine with upfront fruit and spice, oak that is well-integrated, and a long finish.

Ceretto, Alba (CN) *w r sw sp* ☆☆→ ☆☆☆☆ *90 96 97 99 01 03 04* 105ha, 800,000 bottles. Among Piedmont's top estates. Brothers Bruno and Marcello Ceretto are considered pace-setters in Alba, with established Barolo wines from various sites: Barolo Bricco Rocche, Barolo Rocche Prapò, Barolo Asili Bernardot, and Barolo Bricco Rocche Brunate. These are all fabulous wines of stature. Also noteworthy are Barbaresco Bricco Asili, Barbaresco Bernardot, Langhe Rosso Monsordo, Barbera d'Alba Piana, Dolcetto d'Alba Rossana, Nebbiolo d'Alba Bernardina, Langhe Arneis Blangè, and Langhe Bianco Arbarei (a Riesling), as well as Spumante La Bernardina Brut and the Barolo Chinato.

Pio Cesare, Alba (CN) *w r* ☆☆→☆☆☆ *90 93 95 96 97 98 99 00 01 03 04* 45ha, 370,000 bottles. Renowned, long-standing winemaker since 1881, with production stored in historic cellars in the centre of Alba. Wines include the reliable, convincing Barolo Ornato and Barbaresco Il Bricco, as well as Barbera d'Alba Fides, Dolcetto, Nebbiolo d'Alba Il Nebbio, Langhe

Chardonnay Piodilei, and L'Altro.

Michele Chiarlo, Calamandrana (AT) *w r m sw* ☆☆→☆☆☆ *90 96 99 01* 110ha, 1,000,000 bottles. One of Piedmont's largest quality producers, with vines located in some of the most prestigious sites: Cannubi, Cerequio, Brunate, Asili, and Tassarolo. The production includes a range of well-structured Barolos: Cerequio, Cannubi, Brunate, Triumviratum, and Tortoniano, each showing distinctive character. Other wines: Barbaresco Rabajà, Barbaresco Asili, Barbera, Dolcetto, Gavi di Gavi Rovereto, Monferrato Bianco Plenilunio, and Rosso Countacci. Moscato such as Nievole and late-harvest Smentiò, are only produced in top vintages.

Chionetti Quinto & Figlio, Dogliani (CN) *r* ☆☆→☆☆☆ * 14ha, 45,000 bottles. Leading producer of traditional Dolcetto di Dogliani. The production is overseen by consultant oenologist Giuseppe Caviola and top labels include Dolcetto: Briccolero and San Luigi giving deep juicy fruit, with plums, blackcurrant, blueberries, silky tannins and an elegant, fresh, tenacious finish. Vinified in steel, they have the capacity to age well without the presence of oak.

Cieck, Agliè (TO) *w* ☆☆ ›☆☆☆ ** 17ha, 75,000 bottles. Remo Falconieri is partly responsible for putting quality Erbaluce wines on the map. His products reflect good winemaking at reasonable prices. Top label Erbaluce di Caluso Misobolo is fresh, intense, and lively on the palate, with a pleasant, slightly bitter finish. Also very good Passito Alladium and sparkling Erbaluce Metodo Classico.

Fratelli Cigliuti, Neive (CN) *r* ☆☆→☆☆☆ *90 96 97 98 99 00 01 03 04* 7ha, 30,000 bottles. Renato Cigliuti's estate makes superb, firm Barbaresco, Barbera, and Dolcetto d'Alba from vineyards at Serraboella. The top wines are in the classical mould, in particular Barbaresco Serraboella, a finely structured, tannic wine with wonderful cherry, spice and chocolate-mint aromas, with fresh acidity, plus good length. The Barrique-aged Barbera d'Alba Serraboella shows focused depth and a rich, aromatic profile, and it is velvety, with good length. Barbaresco Vigne Erte, aged 22 months in Slavonian oak, is more traditional in style, showing complex mineral character and good tannic structure.

Domenico Clerico, Monforte d'Alba (CN) *r* ☆☆☆→☆☆☆☆ *90 96 98 99 00 01 03 04* 21ha, 85,000 bottles. Fine, modern-style Barolo from one of the top estates in Monforte. Top labels include Barolo: Ciabot Mentin Ginestra, Percristina, and Pajana, all aged 24 months in barrique. These are concentrated wines with spice, dark cherries, bitter chocolate, persistence, and excellent ageing potential. Also impressive are Barbera and Dolcetto d'Alba, plus Langhe Arte, a barriqued, mostly Nebbiolo wine.

Elvio Cogno, Novello (CN) *w r* ☆☆→☆☆☆☆ *96 98 99 00 01 03 04* 9ha, 55,000 bottles. Nadia Cogno and Valter Fissore produce some classy Barolos, including Barolo Vigna Elena, traditional in style, aged 36 months in large Slavonian barrels – slightly austere in character, with an elegant floral bouquet; and Barolo Ravera, aged 12 months in barrique and another 12 in Slavonian oak – dense and concentrated, showing depth and structure. Also good Langhe Rosso Montegrilli and the unusual white Nascetta, made from

100% Nascetta grapes – rich in aromatic profile and minerality.

La Contea, Neive (CN) *w r sp m* ☆☆ * 18ha. Passionate winemaker Tonino Verro uses organically farmed, perfectly manicured vines to produce a fine selection of Nebbiolo Moncastello, Barbaresco Ripa Sorita, Dolcetto Paciocchi, Barbera Caplin, Roero Arneis Tunin, and Moscato Moncastello. The reds are vinous, savoury, with balanced acidity. White Arneis is floral and mineral in character, and has excellent length.

Aldo Conterno, Monforte d'Alba (CN) *r ris* ☆☆→☆☆☆☆ *90 96 98 99 00 01 04* Superb traditional producers. Father and son Aldo and Franco Conterno's top labels include Barolo Granbussia, a wine that ages superbly although austere and closed at first; excellent Barolo Cicala – authentic and dynamic in character, with musk and tobacco; Barolo Colonello – classic, earthy, with depth and layered with structure; and Barolo Bussia – fine aromatic profile and excellent balance. Other labels include Langhe Nebbiolo Il Favot, Langhe Rosso Quartetto, and Barbera d'Alba Conca Tre Pile.

Conterno Fantino, Monforte d'Alba (CN) *w r* ☆☆☆☆→☆☆☆☆ *90 96 97 98 99 00 01 03 04* 25ha, 120,000 bottles. Claudio Conterno and Guido Fantino are expert *Barolisti*. They excel with their top label, a reliable, classy Barolo Sorì Ginestra aged for 24 months in barrique, expressing fine elegance, good structure and balance, with great persistence. Barolo Vigna del Gris is characterized by intense berry aromas, densely textured on the palate with a fine, vibrant finish. Other labels include Langhe Rosso Momprà, Barbera d'Alba Vignota, Dolcetto d'Alba Bricco Bastia, and

Langhe Chardonnay Bastia.

Conterno Giacomo, Monforte d'Alba (CN) *r ris* ☆☆☆→☆☆☆☆ *90 95 97 98 99 00 01 02 03 04* 14ha, 40,0000 bottles. Giacomo Conterno's estate is managed by his son Giovanni and grandson Roberto. His legendary Barolo Monfortino Riserva has a wonderful ethereal nose with hints of ripe, dark berry fruit and marasca cherry, fleshy on the palate with complex layers showing depth and elegance and a long finish. The wine is vinified in oak barrels without temperature control, and matured for seven years in large oak barrels, thus producing an age-worthy Barolo. Barolo Cascina Franca is another outstanding traditional Barolo of great character and structure, expressing individual personality; likewise the powerful Barbera d'Alba Cascina Francia.

Contratto Giuseppe, Canelli (AT) *w r ris sp* ☆☆→☆☆☆ 55ha, 280,000 bottles. This historic estate founded in 1867 is especially known for its Asti De Miranda, which shows fine complexity, wide aromatic profile, and a fresh finish. Giuseppe Contratto Brut Riserva, a Chardonnay/Pinot Noir blend, is characterized by balance, fine perlage, delicate nut and pear aromas, good length. Other labels include a well-structured Chardonnay Sabauda and an elegant Barolo Cerequio.

Luigi Coppo & Figli, Canelli (AT) *w r ris m* ☆→☆☆☆ 24ha, 420,000 bottles. The Coppo brothers are noted for their Barbera: Pomorosso, Camp du Rouss, and Riserva della Famiglia. Good Freisa can be found under the Langhe Rosso Mondaccione label, and a Cabernet/Barbera blend under the Monferrate Rosso Alterego label. In the whites Chardonnay Monteriolo and Coppo Brut Riserva, made with 80% Pinot Noir and 20% Chardonnay are of particular note. They also make a fine Moscato d'Asti Moncalvina.

Giovanni Corino, La Morra (CN) *w* ☆☆☆→☆☆☆☆ *90 96 97 99 00 01 04* 16ha, 55,000 bottles. Corino has won acclaim for excellent Barolo and Barbera. Highlights include Barolo Vecchic Vigne, characterized by wonderful layers of depth and persistence; Barolo Vigneto Arborina; and the Barolo Vigneto Rocche, aged in barrique and characterized by fine tannins, ample aromas, complexity, and great length. Also good Barbera d'Alba Pozzo.

Matteo Correggia, Canale d'Alba (CN) *w r m* ☆☆☆ *95 97 99 01 04* 20ha, 120,000 bottles. Correggia is one of Roero's top winemakers, with a production of interesting Nebbiolo, Barbera, and Arneis. Top of the list is Roero Ròche d'Ampsèj, a 100% Nebbiolo that is modern, elegant, with layered depth, impressive structure, and a classy finish. Also very good Nebbiolo d'Alba La Val dei Preti and Langhe Rosso Le Marne Grigie, a Cabernet/Merlot/Syrah blend aged 18 months in barrique. Langhe Bianco Matteo Correggia is an excellent Sauvignon with plenty of varietal character, vibrant acidity, and a long, clean finish.

Deltetto, Canale d'Alba (CN) *w r ris sp sw* ☆☆→☆☆☆ * 15ha, 120,000 bottles. Passionate winemaker Tonino Deltettooffers precision and quality in his winemaking. Barolo Bussia is modern, fresh, fruity, showing complexity and structure. Roero Braja Nebbiolo, aged 18 months in barrique, shows ripe, fruity, balsamic notes. His whites are driven by elegance and minerality. Rocro Arneis leads with a round, full structure and fine fresh

aromas of white peach, while Extra Brut Riserva and excellent *passito* Bric du Liun, made from overripe Arneis make up this fine range.

Dezzani Fratelli, Cocconato (AT) *w r m* ☆☆ ** 1,200,000 bottles. A rising estate with a large production covering a well-priced range of Barbera, Ruchè, and white Gavi di Gavi, as well as sweet Malvasia and Moscato. Top labels: Barbera d'Asti I Ronchetti and an intriguing local red Ruchè – spicy, fruity red with a peppery touch to it.

Luigi Einaudi, Dogliani (CN) *r* ☆☆→☆☆☆ *90 96 97 98 99 00 01 03 04* 50ha, 250,000 bottles. This house, founded by former Italian president Luigi Einaudi, produces excellent Barolo Nei Cannubi, an earthy, mineral, elegant, and aromatic wine, and Barolo Costa Grimaldi. Also fine Dolcetto di Dogliani, I Filari, Vigna Tecc, and Langhe Rosso, a four-grape blend.

Giacomo Fenocchio, Monforte d'Alba (CN) *r* ☆☆→☆☆☆ * *90 95 96 97 98 99 00 01 03 04* 10ha, 50,000 bottles. Fifth-generation winemakers, Albino and Claudio Fenocchio produce some traditional Barolo, Barbera, and Dolcetto. Their vineyards are divided between Bussia, Villero, and Cannubi, and their Barolos reflect the three sites. These are austere wines that need time to open, but when they do, they are focused, long, and elegant, characterized by earthiness, leather, spice, and tobacco, with ripe underlying fruit, tight tannins and a distinctive, traditional style.

Luigi Ferrando, Ivrea (TO) *w r ris sw* ☆☆☆ * *90 95 97 99 00 01 03 04* 7ha, 50,000 bottles. Established in 1890, the estate is now run by Roberto Ferrando, who is considered a leader in northern Piedmont. He produces Carema made from 100% Nebbiolo, a classy wine characterized by fine elegance, aromatic, with hints of tobacco and spice. Among the highlights is Carema Etichetta Nera – a small production of a *riserva* cultivated in extreme conditions, yielding one of the finest examples of Carema. The whites include good mineral Erbaluce di Caluso Vigneto Cariola, an elegant sweet Passito Cariola and a Solativo Vendemmia Tardiva (late harvest).

Fontanafredda, Serralunga d'Alba (CN) *p w r ris sp sw* ☆☆→☆☆☆ * *90 96 97 99 00 01 03 04* 70ha, 6,500,000 bottles. Former Savoy cellar dating back to the 1870s, the winery is situated in the centre of a large estate and produces a reliable full range of Alba wines. Top labels include Barolo: Gattinara, Vigna La Rosa, Vigna La Delizia, Lazzarito, Paiagallo Vigna La Villa; Barbera Vigna Raimonda; Diano Vigna La Lepre; Nebbiolo d'Alba Marne Brune; and Moscato d'Asti Moncucco; as well as first-rate *spumanti classici* Contessa Rosa Brut and Gattinera Brut (rosé). Fontanafredda's production is one of the largest in Piedmont, and it comes from both company-owned vines and bought-in grapes.

Forteto della Luja, Loazzolo (AT) *w r sw* ☆☆→☆☆☆ 8ha, 45,000 bottles. This estate makes some of Loazzolo's best wines thanks to renowned winemaker/owner Giancarlo Scaglione, who created the rich, sweet *passito* Moscato Piasa Rischei that defines the Loazzolo DOC.

Umberto Fracassi, Cherasco (CN) *w r* ☆☆ * 7ha, 12,000 bottles. Senator Domenico Fracassi established this small estate in the 19th century and it became known for drinkable, reliable wine. Today, managed by Umberto Fracassi, production centres on Barolo, Barbera,

Dolcetto, and a lesser amount of white Langhe Favorita. The wines are fresh, flavoursome, without too much structure, and hence significant ageing potential.

Gaja, Barbaresco (CN) *w r* ☆☆☆→☆☆☆☆ *90 95 96 97 98 99 00 01 04* 84ha, 300,000 bottles. Charismatic Angelo Gaja has been Piedmont's undisputed leader for years, with outstanding wines. Top labels: the classic Nebbiolo-based Langhe Sorì San Lorenzo, Langhe Sorì Tildin, Langhe Costa Russi, Langhe Sperss, Langhe Contesia; also good Langhe Gaja & Rey, from 100% Chardonnay, and Langhe Darmagi (100% Cabernet Sauvignon). Less known are the Alteni di Brassica (Sauvignon), the Langhe Dolcetto Cremes, and Piemonte Barbera Sitorey.

Filippo Gallino, Canale (CN) *w r* ☆☆→☆☆☆ 12ha, 60,000 bottles. Gianni Gallino makes some impressive Barbera d'Alba and Roero Arneis, acclaimed as some of the best Roero wines – classic in style, bold in structure, and tenacious in character.

Ettore Germano, Serralunga d'Alba (CN) *w r* ☆☆ →☆☆☆ *90 93 95 96 97 98 99 00 01 03 04* 11ha, 50,000 bottles. Sergio Germano is both the winemaker and the owner of this estate that produces some of Alba's top Barolos, including Parapò and Cerretta, a typical Serralunga Barolo, aged 24 months in barrique – powerful tight, focused structure, rich in aromas and spice. Dolcetto Pra di Po is a fine example of a rich and powerful Dolcetto with a solid base of ripe fruit. The white Langhe Bianco Binel is a fine barrel-aged Chardonnay and Riesling blend with delicious minerality, well-integrated oak, and excellent persistence.

Bruno Giacosa, Neive (CN) *w r sp*
☆☆☆→☆☆☆☆ *90 95 96 97 98 99 00 01 04* 20ha, 500,000 bottles. Leading traditionalist Giacosa makes exceptional Barolo, Barbaresco, and Roero Arneis. Top labels: Barolo Falletto di Serralunga d'Alba, aged 30 months in large Allier barrels, giving fine, classic elegance. Possessing silky tannins, it is exceptionally long and persistent. Barbaresco Rabaja, also aged 30 months in large Allier barrels is a very elegant wine with ripe fruit and spice. Other labels include Barbaresco Santo Stefano, Barolo Bussia, Barbera Altavilla, Dolcetto Basarin, Nebbiolo Valmaggiore, Roero Arneis, and *spumante classico* Bruno Giacosa Extra Brut.

La Giustiniana, Rovereto di Gavi (AL) *w r* ☆☆ →☆☆☆☆ * 40ha, 200,000 bottles. A well-established estate producing distinguished Gavi. The production is overseen by Donato Lanati. Top labels: Gavi di Gavi Lugarara, Montessora, and Nostro Gavi.

Elio Grasso, Monforte d'Alba (CN) *w r* ☆☆☆→☆☆☆☆ *90 95 96 97 98 99 00 01 04* 14ha, 70,000 bottles. Acclaimed Monforte estate, Elio Grasso's prized Barolo Gavarini Vigna Chiniera, aged 24 months in Slavonian barrels, is powerful and layered, with ripe fruit and sweet spices, velvety, fine, and savoury, with excellent length. Also good Barolo Rüncot, aged 28-30 months in barrique – wonderful complex hints of nutmeg, coffee, and cherry jam, solid in structure, with fine tannins, powerful and long. Other labels include Langhe Nebbiolo, Barolo Ginestra Vigna Casa Maté, Dolcetto d'Alba Vigna Martina, and Langhe Cardonnay Educato.

Giacomo Grimaldi, Barolo (CN) *r* ☆☆☆ 8ha, 30,000 bottles. Ferruccio Grimaldi is a passionate winemaker and a rising Barolo star. His production includes Barolo Le Coste, aged 24 months in barrique – complex, elegant, deep, with luscious layers of back berry fruit and spice. Other labels to note are Barolo Sotto Castello di Novello, a fine Dolcetto d'Alba, and Barbera d'Alba Pistin.

Hilberg-Pasquero, Priocca (CN) *r* ☆☆☆ 5.5.ha, 25,000 bottles. Miklo Pasquero's small estate produces Nebbiolo and Barbera/Barbera Superiore of high standard. Nebbiolo d'Alba has violet and raspberry flavours, a ruby-red colour and mouth-filling tannins. Wines have excellent structure, elegance, balance, and intensity, with plenty of character.

Marchesi Alfieri, San Martino Alfieri (AT) *w r* ☆☆☆→☆☆☆☆ *90 91 94 96 97 98 99 00 01 03* 22ha, 80,000 bottles. The castle of San Martino Alfieri dominates the vines that produce premium-quality wines. In particular fine Barbera d'Asti: La Tota and Alfiera – structured, with fresh acidity, ripe fruit, showing complex aromas. Also good Grignolino Sansoero, and an interesting Monferrato Rosso dei Marchesi (Pinot Noir/Barbera).

Marchesi di Barolo, Barolo (CN) *w m r* ☆☆ →☆☆☆☆ *90 95 97 98 99 00 01 04* 120ha, 1,350,000 bottles. The Abbona family's production covers a wide range of reliable wines, led by Barolo Estate Vineyard – powerful structure, with evident tannins and persistence. Other labels include Barolo: Connubi, Sarmassa, and Vigne di Proprietà; Barbaresco Creja; Grignolino Bricco Prota; and Dolcetto d'Alba: Boschetti and Madonna di Como.

Tenute Cisa Asinari dei Marchesi di Grésy, Barbaresco (CN) *w r m* ☆☆→☆☆☆☆ *90 96 97 98 99 01 03 04*

35ha, 180,000 bottles. Alberto di Grésy's production is overseen by New Zealand winemaker Jeff Chilcott. Highlights include Barbaresco Camp Gros – elegant, spicy, fruity, floral notes, warm and round on the palate, well structured, with subtle tannins and persistent. Other noteworthy labels include Barbera d'Asti Monte Colombo and Langhe Nebbiolo Martinenga.

Mascarello Bartolo, Barolo (CN) *r*
☆☆☆☆ *90 95 96 97 98 99 00 01 04*
5ha, 18,000 bottles. Mascarello – a wine producer/philosopher – was undoubtedly one of the greatest Barolo producers. Today it is his daughter Maria Teresa who supervises the minute estate. Mascarello's Barolo is a traditional wine for purists – a Barolo aged 24 months in Slavonian barrels that needs time to open up. When it does, the aromatic profile is ample, with notes of rose petals, violets, cherry, and spice mingled with tobacco and liquorice. On the palate it is warm, round, and layered with depth and vibrant acidity. The finish is long and persistent.

Giuseppe Mascarello & Figlio, Monchiero (CN) *r* ☆☆☆→☆☆☆☆ *90 95 96 97 98 99 00 01 04* 13ha, 50,000 bottles. A historic estate founded in 1881. The production is supervised by consultant oenologist Donato Lanati, and the wines show lots of character. Masterful, age-worthy Barolo Santo Stefano di Perno leads an impressive range that includes Langhe Rosso, Barbera d'Alba, and Langhe Freisa. Barolo Monprivato and Villero are also noteworthy traditional wines aged 36 months in Slavonian barrels (20–40hl).

Massolino – Vigna Rionda, Serralunga d'Alba (CN) *w r ris* ☆☆☆☆→☆☆☆☆ *90 96 97 98 99 00 01 04* 17ha,

90,000 bottles. The Massolino family is one of the historic Barolo names from Serralunga, producing focused modern Barolos. The top label Barolo Parafada, aged 24 months in barrique, is a structured, powerful, earthy wine with hints of leather and spice and a mineral finish. Barolo Vigna Rionda Riserva, aged 36 months in Slavonian oak, is more traditional in style, very focused, austere. Barolo Serralunga d'Alba is mineral, compact, and powerful; while Barolo Margheria is again classic in style, earthy, with evident tannins.

Moccagatta, Barbaresco (CN) *w r*
☆☆☆→☆☆☆☆ * *90 96 97 98 99 00 01 04* 11ha, 65,000 bottles. One of the top Barbaresco estates, producing reliable-quality wine under the rigorous attention of Sergio and Franco Minuto. Top labels include Barbaresco: Bric Balin and Basarin – powerful, compact, layered, with depth, slightly austere, with fresh acidity and notes of black berry fruit, tobacco, liquorice, elegance, complexity, and individuality.

Mauro Molino, La Morra (CN) *w r*
☆☆→☆☆☆ 10ha, 45,000 bottles. A small, noteworthy estate producing some fine Barolo, Barbera, Dolcetto, and Langhe Nebbiolo. Top labels include Barolo Vigna Conca, a meaty, juicy, ripe, full-bodied wine with complex notes that are well reflected on the palate; and Barolo Vigna Gancia – spicy with hints of liquorice and black pepper, well structured, with a long, clean finish. Even the basic Barolo is fresh and savoury, with great elegance. All are aged 24 months in barrique. Interesting L'Insieme, a Nebbiolo/Barbera/Cabernet/Merlot blend.

Monchiero Carbone, Canale (CN)

w r sw ☆☆→☆☆☆ 10ha, 70,000
bottles. Consultant oenologist
Marco Monchiero produces some
fine Barbera, Langhe Bianco,
Roero, Roero Arneis. He also
makes a new Moscato Passito
Sorì di Ruchin from vines at
Santo Stefano Belbo, derived
from raisined grapes and aged
for two years in barrique. Also
a Langhe Bianco Tamardi, Roero
Printi, and a Roero Sru.

Cordero di Montezemolo Monfalletto,
La Morra (CN) *w r* ☆☆→☆☆☆
90 96 99 00 01 04 30ha, 135,000
bottles. Firm, fine Barolos made
by Gianni and Enrico Corder. Top
labels include Barolo: Vigna Enrico
VI, Monfalletto, and Vigna Bricco
Gattera, all aged 24 months in Allier.

Andrea Oberto, La Morra (CN)
r ☆☆→☆☆☆ *90 96 99 01 04*
16ha, 100,000 bottles. Andrea
and Fabio Oberto's production
includes a range of praised Barolos:
Vigneto Albarella and Vigneto
Rocche, aged 26 months in
barrique – tannic, structured,
with earthy, spicy freshness and
persistence. Good Barbera d'Alba,
Langhe Nebbiolo, and Dolcetto
d'Alba Vantrino Albarella.

Fratelli Oddero, La Morra (CN) *w r*
☆☆→☆☆☆ *90 95 96 97 98 99 00
01 03 04* 64ha, 200,000 bottles.
Historic estate founded in 1878
belonging to the Oddero family,
praised for their powerful
traditional Barolos coming from
historic sites. The top labels are
true classics: Barolo Rocche di
Castiglione is earthy and compact,
with mineral notes and balanced
acidity, giving excellent persistence.
Also good Barolo, such as Vigna
Rionda, Rivera di Castiglione, and
Mondoca di Bussia Soprana.

Orsolani, San Giorgio Canavese (TO)
w r sp sw ☆☆→☆☆☆ * 16ha,
120,000 bottles. A leading estate
producing fine Erbaluce di Caluso,
plus good Passito Sulé, a balanced
fresh aromatic wine aged 36
months in barrique. Also fragrant
La Rustìa and good Spumante
Cuvée Tradizione Metodo Classico
Brut from Erbaluce grapes.

Paitin, Neive (CN) *w r* ☆☆→☆☆☆ *
90 93 95 96 98 99 00 01 03 04 16ha,
60,000 bottles. The Pasqueros are
a dedicated family of winemakers.
Highlights include the focused,
powerful Barbarescos Sorì Paitin
and Serra Boella – opulent and
fruit-forward, with an enticing
melange of aromas and balanced
acidity. Also good Dolcetto Sorì
Paitin, Nebbiolo d'Alba Ca Veja,
Langhe Rosso Paitin, and Roero
Arneis Vigna Elisa.

Armando Parusso, Monforte d'Alba
(CN) *w r* ☆☆→☆☆☆☆ *90 96 97 98
99 00 01* 20ha, 100,000 bottles.
Marco Parusso is a dedicated
winemaker making modern, fruit-
forward Barolos from vineyards
between Castiglione Falletto and
Monforte. Top labels include
Barolo: Bussia Vigne Rocche;
Bussia Vigna Munie; Vigna Fiurin;
Mariondino; and Piccole Vigne.
Also good Barbera, Dolcetto,
Nebbiolo, and Sauvignon.

Fratelli Pecchenino, Dogliani (CN)
w r ☆☆→☆☆☆ *90 91 99 00 01 03 04*
25ha, 80,000 bottles. Brothers
Orlando and Attilio are passionate
about their Dolcetto di Dogliani,
produced in an innovative, rich
style. The flagship Dolcetto di
Dogliani San Luigi is aged ten
months in steel and shows superb
ripeness. The Dolcetto di Dogliani
Sirì D'Jermu is aged in oak for
three months and has depth, and
ripeness. Also good Langhe
Nebbiolo Vigna Botti and a white
Langhe Bianco Vigna Maestro.

Pelissero Giorgio, Treiso (CN) *w r*
☆☆→☆☆☆☆ *90 95 96 97 98 99 00 01
03 04* 35ha, 200,000 bottles. This
estate is known for its modern,
powerful Barbaresco, with
concentrated, solid character
and spicy nature, showing rich,
velvety warmth and finesse.
Top labels include Barbaresco:
Vanotu, Nubiola, and Tulin;
and a series of good Barberas,
Langhe Nebbiolo, and Dolcetto.

Luigi Pira, Serralunga d'Alba (CN) *w r*
☆☆→☆☆☆☆ *97 99 00 01* Giampaolo
Pira and consultant oenologist
Giuseppe Caviola are the driving
forces behind these age-worthy
traditional Barolos from some of
the best Serralunga sites. Top labels
include Barolo: Vigna Rionda,
Vigneto Marenca, and Vigneto
Margheria, aged 24 months in
barrique and characterized by
powerful structure and fine
tannins. They are well-balanced,
slightly austere wines, with good
underlying ripe fruit showing
hints of tobacco and liquorice.
Also high-ranking Roero Trinità,
Mombeltramo, and Arneis Renesio.

Poderi Colla, San Rocco Seno d'Elvio
(CN) *w r* ☆☆☆→☆☆☆☆ *96 97 98 99
00 01 03 04* 27ha, 130,000 bottles.
Tino, Giuseppe, and Federica
Colla make reliable, elegant wines
with good minerality and depth.
The vines at Cascine Drago and
Monforte produce a classy range,
including Langhe Bricco del Drago
(Dolcetto/Nebbiolo) and Barolo
Bussia Dardi Le Rose, plus
Barbaresco Tenuta Roncaglia,
Barbera, Dolcetto, Nebbiolo d'Alba,
and Langhe Bianco Sanrocco.

Produttori del Barbaresco,
Barbaresco (CN) *r ris* ☆☆☆ * *95 96
97 98 99 00 01 03 04* 95ha, 400,000
bottles. Historic 54-member
co-op producing reliable and
relatively well-priced Barbaresco

from nine *crus* of outstanding
quality. Highlights include
Barbaresco: Asili, Montefico,
Montestefano, Rio Sordo, Ovello,
Pajé Rabajà, Moccagatta, and Pora;
as well as Langhe Nebbiolo, Barolo,
Barbera, and Dolcetto.

Produttori di Nebbiolo e di Carema,
Carema (TO) *w p r* ☆☆→☆☆ * 17ha,
70,000 bottles. This 75-member
co-op produces sound, well-priced
Carema, including Carema
Etichetta Nera and a Riserva
Etichetta Bianca, as well as a
barrique version, Carema Barricato.

Prunotto, Alba (CN) *w r* ☆☆☆ *90 97 98
99 00 01 04* 55ha, 650,000 bottles.
An admired house, owned by
Antinori of Tuscany this makes
austere, elegant, mineral wines,
including Barolo Bussia and Barbera
Costamiòle, showing structure,
spicy, fresh, supple tannins, and
characterized by individual terroir
expression. Also good Barbaresco
Bric Turot, Barbera Pian Romualdo,
Dolcetto Mosesco, Nebbiolo
d'Alba Occhetti, and Barbera
d'Asti Costamiòle and Fiulòt.

Carlo Quarello, Cossombrato (AT) *r*
☆☆ * *90 96 97 98 00 01 03* 5ha.
Small traditionalist with vines
producing notable Grignolino
del Monferrato Cré Marcaleone,
rich in colour (unusual for
Grignolino), well structured,
with an intense aromatic profile,
capable of ageing well.

Fratelli Revello, La Morra (CN) *r*
☆☆→☆☆☆☆ * *90 96 97 98 99 00 01*
11ha, 60,000 bottles. Rising stars
Lorenzo and Carlo Revello's
production is overseen by
consultant oenologist Giuseppe
Caviola. They produce fine,
powerful Barolo: Vigna Giachini,
Vigna Conche, Vigna Gattanera,
and Rocche dell'Annunziata – all
of great class, aged in barrique,
showing structure, balance,

depth, and length. Also very well-priced Dolcetto and Barbera.

Giuseppe Rinaldi, Barolo (CN) *p r*
☆☆☆→☆☆☆☆ *90 96 98 99 01*
6.5ha, 30,000 bottles. Charismatic veterinary surgeon/winemaker Beppe Rinaldi is praised by Barolo traditionalists for his individual, genuine Barolo Brunate Le Coste, aged 36 months in Slavonian barrels – a stylized, austere, full-bodied, warm, age-worthy Barolo characterized by an attractive floral bouquet, depth and persistence.

Albino Rocca, Barbaresco (CN) *r w*
☆☆☆→☆☆☆☆ *90 96 97 98 99 00 01 03 04* 10ha, 70,000 bottles. Angelo Rocca's praised production is overseen by consultant oenologist Giuseppe Caviola. He makes increasingly admired Barbaresco, with top label Brich Ronchi expressing finesse and depth, with a rich aromatic profile; and a classic Barbaresco Vigneto Loreto. Both wines are aged 20 months in barrique.

Bruno Rocca, Barbaresco (CN) *w r*
☆☆☆→☆☆☆☆ *90 95 96 97 99 00 01 03 04* 12ha, 12,000 bottles. One of Barbaresco's top producers, tending toward a modernist style, showing finesse, solid structure, and aromatic complexity. Ethereal, complex,warm, and powerful Barbaresco Rabajà leads with wonderful cherry and spice, showing great persistence. Barbaresco Coparossa follows suit with a slightly lighter structure. Very good Langhe Rosso Rabajolo, Barbera, Dolcetto d'Alba Vigna Trifolè, and Chardonnay.

Sandrone, Barolo (CN) *w r*
☆☆☆→☆☆☆☆ 43ha, 95,000 bottles. Luciano and Luca Sandrone, modernist *Barolisti*, produce worldwide acclaimed wines from their excellent, impeccably managed vineyards. Top labels: Barolo Cannubi Boschis – fine

red berries and spice on the nose, velvety, rich, and extracted on the palate, with sweet tannins and persistence; and Barolo Le Vigne – similar in style. Both are aged 24 months in barriques. Also good Barbera, Dolcetto, Nebbiolo d'Alba Valmaggiore, and Langhe Rosso.

San Fereolo, Dogliani (CN) *w r*
☆☆→☆☆☆☆ **97 99 00 01 03 04* 12ha, 46,000 bottles. Nicoletta Bocca's production, overseen by winemaker Giuseppe Caviola, includes a vigorous, extracted Dolcetto di Dogliani of great individual character. Top labels: Dolcetto di Dogliani Superiore, San Fereolo, and Valdibà. Also good Langhe Rosso Brumaio and Langhe Bianco.

Saracco, Castiglione Tinella (CN) *m*
☆☆☆ * 35ha, 360,000 bottles. Paolo Saracco is one of the finest Moscato producers. The two top labels – Moscato d'Asti and Moscato d'Autunno – are fresh, aromatic, and very elegant, with a fine, creamy, persistent perlage.

Paolo Scavino, Castiglione Falletto (CN) *w r ris* ☆→☆☆☆☆ * 25ha, 105,000 bottles. Enrico Scavino produces well-crafted barrique-aged Barolo with layers of complexity and good ageing potential. Legendary label Barolo Bric del Fiasc leads the production. Other labels are Barolo Riserva dell'Annunziata – extracted, rich, with loads of ripe berry fruit, balanced acidity, very persistent; Barolo: Cannubi and Caro Bric. Also good Dolcetto Vigneto del Fiasc, rich Barbera d'Alba, Langhe Rosso, Bianco, and an excellently priced Vino Rosso Scavino.

La Spinetta, Castagnole Lanze (AT) *r m* ☆☆→☆☆☆☆ *93 95 96 97 98 99 00 01 03 04* 100ha, 400,000 bottles. Giorgio and Carlo Rivetti's estate produces excellent single-vineyard Barbarescos: Vigneto Gallina,

Vigneto Staderi, and Vigneto Valeriano, which excel in quality and pleasure. Also good Barolo Campè, aged 24 months in barrique, characterized by a long, elegant finish. Moscato d'Asti Bricco Quaglia and Moscato Vigneto Biancospino round off the excellent range of wines.

Terre del Barolo, Castiglione Falletto (CN) ☆→☆☆☆ ** *90 97 98 99 00 01* 800ha, 1,800,000 bottles. A 450-member co-op producing reasonably priced, reliable Barolo. Among the many labels, Barolo Castello di Grinzane, Rocche, Codana, Baudana, and Monvigliero prevail, along with a full range of Alba and Langhe DOCs.

Terre da Vino, Barolo (CN) *w r sw* ☆→☆☆☆ * *90 93 97 99 00 01 03 04* 390ha, 5,000,000 bottles. This is a model co-op, established in 1980 with a large production covering most Piedmont DOC(G)s, characterized by quality and value. The production and 12 vinification cellars are overseen by a team of oenologists and agronomists using innovative methods and technology.

Travaglini Giancarlo, Gattinara (VC) *r ris* ☆☆☆☆☆☆ *90 95 96 97 98 99 00 01 04* 39ha, 240,000 bottles. Giancarlo Travaglini and consultant oenologist Sergio Molino produce some of Gattinara's top wines. They show traditional class with good complexity, although most need time to open and express their potential, in true Piedmontese style. Top labels are: Gattinara Riserva, with a layered structure, great depth, spicy, balsamic, and floral notes, showing lots of terroir character. Gattinara Tre Vigne follows suit with plenty of elegance and style.

GD Vajra, Barolo (CN) *w r m* ☆☆→☆☆☆ *90, 95, 96, 97, 98, 99, 00, 01, 03, 04* 40ha, 200,000 bottles. Aldo Vajra is a competent producer with a great sense of balance between tradition and innovation. This is evident in his acclaimed range, which expresses elegance, depth, and plenty of aromatic freshness with great balance.

The bottle production includes top labels Barolo Albe, a *cru* from three vineyards; and Bricco delle Viole, from 30-year-old vines, aged 36 months in barrel. Also very good Dolcetto d'Alba Coste & Fossati, Barbera Superiore Bricco delle Viole, Langhe Nebbiolo, Freisa San Ponzio, and a Langhe Bianco from Riesling Renano, plus excellent Moscato d'Asti.

Varaldo, Barbaresco (CN) *r* ☆☆→☆☆☆ 7ha, 45,000 bottles. Rino and Michele Varaldo, rising stars in Barbaresco, make great Barbaresco and Barolo. Top labels include Barolo Vigna di Aldo, and Barbaresco: Bricco Libero, Sorì Loreto, and La Gemma, aged 24–26 months in barrique and characterized by fine complexity backed by solid structure, ripeness, and minerality.

Mauro Veglio, La Morra (CN) *r* ☆☆→☆☆☆☆ * *94 96 97 98 99 00 01 03 04* 11ha, 50,000 bottles. Mauro is a Barolo producer with a classy range of reliable wines. Top of the range are the Barolos: Vigneto Arborina, Bigneto Rocche, Castelletto, and Vigneto Gattera, aged 24 months in barrique and characterized by elegance and fine aromatic profile, structure, and balanced acidity. Nonetheless, most need to be given time to open up and show their full potential.

Viberti Giovanni, Barolo (CN) ☆→☆☆☆ * *98 00 01 04* 10ha, 65,000 bottles. Gianluca Viberti is a young, dynamic winemaker producing traditional-style Barolos. His Bricco delle Viole, San Pietro La Volta, and the top label Buon Padre are based on lengthy fermentation in large 5,000-litre casks, followed by three years of ageing. They show class, elegance, and great depth. A recently released innovative range of well-priced lighter wines includes Nebbiolo, Chardonnay, and a vivacious Barbera.

Giacomo Vico, Canale (CN) *w r sp* ☆☆ 20ha, 110,000 bottles. Good, reliable Arneis and Chardonnay coming from vines on the slopes of Roero. Top labels include Roero Superiore, Nebbiolo d'Alba, and Langhe Chardonnay.

Vietti, Castiglione Falletto (CN) *w r m* ☆☆→☆☆☆ 35ha, 195,000 bottles. Fourth generation winemakers producing a wide range of small vineyard lots of superb Barolo: Rocche, Lazzarito, Bussia, Brunate, and Villero, aged in 20–30hl Slavonian barrels and characterized by precision and persistence. Excellent Barbaresco: Masseria and Rabajà; Dolcetto: Lazzarito, and Tre Vigne; Barbera: Pian Romualdo, Bussia, Scarrone, and Vigna Vecchia; Arneis; and Moscato d'Asti.

Villa Sparina, Monterotondo di Gavi (AL) *w r sp* ☆☆→☆☆☆* 97 99 00 01 03 04 57ha, 300,000 bottles. Villa Sparina, established in the 18th century, was the country residence of the Marchese Franzoni of Genoa, who recognized the importance of Gavi's potential by constructing three, well-built underground cellars for his wines. Today, Mario Moccagatta's production combines tradition with updated technology and makes some pace-setting Gavi di Gavi Etichetta Gialla, Gavi di Gavi Monterotondo sparkling brut, Monferrato Rosso Rivalta, Barbera Sampò, Dolcetto d'Acqui Bric Maioli, and Monferrato Bianco Müller-Thurgau.

Gianni Voerzio, La Morra (CN) *w r m* ☆☆☆ 90 96 97 98 99 00 01 03 04 12ha, 64,000 bottles. Gianni Voerzio produces elegant Barolo La Serra, characterized by delicate floral, berry, and spicy aromas and layers of depth. Also very good Barbera Ciabot della Luna and excellent Dolcetto d'Alba Rocchettevino, with upfront cherry, raspberry, silky tannins, and persistence; Langhe Freisa Sotto I Bastioni; Roero Arneis Bricco Capellina; and Moscato d'Asti Vignasergente.

Roberto Voerzio, La Morra (CN) *r ris* ☆☆☆☆ 12ha, 35,000 bottles. It's amazing what this passionate, perfectionist winemaker achieves year after year in terms of consistent quality. It is hard to pick the best wine from a range of Barolo labels: Brunate, Rocche dell'Annunziata, La Serra, Sarmassa, Cerequio, and Barolo Riserva Vecchie Viti di Capalot, all aged for 24 months in Allier. There are nuances of character, yet all share an excellent, compact structure, with firm tannins, layered depth, and an ample aromatic profile. Voerzio also makes Barbera d'Alba Pozzo dell'Annunziata.

Wine & Food

Piedmontese cooking, like robust red wine, truly comes into its own in the autumn. Hearty, almost chauvinistically traditional, it is a type of refined country cooking that follows the seasons, and autumn provides the largest bounty. There is game from the mountainsides; hams, cheeses, and salami matured to perfection, and a bright array of garden vegetables augmented by what is found in woods and fields. The multitude of antipasti, the ample pastas and risottos, thick soups and stews, roast and boiled meats are the kind of fare that requires generous red wines. But the heartiness can be deceptive, since Piedmontese cooking also has touches of grace distinct from, but equal to, the artistry of the provincial cooking of Burgundy and Lyons. The ultimate luxury is the white truffle, sniffed out by dogs in the Langhe and shaved raw over pastas, risottos, meats, and fondues. Some of the best restaurants are found in the same place as the best wines. Visit when the grapes and truffles are being collected.

Agnolotti piemontesi Square handmade pasta filled with rabbit, veal, pork, and some cabbage.

Bagna caôda "Hot bath" of oil, garlic, and anchovies, bubbling over a burner, into which raw vegetables – peppers, cardoons, fennel, celery, etc. – are dipped.

Bollito misto piemontese Boiled veal and beef with *bagnet piemontese* (a garlicky green sauce).

Brasato al Barolo Beef stewed very slowly in Barolo.

Camoscio alla piemontese Chamois in a savoury stew.

Capretto arrosto Richly seasoned roast kid.

Crudo di vitella delle Langhe

battuta col coltello Finely chopped lean, raw veal, seasoned with salt, pepper, lemon juice, and olive oil. The addition of garlic is optional.

Fonduta di toma con uovo e tartufo Fondue of cheese with a poached egg and plenty of white truffle shavings.

Formaggi con cugnà d'uva moscato Mixed cheeses accompanied by a compote made of cooked must and seasonal fruit.

Fritto misto or fricia Delicacies – brains, sweetbreads, lamb cutlets, chicken breasts, aubergines, courgettes, frogs' legs, sweet pastes, etc. – dipped in batter and fried.

Insalata di carne cruda Minced fillet of beef marinated with oil, lemon, and pepper, sometimes served with mushrooms, Parmesan, or truffles.

Lepre in salmì "Jugged hare", marinated in wine and spices and stewed to rich tenderness.

Ravioli del Plin Very small handmade pasta filled with veal, egg, and cheese.

Tajarin al tartufo Hand-cut egg noodles with butter, Parmesan, and shaved truffles.

Vitello tonnato Thinly cut rosy veal with a tuna fish, anchovy, and caper mayonnaise – the meat used is from the Lissone breed.

Zabaglione Egg yolks whipped with marsala, another sweet wine, or Barolo.

Hotels

Albergo Ristorante del Buon Padre, Frazione Vergne, Barolo € The Viberti family *trattoria* and inn with six rooms are an emblem of warm hospitality and rustic simplicity. Specialties – *tajarin* and *agnolotti al plin, brasato al Barolo*,

wild hare *in salmì*, and fondue with truffle – can be enjoyed with the Viberti family wines.

Cà San Ponzio, Frazione Vergne, Barolo € This typical Langhe farmstead/ bed & breakfast with comfortable rooms is tucked away between vines and garden above the village of Barolo. Maurizio and Luciano are happy to assist with treks, mountain biking, sightseeing, and winery visits. Parking available.

La Contea, Neive €€
Well-preserved hospitable, historic inn in the centre of Neive, with dining on the ground level and steps leading to comfortable upstairs rooms.

La Corte Chiusa, Rocchetta Tanaro €€
This ex-Benedictine monastery converted to country lodgings, with four elegant suites, makes for a truly peaceful setting just a few steps from Rocchetta Tanaro.

Dre´ Castè Il Mongetto, Vignale Monferrato €
This 18th-century family villa with 16ha of vines offering two mini apartments and three spacious, comfortable rooms is a charming sanctuary off the beaten tourist route. Excellent meals are prepared on request.

Locanda del Pilone, Frazione Madonna di Como, Alba €€
An elegant inn amid the vineyards, just 5km (3 miles) from Alba, offering a relaxing stay. Four double rooms, two suites, and a good vaulted restaurant with views onto the hills of Treiso, Barbaresco, and Diano d'Alba.

San Maurizio, Santo Stefano Belbo €€€
A 17th-century Franciscan monastery immersed in an age-old park, housing 32 exclusive rooms-suites decorated with 18th-century furnishings. The vaulted restaurant is run by Guido da Costigliole, one of Piedmont's top chefs, who interprets traditional dishes and flavours from the Langhe.

Villa Carìta, La Morra €
Carìta Strandman's recently renovated farmhouse offers simple, refined hospitality. A large, open terrace offers stunning views over the surrounding vineyards.

Restaurants

Ristorante L'Agrifoglio, Turin €–€€
A traditional *trattoria* not far from the centre, where you can enjoy first-class regional cooking at reasonable prices in a genuine, friendly family atmosphere. The wine list is well-sourced.

Trattoria I Bologna, Rocchetta Tanaro €€
Family run *trattoria* offers traditional Piedmontese recipes, passed down from generation to generation. Excellent traditional salame, *vitello tonnato*, tagliolini with truffles, potato gnocchi, vegetable-filled ravioli served with a poached egg on top and crowned with truffle shavings.

Backed porcini, goat cheese with the local home-made grape must and an exquisite array of desserts. The ambience is relaxed, with a touch of warm, rural elegance.

Trattoria Brezza, Barolo €–€€
Welcoming, genuine *trattoria* set in the heart of Barolo, above Oreste Brezza's cellars, offering some of the lightest *tajarin* with slivers of truffle when in season. Tasty boiled beef and *bagna cauda*, roasts and cheeses, with their ever-present companion, the canonical home-made *cugnà*.

La Ciau del Tornavento, Treiso €€€
Chef Maurilio Garola is one of the Langhe's best chefs. He bases his

dishes on local ingredients, has a great cheese board and when truffles are in season he makes a delicious cheese fondue with egg and truffles. His basement cellar is well stocked, with some 700 labels. Book ahead. There is also a fine garden for alfresco dining.

Trattoria del Peso, Belvedere Langhe, Dogliani €

Feel like stepping back a few decades to a rare glimpse of a real Italian/Piedmontese *trattoria*? This place's old-fashioned charm and simplicity are reminders of authentic Italian hospitality, which prides itself on traditional values and home-made recipes. Trattoria del Peso offers a few rooms above the restaurant and there is a shop on the same level selling local cheeses. Only open for lunch. Essential to book – especially Sunday lunch.

Enoclub Ristorante, Alba €€

In the centre of Alba, on Piazza Savona, Enoclub is a downstairs cellar with stone walls and vaulted ceilings. Attentive, courteous service and traditional food come with an innovative touch. The wine list is ample and well priced. It is advisable to book ahead.

All' Enoteca di Davide Palluda, Canale €€€

Davide Palluda is the Langhe's most creative chef: he has an excellent sense of style and matches flavours based on local cuisine. Housed above the Enoteca Regionale del Roero, the restaurant offers an ample wine list with about 400 labels from Piedmont, but also from other parts of Italy. Book ahead.

Ristorante Gener Neuv, Asti €€€

Traditional, elegant dining offering a hospitable, convivial atmosphere, attentive service and excellent Piedmontese dishes prepared with a touch of class. Excellent wine list. Book ahead.

Ristorante Guido, Pollenza €€€

Situated on the Slowfood University premises, Guido's classy restaurant offers some of Piedmont's eclectic dishes, prepared with simplicity and fine ingredients. Excellent wine list.

Osteria La Lumaca, Cherasco €

Traditional *trattoria* with well preserved elegant-rustic interior offering good array of Piedmontese dishes, as well as snails which as the name suggests (Lumaca) is the specialty of Cherasco. Excellent wine list.

Osteria Veglio, Morra €€–€€€

A favourite with wine producers. The austere dining room has been carefully restored to create an authentic old-style *trattoria* for serious eating and drinking. Excellent wine list, but can get busy, so book ahead.

Trattoria della Posta, Monforte d'Alba €€–€€€

Elegant setting overlooking Barolo's vineyards offers excellent *agnolotti del plin*, *tajarin*, quail risotto, finely chopped lean, raw veal, seasoned with salt, pepper, lemon juice and olive oil, braised oxtail in Barbera reduction served with mashed potatoes, excellent cheese board and a tempting choice of desserts, including zabaglione and nut cake.

Al Vecchio Tre Stelle, Barbaresco €€€

A traditional country house tucked away in a small side street, known for its classic dishes. Specialties include *ravioli del plin al burro e salvia*, *tajarin al ragù di carne*, and *coniglio ai peperoni* (rabbit and peppers). There is an excellent wine list. There are also some rooms above the restaurant.

Liguria *Liguria*

Liguria's wine production is among the lowest in Italy (only Valle d'Aosta trails). This may be due to the region's vertiginous topography: mountains rise dramatically from a spectacularly jagged coastline, making mechanized viticulture virtually impossible. Still, more than 100 types of vine are grown on the rocky hillsides of this slender crescent arching along the Ligurian Sea from France past the capital Genoa to Tuscany.

The region is known as a rather introspective place, which may explain the obscurity of its wines, very few of which are exported beyond its shores. The exception is Cinqueterre, the reputation of which derives more from past than present achievements. Pre-phylloxera, the Cinqueterre (a UNESCO World Heritage site comprising the villages of Monterosso, Vernazza, Corniglia, Manarola, and Riomaggiore) on the eastern coast (Riviera di Levante) boasted some 1,500 hectares of terraced vineyards; today this "endangered" viticulture has diminished to a mere eighty hectares, with a group of winemakers determined to revive the wealth of its ancient traditions, including rare Sciacchetrà and a new surge of blended Granaccia and Syrah wines.

Other wines merit more attention: under the sprawling Riviera Ligure di Ponente DOC (the western coast) are the intriguing red varieties Rossese and Ormeasco (a clone of Dolcetto), the unique white Pigato, and the leading white Vermentino, which is gaining prominence everywhere, most notably in the Colli di Luni DOC to the east. Rossese also has its own DOC, Rossese di Dolceacqua, in a small area near the French border. Wines from Liguria's other DOCs – Colline di Levanto, Golfo del Tigullio, and Val Polcevera (with its sub-zone Coronata) – are rarely seen. The region has few IGTs: Colline Savonesi, Golfo dei Poeti, and Colline del Genovesato. Most other wine is called simply, but proudly, *nostrani* (ours).

Visitors may find the rusticity of the westerly Dolceacqua zone a relaxing counterpoint to the crowds of Portofino and Portovenere. The Vinoteca Sola in Genoa provides a wide range of Ligurian wines along with the best from elsewhere. Also recommended are Enoteca Gran Caffè Defilla in Chiavari, Enoteca Lupi in Imperia, and Enoteca Bacchus in San Remo. Enoteca Internazionale in Monterosso is the reference point for Cinqueterre.

Recent Vintages

Recommended vintages appear next to appellation wines capable of ageing.

Appellations

DOC

CINQUETERRE *w sw*
Bosco, Albarola, Vermentino.

CINQUETERRE SCIACCHETRÀ
w sw ris 95 96 97 98 99 00 01 04
Bosco, Albarola, Vermentino.

COLLI DI LUNI *w r ris 98 99 00 01 02 03 04*
Vermentino, Trebbiano, Sangiovese, Canaiolo, Ciliegiolo.

COLLINE DI LEVANTO *w r nov*
Vermentino, Albarola, Bosco, Sangiovese, Ciliegiolo.

GOLFO DEL TIGULLIO *w r fz*
sw pas nov sp m 00 01 02 03 04
  Vermentino, Bianchetta Genovese,
  Dolcetto, Ciliegiolo

PORNASSIO/ORMEASCO
r sw sup liq pas 98 01 02 03 04
  Dolcetto, Bosco.

RIVIERA LIGURE DI PONENTE
w r
  Pigato, Rossese, Vermentino.
  Sub-zones: Albenga (Albenganese),
  Finale, Riviera dei Fiori.

**ROSSESE DI DOLCEACQUA/
DOLCEACQUA** *r sup 98 00 01 04*
  Rossese.

VAL POLCEVERA *w r pas nov fz sp*
  Vermentino, Bianchetta Genovese,
  Albarola, Dolcetto, Sangiovese,
  Ciliegiolo, Barbera.
  Sub-zone: Coronata.

IGT
  Colline del Genovesato
  Colline Savonesi
  Golfo dei Poeti

Producers

*The key provinces have been
abbreviated as follows: GE =
Genova; IM = Imperia; SP =
La Spezia; SV = Savona.*

Walter De Battè, Riomaggiore (SP) *w r
sw* ☆☆→☆☆☆ 1ha, 2,500 bottles.
Walter De Batté's Cinqueterre
Bianco exemplifies the potential of
"extreme" terraced viticulture. His
400-bottle production of Sciacchetrà
is perhaps the only authentic
example of the Cinqueterre's
tradition of the variety – intense,
elegant aromatic profile, balanced
structure, and acidity.

Bisson, Chiavari (GE) *w r sw* ☆☆→☆☆☆ *
10ha, 80,000 bottles. Piero Lugano's
production includes Golfo del
Tigullio Vermentino Vigna
Intrigoso, Vermentino Vignerta,
Cinque Terre Vigna Marea – all
showing flinty, mineral character.
Also good Rosso Musaico Vigna
Intrigoso and Passito Acinirari.

Riccardo Bruna, Ranzo (IM) *w r*
☆☆→☆☆☆ 5ha, 38,000 bottles.
Francesca Bruna produces Riviera
Ponente Pigato, in particular Pigato u
Baccan, only made in top vintages –
fine citrus, mineral elegance, body
and persistence. Also good Pigato Le
Russeghine – complex, floral, full,
round, austere terroir expression.

Buranco, Monterosso al Mare (SP) *w r
sw* ☆☆→☆☆☆ 1ha, 6,000 bottles.
The Wachter family's organic
production is based on Cinqueterre
Bianco (Bosco/Vermentino/
Albarola) – citrus and herbs, round,
and long; an international-style
Rosso – cassis, prune, and liquorice;
and exotic and sensual Sciacchetrà.

Mandino Cane, Dolceacqua (IM) *r*
☆☆→☆☆☆ Good Rossese
producer. Top labels: Rossese
Vigneto Arcagna – sapid on the
nose, good cherry, delicate, firm
tannins, persistent; and Rossese
Vigneto Morghe – mineral, complex
nose, soft, full fruit, medium length,
good acidity.

Forlini Cappellini, Manarola (SP) *w sw*
☆☆☆ 8,000 bottles. Giacomo
Forlini's production includes praised
Cinqueterre Bianco – fresh, floral
aromas, vibrant acidity; a deep
amber-hued Sciacchetrà; and
Albarola – rich and complex notes
of chestnut honey and dried fruit.

Cascina du Fèipu dei Massaretti,
Albenga (SV) *w r sw* ☆☆☆ 6ha,
60,000 bottles. One of the Ponente's
historic producers. Highlights:
Pigato – varietal character marked
by good minerality; Rossese – cherry
aromas, depth, and persistence;
passito La Bice – delicate, floral.

Co-op Agricoltori Vallata di Levanto (SP) *w r sw* ☆☆→☆☆☆ * 80,000 bottles. Co-op producing the lesser-known Colline di Levanto DOC. Of particular interest: Bianco Costa di Matelun Etichetta Nera – good mineral character, citrus, racy, and full on the palate. Also good Costa di Matelun Lievàntu (white) and Passito Rosso – hints of blackberry, with velvety texture.

Maccario Dringenberg, Dolceacqua (IM) *w r* ☆☆→☆☆☆ 2ha, 15,000 bottles. Production includes two excellent Rossese Superiore reds: Posaù and L'Uvaira – crushed berries, spice, tobacco, liquorice. Intriguing fresh, zesty, late-harvest white Masaira – floral, strawberry aromas.

Ottaviano Lambruschi, Castelnuovo Magra (SP) *w r* ☆☆→☆☆☆ 5ha, 35,000 bottles. Fabio Lambruschi was one of the first winemakers to produce local monovarietal wines, in particular Costa Marina, a 100% Vermentino – elegant, structured, crisp finish. Also good Vermentino Sarticola – mineral, sapid, zesty; and Rosso Manicro (Sangiovese/Merlot/Cabernet/Canaiolo) .

Lupi, Pieve di Teco (IM) *w r sw* ☆☆→☆☆☆ 10ha, 140,000 bottles. Historic producer of Riviera di Ponente Liguria. Top labels: Ormeasco di Pornassio, from a Dolcetto clone – herbaceous, sapid, and vibrant; Pigato Le Petraie and Vignamare – dandelion, honey, good aromatic persistence; Vermentino Le Serre – hints of exotic fruit and wild flowers.

La Pietra del Focolare, Ortonovo (SP) *w r* ☆☆ Small estate run by Stefano Salvetti. Highlights: Colli di Luni Vermentino – terroir character with ample aromatic profile; Colli di Luni Vermentino Solarancio – aromatic complexity, tropical fruit, round, full, with long, mineral, bitter-almond finish; and good Vermentino Villa Linda from 35-year-old vines.

La Polenza, Corniglia (SP) *w sw* ☆☆ 8ha, 10,000 bottles. A growing gem with a production of Bosco-based Cinque Terre Polenza – minerality, aromatic complexity, zesty, persistent palate. An experimental Sciacchetrà is currently under way at the property.

Santa Caterina, Sarzana (SP) *w r* ☆☆→ ☆☆☆ 7ha, 20,000 bottles. Andrea Kihlgren's top labels include Colli di Luni Vermentino Poggi Alti – fresh and crisp; Giuncarò (Sauvignon/Tocai/Vermentino) – elegant, mineral character; and Fontananera (Merlot-based with Ciliegiolo) – ripe berry fruit, vibrant and full.

Tenuta Giuncheo, Camporosso (IM) *w r* ☆☆→☆☆☆ Arnold Schweizer and Marco Romagnoli produce good Rossese di Dolceacqua Vigneto Pian del Vescovo – ample aromatic profile, ripe brambly fruit, vibrant with depth; and Vermentino Le Palme – fruity apple, citrus, flowery bouquet, racy and crisp.

Terre Bianche, Dolceacqua (IM) *w r* ☆☆→☆☆☆ 8ha, 55,000 bottles. Filippo Rondelli's Rossese di Dolceacqua Bricco Arcagna shows complex aromas of cherry, tobacco, cassis, and vanilla. Also good Arcana Rosso (Rossese/Cabernet Sauvignon) and Arcana Bianco (Pigato/Vermentino).

Terre Rosse, Finale Ligure (SV) *r w* ☆☆→☆☆☆ 30,000 bottles. Vladimiro Galluzzo's production is based on Riviera Ponente Pigato Apogeo and Le Banche, a well-crafted oak-fermented Pigato. Also Vermentino and an interesting Cerbina made from local variety Lumassina.

Testalonga at Dolceacqua (IM) *w r* ☆☆→☆☆☆ * 1,5ha, 6,500 bottles. Antonio Perrino's production focuses on Rossese, barrel-fermented and aged – slightly rustic, but wonderful fabric, rich, vibrant, full , good acidity, fresh, and lively.

Wine & Food

Ligurian cuisine blends ingredients such as eggs, nuts, cheese, vegetables, and olive oil (as well as fresh herbs). Recipes change with the seasons: in autumn, chestnut flour is used to make cakes such as *castagnaccio*, and chickpea flour is used to make *farinata*, a pizza-like flatbread. In summer, vegetable *frittate* (omelettes) are made with courgettes, potatoes, and onions, or chard and cream cheese. *Pesto* (a sauce of basil, olive oil, pine nuts, and cheese) appears on most menus. Ligurians rely on fish prepared in artistic and savoury ways. Meat is secondary, though rabbit in Rossese with olives is traditional in the countryside of the Riviera di Ponente.

Branzino in tegame Sea bass cooked with white wine, tomato, and seasonings.

Cappon magro At least 12 types of fish are piled pyramid-style on a base of ship's biscuits and topped with oysters and lobsters.

Cima alla genovese Veal breast rolled with vegetables, nuts, herbs, spices, eggs, and cheese.

Stoccafisso Dried cod with pine nuts, olives, potatoes, herbs and anchovies, in white wine and tomato sauce.

Hotels

Grand Hotel dei Castelli, Sestri Levante (GE) €€€ Exclusive hotel in a park overlooking Golfo Tigullio. Good pool, plus a small private bay in the rocks facing the sea.

Cenobio dei Dogi, Camogli (GE) €€–€€€ Set in a park on the seafront, this hotel offers great views, pool, and a private beach.

Locanda Ca' Peo, Leivi (SP) € Simple but charming, set among olive groves. The restaurant serves good local fare.

La Luna di Marzo, Volastra, (SP) €€ Charming small hotel with views of the Cinqueterre coastline.

Le Palme, Zoagli (GE) € Charming family villa with spacious rooms (in the old part). Nice garden.

Hotel Splendido, Portofino (GE) €€€ The Riviera's most exclusive hotel. Exceptional service, very romantic, and very expensive!

Hotel Suisse Bellevue, Monterosso (SP) €–€€ A serene oasis with great views from the sea-facing rooms.

Restaurants

Antica Trattoria dei Mosto, Conscenti di Ne (GE) €€ Excellent local dishes including *mandilli* (lasagne) *al pesto*. Good wine list.

Cappun Magro, Groppo di Riomaggiore (SP) €€ Local flavours and recipes presented with a twist.

La Lanterna, Riomaggiore (SP) € Fresh fish and local wines at this restaurant perched above the sea.

Da Luchin', Chiavari (GE) € Characteristic *osteria* serving *farinata* and other regional dishes.

I Matteti, Alassio (IM) € Simple home-cooking: *farinata*, octopus in a tomato sauce, and other specialties.

Il Mulino Del Cibus, Castelnuovo Magra (SP) €–€€ Creative dishes such as a soufflé of aubergines with *raschera* fondue. Great wine list.

Il Palma, Alassio (IM) €€€ This Michelin-starred restaurant boasts some of Liguria's most creative cooking. Small, eclectic wine list.

Lombardy *Lombardia*

Lombardy is a moderate wine producer compared to its neighbours of Piedmont, the Veneto, and Emilia-Romagna. As consumers, however, Lombards are second to none. Milan, capital of fashion, industry, and finance, is a most active wine market, the pace-setter in food and drink. This influence has contributed to Lombardy's lead in the production of classic-method sparkling wine, of which Franciacorta and Oltrepò Pavese are the centres. But otherwise, the Milanese often turn to regions such as Piedmont, Tuscany, or Bordeaux for premium reds; Friuli, Trentino-Alto Adige, or Burgundy for premium whites, and for special occasions, Champagne.

Still, Italy's most industrialized region does have hillsides between the Alps and Apennines and the Po Valley where vines excel. To the southwest is the Oltrepò Pavese, which boasts Lombardy's most productive vineyards. As a supplier of everyday wines to Milan and of Pinot grapes to sparkling wine producers elsewhere, the Oltrepò has never enjoyed much prestige, despite vastly improved wines. To the north is the Valtellina, where vines grow on a south-facing hill overlooking the Adda River; its sub-zones of Grumello, Inferno, Sassella, and Valgella are covered by the Valtellina Superiore DOCG. Its apogee is the powerful Sfursat, from semi-dried grapes, it too DOCG.

To the east are the provinces of Brescia, Bergamo, and Mantova (Mantua), with the vast majority of the region's fifteen DOC zones; Franciacorta (DOCG), producing Italy's best sparkling wine, lies not far from Brescia. To the east, along Lake Garda, are Riviera del Garda Bresciano, lying within the province of Brescia, and Garda Colli Mantovani, covering the province of Mantova. The small zone of Lugana nestles under the south shores of the lake. There is also an umbrella DOC, Garda, that spreads over all the wine-growing territories under the lake's climatic influence, in both Lombardy and the Veneto, but its *classico* sub-zone is restricted to lands in the Brescia area.

Visitors to Lombardy's lake country can take in Garda, Lugana, and Franciacorta, which touches on the pretty Lake Iseo. The Valtellina is a gorgeous valley in the Alps with steeply terraced vineyards overlooking the Adda River. The Oltrepò Pavese lies amid rustically scenic hills south of Pavia. Lombardy has some of Italy's best-stocked *enoteche*, including Emporio Solci, Cotti, Ronchi, N'Ombra de Vin, Peck, Vino Vino (all in Milan), Longo in Legnano, Enoteca 77 in Meda, and Meregalli in Monza. In the provinces you'll find Delizie di Bacco in Como, Castelletti in Ponte San Pietro (Bergamo), Il Carato and Creminati in Brescia, Marino in Chiavenna (Sondrio), Malinverno in Isola Dovarese (Cremona), Re Carlo Alberto in Mantova, L'Enoteca in Voghera (Pavia), and L'Uva In Bottiglia in Vercelli.

Recent Vintages

Lombardy's longest-lived wines are the reds from Valtellina, which may mature and improve for a decade or more. In Oltrepò Pavese, Brescia, and other eastern zones of the region, most reds are made with a view to drinking within six or seven years.

2004 A long, balanced ripening season ensured good levels of acidity, sugar, and ripe tannins. Generally higher yields and good homogenous quality.

Wine Areas

1   Valtellina
2   Valcalepio
3   Garda Bresciano
4   Franciacorta
5   Cellatica
6   Botticino
7   Garda Classico
8   Lugana
9   San Martino della Battaglia
10 Mantovani Garda Colli Mantovani
11 San Colombano al Lambro
12 Oltrepò Pavese
13 Lambrusco
14 Moscato di Scanzo

2003 Early ripening due to lack of rain and intensive heat throughout the summer, producing some powerful, alcoholic wines.

2002 A wet summer with widespread hailstorms followed by a fine autumn resulted in variable grape quality, but there were good results for the more assiduous producers who selected stringently. The notable exception was Valtellina, which escaped the worst of the weather and gained excellent wines.

2001 A rainy spring followed by a hot summer brought gratifyingly good wines throughout the region, with whites especially excelling.

2000 Very good throughout, except in Lugana, where hail struck; particularly good for reds.

1999 Good vintage for Valtellina thanks to cold nights and sunny days in autumn; excellent Chardonnay wines in Franciacorta.

1998 Small crop with some wines rated at the same levels of 1997.

1997 Outstanding vintage in Valtellina and the Brescia area; very good in Oltrepò Pavese.

1996 Good to excellent harvest for reds throughout the region.

1995 Small crop of generally good quality; Valtellina reds show fairly full structure.

Notes on earlier vintages: Earlier good vintages in Valtellina include 1994, 93, 92, 90, 89, 88, 86, 85, 83, 80, 79, 78, 71, and 70.

Appellations

DOCG

FRANCIACORTA *w sp mc r*

The low hills west of Brescia fronting Lake Iseo were once noted for rustic reds, but over the last two decades Franciacorta has gained a reputation as a miniature Champagne. Although still wines are also produced (*see* Terre di Franciacorta DOC), Franciacorta DOCG applies only to its classic-method sparkling wines. Its requirements are strict: the label does not allow mention of the terms *metodo classico, metodo tradizionale*, or *spumante*, and, like Champagne, the wine is identified only by the name of a place. Ageing requirements are more demanding than for Champagne. The non-vintage must age at least 25 months from the latest vintage in the *cuvée* before being sold, and this includes a minimum of 18 months in bottle after the second fermentation. Vintage Franciacorta (*millesimato*) must age for 37 months, of which 30 must be in bottle. The better wines all age for at least three years in bottle.

Franciacorta is produced from any or all of Chardonnay, Pinot Bianco, and Pinot Nero. Chardonnay, noted for its finesse, often dominates blends or stands alone as blanc de blancs. Franciacorta Rosé must contain at least 15% of Pinot Nero. This variety cannot be used in the growingly esteemed *satèn*, the registered term for *crémant*, the "creamy" texture and gentle perlage of which come from lower CO_2 pressure. Typically it covers a range of tastes, from brut (dry) and extra dry (lightly sweet), to demi-sec (medium-sweet) and sec (quite sweet). However, the vast majority of Franciacorta is brut. This includes the wines that receive no final dosage or *liqueur d'expédition* and may be described as extra brut, *pas dosé*, dosage zéro, etc. Production has surpassed 5 million bottles annually, and overall quality is remarkably fine.

SFORZATO (SFURSAT) DI VALTELLINA *r 90 93 94 95 96 97 98 99 00 01 04*

The names are dialect versions of the vinification process that semi-dries the Valtellina grapes to bring alcohol to a minimum of 14%. Ample in body, with a rich, ruby-garnet colour, Sforzato becomes warm and perfumed after four to five years and can age for a decade or more. Considered by many as Valtellina's best wine. Age: 2 years.

VALTELLINA SUPERIORE *r ris 93 94 95 96 97 98 99 00 01 04*

DOCG for wines from four sub-regions within Valtellina: Grumello, Inferno, Sassella (considered the best of the four), and Valgella. Must contain at least 90% Nebbiolo (here called Chiavennasca). Though there are differences between them, the basic traits are similar: ruby-red colour, which tends to garnet with age, the bouquet becoming complex, and the dry, tannic taste more mellow and rounder (very good vintages keep for a long time). First-class Valtellina has an ageing potential that compares well with that of Barolo and Barbaresco. Age: 2 years (1 in barrel); *riserva* 3 years.

DOC

BOTTICINO *r ris 99 00 01*

Barbera, Marzemino, Schiava, Sangiovese.

CAPRIANO DEL COLLE *r ris nov 97 98 00 01*

Sangiovese, Marzemino, Barbera, Merlot, Trebbiano.

CELLATICA *r sup 98 99 00 01*
Schiava Gentile, Barbera,
Marzemino.

GARDA COLLI MANTOVANI
w r p
Trebbiano, Garganega,
Chardonnay, Sauvignon Blanc,
Merlot, Rondinella, Cabernet Franc,
Cabernet Sauvignon, Tocai Italico.

GARDA *w r p fz cl ris*
Barbera, Cabernet Sauvignon,
Cabernet Franc, Carmenère,
Chardonnay, Cortese, Corvina,
Garganega, Marzemino, Merlot,
Pinot Bianco, Pinot Grigio, Pinot
Nero, Riesling, Gropello,
Sangiovese, Sauvignon Blanc,
Tocai.

**RIVIERA DEL GARDA
BRESCIANO/GARDA
BRESCIANO** *w r p sup sp nov*
Riesling Italico, Riesling Renano,
Groppello, Sangiovese, Marzemino,
Barbera, Gentile, Santo Stefano,
Mocasina, Croatina, Pinot Nero,
Uva Rara, Ughetta.

LAMBRUSCO MANTOVANO
r p fz sw
Lambrusco Viadanese (Grappello
Ruperti), Lambrusco Maestri,
Lambrusco Marani, Lambrusco
Salamino, Ancellotta.
Sub-zones: Oltrepò Mantovano,
Viadanese-Sabbionetano

LUGANA *w sp*
Trebbiano di Lugana and other
local non-aromatic white varieties.

MOSCATO DI SCANZO *r sw pas*
Semi-dried Moscato di Scanzo.

OLTREPÒ PAVESE *r p fz sp mc sw
pas liq ris*
Barbera (*96 97 98 99 00 01 02 03
04*), Bonarda (*98 99 00 01 02 03 04*),
Buttafuoco (*99 00 01 03 04*),
Pinot Nero (*97 98 99 00 01*), Sangue
di Giuda (*99 00 01 02 03 04*),

Cabernet Sauvignon, Chardonnay,
Cortese, Malvasia, Moscato, Pinot
Grigio, Pinot Bianco, Riesling
Italico, Riesling Renano, Sauvignon
Blanc, Croatina, Ughetta.

**SAN COLOMBANO AL LAMBRO/
SAN COLOMBANO** *w r fz ris
98 99 00 01 03 04*
Chardonnay, Pinot Nero, Croatina,
Barbera, Bonarda.

**SAN MARTINO DELLA
BATTAGLIA** *w sw liq*
Tocai Friulano and other varieties.

TERRE DI FRANCIACORTA
w r
Chardonnay, Pinot Bianco, Pinot
Nero, Cabernet Franc, Cabernet
Sauvignon, Merlot, Barbera,
Nebbiolo.

VALCALEPIO *w r m pas ris 97 98 99
00 01 04*
Chardonnay, Pinot Bianco, Pinot
Grigio, Merlot, Cabernet
Sauvignon.

VALTELLINA *r 97 98 00 01 02 04*
Nebbiolo (here called
Chiavennasca).

IGT
Alto Mincio
Benaco Bresciano
Bergamasca
Collina del Milanese
Montenetto di Brescia
Provincia di Mantova
Provincia di Pavia
Quistello
Ronchi di Brescia
Sabbioneta
Sebino
Terrazze Retiche di Sondrio
Valcamonica

Producers

The key provinces have been abbreviated as follows:
BG = Bergamo; BS = Brescia; CO = Como; CR = Cremona; LO = Lodi; MI = Milano; MN = Mantova; PV = Pavia; SO = Sondrio; VA = Varese.

Fratelli Agnes, Rovescala (PV) *p r sw fz* ☆→☆☆ * 18ha, 80,000 bottles. Sergio and Cristiano Agnes are consciously reviving some of the lesser-known and forgotten clones of local Bonarda Pignolo, such as Poculum, a vibrant, spicy balsamic wine, well balanced and with medium length. Good Croatina Loghetto and very refreshing *frizzante* Campo del Monte and Il Cresta del Ghiffi.

Albani, Casteggio (PV) *w r fz* ☆→☆☆ 16ha. An estate at 250m (820ft) in an area known for its full-bodied reds – producing top-notch Oltrepò wines and sensibly avoiding the temptation to produce innumerable labels – or to overoak. Impeccable, long-lived Rosso Vigna della Casona from 40-year-old Barbera, Croatina, Uva Rara, and Pinot Nero vines, expressing terroir character. Exhilarating Rosso Costa del Morone and refined age-worthy Riesling Renano and Pinot Nero.

Antica Tesa, Botticino Mattina (BS) *r* ☆→☆☆ 6ha, 40,000 bottles. Pierangelo Noventa's small property with manicured vineyards produces some fine blends of Sangiovese, Marzemino (which is partly raisined), and Schiava aged for 24 months. The wines are rich, full, and powerful, yet show elegance and good aromatic profile with hints of prune, vanilla, cloves, and sour cherries. Highlights include Botticino Vigna Gobbio, Botticino Vigna Pià de la Tesa, and Botticino Vigna degli Ulivi.

Barone Pizzini, Corte Franca (BS) *w pr sp* ☆☆→☆☆☆ 40ha, 310,000 bottles. Historic estate producing some smartly styled Franciacorta (brut, extra brut, *satèn*), showing structure and elegance, in particular Franciacorta Satèn made from 100% Chardonnay, with a melange of apple and exotic fruit and buttery biscuit, soft and round, with a fine perlage. It's vinified in steel and barrique and left on the lees for 36 months. Also good sparkling rosé made from Chardonnay and Pinot Nero.

Bellaria, Casteggio (PV) *w r fz* ☆☆→☆☆☆ * 20 ha, 65,000 bottles. Paolo Massone's production comes from low-cropping, well-manicured vines. It includes very good Bricco Sturnel – an intense, tenacious Cabernet/Barbera blend with ripe berry fruit; La Macchia – a Merlot, slightly international in style; and the remarkable barrel-fermented Chardonnay Costa Soprana, characterized by delicate hints of peach, apricot, vanilla, and honey – full, soft, and fresh on the palate. The grapes are picked at dawn and macerated at low temperatures to extract the aromas.

Bellavista, Erbusco (BS) *w p r sp* ☆☆☆ ›☆☆☆☆ 180ha, 950,000 bottles. Winemaker Mattia Vezzola maintains high standards at this renowned estate with a number of top Franciacorta labels (brut, *satèn*, *pas opéré*, rosé): Brut Gran Cuvée, made from Chardonnay and Pinot Nero – richly layered, with hints of apricot, mango, and bread crust, round, soft, and aristocratic, with excellent balance; Gran Cuvée Pas Operé – very good, showing structure and elegance, with citrus notes, creamy and persistent, and good ageing potential. Also good

Brut Satèn Cuvée, Brut Rosé Gran Cuvée, perfectly honed Terre di Franciacorta Bianco and Rosso, and IGT Rosso del Sebino.

Fratelli Berlucchi, Borgonato di Cortefranca (BS) *w p r sp* ☆☆ 40,000 bottles. Pia Donata Berlucchi's estate produces fine sparkling Franciacorta. Leading labels include: Satèn Millesimato – soft, fruity; and Pas Dosé, a dry Millesimato with only 3g/l of residual sugar. Both are produced from highly selected grapes. Also good Rosé and Terre di Franciacorta Dossi delle Querce.

Guido Berlucchi, Borgonato di Cortefranca (BS) *w r sp* ☆☆→☆☆☆ 5,000,000 bottles. Italy's largest *metodo classico* sparkling-wine house. Main production covers the Cuvée Imperiale Brut (not made under the Franciacorta DOCG), which enjoys great commercial success for its dependable quality. Also, Brut Extrême – fine, fresh, mineral character from Chardonnay, Pinot Nero, and Pinot Blanc; and Brut Cuvée Storica – well-balanced sparkling showing structure and class.

Bersi Serlini, Provaglio d'Iseo (BS) *w sp* ☆☆ 30ha, 250,000 bottles. This historic estate is completing the building of a new cellar, as well as restoring the 14th-century Benedictine monastery. Both good normal Cuvée and Franciacorta (brut, *satèn*, brut *riserva*), made from Chardonnay with small percentages of Pinot Bianco. The Extra Brut Riserva is left on the lees for up to 50 months, producing fragrant, structured *spumante*.

Fattoria Cabanon, Godiasco (PV) *w p r fz* ☆☆ 30ha, 85,000 bottles. Elena Mercandelli's organically farmed land produces some top labels. Oltrepò Pavese: late-harvest Rosso Infernot Riserva, a Bonarda/Uva Rara/Barbera blend aged 12–18 months in barrique – warm, full-bodied. Also good Barbera Prunello showing varietal character; and a fine Cabanon Blanc Opera Prima from 100% Sauvignon Blanc with crisp acidity.

Ca' del Bosco, Erbusco (BS) *w r sp* ☆☆☆→☆☆☆☆ 147ha, 1,500,000+ bottles. Leading Franciacorta estate producing an outstanding array of Franciacorta (brut, rosé, *satèn*, dosage zero, brut *millesimato,* and the superb Cuvée Anna Maria Clementi). Still wines earn similar praise: Terre di Franciacorta Chardonnay and Curtefranca Rosso and Bianco blends; Sebino IGT Pinèro (Pinot Nero) and Carmenèro (Carmenère); plus the signature red Maurizio Zanella (Cabernet Sauvignon/Cabernet Franc/Merlot).

Ca' di Frara, Mornico Losana (PV) *w r ris sw* ☆☆→☆☆☆ 42ha, 24,000 bottles. Luca Bellani's production covers a range of Oltrepò DOCs, including unusual late-harvest Pinot Grigio Vendemmia Tardiva. Other labels: Il Frater Riserva, a Croatina/Barbera/Uva Rara/Pinot Nero blend aged 18 months in barrique – sapid, rich berry fruit, cherry with balsamic notes, showing structure and elegance. Also good Pinot Nero, plus Rosso and Bianco.

Ca' dei Frati, Lugana di Sirmione (BS) *w p r* ☆☆→☆☆☆ * 68ha, 550,000 bottles. Anna Maria dal Cero, together with Brescia's Institute for Experimental Viticulture, has revived some interesting local varieties. Highlights: late-harvest barrique-fermented Brolettino Grand'Annata Trebbiano di Lugana – floral, peaches, buttery, vanilla and spice, slightly smoky, round and full; and rich Ronchedone Grand'Annata, a Sangiovese/Marzemino/Cabernet blend showing good ageing potential.

Ca' Montebello, Cigognola (PV) *w r fz sp* ☆☆ * 32ha, 200,000 bottles. Luigi Scarani's production includes an interesting range of Oltrepò Pavese wines: Pinot Nero Brut made by the *metodo classico*, and the *frizzante* Bonarda. Top reds: Rosso Custiò – fresh, savoury with pepper, tobacco, and ripe berry fruit; and Sangue di Giuda – body, delicate rose petal and plummy aromas balanced by crisp acidity.

Cantina Sociale La Versa, Santa Maria della Versa (PV) *w r sp fz* ☆☆ * 1,300ha, 6,500,000 bottles. This large co-op produces a range of Oltrepò wines, in addition to *metodo classico spumante*. The I Roccoli range produces some interesting Sangue di Giuda *frizzante* and Barbera. Good Buttafuoco Roccolo delle Viole is a Barbera/Croatina/Uva Rara blend – intense blackberry, tobacco, and earthy bouquet, structure, balanced acidity, and persistence. Also good Chardonnay Terre d'Alteni.

Cascina La Pertica, Picedo di Polpenazze (BS) *w r* ☆→☆☆ 15ha, 65,000 bottles. Emerging winemaker Ruggero Brunori produces Garda classics, guided by consultant Franco Bernabei. Impressive, elegant Cabernet Le Zalte leads the range. Also good Rosso Le Sincette – hints of cherry, pomegranate, liquorice, and tobacco, tannic, fresh, and long; Chardonnay Le Sincette; and Groppello Il Colombaio.

Castel Faglia, Cazzago San Martino (BS) *w r sp* ☆☆ 20ha. The Cavicchioli family produce sound Franciacorta: Satèn Cuvée Monogram and Brut Cuvéè Monogram, as well as the still Terre di Franciacorta Bianco Campo Marte, a Chardonnay-based wine with good varietal character and fresh minerality.

Castelveder, Monticelli Brusati (BS) *w r sp* ☆☆ 13ha, 100,000 bottles. Franciacorta 100% Chardonnay brut, extra brut, and *millesimato* are among Renato Alberti's production made near a medieval castle. Also rich Terre Rosso Curtefranca and Rosso Curtefranca Monte delle Rose (Cabernet/Merlot/Barbera/Nebbiolo).

Cavalleri, Erbusco (BS) *w p r sp* ☆☆☆ * 37ha, 250,000 bottles. The Cavalleri family settled here in 1300 and has been making beautifully refined Franciacorta (brut, *pas dosé*, *satèn*, Collezione Rosé, and the acclaimed Collezione Brut) for generations. Also good structured, aromatic, persistent Blanc de Blancs and mineral, crisp Terre Bianco Rampaneto, Seradina, Rosso Vigna Tajardino, and IGT Sebino Corniole (Merlot).

Contadi Castaldi, Adro (BS) *w p r sp sw* ☆☆☆ * 60ha, 500,000 bottles. Vittorio Moretti and Martino De Rosa's production yields an impressive range of Franciacorta, in particular: Franciacorta Zero – apple and peach, citrus with hints of dough, fine fresh, finish; Franciacorta Rosé – raspberry, strawberry, and floral fragrance; Franciacorta Satèn – structured with persistence. Also good Terre Bianco and Rosso, as well as Marco Nero – a full-bodied, succulent Cabernet Sauvignon with spice, tobacco, ripeness, and elegance.

Conti Sertoli Salis, Tirano (SO) *w r* ☆☆→☆☆☆ 13ha, +55ha of bought grapes, 300,000 bottles. Small estate producing excellent Valtellina Superiore: Capo di Terra, made from 100% Nebbiolo and aged in barrique 16 months – mineral, spicy, ripe, with black pepper, showing well-integrated oak; and Grumello – inky, violets and liquorice, full-bodied, elegant silky tannins. Also Sforzato di Valtellina Canua, aged 18 months in barrique and tonneau – opulent and powerful, with ample aromatic complexity, fine tannins, and final acidity.

Cornaleto, Adro (BS) *w p sp* ☆☆→☆☆☆ 16ha, 100,000 bottles. Elegant Franciacorta (brut, rosé, *satèn, pas dosé*) millesimée showing excellent ageing potential, in particular Franciacorta Brut 1994, kept in steel on the lees for nine years, showing delicate fruity notes with minerality backed by a creamy, well-balanced silky perlage. Also good Rosé Brut 1997 and Satèn Brut 1999.

Sandro Fay, San Giacomo di Teglio (SO) *r* ☆☆☆ 13ha, 30,000 bottles. Known for quality Valtellina Nebbiolo reds. Highlights include: Sforzato di Valtellina Ronco del Picchio – richly extracted, sapid and ripe, vibrant and balanced, with persistence; Valtellina Superiore Il Glicine – powerful, balsamic, and spicy; and Valgella Ca' Morei – cherry, leather, and tobacco notes, fairly opulent but well balanced. The new La Faya is a Syrah/Nebbiolo/Merlot blend.

Le Fracce, Mariano di Casteggio (PV) *w r fz* ☆☆→☆☆☆ 45ha, 180,000 bottles. Highlights include Oltrepò Pavese Rosso Bohemi made from Barbera, Croatina, and Pinot Nero, aged 15 months in barrique – attractive spicy bouquet, while vigorous, fresh, and tannic on the palate, with exceptional length; good Bonarda La Rubiosa – fresh and long; and Rosso Garboso – savoury with berry character, fine tannins, persistent. In the whites, good Pinot Grigio Levriere and Riesling Landò.

Frecciarossa, Casteggio (PV) *w r* ☆☆ 26ha, 80,000 bottles. Reliably good Oltrepò across the board, overseen by consultant winemaker Franco Bernabei. New replanting project and cellar currently under way. Highlights include: Pinot Nero Giorgio Odero – good varietal character with small wooded

berries; Riesling degli Orti – floral, mineral character, fresh and sapid on the palate; and Roso Praielle – showing terroir typicity.

Enrico Gatti, Erbusco (BS) *w r sp* ☆☆→☆☆☆ 17ha, 100,000 bottles. Reliable production of Franciacorta Satèn, Brut, and Millesimato, as well as Terre di Franciacorta Rosso Curtefranca, characterized by cassis and green pepper, with a balsamic finish. Also good Terre Gatti Bianco Riserva and Bianco Curtefranca.

Isimbarda, Santa Giuletta (PV) *w r* ☆☆ 36ha, 100,000 bottles. The Meroni family's vines are divided between Santa Giulietta and Mornico Losana. Highlights: Oltrepò Pavese Rosso Montezavo Riserva – full-bodied, warm, and spicy, with complex aromas, sustained acidity; Pinot Nero – delicate, mineral, cranberry, cold-maceration, non-filtered. Also good, crisp, citrus Riesling Vigna Martina.

Mamete Prevostini, Mese (SO) *w r* ☆☆☆ * 12ha, 80,000 bottles. Emerging Valtellina producer with small parcels perched on rocky terrain. A "heroic viticulture" yielding superb Sforzato and Superiore Sassella, characterized by terroir elegance. Sforzato Albareda is 100% Nebbiolo aged 18 months in barrique – complex, full-bodied elegance, ample aromatic profile, and long finish. Very good Corte di Cama from part-dried grapes; and a partly barrel-fermented Chardonnay called Opera.

Mirabella, Rodengo Saiano (BS) *w p r sp sw* ☆☆→☆☆☆ 50ha, 450,000 bottles. Elegant Franciacorta production includes Franciacorta Non Dosato Millesimato, Brut Wertmuller, and Brut Satèn. Also good Terre Rosso Maniero and Nero d'Ombra from late-harvest Cabernet Sauvignon, Cabernet Franc, Merlot, and Nebbiolo, aged 12 months in barrique – cassis, tobacco, spice; elegant structure and fine tannins.

Monsupello, Torricella Verzate (PV) *w r sp fz* ☆→☆☆☆ * Well-priced, elegant Oltrepò DOCs. Highlights include: Riserva Mosaico, Cabernet Sauvignon Aplomb, Pinot Nero 3309, solid Barbera I Gelsi, *frizzante* Bonarda, Rosso La Borla, as well as excellent Riesling, Pinot Grigio, and Sauvignon, and an excellent Brut Cuvée Ca' del Tava *spumante*.

Monte Rossa, Cazzago San Martino (BS) *w p* ☆☆☆☆ 45ha, 220,000 bottles. Cesare Ferrari produces premium Franciacorta: brut, extra brut *millesimato*, *satèn*, and especially brut cabochon – showing a fine, fruity bouquet, with a buttery texture and fine mousse, matured on yeast for 40 months.

Il Mosnel Carmignone (BS) *w p r sp sw* ☆☆☆ * 40ha, 250,000 bottles. Established in 1840, this historic estate produces high-quality wines, including Brut, Satèn, Extra Brut, and Millesimato, and has added a Rosé Pas Dosé – good complexity with strawberry, citrus, pineapple aromas, fresh, with good mousse on the palate. Also good Terre Rosso and Bianco Curtefranca Campolarga.

Nino Negri, Chiuro (SO) *w r* ☆☆☆☆→ ☆☆☆☆ 34ha, 1,200,000 bottles. Part of the Gruppo Italiano Vini. Stunning Valtellina Sfursat 5 Stelle – produced only in top vintages with partially raisined grapes, shows the full potential and character of Sfursat. Impressive Valtellina Superiore; Inferno Mazer – raspberry, earthy, and gamey, with elegance; Vigneto Fracia – sapid, with fine tannins and elegant finish; Sassella Le Tense – vibrant and structured. Also good Grumello Sassorosso and white Ca' Brione, from Sauvignon – apple blossom, tropical hints, citrus, and

spice, with mineral finish.

Nera, Pietro (SO) *w r* ☆☆ 47ha, 600,000 bottles. Nera is a historic name in Valtellinese winemaking, producing some solid Valtellina Superiore Inferno Riserva and good Sfurzat with international-style Rosso Sorèl (Cabernet/Nebbiolo) and Sassella Alisio. Interesting white Rezio from Chiavennasca and Chardonnay.

Pasini Produttori, Puegnago sul Garda (BS) *w p r sp sw* ☆☆ 40ha, 400,000 bottles. Emerging producer making reliable Garda and Garda Classico wines, such as Garda Cabernet Sauvignon Vigneto Montezalto – cassis, herbs, chocolate, balsamic, with mineral elegance. Also good *metodo classico* Ceppo 326 Brut and sweet San Gioan Brinat from Chardonnay and Torbiana – floral with good acidity.

Provenza, Desenzano del Garda (BS) *w p r sp* ☆☆☆ 85ha, 800,000 bottles. Fabio Contato produces some of Garda's top wines. His eponymous red Garda Classico shows mineral character, elegance, and balance. Also premium oak-fermented Lugana Superiore Fabio Contato – peach, mango, floral bouquet, full, round, and persistent. Good Lugana Brut Ca' Maiol and Lugana Tenuta Maiolo.

Quaquarini Francesco, Canneto Pavese (PV) *w p r sp fz* ☆☆ Dedicated winemakers with praised production of Sangue di Giuda – sweet red *frizzante* showing terroir character, red berry fruit, clean finish, with good acidity. Also good production of Oltrepò Pavese: Rosso Magister, Bonarda, and Buttafuoco.

Rainoldi Aldo, Chiuro (SO) *w p r sp* ☆☆☆ 9ha, 200,000 bottles. Family-run estate with a production of crafted Valtellina Superiore: Grumello, Sassella, Inferno, and a modern Crespino from Nebbiolo grapes. The Valtellina Superiore wines show good varietal character, elegance, and sapidity, with 15–28 months ageing in barrique. Interesting Sauvignon Ghibellino IGT with citrus and freshly cut grass bouquet, aged five months in barrique.

Ricci Curbastro, Capriolo (BS) *w p r sp* ☆☆→☆☆☆ 24ha, 180,000 bottles. Renowned Franciacorta Satèn, Brut, and Demi Sec. Also good production of Terre di Franciacorta, in particular Bianco Vigna Bosco Alto, Bianco Curtefranca, Rosso Curtefranca, and a Pinot Nero.

Ronco Calino, Torbiato di Adro (BS) *w r sp* ☆☆ 10ha, 40,000 bottles. Friendly, small winery run by Paolo Radichi with the help of oenologist Francesco Polastri and agronomist Leonardo Valenti. 10 ha are planted to vines of Chardonnay, Pinot Bianco, Pinot Noir, Cabernet Sauvignon, Merlot, Barbera and Nebbiolo. Good Franciacorta Satèn from Chardonnay and Pinot Bianco, from yields of 55hl/ha, characterized by a slightly fruity, floral fragrance, round and persistent. Also very good Terre di Franciacorta Bianco Curtefranca and Rosso.

Ruiz de Cardenas, Casteggio (PV) *w r sp* ☆☆ 5ha. Gianluca Ruiz de Cardenas's vineyard reflects his passion for Pinot Nero- and Chardonnay-based *spumante*. The production includes 25,000 bottles of Pinot Nero Vigna Brumano with good varietal character, ripe cassis, and fine finish. Also good is Blanc de Blanc Brut Nature (100% Chardonnay) and Galanta Brut – both *metodo classico* showing fresh, balanced structure.

Fratelli Triacca, Villa di Tirano (SO) *r* ☆☆☆ 47ha, 700,000 bottles. Domenico Triacca is a quality conscious winemaker, and this shows throughout the range of Nebbiolo monovarietal Valtellina Superiore with particular emphasis on the Sforzato San Domenico. Also very good: Prestigio, Grumello, Inferno, Sassella, and La Gatta Riserva – full, round, ripe wines with good complexity and persistence.

Uberti, Erbusco (BS) *w p r sp* ☆☆☆→☆☆☆☆ 23ha, 145,000 bottles. Producer of premium Franciacorta sparkling and Franciacorta Terre, admired for their complexity and elegance. Excellent Extra Brut Comari del Salem, Satèn Magnificentia Brut, and Brut Rosé Francesco I. In the still wines, good Rosso dei Frati Priori, Rosso Augusta, Rosso and Bianco Curtefranca.

Vercesi, Montù Beccaria (PV) *w r fz* ☆☆ 15ha, 80,000 bottles. Gianmaria Vercesi produces reliable Oltrepò Pavese. Highlights: Pinot Nero Luogo dei Monti – attractive bouquet of dried flowers and small berry fruit, elegant and persistent; Castellazzo Rosso, Pezzalunga Rosso, Bonarda Luogo Della Milla, and Barbera Clà.

Bruno Verdi, Canneto Pavese (PV) *w p r fz* ☆☆→☆☆☆ * 8ha, 100,000 bottles. Paolo Verdi produces fine Oltrepò Pavese wines, including lively Buttafuoco and Sangue di Giuda,led by Rosso Riserva Cavariola, aged 20 months in barrique – floral, fruity, with body, structure, and fine tannin. Good Bonarda, Pinot Nero, Barbera, and Riesling Vigna Costa.

Villa Franciacorta, Monticelli Brusati (BS) *w r sp* ☆☆ 35 ha, 230,000 bottles. Alessandro Bianchi's ever-improving Franciacorta (brut, extra brut, *satèn*, rosé, Brut Millesimato, and extra dry *cuvette*) and Terre red and white are based on fresh, elegant aromas. Also good Rosso Gradoni, Merlot Querqus, and Bianco Pian della Villa.

Wine & Food

Natural opulence is reflected in Lombardy's multifarious diet. Milan, unavoidably, instigates food forms called "fast", "international", and "nouvelle", but the city also has more fine Italian restaurants than any other. Gourmets still relish their *ossobuco*, *cotoletta*, and *risotto alla milanese* in the city that deserves recognition as Italy's rice capital. The seven provinces have so clung to tradition that Lombardian cooking is more accurately described as provincial than regional. Still, everybody eats veal, beef, pork (though cuts and cooking differ), and cheese (besides blue-veined gorgonzola, there are Grana Padano to rival Parmigiano Reggiano, stracchino, taleggio, robiola, and bitto). Risotto reigns in the flatlands, and polenta and pasta in the hills, though there is plenty of crossover. In Pavia, they eat frogs and snails, in Bergamo small birds, in Mantua pasta with pumpkin, in Cremona candied fruit with mustard. Perhaps the leading preserve of provincial cooking is the Valtellina around Sondrio, where, among other nutritious eccentricities, buckwheat is used for pasta and polenta.

Bresaola Beef cured much as prosciutto and served in thin slices.

Busecca A richly flavoured Milanese tripe soup.

Casônsei Ravioli filled with sausage, cheese, and bread; a specialty of Brescia and Bergamo.

Cassoeula Cuts of pork cooked with cabbage, celery, and carrots, and often served with polenta.

Cotoletta alla milanese Breaded veal cutlet with mashed potatoes.

Ossobuco e risotto alla milanese Braised veal shank with saffron risotto – the pride of Milan.

Panettone Milan's dome-shaped Christmas cake.

Pizzoccherl Rustic buckwheat noodles served with boiled potatoes, cabbage, and melted cheese in the Valtellina.

Polenta e osei alla bergamasca Polenta with small game birds cooked with butter and sage – a specialty.

Risotto alla certosina Risotto with freshwater prawns, frogs, perch, and vegetables, cooked in white wine.

Sciatt Fritters of buckwheat and white flour, bitto cheese, and grappa.

Tortelli di zucca Pasta filled with pumpkin paste flavoured with Amaretto and nutmeg, served with butter and grated grana.

Vitello tonnato Veal fillet dressed with a tuna-flavoured cream sauce.

Hotels

L'Alberta with Gualtiero Marchesi, Erbusco (BS) €€€
Elegant villa residence set between the Alps and Lake Iseo – a good starting point for Franciacorta wine estates. Enjoy the surrounding countryside and Marchesi's refined cuisine and excellent wine list.

Altavilla Trattoria con Locanda, Bianzone (SO) € This *trattoria* 21km (13 miles) east of Sondrio offers four comfortable bedrooms, excellent local fare, and a good wine list.

Hotel de Charme Cappuccini, Cologne (BS) €€ This 16th-century family-run convent in the heart of Franciacorta offers comfortable rooms and fine dining. Ideal for visiting Franciacorta vineyards. Lake Garda, surrounded by a large park – luxurious and magnificent.

Hotel Villa D'Este, Lago di Garda

(BS) €€€ Former 16th-century princely residence, on the shores of **Hotel Villa Fiordaliso,** Gardone Rivera (BS) €€€ A 17th-century

Relais & Châteaux villa, with antique-furnished rooms facing the lake. Relaxed elegance, with a good restaurant serving local specialties.

Restaurants

Al Gambero, Calvisano (MN) €€–€€€ Small elegant restaurant offering traditional Lombard fare and regional specialties: *tagliatelle alla zucca* (pumpkin) *e amaretti; capretto da latte* (young kid) *con polenta; meringa* (meringue) *al Grand Marnier.* Good wine list.

Antica Osteria del Ponte, Cassinetta di Lugagnano (MI) €€€ 17th-century family-run country *osteria* 30km (18.6 miles) outside Milan on the shores of the Naviglio, offering a hybrid of creative Lombard and French cuisine. Excellent wine list.

Antica Trattoria La Pergolina, Capriano del Colle (BS) € Hospitable, family-run *trattoria*, with three dining rooms serving traditional recipes, such as ravioli with pheasant butter and thyme, polenta and gorgonzola, veal, venison, snails, and a vast selection of cheese and local wine.

I Castagni, Vigevano (PV) €€–€€€ Situated in the countryside south of Vigevano. Enrico Gerli is a master in the rich, tasty territorial Lomellina cuisine: goose, foie gras, pigeon, and a range of risottos.

Dal Pescatore, Canneto sull'Oglio, Runate (MN) €€€ One of Italy's prime dining locations. Excellent fish and traditional dishes such as *tortelli di zucca* (pumpkin parcels), *agnolini in brodo* (tiny meat ravioli in broth), and *anguilla alle braci* (chargrilled eel).

Da Vittorio, Bergamo €€–€€€ Traditional meat dishes with excellent salamis, and sophisticated fish dishes with fresh raw scampi and *branzino* carpaccio.

La Lanterna Verde, Villa di Chiavenna (SO) €€–€€€ Family-run restaurant with local cuisine such as *tajadin* (pasta made with chestnut flour), truffled partridge breast in filo pastry with garden vegetables, trout, and foie gras.

Locanda Vecchia Pavia al Mulino, Certosa di Pavia (PV) €€€ Offering a rich selection of dishes with a good five-course tasting menu, including *ventresca di tonno* (tuna) *marinata con salmone e avocado* and *maialino da latte farcito* (stuffed suckling pig) with apples, foie gras and truffles.

Il Luogo di Aimo e Nadia, Milan €€€ Top fine-dining location in central Milan. Specialties include carpaccio with red chicory and cream of white truffle; risotto with sausage and artichokes; roast duck with *vin santo* reduction and goose liver; raw amberjack marinated in ginger and aromatic herbs.

La Rucola, Sirmione (BS) €€–€€€ Gionatha Bignotti's romantic setting on Lake Garda specializes in creative cooking, such as lobster with sweetbread.

Ristofante, Alzano Lombardo (BG) €€–€€€ Giambattista Manzini will entertain you with traditional recipes, many based on fresh fish, excellent cheeses, and local fare. Good and reasonably priced wine list.

Il Sole, Ranco (VA) €€–€€€ Sited on the shores of Lake Maggiore, where the Brovelli family, leaders in the *nuova cucina italiana,* have been restaurateurs for generations. Their cuisine is based on tradition, presented with an inventive twist.

Trentino-Alto Adige *Trentino-Alto Adige*

The northernmost region of Italy, with its fragrant white wines and German-accented syllables, is sometimes compared with Alsace. As well as having vines in common – Riesling, Sylvaner, Pinot Blanc, Pinot Noir, Pinot Gris, and Muscat – it is said that the Traminer variety, a superior clone of which became Gewürztraminer in Alsace, took its name from the Alto Adige village of Tramin. But analogies should not be overdrawn, for Trentino-Alto Adige has its own clear styles and a strong line in reds.

Trentino (the province of Trento, or Trent) and Alto Adige (the more northerly province of Bolzano, or Bozen, also known as South Tyrol or Südtirol, bordering Austria) share a gorgeous region of Alps by the Adige River. The two provinces are, however, quite distinct (Alto Adige vaunts autonomous status and official Italian–German bilingualism), and there is little collaborative overlap among wine producers.

Nevertheless, despite ethnic contrasts between Alto Adige's German-speaking citizens, who cling tenaciously to Austrian traditions, and the Italian-speaking majority, the entire region is a model of oenological efficiency, with more than eighty per cent of the wine produced under the two blanket Trentino and Alto Adige DOCs handling a multitude of grape varieties with aplomb.

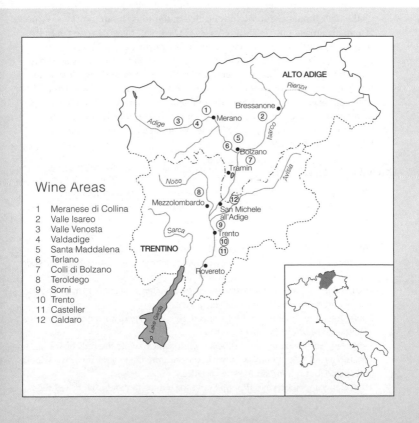

Wine Areas

1   Meranese di Collina
2   Valle Isareo
3   Valle Venosta
4   Valdadige
5   Santa Maddalena
6   Terlano
7   Colli di Bolzano
8   Teroldego
9   Sorni
10 Trento
11 Casteller
12 Caldaro

Both Trentino and Alto Adige produce notable amounts of Pinot Grigio, Chardonnay, and Sauvignon Blanc, as well as Pinot Bianco and the sometimes deliberately understated Riesling and Müller-Thurgau. Gewürztraminer, Moscato, and Sylvaner can be enticingly perfumed and long-lived. Trentino, which pioneered sparkling winemaking by the classic method early in the century, has retained its leading position, and these sparklers, which are predominantly Chardonnay-based, are now grouped under the Trento DOC. Distinctive reds come from Alto Adige's indigenous Lagrein and Trentino's native Teroldego and Marzemino, which can be matched in class by Cabernet, Merlot, and, rarely, Pinot Nero. Some winemakers have achieved a note of complexity with the pleasant but lightweight Schiava (Vernatsch).

Trentino's ideal climate and range of varietals account for its great white wines. Although reds do not always match the whites, they are not lacking in flavour. In recent years there has been an improvement with many varietals, in particular indigenous ones such as Refosco, Pignolo, Schioppettino, and Tazzelenghe, as well as a good showing for Bordeaux-style blends. In addition many wine producers rate high quality over high yields and make the most of the cool Alpine slopes to extract refined reds and graceful whites that could rank with Europe's elite.

With its towering Dolomites, glacier lakes, and forests, Trentino-Alto Adige is a favourite holiday spot in both summer and winter. Millions of tourists come here every year to ski, climb, and relax amid the beauty of Gothic and Romanesque villages nestled in the steep mountainsides. Wine is a major attraction. The Adige Valley is traversed by wine roads in both provinces, leading to an imposing array of vineyards. The Merano Wine Festival is held every November in Merano, while late April/May sees two important wine fairs: the Bozner Weinkost in Bolzano and the Mostra dei Vini Trentini in Trento. South Tyrol's wines are displayed in the Castel Mareccio/Maretsch in Bolzano. Recommended shops are Vinoteque Alois Lageder in Bolzano, Enoteca Johnson & Dipoli in Egna/Neumarkt, Lo Scrigno del Duomo in Trento, Meraner Weinhaus in Merano, and Schondorf in Brunico.

Recent Vintages

2004 A good year, with a long ripening season with good temperature variation between night and day making for balanced, aromatic wines.
2003 Scarce rains and heat brought an early harvest, with better results for reds than for whites.
2002 A difficult year in Trentino, with poor weather making stringent selection essential, but many fine wines were produced nonetheless. Alto Adige escaped the rains and produced excellent wines.
2001 A very good year, though without the excellence of 2000. Whites of good acidity and aroma; reds tending to elegance.
2000 Outstanding vintage with balanced, ripe, healthy grapes giving exceptional reds and excellent whites.
1999 Very good year in Alto Adige for white wines, while the reds in Trentino suffered as a result of rainy weather in the autumn. Good year for white wines in Trentino, but rather bad for late varieties.
1998 Generally good year, though better for whites than late-harvested reds.

1997 Outstanding harvest for Cabernet, Merlot, Lagrein, and Teroldego; it was also favourable for whites.

1996 An ample crop of generally good-quality whites and reds.

1995 A small crop, good to excellent for whites and reds, particularly Cabernet and Merlot.

1994 Though limited in size, quality was good to very good for both whites and reds.

1993 Attractive whites, though sometimes lacking structure; mixed results with reds.

Notes on earlier vintages: Other, earlier fine vintages include 1990, 86, 85, 83, 82, 79, 76, 75, 74, 71, and 70.

Appellations

DOC

ALTO ADIGE *w p r pas vt ris sw sp mc*
Cabernet Sauvignon, Cabernet Franc, Lagrein, Chardonnay, Gewürztraminer, Kerner, Malvasia (Malvasier), Merlot, Moscato Giallo (Goldenmuskateller), Moscato Rosa (Rosenmuskateller), Müller-Thurgau, Pinot Bianco (Weissburgunder), Pinot Grigio (Ruländer), Pinot Nero (Blauburgunder), Riesling Italico (Welschriesling), Riesling Renano (Rheinriesling), Sauvignon Blanc, Schiava (Vernatsch), Schiava Grigia (Grauvernatsch), Sylvaner (Silvaner), Traminer Aromatico.
Sub-zones: Colli di Bolzano, Meranese di Collina, Santa Maddalena, Terlano, Val Venosta, Valle Isarco.

CALDARO/LAGO DI CALDARO/ KALTERERSEE *r cl sup*
Schiava Grossa, Schiava Gentile, Schiava Grigia, Lambrusco, Merlot, Lagrein, Teroldego.

CASTELLER *r sup sw*
Schiava Grossa, Schiava Gentile, Lambrusco, Merlot, Lagrein, Teroldego.

TEROLDEGO ROTALIANO *p r ris sup 95 96 97 98 99 00 01 04*
Teroldego.

TRENTINO *w p r sup ris vt m sw liq*
Cabernet Franc (*97 98 99 00 01 04*), Cabernet Sauvignon (*90 91 93 94 95 96 97 98 99 00 01 04*), Chardonnay (*97 98 99 00 01 04*), Lagrein, Marzemino, Merlot (*97 98 99 00 01 04*), Moscato Giallo, Moscato Rosa, Müller-Thurgau, Nosiola, Pinot Bianco (*95 96 97 98 99 00 01 04*), Pinot Grigio, Pinot Nero (*97 98 99 00 01 04*), Rebo, Riesling Renano, Riesling Italico, Sauvignon Blanc (*99 00 01 04*), Traminer Aromatico (*99 00 01 02*).

TRENTO *w p sp ris mc*
Chardonnay, Pinot Bianco, Pinot Meunier, Pinot Nero.

VALDADIGE *w r fz ris*
Pinot Bianco, Pinot Grigio, Müller-Thurgau, Chardonnay, Trebbiano, Nosiola, Sauvignon Blanc, Garganega, Schiava, Lambrusco, Merlot, Pinot Nero, Lagrein, Teroldego, Cabernet Franc, Cabernet Sauvignon.
Sub-zone: Terre dei Forti.

IGT
Atesino delle Venezie
Delle Venezie
Mitterberg
Vallagarina
Vigneti delle Dolomiti

Producers

Producers are divided between Alto Adige and Trentino.

ALTO ADIGE

All Alto Adige producers are in the province of Bolzano/Bozen. Town names are given in Italian rather than German, as are DOC zones and wines (for the German names, see the wine listings). "AA" stands for Alto Adige.

Abbazia di Novacella/Stiftskellerei Neustift, Varna *w r ris sw* ☆☆☆ *
21ha, 500 bottles. Wines from this landmark abbey set quality standards in the Isarco Valley. Tautly aromatic Sylvaner, Sauvignon, and Gewürztraminer are matched by fine Kerner, Pinot Grigio, Lagrein, Pinot Nero, and Moscato Rosa. Also elegant Pinot Noir Riserva and a powerful Lagrein Riserva. The top wines are grouped in the Praepositus line.

Baron Widmann, Cortaccia *w r* ☆☆☆
15ha. Andrea Widmann's estate is noted for its Gewürztraminer, which shows a pure aromatic profile. Top production includes AA Cabernet/Merlot Rot, aged 15 months in barrique – elegant, with hints of leather, cedar, tobacco, and capsicum, structured and long; and Schiava – light-coloured, with flowery bouquet, spicy, unchallenging structure, refreshing, an excellent match for the local smoked hams and cheese.

Brigl Josef, Appiano *w r* ☆☆ *
2,000,000 bottles. Historic estate dating back to 1300, with excellent vineyard sites. Top labels include Gewürztraminer Windegg – ripe, with floral and mineral notes; and barrel-aged Chardonnay Briglhof. Also well-flavoured, ripe and fresh Pinot Noir. The top line is bottled under the Brigl label.

Caldaro, Caldaro *w r ris* ☆☆→☆☆☆☆
290ha, 1,400,000 bottles. Turn-of-the-century co-op with a production of exemplary AA Sauvignon Castel Giovanelli; Cabernet Sauvignon: Riserva Pfarrhof and Riserva Campaner; Moscato Giallo Passito Serenade; Lagrein Spigel; Chardonnay Wadleith; Gewurztraminer Campaner; and Pinot Bianco Vial.

Cantina Convento Muri Gries, Bolzano *w p r ris* ☆☆→☆☆☆☆ Situated above Bolzano, in Lagrein's heartland, this winery naturally concentrates on red wines, in particular AA Lagrein Abtei Muri Riserva – full-bodied, sapid, balsamic, elegant, with excellent structure and individual personality. Also a good Lagrein Moscato Rosa Abtei Muri – hints of rose petals; and AA Santa Magdalener Classico in the Tröglerhof collection.

Cantina H. Lun, Egna *w r ris* ☆☆→☆☆☆☆
30ha, 250,000 bottles. Historic winery established in 1840 with a production of reliable AA varietals in three lines: basic, Sandbichler, and the top Albertus. Among the prime labels: AA Lagrein Albertus Riserva – blueberries, vibrant, balanced, long. Also good Cabernet Sauvignon Albertus Riserva and Gewürztraminer Albertus.

Cantina Produttori di Andriano, Andriano *w r* ☆☆☆ 132ha, 675,000 bottles. Quality driven co-op founded in 1893. The range includes a fine line of organic AA varietals: Lagrein Scuro, Merlot, Cabernet, Gewürztraminer, Chardonnay, and Terlano Sauvignon. Highlights within the premium range: Tor di Lupo; in the medium range: Selection Sonnengut.

Cantina Produttori Bolzano, Bolzano *w p r ris sw* ☆☆→☆☆☆ 130ha, 950,000 bottles. Quality co-op formed from the fusion of the Gries and Santa Maddalena co-ops. The production is overseen by Stephan Filippi. Among the top labels: AA Lagrein Taber Riserva – ripe, warm, round, and full, balanced by elegance and length. Cabernet Mumelter Riserva and Lagrein Dunkel Prestige Riserva are in a class of their own. Also good Moscato Giallo Passito Vinalia.

Cantina Produttori Burggräfler, Marlengo *w r* ☆☆→☆☆☆ * 135ha, 1,100,000 bottles. Quality-directed co-op with well-sited vineyards and a fairly large production. Good whites, especially a citrus-noted AA Moscato Giallo Schinkenburg; late-harvest Pinot Bianco MerVin – sapid, with a grapey quality, fresh and mineral character; Merlot-Lagrein – blackberry jam, green pepper, and spice, with silky tannins.

Cantina Produttori Colterenzio, Cornaiano *w r ris* ☆☆☆→☆☆☆☆ 300ha, 1,300,000 bottles. Wolfgang Raifer ably manages this leading AA co-op with a production of superb quality. Excellent Chardonnay Cornell and Cabernet Sauvignon Lafoà, as well as Pinot Bianco Praedium Weisshaus, Gewürztraminer Cornell, Lagrein Cornell, Merlot Cornell, Cabernet/Merlot Cornelius, Pinot Noir Praedium St Daniel Riserva, and more.

Cantina Produttori Cornaiano, Cornaiano *w p r* ☆☆→☆☆☆ 230ha, 2,000,000 bottles. Massive range of reliably good AA varietal wines from selected vineyards. Top wines from the SelectArt Flora label include good Gewürztraminer – rose petal, spicy exotic aromas, vibrant and round; and Lagrein – berry fruit,

compact, full, with hints of bitter chocolate. Also good Sauvignon, Merlot and Schiava Botte N.9.

Cantina Produttori Cortaccia, Cortaccia *w p r sw* ☆☆☆ 220ha, 900,000 bottles. Early 20th-century co-op with a production of excellent AA reds from Lagrein, Cabernet, and Merlot; whites from Sauvignon and Gewürztraminer, all from well-sited vineyards. The top range comes under the Brenntal label, with particularly good Gewürztraminer and Merlot. Also good Sauvignon and late-harvest Moscato Rosa in the Fohrhof label.

Cantina Produttori di Merano, Merano *w p r ris* ☆☆☆ * 142ha, 1,000,000 bottles. Quality-driven ranges of red and white AA varietals. The Sauvignon Blanc, Riesling, and Gewürztraminer, under the Graf von Meran label, are of particular interest, as well as the Merlot Riserva Freiherr and the Pinot Noir Zeno Riserva. Good Moscato Giallo Passito Sissi Graf von Meran.

Cantina Produttori Nalles & Magré Niclara, Nalles *w r sw* ☆☆→☆☆☆☆ * 150ha, 700,000 bottles. 1930's co-op producing quality AA Chardonnay, Pinot Grigio, Terlano, and Pinot Bianco. Top label Baron Salvadori includes an excellent Moscato Giallo Passito – dense, citrus, vanilla, and mineral, full and rich on the palate. Also good barrel-matured Chardonnay with well-integrated oak and commendable Anticus (Merlot/Cabernet).

Cantina Produttori San Michele Appiano, Appiano *w p r sw ris* ☆☆☆→☆☆☆☆ * 340ha, close to 2,000,000 bottles. Fabulous AA wines from choice vineyards. The production is masterfully managed by winemaker Hans Terzer. Top AA varietal selections come under the Sanct Valentin label, with superb

Sauvignon, Gewürztraminer, Lagrein, Cabernet, Pinot Grigio, and Gewürztraminer Passito Comtess. The wines are very focused, with excellent varietal character, vibrance, balance, and length even in the lesser ranges.

Cantina Produttori Terlano, Terlano *w r* ☆☆→☆☆☆☆ * 140ha, 850,000 bottles. A 100-member cooperative established in 1893 and based in the small village of Terlano, where the land is divided into small parcels of steep vineyards, many not even reaching a hectare. Here Lagrein and other local grapes grow better as pergolas at an altitude. Both red and white AA varietals make up the production, with a special selection of age-worthy aged whites called Le Rarità, including excellent bottlings of Terlaner, Sauvignon, and Pinot Bianco.

Cantina Produttori Termeno, Termeno *w r sw* ☆☆→☆☆☆☆ * 220ha, 900,000 bottles. Impressive AA co-op with a production led by the fabulous Gewürztraminer Nussbaumerhof – refined elegance with exotic lychee, roses, mangoes, floral bouquet, fresh and vibrant, full, round, and persistent. Also very good late-harvest Gewürztraminer Roan. The top range is labelled Terminum, with worthy Lagrein Urban, Pinot Grigio Unterebner, and Cabernet Freising.

Cantina Produttori Valle Isarco, Chiusa *w r* ☆☆→☆☆☆ 130ha, 650,000 bottles. Thomas Dorfmann heads the winemaking at this co-op with a production featuring Valle Isarco's range of varietals, with the emphasis on crisp whites. The Aristors range is of particular interest: elegant wines, especially Kerner and Sylvaner, showing finesse, structure, and complexity. Also good Gewürztraminer and Veltliner.

Castel Schwanburg, Nalles *w p r ris* ☆☆→☆☆☆☆ 27ha, 500,000 bottles. Historic estate and castle founded in 1556. Red wines top the ranks, with AA Cabernet Sauvignon Privat, an elegant wine with some Cabernet Franc and Petit Verdot. Also a very good Merlot/Cabernet blend and a Lagrein Riserva. Among the whites, AA Terlano and Riesling rank high.

Peter Dipoli, Egna *w r* ☆☆☆ Alto Adige's wine guru Dipoli is principally an apple grower, but he also makes some excellent wines from vineyards in Cortaccia. Very good AA Sauvignon Voglar, Merlot, and Cabernet Sauvignon Yugum.

Franz Gojer Glögglhof, Bolzano *r ris* ☆☆☆ Glögglhof's family vineyards are centrally located in the St Magdalener Classic appellation, where the moraine-covered southeastern slopes guarantee ideal ripening for red varieties. Top labels: well-structured, warm, round, red AA St Magdalener Rondell, Lagrein Scuro, and Merlot Spitz.

Franz Haas, Montagna *w p r* ☆☆☆→☆☆☆☆ 35ha, 240,000 bottles. Haas produces consistently stylish, well-honed AA varietals. Top labels: Moscato Rosa – elegant, with great varietal character and clear, intense aromas; and Pinot Nero Schweizer – spice, tobacco, leather, elegant, silky tannins. Also stylish Mittenberg Manna, a blend of Chardonnay, Gewürztraminer, and Sauvignon.

Haderburg, Salorno *w r sp* ☆☆ Hausmannhof and Stainhauser vineyards yield sound AA wines, especially the brut and *pas dosé* sparklers. Also good Pinot Noir Hausmannhof – crushed cherry, warm and full on the palate, elegant, and long.

Hofstätter, Termeno *w r sw* ☆☆☆→
☆☆☆☆ 53ha, 750,000 bottles.
Dynamic family estate founded
in 1907 in the heart of Termeno
and managed by Martin Foradori.
Leading labels: Gewürztraminer
Kolbenhof, with excellent late-
harvest version Gewürztraminer
Joseph; and impeccable Pinot Nero
Barthenau Vigna San Urbano –
fine clove, cherry, chocolate,
and balsamic aromas, round
and silky, classy long finish.

Köfererhof, Varna *w sw* ☆☆☆ * 5,5ha,
40,000 bottles. Emerging estate in
Valle Isarco making waves with
wines that are stylish, vibrant,
and varietally intense throughout.
Top labels: AA Valle Isarco Riesling
– grapefruit and mineral, finesse
and balance; Kerner – aromatic,
with herbs, citrus, and peach,
mineral, full, and sapid; and
Gewürztraminer Passito Brixner –
aromatic, full, and persistent.

Kuenhof, Bressanone *w* ☆☆☆ Peter
Pliger's wines are fine, complex,
age-worthy Valle Isarco whites,
showing genuine structure,
aromatic profile, and individual
character. The wines show their
class after some months of bottle-
ageing. Top labels: AA Valle
Isarco Kaiton; Veltliner;
Sylvaner; Gewürztraminer.

Alois Lageder, Magrè *w p r sw ris*
☆☆→☆☆☆☆ 150ha, 1,200,000
bottles. Large and influential
estate established in 1855 making
archetypal AA wines in three lines:
classic varietals, single-vineyard
selections, and the flagship single-
estate of Tòr Löwengang, from
exceptional sites with low-yielding
grapes matured in barrique. Fine,
complex wines include the Pinot
Nero, Chardonnay, and Cabernet
Sauvignon. Casòn Hirschprunn,
also in Magrè, is Lageder's second
estate. It focuses on *cuvée* wines

and brings together a balanced
selection of several varieties of
grapes – Mitterberg IGT blends
Contest and Etelle (both based
on Pinot Grigio and Chardonnay),
and Casòn and Corolle (both based
on Merlot and Cabernet).

Loacker, Bolzano *w r sw* ☆☆ 7ha,
80,000 bottles. Rainer and Hayo
Loacker's estate boasts a production
of organically farmed wines,
including a good AA selection of
Cabernet/Lagrein, Gewürztraminer
Atagis, Sauvignon Tasmin,
Chardonnay Ateyon, Sylvaner
Ysac, and a late-harvest Tagis.

Gummerhof Malojer, Bolzano *w r ris*
☆☆☆ 28ha, 100,000 bottles. Alfred
Majoler's production is known for
robust fruity reds, in particular AA
Cabernet Riserva, aged 15 months
in barrique – powerful, with hints
of violets prunes, balsamic, fine
tannins, long finish; and
Bautzanum Riserva, a Cabernet/
Lagrein blend – vegetal hints
mingled with spice, vanilla, and
crushed berries, round and full
on the palate. Also good Lagrein
Riserva and Lagrein Gummerghof.

Manincor, Caldaro *w p r sw* ☆☆☆ 40ha,
120,000 bottles. Count Michael
Goëss-Enzenberg's vines overlook
Lake Caldaro; the grapes are
vinified in high-tech new cellar. Top
labels: a refreshing Moscato Giallo
that makes a perfect apéritif; Castel
Campan IGT – Merlot-based with
Cabernet Sauvignon; excellent
Pinot Noir Mason di Mason –
toasted, with ripe fruit, gamey,
structured, balanced, with long, soft
finish; elegant Cassiano (Cabernet
Sauvignon/Cabernet Franc/Merlot)
– capsicum, balsamic, velvety.
Also good Schiava.

Josephus Mayr, Cardano *r ris*
☆☆→☆☆☆ Josephus Mayr is
a small artisan producer with a
passion for his vines, winery, and

wines. His production focuses on ripe, structured, tenacious reds with some bottle-ageing. AA Santa Maddalena, Lagrein, and Cabernet of notable class. Top labels: Composition Reif, Lagrein Riserva, and Lamarein.

Niedermayr, Cornaiano *w r ris sw* ☆☆☆→☆☆☆☆ 25ha, 400,000 bottles. Josef and Johanna Sölva produce some of the region's top labels. AA Lagrein Riserva Aus Gries; Sauvignon Allure; Euforus Rosso (a Lagrein/Cabernet/Merlot blend), Gewürztraminer Doss, and IGT Aureus (*passito* Chardonnay/ Sauvignon) set the pace here.

Prima & Nuova/Erste & Neue, Caldaro *w p r sw* ☆→☆☆☆ Admirable co-op with good Caldaro and Puntay AA selections. Top labels: Passito Anthos – ripe honeydew melon, vibrant acidity, and excellent length; and Lagrein Puntay – modern style, punchy, structured, fresh and fruity.

Rottensteiner, Bolzano *w r ris sw* ☆☆→☆☆☆ 10ha, 400,000 bottles. Fine AA selection of wines from this estate. The top label is the intense, sweet Gewürztraminer Passito Cresta – almonds, ginger, honey, and apricot, dense and long. Also good Lagrein Scuro, Santa Maddalena Premstallerhof, Cabernet Select Riserva, Pinot Noir Mazzon Select Riserva, and an old-fashioned, tart Moscato Giallo.

Peter Sölva & Söhne, Caldaro *w r* ☆☆☆ 9ha, 60,000 bottles. A small estate producing fine reds and whites under the Amistar label. A Lagrein/Cabernet/Merlot blend (Amistar Rosso) shows complex notes with vegetal character, liquorice, tobacco, plums, full, and elegant. Good new Cabernet Franc Amistar and crisp Amistar Bianco.

Tiefenbrunner *w r ris* ☆☆→☆☆☆☆ * 20ha, 800,000 bottles. Castle estate founded in 1848 and renowned for

Feldmarschall – superbly pure-toned, aromatic Müller-Thurgau. Excellent AA Gewürztraminer, Moscato Rosa, Cabernet Sauvignon, and Chardonnay. Good Lagrein Riserva and AA Cuvée (all under the Linticlarus label). Also aromatic Gewürztraminer Castel Turmhof – hints of tropical fruit and rose water.

Elena Walch-Castel Ringberg & Kastelaz, Termeno *w p r ris sw* ☆☆☆→☆☆☆☆ 30ha, 350,000 bottles. Renowned estate making exemplary wines. Top labels: impeccable AA Gewürztraminer Kastelaz, AA Bianco Beyond the Clouds, Lagrein Riserva Castel Ringberg, new Pinot Noir Ludwig, Merlot Kastelaz Riserva, Riesling Castel Ringberg, and Bianco Passito Cashmere.

Ansitz Waldgries, Bolzano *w p r sw* ☆☆☆ 6ha, 50,000 bottles. Small estate with a production of classy reds, including AA Santa Maddalena Classico, Lagrein Scuro Mirell, Cabernet Sauvignon Laurenz, and Moscato Rosa Passito – delicate aromas, vibrant structure. Also elegant Pinot Bianco Riol.

Peter Zemmer, Cortina *w r ris* ☆☆→☆☆☆ 100ha, 650,000 bottles. Helmuth Zemmer's production is divided into two ranges (Zemmer and Kupelwieser), focusing on AA varietals, which all show well. Top labels include Santa Maddalena, Lagrein Riserva, Chardonnay Riserva, and Lagrein Kretzer.

TRENTINO

All Trentino producers are in the province of Trento. Unless otherwise specified, varietals come under the Trentino DOC and IGTs under Vigneti delle Dolomiti.

Balter Nicola, Rovereto *w r ris sp* ☆☆☆ 10ha, 54,000 bottles. This historic estate (est. 1872) is seeing improvement in vineyard management, with old pergolas being replaced with Guyot vines planted to a higher density. Fine Barbanico (Lagrein/Cabernet Sauvignon/Merlot), rich and concentrated, with fruit-forward character, fine tannins, and a fresh, long finish. Also good Spumante Brut Riserva and a Lagrein/Merlot blend.

Bolognani, Lavis *w r* ☆☆ 4.5ha, 65,000 bottles. Diego Bolognani's small estate is noted for its Bordeaux blend of Gabàn – sapid, powerful, with brambly fruit and elegance; Moscato Giallo – jasmine, sage, white peach, juicy, balanced, and crisp; and Teroldego Armillo, aged eight months in oak – spicy, rich, evident tannins, berry fruit, fresh, medium length.

Cantina d'Isera, Isera *w r* ☆→☆☆☆ 200ha, 700,000 bottles. Co-op founded in 1907, with 200 members and a production covering a wide range of Trentino varietals. Top wines come under the Selezione 907 label, which includes Superiore Marzemino D'Isera; Rebo; Moscato Giallo; and very interesting Pinot Grigio Agiato, left on the skins, with good individual character.

Cantina di Toblino, Sarche di Calavino *w r* ☆→☆☆☆ * 650ha, 280,000 bottles. Quality co-op with 480 members growing a wide selection of varietals. Particularly good Nosiola and Müller-Thurgau, along with *vin santo* made from 100% Nosiola, aged six years in casks – ripe, dried fruit, nuts, well-balanced acidity and sugar.

Cantina Rotaliana, Mezzolombardo *w r ris* ☆→☆☆☆ * 350ha, 1,000,000 bottles. Large, well-run co-op with 325 members, representing most Trentino varietals and showing good quality/price ratio. Top labels include the Principe range and a classy Teroldego Rotaliano Riserva.

Cantine Mezzacorona, Mezzacorona, *w r sp* ☆☆→☆☆☆ * 2,600ha, 30,000,000 bottles. Large co-op (1,500 members) exporting 70% of its production. Good *metodo classico spumante* made under the Rotari label, plus a range of well-priced quality-conscious local red (Teroldego) and white wines (Chardonnay and Pinot Grigio).

Castel Noarna, Nogaredo *w r* ☆☆→☆☆☆ * 7ha, 30,000 bottles. Marco Zani's medieval castle is noted for impressive Cabernet Romeo, a sapid Cabernet Sauvignon/Cabernet Franc/Merlot/Lagrein blend aged two years in barrique – structure, balance, and elegance. Also good Nosiola, and Bianco di Castelnuovo, a white four-grape blend.

Cavit, Trento *w p r ris sw* ☆→☆☆☆ * 72,000,000 bottles. Cavit groups 12 co-ops that produce and sell a large share (70% of total production) of reasonably priced Trentino wines. Wines from individual vineyards, prefixed "Maso", include good Teroldego and other varietals. Also Cuvée Maso Torsella and well-priced Bottega Vinai range, covering varietal Chardonnay, Traminer, Pinot Grigio, Sauvignon, Merlot, Lagrein, and classy Trento Brut Alte Masi Riserva Graal.

Cesconi, Pressano di Lavis *w r* ☆☆→☆☆☆ 16ha, 75,000 bottles. Lorenzo and Roberto Cesconi are firm supporters of vineyard management. Chardonnay, Pinot Grigio, Nosiola, and Traminer lead a stylish range. Top labels: elegant Olivar, a four-grape *cuvée* aged in barrique and tonneau; Traminer Aromatico – great aromatic profile; and Pivier, 100% Merlot.

De Tarczal, Isera, *w r* ☆☆→☆☆☆ 17ha, 120,000 bottles. One of Trentino's historic estates, established in the 18th century.

The main focus is a selection of classy, well-balanced Marzemino. Top labels: Trentino Superiore Marzemino di Isera, Marzemino Husar, Cabernet Sauvignon Selezioni Pianilonghi, and Merlot Campiano.

Giuseppe Fanti, Pressano di Lavis *w* ☆☆→☆☆☆☆ 3,5ha, 19,000 bottles. Alessandro Fanti's small estate reflects dedicated vineyard management. Top wines are led by Manzoni Bianco, Chardonnay Robur, and Nosiola.

Ferrari, Trento *w p sp* ☆☆→☆☆☆☆ 120ha, 4,500,000 bottles. Leading sparkling wine house founded in 1902. Excellent Trento Classico, including outstanding Giulio Ferrari Riserva del Fondatore, made only in top vintages. Good Brut, Brut Perlé, Brut Rosé, and Maximum Brut.

Foradori, Mezzolombardo ☆☆☆→ ☆☆☆☆ 25ha, 200,000 bottles. Elisabetta Foradori manages her production with a firm grip. She has achieved an exemplary production of Teroldego Rotaliano, in particular with her Granato (100% Teroldego) – complex notes of berry fruit, smoky, tobacco, tar, aristocratic elegance. Also refined, long-ageing Pinot Bianco and Pinot Bianco-based blend Myrto.

Fratelli Dorigati, Mezzocorona *w r sp* ☆☆→☆☆☆☆ 100,000 bottles. Established in 1858 and focusing on stylish wines. Top labels: Trento Brut Riserva Methius Talento Metodo Classico, stylish Teroldego Rotaliano Diedri, good Rebo/Pinot Grigio, and Cabernet Grener.

Fratelli Lunelli, Trento *w r ris* ☆☆→☆☆☆☆ 29ha, 110,000 bottles. Owners of Ferrari, making impressive Bordeaux-style blend Maso Le Viane – ripe berries, with toasted and mint nuances, structure, fine tannins, very persistent. Also good Pinot Noir

Maso Montalto, Chardonnay Villa Gentilotti, Sauvignon Villa San Nicolò, and four-varietal blend Bianco Superiore Villa Margon.

Instituto Agrario Provinciale, San Michele all'Adige *w p r* ☆☆→☆☆☆☆ * 50ha, 250,000 bottles. Historic school established in 1874 producing reliably good varietal wines with good quality/price ratio. Top labels: Traminer Aromatico Vigneto Doss, Bianco Castel San Michele, Chardonnay Vigneto Molini, and Pinot Bianco Vigneto San Donà.

Letrari, Rovereto *w p r sp* ☆☆→☆☆☆☆ 23ha, 160,000 bottles. Family-run estate producing solid, reliable wines spanning a range of varietals, including Terra dei Forti Enantio from Valdadige – youthful berry fruit, balsamic, capsicum; spicy Good Moscato Rosa – reminiscent of rose petals; and Teroldego Cervaia del Fovo – sapid, with marked varietal character.

Longariva, Rovereto *w r ris* ☆☆→☆☆☆☆ 17ha, 100,000 bottles. Marco Manica's production is best noted for its fine whites, including Pinot Bianco Pergole – floral, with white peaches, sapid, and fresh; Pinot Grigio Perer; and oak-fermented Chardonnay Praistél. In the reds, Cabernet Sauvignon Marognon, as well as a fine three-varietal blend: Rosso Tre Cesure Marco Manica Riserva.

Marco Donati, Mezzocorona *w r* ☆☆→☆☆☆☆ 100,000 bottles. Estate founded in 1863. Classy, individual Teroldego Rotaliano Sangue di Drago and Bagolari lead this intriguing range. Also good Lagrein Rubino, Marzemino Orme, Syrah Costa dei Sauri, and Torre del Noce, a Sauvignon/ Chardonnay blend with mineral qualities.

Maso Bastie, Volano *w p r sw* ☆☆→☆☆☆☆ 14ha, 20,000 bottles.

Giuseppe Torelli's production focuses on a small number of quality wines. Excellent Traminer Aromatico – good varietal character and mineral quality; good Rosso Bastile Alte, a Merlot/Cabernet Sauvignon blend aged 24 months in barrique; and delightful Moscato Rosa – delicate bouquet of red roses, small berry fruit, structure and persistence.

Maso Furli, Lavis *w r* ☆☆☆ 4ha, 14,000 bottles. Marco Zanoni produces fine, fresh, elegant wines. Top labels: a Trentino Traminer characterized by sapidity and pretty floral aromas; a structured Sauvignon, partly fermented and aged in Allier to give it a richer consistency; and a Rosso Furli blend of Cabernet Sauvignon and Merlot – balsamic, spicy, with vegetal notes, round, and long.

Maso Martis, Trento *w p sp sw* ☆☆☆ 12ha, 60,000 bottles. Antonio Stelzer's production is known for high-quality sparklers: Trento Brut, Brut Riserva, Brut Rosé, all characterized by great finesse. Also good still Chardonnay L'Incanto – barrique-fermented, showing well-integrated oak; and Moscato Rosa, which is quite intense and vinous in character.

Gino Pedrotti, Cavedine *w r sw* ☆☆☆ 5ha, 22,000 bottles. Small family estate near Lake Garda with a production specializing in *vin santo* aged in barrique 48 months – botrytized, honey, apricots, nuts, figs, fresh, vibrant and long. Also good Chardonnay, Schiava Nera, and Nosiola.

Fratelli Pisoni, Sarche di Lasino *w r* ☆☆☆ 16ha, 100,000 bottles. A family estate specializing in *vin santo* showing good complexity, aromas, structure, elegance, and length. Also good Trentino Pinot Noir, Rebo, Nosiola, and

an interesting Sarica Rosso, a Syrah-based wine with Pinot Noir, aged 18 months in barrique – good aromatic profile, balance, and persistence.

Pojer & Sandri, Faedo *w r sw* ☆☆→☆☆☆ 24ha, 250,000 bottles. Family-run estate with some vineyards focusing on unusual varieties, such as Groppello from Val di Non, Negara Trentino, and Rotenberg (a cross of Schiava and Riesling). First-class finely toned wines include Müller-Thurgau, Chardonnay, Pinot Nero, Nosiola, Traminer Aromatico, IGT Bianco Fayè (Chardonnay/Pinot Bianco), Rosso Fayè (Cabernet/Merlot/Lagrein), and sweet Essenzia from a blend of botrytized late-harvested white grapes.

Giovanni Poli, Santa Massenza di Vezzano *w r sw* ☆☆→☆☆☆☆ * 6ha, 42,000 bottles. Small estate specializing in aromatic grappas, some aged in barrique, and excellent *vin santo* from Nosiola, both in the dry (Vigneto Goccia d'Oro) and sweet version (Vin Santo). Also fine Nosiola, Rebo Rigotti, and Cabernet Fuggé.

Pravis, Lasino *w r sw* ☆☆→☆☆☆ 32ha, 180,000 bottles. The terraced vineyards of this estate focus on a revival of some unusual local varietals, including red Niergal and white Stravino – late-harvest. Deep, modern-style wines: Lagrein Niergal, Nosiola Le Frate, Rebo Rigotti, Cabernet Frata Granda, Müller-Thurgau San Thomà, Pinot Grigio Polin; plus IGT Syrae Syrah, Stravino di Stravino, a five-grape white blend, and Vin Santo Arèle.

Tenuta San Leonardo, Borghetto all'Adige *r* ☆☆☆→☆☆☆☆ 20ha, 140,000 bottles. Marchese Guerrieri-Gonzaga's estate is considered the "Sassicaia of Trentino". Production focuses on four grapes – Merlot, Cabernet Sauvignon, Cabernet Franc, and Carmenère – and three wines: Merlot di San Leonardo, Villa Gresti (mainly Merlot), and San Leonardo (a Bordeaux blend). All are powerful and age-worthy.

Enrico Spagnolli, Isera *w r* ✩✩ * 150,000 bottles. Family estate with production focusing on local Trentino varieties, led by good Moscato Giallo made using a process of cold maceration to extract the aromatic profile. Marzemino selezione Don Giovanni shows classic tipicity – earthy, violets, medium structure.

Vallarom, Avio *w r* ✩✩→✩✩✩ 8ha, 40,000 bottles. Viticultural expert Attilo Scienza and family make carefully-crafted wines at this property close to the river Adige, including Cabernet Sauvignon, Pinot Nero, Chardonnay Vigna Brioni, white blend Vadum Caesaris, and a delicious Marzemino. Campi Sarni Rosso is a blend of Cabernet Sauvignon, Cabernet Franc and Merlot, with fine tannins, and an elegant finish.

La Vis, Lavis *w p r* ✩→✩✩✩ * 1,350ha, 5,500,000 bottles. High ranking co-op producing wines with incisive varietal character across the board, especially with the leading Ritratti range – excellent Ritratto Bianco (Chardonnay/Pinot Grigio) and Rosso (Teroldego/Lagrein). Cantina Valle di Cembra was recently bought out by La Vis and is now labelled La Vis-Valle di Cembra. La Vis also owns Cesarini Sforza Spumante and Maso Franc, as well as estates in Tuscany.

Zeni, San Michele all'Adige *w p r sw sp* ✩✩→✩✩✩ * 20ha, 195,000 bottles. Estate founded in 1882 with some vines situated in the top Campo Rotaliano sites, famous for Teroldego and Pinot Bianco. Top labels: fine, Teroldego Rotaliano (Pini and Vigneto Lealbere), good Pinot Nero Spiazol, Müller-Thurgau Vigneto Lecroci, Pinot Bianco Sorti, Moscato Rosa, and a small production of excellent Metodo Classico Brut.

Wine & Food

The cooking of Trentino and the Alto Adige derives from distinct heritages: one Italian-Venetian, the other Austro-Tyrolean; but the intermingling of people drawing on shared resources along the Adige Valley has taken the sharp edges off the contrasts. Something akin to a regional style of cooking has emerged. True, the Italian-speaking population still relies more heavily on polenta, gnocchi, and pasta, and the German-speaking on wurst, black bread, and soups. But the fare found in both *ristoranti* and *Gasthäuser* here has been enriched by the points in common. The *Knödel*, for example, has become *canederli* in Italian and savoured just as avidly. The same can be said for sauerkraut, or *crauti*. Game, trout, speck (smoked pork flank), and Viennese-style pastries are further evidence of a unity of taste that makes the long hours spent at table in the warm, wood-panelled *Stuben* so enjoyable.

Biroldi con crauti Blood sausages with chestnuts, nutmeg, and cinnamon, served with sauerkraut.
Blau Forelle Alpine trout boiled with white wine and flavourings.
Carne salata Beef marinated with herbs and spices, served with polenta and beans.
Gerstensuppe Barley soup with bacon, onions, and celery.
Gröstl Beef, potatoes, and onions cooked together in a mould.

Krapfen Tirolese Fried pastry with marmalade and sugar.
Leberknödelsuppe Bread dumplings flavoured with calf's liver and herbs, served in broth.

Säuresuppe Flavoursome tripe soup traditionally eaten mid-morning on market days.
Speck Smoked pork flank.

Hotels: Alto Adige

Gasthof Ristorante Kirchsteiger, Lana €€
Excellent value *Gasthof* with spacious rooms and balconies in the hills 12km (7.5 miles) above Merano, plus traditional *Stube* with regional specialties and courteous service.

Krone, Aldino (BZ) €–€€
Small *Gasthof* with a few old-fashioned rooms above the *Stube*, where you can enjoy excellent local fare. Great cheeses and speck. Excellent selection of wines.

Hotel Park Laurin, Bolzano €€–€€€
A central and comfortable hotel with spacious rooms and a good restaurant.

Hotel & Spa Rosa Alpina/Restaurant St Hubertus, San Cassiano (BZ) €€€
Traditional, elegant spa hotel run by the Pizzinini family. Comfortable rooms with mountain views and two good in-house restaurants – one offering pizza and local fare, and the other, the renowned Michelin-starred St Hubertus, refined elegance and eclectic local dishes. Excellent wine list.

Restaurants: Alto Adige

Enoteca Johnson & Dipoli, Egna (BZ) €–€€
This elegant restaurant-wine bar focuses on creative, innovative cooking, with dishes such as swordfish carpaccio with grapefruit, filet steak, caviar, and fois gras. Good wine list.

Gasthaus Zur Rose, Cortaccia (BZ) €€
Traditional *Stube* with good home cooking, featuring speck, mushrooms, *tagliolini* with black truffle, *canederli*, ricotta and spinach ravioli, apple strudel, and home-made cakes.

Kupperlain, Castelbello (BZ) €€
Jörg Trafojer's restaurant in Val Venosta is located within an old *maso* (a typical northern Italian mountain farmhouse) with four dining rooms. Excellent pappardelle with hare ragout, plus creative dishes with vegetables and flowers. Good wine list.

La Passion, Vandoies di Sopra (BZ) €€
Seventeenth-century *Stube* in Val Pusteria with local seasonal fare. Specialties on the menu include saddle of hare with savoy cabbage on a veil of cranberry sauce. It's a small establishment, so make sure you book well in advance.

Restaurant Marklhof – Bellavista, Cornaiano €–€€
Excellent regional cuisine with prime selection of hams and cheese, asparagus when in season, special bouillon with egg and venison cooked in wine and more. Good wine list.

Schöneck, Frazione Molini (BZ) €€–€€€
Traditional chalet with three *Stuben*, an open fireplace and a veranda offering local Val Pusteria dishes. Excellent desserts and wine list.

Zur Rose, San Michele Appiano
(BZ) €€€
Chef Herbert Hintner is one of
northern Italy's gastronomic

stars. His excellent restaurant
offers traditional hospitality,
creatively combining local
ingredients. Excellent wine list.

Hotels: Trentino

Boscolo Grand Hotel Trento,
Trento €–€€
This large four-star hotel in the
centre of Trento offers comfortable,
spacious rooms sumptuously
decorated with antiques. Some
rooms have splendid views of
the city.
Locanda dello Scalco,
Segonzano €–€€
Wonderfully restored *maso* dating
back to 1681 and part of the
Castello di Segonzano, situated
in the Valle di Cembra.

Locanda San Martino,
Cavizzana €
Lina and Fabrizio Franceschi's
hospitable *locanda* in Val di Sole
offers four rooms. Also available
are home-made cheeses, hams
and speck, steaks, polenta, and
strudel
Hotel Rovereto, Rovereto
€–€€
An elegant palazzo dating back
to 1889, with comfortable rooms,
charm, and good service.
Hospitable family ambience.

Restaurants: Trentino

Locanda delle Tre Chiavi, Isera
€–€€
Isera is the home of Marzemino,
and here, your host Sergio
Valentini will regale you with
carne salata, tagliatelle with
mushrooms, trout and grilled
meats, as well as excellent cheeses
and wines stored in the restaurant's
historic underground cellars.
Maso Cantanghel, Civezzano €–€€
Warm hospitable, elegant *trattoria*
serving typical Trentino fare with
a tasting menu featuring leek and
cabbage flan, polenta and cod,
risotto with vegetables, roast
pheasant, good wines, and more.
Orso Grigio, Ronzone €€

Local cuisine with foie gras, ravioli,
gnocchi, venison in juniper berry
sauce, fillet in Teroldego reduction,
vegetable quiches, and strudel.
Good wine list.
Osteria del Pettirosso,
Rovereto €€
Excellent local fare served with
flare, using local seasonal
ingredients. Good wine list.
Lo Scrigno del Duomo, Trento
€€–€€€
Centrally located just off Trento's
main square, facing the Duomo.
This one-starred Michelin
restaurant offers an elegant setting,
excellent local fare, attentive service,
and a well-selected wine list.

Veneto *Veneto*

This verdant land of vines that flourish in hills and plains is northern Italy's most abundant source of wine. It also ranks top in Italy for DOC(G) output, producing about a quarter of the country's total. Two-thirds of that comes from the province of Verona, where the famous trio of Soave, Valpolicella, and Bardolino is complemented by Bianco di Custoza, Lugana, the extensive Garda, and the recent Arcole.

After years of making cheap and cheerful wines, the large Veronese producers have now become more quality-directed, and the wines, most notably Soave and Valpolicella, show a far more distinct character. Soave Superiore has finally been upgraded to DOCG, following close on the heels of Bardolino Superiore. Verona's flagship wine is Amarone della Valpolicella, a strong, powerful red of uniquely dynamic dimensions. But the revival is bringing new class to all the traditional Veronese wines, which, creditably, remain predominantly based on native vines.

But Verona by no means stands alone in the region. The central hills around Vicenza and Padova (Padua) boast an eclectic mix of native and foreign varieties in wines from the DOC zones of Gambellera, Lessini Durello, Breganze, Colli Berici, Colli Euganei, Merlara, and Bagnoli. The Prosecco grape, grown on the steep hills between Conegliano and Valdobbiadene, makes lightly and fully sparkling wines that have become Italy's favourite. There are also some highly characterful still wines from DOC Colli di Conegliano, in the same area. The province of Venice extends northeast along the Adriatic across the DOC zones of Piave and Lison-Pramaggiore, bountiful sources of Merlot and Cabernet. The Pinots, Sauvignon Blanc, and increasingly Chardonnay thrive here too, alongside such native varieties as white Verduzzo and Tocai, and red Raboso.

The Veneto's twenty-seven DOC(G)s include five that extend into adjacent regions: Lison-Pramaggiore (shared with Friuli-Venezia Giulia), Valdadige (Trentino-Alto Adige), and Garda, Lugana, and San Martino della Battaglia (Lombardy). There are also ten IGT areas contained wholly or partly within the region.

Those who visit Venice's hinterland in quest of wine and food will also find a heritage of art, architecture, and history amid inspiring landscapes. Wine roads lead through Verona's hills, as well as through Breganze, the Piave Valley, and the splendid hills of the Prosecco zone northwest of Treviso. A local habit that is easy to take to is to call at a bar for a small glass of wine, called an *ombra*, at any time of day. VinItaly, held each April in Verona, is the nation's main wine fair. Impressive wine shops include Bei Leo and La Caneva in Jesolo, Enoteca La Mia Cantina in Padova, Enoteca Regionale Veneto in Pramaggiore, Mario Rossi in Treviso, Al Volto in Venice, and Bottega del Vino and Bottiglieria Corsini in Verona.

Recent Vintages

In a region where whites account for more than seventy-five per cent of production, most wines are designed to be drunk young. Certain Cabernets, Merlots, and other reds of the eastern Veneto age well. Verona's sweet Recioto della Valpolicella often improves with time, and its dry counterpart, Amarone, is one of the world's great wines for ageing. Some sturdy Valpolicella can age well, too, as can Custoza, Lugana, Soave Classico, and Recioto di Soave.

2004 A later ripening season with generally high yields. Some vineyards suffered from summer hail. On the whole, a good, healthy crop.

2003 Average rainfall was down by thirty per cent and summer temperatures up by about forty per cent, which contributed to wines with a high sugar/alcohol content.

2002 A rainy late summer with hailstorms led to great variability. However, most producers picked the healthiest grapes and thereby gained fine quality.

2001 A good year throughout the region but without the quality peaks of 2000.

2000 Excellent vintage for white and red wines in the whole of the Veneto. Poor weather after the vintage compromised some Amarone.

1999 Showers in mid-September affected the quality of certain grape varieties (especially Pinot Grigio), while the reds are satisfactory to good.

1998 Large crop harmed by hail and harvest rains; mixed quality.

1997 Reduced crop of excellent quality; superb year for Amarone.

1996 Abundant harvest, good to very good throughout the region.

1995 Fine year in general; grapes of exceptional concentration made what some are calling the vintage of the century for Amarone.

Earlier good vintages for Amarone: 90, 88, 86, 85, 83, 79, 76, 74, 71, 70, 67, 64.

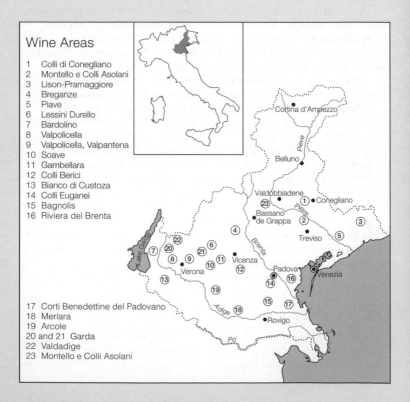

Wine Areas

1   Colli di Conegliano
2   Montello e Colli Asolani
3   Lison-Pramaggiore
4   Breganze
5   Piave
6   Lessini Durello
7   Bardolino
8   Valpolicella
9   Valpolicella, Valpantena
10 Soave
11 Gambellara
12 Colli Berici
13 Bianco di Custoza
14 Colli Euganei
15 Bagnolis
16 Riviera del Brenta

17 Corti Benedettine del Padovano
18 Merlara
19 Arcole
20 and 21 Garda
22 Valdadige
23 Montello e Colli Asolani

Appellations

DOCG

BARDOLINO SUPERIORE *r cl 98 99 00 01 04*

From the same grapes as Bardolino DOC, with a lower maximum yield, higher minimum alcohol, and at least one year's ageing.

RECIOTO DI SOAVE *w sw sp 95 96 97 98 00 01 04*

This prized dessert wine from semi-dried grapes comes from the same zone and varieties as Soave. Light golden to amber, after two to three years of ageing the wine develops an aroma of currants and, in particularly good years, of botrytis; supple, full-bodied, and sweet.

SOAVE SUPERIORE *w ris cl*

The rehabilitation of Soave from an attractive but forgettable drink to a wine of class has been taken one stage further with this DOCG for *superiore* versions with lower yields. There is also a *riserva* category for wines with two years of ageing, which mainly embraces oak-fermented Soave. Grape varieties are as for Soave DOC.

DOC

ARCOLE *w fz ris nov*

Cabernet Franc, Carmenère, Cabernet Sauvignon, Merlot, Chardonnay, Garganega, Pinot Bianco, Pinot Grigio.

BAGNOLI/BAGNOLI DI SOPRA *w r p cl ris vt sp pas*

Chardonnay, Tocai Friulano, Sauvignon Blanc, Merlot, Raboso, Cabernet Sauvignon, Cabernet Franc, Carmenère, Friularo.

BARDOLINO *w r p cl sp*

Corvina, Rondinella, Molinara, Negrara, Rossignola, Barbera, Sangiovese, Garganega.

BIANCO DI CUSTOZA *w sup*

Trebbiano, Garganega, Tocai.

BREGANZE *w r sup ris sw*

Cabernet Franc, Cabernet Sauvignon, Carmenère, Merlot, Chardonnay, Marzemino, Pinot Bianco, Pinot Grigio, Pinot Nero, Sauvignon Blanc, Torcolato, Vespaiolo, Cartizze, Prosecco di Conegliano-Valdobbiadene, Tocai Friulano.

COLLI BERICI *w r ris sp*

Cabernet Franc, Cabernet Sauvignon, Chardonnay, Merlot, Garganega, Pinot Bianco, Pinot Grigio, Sauvignon Blanc, Tocai Italico, Tocai Rosso.

COLLI DI CONEGLIANO *w r sw pas m fz*

Incrocio Manzoni (Riesling/Pinot Bianco), Pinot Bianco, Chardonnay, Sauvignon Blanc, Riesling, Marzemino, Merlot, Prosecco, Verdino, Boschera, Refrontolo Passito, Torchiato di Fregona.

COLLI EUGANEI *w sp r ris sw pas*

Garganega, Prosecco, Merlot, Cabernet Franc, Cabernet Sauvignon, Barbera, Raboso, Chardonnay, Pinot Bianco, Serprino, Riesling Italico, Fior d'Arancio (from a strain of Moscato).

CORTI BENEDETTINE DEL PADOVANO *w r p ris fz sp sw m pas nov*

Tocai Friulano, Chardonnay, Pinot Bianco, Pinot Grigio, Sauvignon, Tocai Italico, Cabernet Sauvignon, Merlot, Moscato Raboso, Refosco.

GAMBELLARA *w cl sp sw*

Garganega and other local non-aromatic white varieties.

GARDA

See Lombardy.

MONTI LESSINI/LESSINI

w r p sup sp pas ris

Merlot, Pinot Nero, Cabernet Franc, Corvina, Cabernet Sauvignon, Carmenère, Durello, Garganega, Trebbiano, Pinot Bianco, Chardonnay.

LISON-PRAMAGGIORE *w r ris fz sp nov cl sw*

Chardonnay, Pinot Bianco, Pinot Grigio, Pinot Nero, Cabernet Sauvignon, Cabernet Franc, Merlot, Corvina, Carmenère, Tocai Friulano, Malbec, Riesling, Tocai, Verduzzo.

LUGANA *See* Lombardy

MERLARA *w r fz nov*

Tocai Friulano, Merlot, Cabernet Sauvignon, Malvasia, Marzemino, Tocai.

MONTELLO E COLLI ASOLANI

w r sup sp fz

Cabernet Sauvignon, Cabernet Franc, Merlot, Chardonnay, Pinot Bianco, Pinot Grigio, Prosecco, Riesling.

PIAVE/VINI DEL PIAVE *w r ris sw*

Cabernet Franc, Cabernet Sauvignon, Chardonnay, Merlot, Pinot Bianco, Pinot Grigio, Pinot Nero, Raboso, Tocai Italico, Verduzzo.

PROSECCO DI CONEGLIANO-VALDOBBIADENE *w sp fz sup sp*

Prosecco, Verdisio, Bianchetta, Perera, Prosecco Lungo.

RIVIERA DEL BRENTA *w r p fz sp ris nov*

Merlot, Raboso, Cabernet Franc Cabernet Sauvignon, Refosco, Pinot Grigio, Pinot Bianco, Chardonnay, Tocai.

SAN MARTINO DELLA BATTAGLIA *See* Lombardy.

SOAVE *w sp cl*

Garganega, Trebbiano di Soave, Chardonnay, Pinot Bianco.

VALDADIGE *See* Trentino-Alto Adige.

VALPOLICELLA *r cl sup fz sp sw sup 97 98 99 00 01 04*

Corvina, Rondinella, Molinara, Barbera, Negrara, Rossignola, Sangiovese.

Amarone della Valpolicella *83 85 88 90 95 97 98 00 01 04*

Important variant of Valpolicella. Preferably Corvina, dried on racks for an average of three months after harvest, then fermented to almost dryness to give a powerful wine with an ageing potential of 20 years or longer. Age: 2 years.

Recioto della Valpolicella *95 97 98 00 01 04*

From semi-dried grapes, as for Amarone, but those that are semi-sweet, not dry. Deep purple with ample bouquet and structure, a semi-sweet flavour and a bitter aftertaste.

VICENZA *w r p fz sp m sw ris nov*

Cabernet Franc, Cabernet Sauvignon, Carmenère, Chardonnay, Garganega, Manzoni Bianco, Merlot, Moscato, Pinot Bianco, Pinot Grigio, Pinot Nero, Raboso, Riesling, Sauvignon Blanc.

IGT

Alto Livenza,
Colli Trevigiani,
Conselvano,
Delle Venezie,
Marca Trevigiana,
Provincia di Verona/Veronese,
Vallagarina,
Veneto,
Veneto Orientale,
Vigneti delle Dolomiti

Producers

The key provinces have been abbreviated as follows: BL = Belluno; PD = Padova; RO = Rovigo; TV = Treviso; VE = Venezia;
VR = Verona; VI = Vicenza.
"V" stands for Valdobbiadene;
"C" stands for Conegliano.

Igino Accordini, Pedemonte (VR) *r sw* ☆☆→☆☆☆ 6ha, 72,000 bottles. Estate founded in 1950 producing classic Amarone and Valpolicella. Top labels include Amarone Classico Alzaro, aged 25 months in barrique – round and ripe, with cherry, plum, and blackberry fruit, full, warm, and persistent. Also good Valpolicella: Classico Le Bessole and Classico Superiore Ripassà; and Recioto Le Viole.

Stefano Accordini, Pedemonte (VR) *r sw* ☆☆→☆☆☆☆ 90 95 97 98 00 04 7ha, 55,000 bottles. Stefano and Daniele Accordini's vines in Fumane produce fine Valpolicella, Amarone, and Recioto under the Acinatico and Fornetto labels. The wines are complex, sapid, and compact, showing fine ageing potential and terroir character.

Adami, Colbertaldo di Vidor (TV) *w sp* ☆☆→☆☆☆ 7ha, 420,000 bottles. Well-established estate with a production of Prosecco V, in particular Vigneto Giardino – elegance, peach, apricot, and flowery bouquet, fine, fresh, and creamy on the palate, balanced and long. Also good Cartizze, Prosecco Tranquillo, and Brut Bosco di Gica.

Allegrini, Fumane (VR) *r sw* ☆☆☆→ ☆☆☆☆ 95 97 00 100ha, 900,000 bottles. Marilisa and Franco Allegrini lead this renowned Fumane estate (est. 1854). Lively, youthful Valpolicella; impressive Amarone; 100% Corvina IGT La Poja; and a sapid IGT blend Villa Giona (Cabernet/Merlot/Syrah), as well as La Grola IGT (Corvina/Rondinella/Syrah/Sangiovese).

Anselmi, Monteforte d'Alpone (VR) *w r sw* ☆☆☆→☆☆☆☆ 90 92 98 00 01 02 03 70ha, 500,000 bottles. Roberto Anselmi is one of Soave's most dynamic and quality-orientated producers, famed for his use of oak on Garganega. Capitel Foscarino, Capitel Croce, Recioto, and Recioto I Capitelli all excel. The wines show elegance, balance, and harmony, ripeness and full aromatic complexity. I Capitelli is particularly long-lived.

Armani, Dolcè (VR) *w r* ☆☆→☆☆☆ Albino Armani comes from a long line of winemakers dating back to 1600. He is a man with a vision – to produce a red from unique Foja Tonda (Vitigno Casetta) on old pergola vineyards close to the River Adige, near the Trentino border. Also good Terre dei Forti Chardonnay, Corvara (a Corvina/Cabernet/Merlot blend), and Valdadige Pinot Grigio.

Lorenzo Begali, San Pietro in Cariano (VR) *r sw* ☆☆→☆☆☆☆ 90 95 97 00 04 7ha, 40,000 bottles. New rising Amarone and Valpolicella Classico star with a production focusing on fruit-driven wines with great character and individual expression. Top labels: Amarone Monte Ca' Bianca, a single-vineyard – wonderful complexity, hints of cherry, tobacco, liquorice, and spice, round, full, elegant, and long – excellent for ageing.

Bellenda, Vittorio Veneto (TV) *w r sp* ☆☆→☆☆☆ * 35ha, 1,000,000 bottles. Luigi Cosmo's production covers a wide range of Colli di Conegliano reds and whites, as well as good Metodo Classico Brut Bellenda and Prosecco di CV Miraval. Good Conegliano Rosso

Contrada di Concenigo, aged in barrique 18 months – well-extracted, fine aromas, leather, and tobacco.

Bepin de Eto, San Pietro di Feletto (TV) *w sp sw* ☆→☆☆☆ 95ha, 800,000 bottles. An estate in the heart of Colli di Conegliano. Notable Colli di Bianco Il Greccio and Rosso Croda Ronca. Also fine Prosecco di C and a Passito Faè.

Bertani, Negrar (VR) *w r sp sw* ☆☆→☆☆☆ 90 93 94 95 97 98 99 00 01 03 04 135ha. Historic Valpolicella estate (est. 1857), said to have created Amarone in the dry version. Noted for Valpolicella Classico and Valpantena Secco-Bertani, Soave, Bardolino, and especially for its cask-aged Amarone. Also white IGT Le Lav (Garganega/Chardonnay), red IGT Ripasso Catullo (Corvina/ Cabernet Sauvignon), and Villa Novare (Cabernet).

Bisol, Santo Stefano di Valdobbiadene (TV) *w sp sw* ☆☆→☆☆☆☆ * 50ha, 500,000 bottles. Bisol is a well-reputed estate with a production exported worldwide. Top labels: Prosecco di V; Granei – elegant, crisp, persistent, with fine aromas; and Vigneti del Fol – mineral, citrus, sapid, and creamy. Also good Brut Crede and Passito Duca di Dolle – delectable nectar.

Borin, Monselice (PD) *w p r ris fz sw* ☆→☆☆ * 29ha, 130,000 bottles. Emerging Colli Euganei estate. Gianni Borin focuses on Moscato Giallo and Prosecco. Top labels: *passito* Fior d'Arancio (Moscato Giallo) – flowery, citrus, with spice and crisp acidity, fresh; Colli Euganei Cabernet Mon Silicis Riserva; and Merlot Rocca Chiara Riserva.

Bortolin, Valdobbiadene (TV) *r w sp* ☆→☆☆☆ * 20ha, 300,000 bottles. This estate at the foothills of the Cartizze area produces an impressive Prosecco di V and

Cartizze. Top labels: Cartizze Dry – reminiscent of wisteria, golden apples, and acacia, balanced and persistent; Prosecco di V Extra Dry – crisp elegance, with fine perlage.

Bosco del Merlo, Anone Veneto (VE) *w r* ☆☆→☆☆☆ 130ha, 650,000 bottles. Promising Lison-Pramaggiore estate with an organic production. Top labels: a white Priné (a blend of Chardonnay, Pinot Bianco, and Riesling), Lison Pramaggiore Refosco Roggio dei Roveri, Classico Tocai Juti, and 360 Ruber Capite (Merlot/Malbec/Cabernet) – full-bodied, delicious.

Brigaldara, San Floriano (VR) *r sw* ☆☆☆→☆☆☆☆ 90 91 95 97 98 00 01 34ha, 150,000 bottles. Stefano Cesari's production is praised particularly for his exceptional Amarone, Valpolicella, and Recioto. Top labels: Amarone Case Vece, aged 12 months in barrique and 24 in larger barrels – explosive aromas, compact and structured, depth, harmony, and elegance.

Luigi Brunelli, San Pietro in Cariano (VR) *w r sw* ☆☆→☆☆☆ 90 91 95 96 97 00 01 04 10ha, 100,000 bottles. Luigi Brunelli's production is based on Valpolicella, Amarone, and Recioto Classico. His style is modern and highly extracted, showing concentration and muscle. Top Amarone labels: Campo del Titari and Campo Inferi Cengia.

Tommaso Bussola, Negrar (VR) *r sw* ☆☆☆→☆☆☆☆ 90 93 95 97 99 00 03 Bussola's meticulous vineyard management results in superb Recioto and very good Valpolicella and Amarone Classico. Highlights: Valpolicella Vigneto Alto TB, made only in top years; and the other Classico TB labels – complex, fresh, and sapid, balanced by elegance.

Ca' Lustra, Faedo di Cinto (PD) *w r sw* ☆☆→☆☆☆ * 29ha, 180,000 bottles. Dynamic producer Franco

Zanovello has a production of Colli Euganei: Pinot Bianco, Cabernet, Chardonnay, Merlot, and Moscato Fior d'Arancio, all of notable quality and reasonable price.

Giuseppe Campagnola, Valgatara di Marano (VR) *r sw* ☆→☆☆☆ 5,000,000 bottles. Large winery for major Verona DOCs, especially all Valpolicella types. Top Valpolicellas: Caterina Zardini and Le Bini Vigneti di Purano Ripasso.

Cantina del Castello, Soave (VR) *w r sw* ☆☆☆ 12ha, 120,000 bottles. Arturo Stochetti is among the leading Soave producers, with Soave Classico Superiore: Acini Soavi, Carniga, and Pressoni. Also good Valpolicella Casotto del Merlo, Amarone Classico, and Recioto.

Cantina della Valpantena, Quinto di Verona (VR) *r sw* ☆☆→☆☆☆ * 700ha, 3,500,000 bottles. Prime source of wines from the Valpantena sub-zone of Valpolicella. The reliable-quality range includes top labels Valpolicella Tesauro and Ripasso, and Amarone Falasco.

Cantina di Soave, Soave (VR) *w r fz sw* ☆→☆☆ * 3,500ha, 30,000,000 bottles. Enormous winery with the aim of producing quality wines at competitive prices. Soave, Amarone, Recioto, Bardolino, and a range of other labels.

Cantina Sociale Valpolicella, Negrar (VR) *w r sw* ☆☆→☆☆☆ * 500ha, 6,000,000 bottles. Quality-conscious co-op selects Amarone, Recioto (Domini Veneti), Valpolicella Classico, and Soave by site. Daniele Accordini oversees the production. Top ranges: Domini Veneti and the Classico Selezione Milo Manara.

La Cappuccina, Costalunga di Monteforte (VR) *w r* ☆☆→☆☆☆ * 28ha, 190,000 bottles. The Tessari family estate produces wines of elegance and style. Among its range of four Soaves, San Brizio is especially noteworthy – aromatic, with good minerality. Also good international-style IGTs from Sauvignon, and Cabernet and Carmenère, such as Campo Buri – blackberry, green pepper, round and full. Good Arzimo *passito*.

Carpenè Malvolti, Conegliano (TV) *r w sp* ☆→☆☆ Historic estate, pioneer of sparkling wine in Veneto, has a respected range of Prosecco di C, *metodo classico spumante* Carpenè Malvolti Brut, and other labels.

Ca' Rugate, Montecchia di Crosara (VR) *w r sw* ☆☆☆ * 50ha, 450,000 bottles. Estate between Valpolicella and Soave with many vines planted to traditional pergolas. Good late-harvest Garganega Bucciato – structure and vibrance; and Soave Monte Alto – floral with nuances of peach. Also good Recioto di Soave La Perlara and Recioto della Valpolicella L'Eremita.

Michele Castellani, Valgatara di Marano (VR) *r sw* ☆☆☆ 48ha, 260,000 bottles. Sergio Castellani's production is esteemed for Recioto, Amarone, and Valpolicella Classico from Casalin I Castei and Ca' del Pipa vineyards. The wines have a bold, fruity structure, with ample aromatic complexity; they are warm, full, and long on the palate.

Domenico Cavazza, Montebello (VI) *w r sw* ☆☆→☆☆☆ * 140ha, 800,000 bottles. A leading light in Colli Berici with Cicogna (Merlot), good Cabernet, and Pinot Bianco; and in Gambellara, with Recioto. Top label: Capitel Santa Libera Recioto di Gambellara Classico – intense, ethereal, and fruity, round, full, balanced, and persistent.

Coffele, Soave (VR) *w sw* ☆☆→☆☆☆ 30ha, 90,000 bottles. Situated in Soave's historic centre, with vines in the *classico* area. Top label: Recioto Le Sponde – flowery bouquet, with a velvety texture. Also good Soave

Classico: Ca' Visco, Alzari, and a basic, well-priced Soave Classico.

Col Vetoraz, Santo Stefano di Valdobbiadene (TV) *w sp* ☆☆→ ☆☆☆ 11ha, 633,000 bottles. An emerging Prosecco di V producer with a fine south–southeast exposition, producing fragrant, structured wines with individual character and elegance. The production includes finely honed brut, extra dry, dry, *frizzante*,Cartizze, and still Prosecco.

Conte Loredan-Gasparini, Volpago del Montello (TV) *r w sp* ☆☆→☆☆☆ 80ha, 350,000 bottles. Historic Venegazzù estate. Highlights include great Montello e Colli Asolani Prosecco Brut, and two red IGT Bordeaux-style blends: Capo di Stato and Venegazzù della Casa.

Corte Gardoni, Valeggio sul Mincio (VR) *w p r fz* ☆☆→☆☆☆ 25ha, 200,000 bottles. Gianni Piccoli's vines are planted to both indigenous and international varietals. Top labels: Bardolino Chiaretto; Bianco di Custoza; Rosso di Corte, a Bordeaux blend – concentrated and fruity, with fine finish; and Fenili – Garganega-based, made with partly raisined grapes and oak-fermented.

Corte Sant' Alda, Mezzane di Sotto (VR) *w r sw* ☆☆☆→☆☆☆☆ *90 95 97 98 00* 16ha, 100,000 bottles. Marinella Camerani is one of Valpolicella's rising stars, with excellent Amarone, Recioto, and Valpolicella Superiore Mithas – ripe cherry and mineral notes, depth and structure. Also good Soave Vigne di Mezzane.

Fratelli Degani, Valgatara di Marano (VR) *r sw* ☆☆→☆☆☆ * 5ha, 30,000 bottles. Small estate producing admired Amarone, Recioto, and Valpolicella Classico with individual personalities. Of particular interest: Amarone la Rosta – intense, complex, plums and tobacco, smoky finish; and Recioto La Rosta – ripe berries, round and long. Good Valpolicella Ripasso Cicilio.

Fasoli Gino, Colognola ai Colli (VR) *w r sw* ☆☆☆→☆☆☆☆ * 14ha, 200,000 bottles. Emerging Soave and IGT Merlot from organic vineyards. Of particular interest: Amarone Altero – focused, rich, spicy, and full; Soave Pieve Vecchia – late-harvest, hints of grapefruit. Also good Pinot Nero Sande and Merlot Calle.

Nino Franco, Valdobbiadene (TV) *w sp* ☆☆☆→☆☆☆☆ 836,000 bottles. Established in 1919 and today managed by Primo Franco. The production covers a range of reliable-quality Prosecco di V, including brut, dry, Cartizze, old-style *rustico* (bottle-fermented), and still.

Gini, Monteforte d'Alpone (VR) *w cl sw* ☆☆→☆☆☆☆ Sandro and Claudio Gini's wines come from good soil, rich in black tufaceous rock and limestone, which makes for mineral elegance and crisp acidity. Sound Soave Classico: La Froscà and Contrada Salvarenza; and Recioto Col Foscarin – rich tropical notes.

Gregoletto, Premaor di Miane (TV) *r w sp* ☆☆→☆☆☆☆ * Giovanni Gregoletto produces irresistibly refreshing Prosecco di C, including a traditional Frizzante Sur Lie, which, as tradition requires, is fermented in bottle, often leaving a yeast residue at the bottom. Also good Colli di Conegliano Rosso and Bianco.

Guerrieri Rizzardi, Bardolino (VR) *w r* ☆☆→☆☆☆☆ 90ha, 500,000 bottles. The only estate with vineyards spread over the three Verona DOCs (Bardolino, Valpolicella, and Soave), producing fine Bardolino Classico: Fontis Vineae Munus and Tacchetto; plus IGTs Castello Guerrieri, Valpolicella Classico Superiore Pojega, as well as delicious Soave Classico Superiore Costeggiola.

Inama, San Bonifacio (VR) *w r sw*
☆☆☆→☆☆☆☆ * *92 93 95 96 98 00
01 03* 40ha. Stefano Inama's wines
come from low-yielding vines
planted in the centre of the Soave
Classico DOC. The intensity of
these wines comes from scrupulous
vineyard management. Top wines
include Soave Classico: Vigneti di
Foscarino, Vigneto du Lot, and Vin
Soave. Also remarkable IGT
Sauvignon Vulcaia, including a rich
Fumé and a late-harvest Aprés, and
fine IGT Cabernet and Chardonnay.

Giuseppe Lonardi, Marano (VR) *r sw*
☆☆☆ 7ha, 40,000 bottles. Small
production of fine Valpolicella
Recioto and Amarone Classico,
plus IGT Privilegia Rosso (Cabernet
Franca, Corvina) – a rich, fruit-
forward wine with floral bouquet.

Luigino Dal Maso, Montebello
Vicentino (VI) *w r sw sp* ☆☆☆ *
30ha, 450,000 bottles. Family-run
estate with a production from the
Colli Berici and Gambellara. Top
labels include Colli Berici: Merlot
Casara Roveri – spicy, concentrated,
and long; and Cabernet Casara
Roveri – juicy fruit, focused, with
complexity. Also good Bordeaux
blend Terra dei Roveri Rosso and
Gambellara Recioto.

Maculan, Breganze (VI) *w r sw* ☆☆☆☆
90 95 97 98 99 00 01 03 35ha. A
huge range (17 wines) of
international and local blends.
Highlights include intense Fratta
(Cabernet/ Merlot) and Cabernet
Palazzotto; stylish white Breganze
di Breganze; spicy, rich Acininobili
from local Vespaiola, Tocai, and
Garganega; sweet Torcolato and
Dindarello Moscato Fior d'Arancio.

Marion, San Martino (VR) *r sw*
☆☆→☆☆☆☆ * 6ha, 20,000 bottles.
The Campedelli family estate likes
to keep things small so that their
quality-driven wines can express
individual character. Besides

Amarone, top labels include
Teroldego, Cabernet Sauvignon,
and good Passito Bianco.

Masi, Gargagnago (VR) *w r sw* ☆☆→
☆☆☆ *90 93 94 95 97 99 00 01 03 04*
3,500,000 bottles. The Boscaini
family own one of Veneto's most
important estates. Their production
includes a range of premium to
everyday drinking wines. Top
selections: Amarone Mazzano,
Amarone Campolongo di Torbe,
and Recioto Mezzanella. Oddities
extend to Osar, based on the rare
Oseleta grape, and wines from the
historic estate of Pieralvise Serègo
Alighieri (a descendant of Dante),
which include notable Valpolicella,
Amarone, and Recioto Classico.

Masottina, San Fior (TV) *w r ris sp*
☆→☆☆ 2,000,000 bottles. Reliable
wines from the Piave area, especially
Prosecco di CV and Colli di C.
Interesting labels include Colli di
C: Rosso Vigneto Montesco and
Bianco Vigneto Rizzardo; good
Brut di Pinot; Piave Chardonnay;
Vigneto Ai Palazzi Cabernet
Sauvignon Riserva; Pinot Grigio
Riserva; and IGT Incrocio Manzoni.

Roberto Mazzi, Negrar (VR) *r sw*
☆☆→☆☆☆☆ *90 95 97 00 01 03 04*
7ha, 50,000 bottles. Estate in the
heart of Valpolicella Classico with a
production of admired Valpolicella
Classico Poiega, Recioto Le
Calcarole, and Amarone Punta di
Villa. The wines (aged in barrique
and larger French oak for the
Amarone) show classic complexity,
fine balance, and character.

Molon Traverso, Salgareda (TV) *w r*
☆☆→☆☆☆☆ 40ha, 350,000 bottles.
Ornella Molon's 17th-century villa –
once the property of the Doge
Giustinian – is one of Piave's most
innovative estates, with particular
emphasis on vineyard management
and wines showing terroir character.
Good Piave: Merlot Rosso di Villa,

Raboso, Vite Rossa, Vite Bianca, and white Traminer.

La Montecchia, Selvazzano Dentro (PD) *w r sw* ☆☆ 23ha, 110,000 bottles. Aristocratic estate producing reliably elegant wines from the Colli Euganei, with good Rosso Villa Capodilista and a number of single-varietal wines including Chardonnay, Pinot Bianco, Merlot, and the traditional Raboso. Very good Fior d'Arancio Passito.

Montresor, Verona *w r sw sp* ☆☆→☆☆☆ * 150ha, 3,500,000 bottles. Large, historic estate (est. 1880) focusing on quality production. New cellars have recently been completed. Top labels: Amarone Castelliere delle Guaite, Valpolicella Castelliere delle Guaite, and Recioto Re Teodorico, in the Classico range. Also good Soave Classico Capitel Alto, Bianco di Custoza Montifiera, and Lugana Gran Guardia.

Tenuta Musella, San Martino Buon Albergo (VR) *w r sw* ☆☆→☆☆☆ 33ha, 120,000 bottles. Emilio and Graziella Pasqua di Bisceglie's production focuses on quality Valpolicella, Amarone, and Recioto. Also interesting Monte del Drago, a Corvina/Cabernet Sauvignon blend – dark berry fruit, warm on the palate, with silky tannins, juicy, long, and elegant; and Chardonnay Garda Bianco del Drago.

Pasqua, Verona *w r* ☆→☆☆☆ 90ha, 200,000 bottles. Established winery making an array of sound Verona wines under the Pasqua label, while Cecilia Beretta is a brand name for a line of estate wines led by Valpolicella and Amarone from Terre di Cariano, Roccolo di Mizzole, and Recioto di Soave Case Vecie.

Pieropan, Soave (VR) *w sw* ☆☆→ ☆☆☆☆ * 90 93 97 98 00 04 33ha, 350,000 bottles. Leonildo Pieropan is one of Soave's most respected producers. His Soave Classico is of unusual style and integrity, especially the single-vineyard Calvarino and La Rocca versions. Also exquisite Recioto Le Colombare, IGT Passito della Rocca (a four-grape blend), and Santa Lucia late-harvest Garganega.

Prà, Monteforte d'Alpone (VR) *w* ☆☆☆ * 30ha, 200,000 bottles. Graziano and Flavio Prà's vines, in the heart of Soave, make impressive Soave Classico Superiore: Colle Sant'Antonio and Vigneto Monte Grande, aged in Allier – excellent aromatic profile expressing ripeness, tropical scents, and a clean, elegant, mineral finish.

Provolo, Mezzane di Sotto (VR) ☆☆ * 20ha, 120,000 bottles. Luigino and Marco Provolo's vines are situated on the slopes of Mezzane. This is an emerging Valpolicella, Amarone, and Recioto estate with a quality-orientated production showing good potential with well-priced wines.

Quintarelli, Negrar (VR) *r ris sw* ☆☆☆☆ *90 95 97* "Bepi" Quintarelli is a mentor to a new generation of Valpolicella winemakers for constantly producing exceptional-quality wines. Singularly rich and complex Valpolicella Classico, unforgettable Amarone (the *riserva* is exceptional), and Recioto from Monte Ca' Paletta vineyards; plus super-concentrated IGT Alzero (Cabernet Franc) and *passito* Amabile del Cerè.

Le Ragose, Arbizzano di Negrar (VR) *r sw* ☆☆☆ *90 95 98 01 03 04* 18ha, 120,000 bottles. Arnaldo Galli's production focuses on refined Valpolicella Classico, Amarone, and Recioto; also fine Garda Cabernet. Top labels: Amarone Marta Galli – rich aromas of berry fruit, spice, tobacco, with balsamic notes, silky, full, and persistent; and Amarone Le Ragose – harmony and elegance.

Roccolo Grassi, Mezzane di Sotto (VR) *w r* ☆☆☆ 12ha, 29,000 bottles. Bruno and Marco Sartori's small production of quality-driven Valpolicella and Amarone shows balance, class, and elegance.

Romano Dal Forno, Illasi (VR) *r sw* ☆☆☆☆ *90 95 97 98 00 03 04* 25ha, 45,000 bottles. Dal Forno produces expensive, but age-worthy wines of individual character, including an impressive, richly fruited DOC Valpolicella and a signature Amarone from Vigneto di Monte Lodoletta. His bottles age in a new, vaulted cellar.

Ruggeri, Valdobbiadene (TV) *w fz* ☆☆→☆☆☆ 1,200,000 bottles. Paolo Bisol's estate is a large, modern, efficient winery with worldwide exports. Selected grapes come from 80 growers for the production of high-quality Prosecco di V, led by Extra Dry Giustino B, Dry Santo Stefano, Extra Dry Giall'Oro, and Superiore Cartizze.

Le Salette, Fumane (VR) *r sw* ☆☆☆ *90 95 97 00 01 03* 40ha, 190,000 bottles. Franco Scamperle's vines are situated in the heart of Valpolicella. Production focuses on top-quality Amarone: La Marega and Pergole Vecie; Recioto: Le Traversagne and Pergole Vecie, and Valpolicella Classico Ca' Carnocchio. Also good Cesare Passito from Garganega, Malvasia, and Moscato.

Speri, Pedemonte (VR) *r sw* ☆☆☆→☆☆☆☆ *90 93 95 97 98 00 01 03 04* 60ha, 350,000 bottles. The Speri family's manicured vineyards are situated in some of Valpolicella's best sites. Production includes a number of top-label Valpolicella, Amarone, and Recioto, from their I Comunai, Monte Sant'Urbano, La Roggia, and La Roverina vineyards.

Suavia, Soave (VR) *w sw* ☆☆☆ * 12ha, 100,000 bottles. Giovanni Tessari's estate is named after the ancient moniker given to Soave, a land of volcanic nature, giving a mineral character to its wines. Impeccable Soave Classico Superiore: Le Rive and Monte Carbonare; and superb Recioto Acinatium – aromatic fruit and floral aromas, balanced acidity and minerality.

Tedeschi, Pedemonte (VR) *r sw* ☆☆☆☆→☆☆☆☆☆ *90 91 93 95 97 98 00 01 03 04* 42ha, 400,000 bottles. One of Valpolicella's historic estates (est. 1630), with wines showing individual character. Top labels: Valpolicella Classico Superiore Capitel dei Nicalò, made with a small percentage of raisined grapes; Amarone Capitel Monte Olmi; and Recioto Capitel Monte Fontana. Also acclaimed IGT Rosso della Fabriseria and Capitel San Rocco.

Tenuta Sant'Antonio, Mezzane di Sotto (VR) *r sw* ☆☆☆ *95 97 00 03 04* 48ha, 300,000 bottles. A rising Veneto star. The production of impressive Cabernet Sauvignon Capitello from semi-dried grapes complements that of esteemed Amarone Campo dei Gigli. Also excellent Valpolicella Superiore La Bandina – rich and aromatic on the nose, with hints of cedar wood, balanced, full on the palate, persistent, and elegant.

Tezza, Poiano di Valpantena (VR) *r sw* ☆☆☆ 25ha, 100,000 bottles. The Tezza cousins are rising to new heights with their Amarone, Valpolicella, and Recioto. Top labels include Amarone Brolo delle Giare – wonderful, intense, dark berry fruit, plums, and spice, robust and structured, grippy tannins, persistence. A wine to age.

Tommasi, Pedemonte (VR) *w r sw* ☆☆☆ 135ha, 900,000 bottles. Production covers a range of Valpolicella Classico wines showing excellent potential, in particular Vigneto

Cà Florian – pepper, tobacco, and crushed berries. Also unusual Crearo della Conca d'Oro, a Corvina/Oseleta/Cabernet Franc blend – ripe, structured, and elegant; and good Recioto Vigneto Fiorato.

Trabucchi, Illasi (VR) *w r sw* ☆☆☆ 20ha, 40,000 bottles. Trabucchi's vines, situated at San Colombano, bordering with Soave, produce traditional Amarone and Recioto, along with good Valpolicella Cereolo and Terre di San Colombano.

Massimino Venturini, San Floriano (VR) *w r sw* ☆☆☆ 11ha, 70,000 bottles. With vineyards in the heart of Valpolicella Classico, the Venturini family annually increase their quality-driven production, which is divided between Amarone, Recioto, and Valpolicella – cherry aromas, firm tannic structure, and persistence, balanced, fresh finish.

Vignalta, Arqua Petrarca (PD) *w r sw ris* ☆☆☆→☆☆☆☆ 95 99 00 01 02 04 05 47ha, 250,000 bottles. A leading light in the Colli Euganei area, with consistency throughout a really impressive range. Highlights include Cabernet Sauvignon Riserva, produced in top vintages; Agno Tinto, a Syrah-based wine with Marzemino, aged in American oak; and Fior d'Arancio, which is delicate and delicious.

Le Vigne di San Pietro, Sommacampagna (VR) *w r sw* ☆☆→☆☆☆☆ 90 93 97 00 01 04 10ha, 70,000 bottles. Carlo Nerozzi's production is noted for excellent Bianco di Custoza and IGT Refolà Cabernet Sauvignon. This wine offers complexity, structure, balance, and persistence. Duecuori is the name given to a fine *passito* made from Moscato Giallo, aged in Allier and acacia for 18 months – delicate aromas, balanced acidity.

Viviani, Negrar (VR) *r sw* ☆☆☆→☆☆☆☆ 90 95 97 00 10ha, 60,000 bottles. One of Valpolicella Classico's top estates, with a history of fine wines from the vineyards in Mazzano showing power, elegance, and personality. Top labels: Valpolicella Superiore Campo Mohar – balsamic hints of cedar; excellent Amarone Casa dei Bepi – floral hints, tobacco, and berries, very balanced and extremely long, a wine to age.

Zenato, San Benedetto di Lugana (VR) *w r ris* ☆☆☆ * 90 95 97 00 01 04 70ha, 1,200,000 bottles. Classy range of Verona DOCs from select vineyards. Top labels include an impressive Amarone Riserva Sergio Zenato – a melange of ripe fruit and spice, elegant, balanced, and very persistent. Also good Valpolicella Superiore Ripassa, Lugana Riserva Sergio Zenato, and *passito* Rigoletto.

Fratelli Zeni, Bardolino (VR) *w p r sw* ☆☆→☆☆☆ 26ha, 860,000 bottles. Historic estate established in 1870 with its own wine museum and a production of classic Veronese wines, including solid Bardolino: Marogne and Vigne Alte; Valpolicella Classico; Bianco di Custoza; Lugana; and two interesting IGTs: Merlar (Cabernet Sauvignon) and Corvar, a Cabernet/Corvina blend.

Zonin, Gambellara (VI) *w r sp sw* ☆☆ 25,000,000 bottles. The Zonin family empire produces a wide range of Veneto DOC, IGT, and sparkling wines. They specialize in estate bottlings from Gambellara, such as Recioto Il Giangio and Valpolicella Il Maso. The company also owns estates in Piedmont, Lombardy, Friuli, Tuscany, and Sicily; Virginia and California in the United States.

Wine & Food

Whether the setting is a smart *ristorante* on the Grand Canal or a country *trattoria* with a spit turning on an open fire, dining in the Veneto is a civilized pleasure. Few regions have such equilibrium in food sources – from fertile plains, lush hillsides, woods, lakes, streams, and the Adriatic – and few other cooks combine them with such easy artistry. Dishes can be lavish, ornate, exotic (it was the Venetians who introduced spices to Italy), but the elements of the cooking are simple: rice, beans, polenta, sausages, salami, poultry, game, fish, mushrooms, and mountain cheese. Venice is the showcase, but the food is every bit as delicious in Verona, Vicenza, Padua, Belluno, Rovigo, and most of all in Treviso, a true sanctuary of Veneto gastronomy.

Baccalà alla vicentina Dried cod stewed in milk

Bigoli con l'anatra Thick, spaghetti with a duck ragout.
Carpaccio Raw beef sliced thin and served with mayonnaise or other sauces (named after the Venetian Renaissance painter).
Fegato alla veneziana Calf's liver cooked with onions and wine.
Granseola alla veneziana Spider crab with oil and lemon.
Pasta e fasioi Soup of pasta and beans, very popular throughout the Veneto region.
Pastissada a caval Horse meat stewed with wine and served with gnocchi or polenta.
Risi e bisi Rice and peas.
Risotto al nero di seppia The rice is cooked with squid and blackened by its ink.
Sardine in saor Pickled marinated sardines with onions
Torresani all peverada Spit-roasted pigeons with a sausage-liver-anchovy-herb sauce served on a bed of polenta.

Hotels

Hotel Accademia, Verona €€
Just off the central Via Mazzini and main Piazza delle Erbe, this hotel offers a touch of "old worldliness". Rooms 302 and 360 are set out under an attractive dome ceiling.
Hotel American, Venice €€–€€€
A charming small hotel just off the Salute, on the picturesque canal of San Vio. An ideal sanctuary, with comfortable rooms away from the constant bustle and flow.
Agriturismo Pozzo di Mazza, Negrar (VR) € This charming family villa with a 16th-century mill is set amid vineyards that form part of the Mazza wine estate. The restaurant serves excellent traditional cuisine. Good parking.

Relais Villabella, San Bonifacio (VR) €€ A 17th-century country villa near Soave with ten elegant bedrooms, surrounded by a park with a good pool.
Hotel Villa Abbazia, Follina (TV) €€–€€€ This 17th-century villa is surrounded by a lush garden and courtyard. The hotel is situated in the historic centre of Follina, a picturesque village at the foothills of the Venetian pre-Alps.
Villa Giona, San Pietro in Cariano (VR) €€–€€€ A beautiful 15th-century villa in a park belonging to the Allegrini estate. First-class service, comfortable rooms, and meals served under the loggia. Also on offer are wine and cookery courses. Good parking.

Hotel Villa Margherita, Mira Porte (VE) €€–€€€ This 16th-century villa set in a scenic park offers relaxed, elegant accommodation. Comfortable rooms and sitting rooms, and an outdoor terrace for alfresco dining.

Restaurants

Al Pompiere, Verona €–€€ Impressive choice of up to 120 Italian cheeses, and an excellent assortment of salamis, hams, and other regional cuts from small artisan producers. Good daily specials and an excellent wine list.

Antica Trattoria Da Bepi, Marano di Valpolicella (VR) €–€€ This traditional family-run country *trattoria* has great character and serves excellent *risotto all'Amarone* and lamb stewed in Amarone.

Bottega del Vino, Verona €€ When in Veneto, a visit here is *de rigueur*. The place buzzes with atmosphere. A large selection of wines is available by the glass, there is a massive wine list, and the food is not bad either.

Da Giggetto, Miane (TV) €€ Excellent regional cuisine. Top-quality ingredients are used masterfully to create traditional recipes with a touch of innovation. Commendable wine list. The underground cellar (up to 18m/ 59ft deep) is well worth a visit!

Enoteca della Valpolicella, Fumane (VR) €€ Wine is at the heart of this *enoteca*, where you can find almost every good label of Valpolicella and Amarone. Excellent well-prepared seasonal recipes are based on prime ingredients and traditional cuisine.

Enoteca Realda, Albareto d'Adige (VR) € This charming wine bar with six tables serves typical local cuisine. There is an excellent selection of local wines, local cheeses, hams, polenta, *bigoli* and more.

Groto de Corgnan, Sant'Ambrogio Valpolicella (VR) €–€€ Great hospitality and regional recipes make this an excellent eating experience. Enjoy a wide range of antipasti and pasta-based main courses. Good wine list.

La Locanda di Piero, Montecchio Precalcino (VI) €€ Excellent, creative cuisine using local ingredients, such as spaghetti with prawns, peppers, and wild fennel; and pheasant breast stuffed with black truffle with tepid bean salad with sour cream.

Naranzaria, Venice € Located just in the shade of the Rialto bridge, this *osteria* is named after the *naranzaria*, the old warehouse for storing citrus fruits. It has an outside terrace offering superb views of the Grand Canal, good wine and great starters.

L'Oste Scuro, Verona €€–€€€ This restaurant features fresh seafood with exotic crudités: scallops, scampi, salmon tartar, marinated angler, tender grilled calamari, and wonderfully prepared sea bass and seabream. Fine wine list.

La Peca, Lonigo (VI) €€€ Renowned one-star Michelin restaurant with a creative menu based on sound ingredients. Specialties include *riso nero*, cod fish with melted Asiago cheese and anchovy sauce, and pigeon with pea purée.

Friuli-Venezia Giulia *Friuli-Venezia Giulia*

Friuli's hills are Italy's sanctuary of modern white wine. The climate of this northeastern corner of the country benefits from the mingling of cool air flowing down from the Alpine north and warm Adriatic air wafting inland from the south. This creates propitious conditions for vine growth in Collio, Colli Orientali del Friuli (COF), Carso, and the sweet late-harvest Ramandolo DOCG, enclosed in the narrow band of hills that rise gently into the border with Slovenia. But nature's gifts aren't limited to the hills. The rising status of Isonzo, nestling under Collio on the plain, has helped further the reputation of Friuli's eastern frontier as one of Italy's prime wine territories.

The region emerged in the early 1970s, with revelatory white wines that were acclaimed as "the Friuli style" but that were as nothing compared to the classy, distinctive wines of today. Pinot Grigio popularized the mode, but now Pinot Bianco, Chardonnay, Sauvignon Blanc, and local favourite Tocai Friulano often show greater character. Dessert wines – legendary Picolit and rejuvenated Verduzzo – also show unmistakably Friulian grace. Tocai is now gaining recognition abroad, but its name is under notice of prohibition by the EU because of potential confusion with Hungary's Tokaj. Friulian producers have to find a pseudonym for their historic vine by 2007.

Wine Areas

1 Friuli Grave
2 Colli Orientali del Friuli
3 Collio Goriziano
4 Friuli Annia
5 Carso
6 Ramandolo
7 Friuli Isonzo
8 Friuli Latisana
9 Lison Pramaggiore

Today's Friuli style is represented by low-yielding, polished whites of pure, soft, yet fresh aromas, smooth textures, and alluring flavours, a fine-tuned balance that depends on picking perfectly ripe grapes and having them processed by creative tacticians able to pay minute attention to detail. When it works – which it does ever more often – few whites anywhere are as exquisite as those of Friuli. Their refinement and poise are sometimes lost on palates attuned to bolder tastes, so some winemakers are now fermenting and ageing some or all of their wines in oak barrels, to give them the depth and complexity that critics often regard as essential in world-class whites.

Friuli's wine production is by no means confined to whites, however. The region also makes a major share of Merlot and Cabernet, along with distinctive reds from the native Refosco grape, and such local curiosities as Schioppettino, Pignolo, and Tazzelenghe. Most of these reds have weight, firm structure, excellent fruit, and incisive character. Overall, Friuli produces much less wine (just over one million hectolitres) than neighbouring Veneto and accounts for only twenty per cent of northern Italian wine exports. Prices tend to be high, but demand still outstrips supply for the better wines, and few other producers share the foresight, versatility, and grit of Friulian winemakers in their devotion to raising standards.

There are nine DOC(G) zones in Friuli (plus a slice of Veneto's Lison-Pramaggiore), but all are sub-divided into numerous varietal versions, with most varieties common to most of the denominations. Many comprise a red, white, and rosé blend, too. Thankfully, local producers no longer aim to make all styles but only those best suiting their particular vineyards. The names of the five DOC zones on the broad Adriatic plains – the small Annia, Aquileia, Isonzo, and Latisana, and the large Grave – are preceded by the term Friuli to enhance the regional identity. There are also three IGTs: Alto Livenza, in the province of Pordenone; Venezia Giulia, for wines produced in the coastal area; and Delle Venezie, which spreads across the whole region as well as Veneto and Trentino (but not Alto Adige).

Friuli-Venezia Giulia is a crossroads of Germanic, Slavic, and Italianate cultures. There is a prominent Slovenian minority in the southeast around Gorizia and in the capital of Trieste, where the West meets Central Europe with great self-assurance. For a selection of the region's wines try Enoteca La Serenissima in Gradisca d'Isonzo, Enoteca di Cormòns in Cormòns, La Casa Degli Spiriti in Udine, and Enoteca Nanut in Trieste.

Recent Vintages

As a rule, Friulian dry whites are best at up to three years old, though Pinot Bianco, Chardonnay, and Sauvignon Blanc often defy the rule. Friulian reds are usually styled to age at least a few years, many longer.

2004 Ample harvest with mixed results: excellent whites and good reds, though some may lack balance and structure for ageing.
2003 Lack of rain in winter and a torrid summer brought early ripening. Reds did better than whites, some with excellent results; whites generally full-bodied and not age-worthy. Good late-harvest Ramandolo and Picolit.
2002 Sporadic rains in August and September caused difficulties, especially with Pinot Grigio and other early ripeners. The exception was in Colli Orientali, where the reds were more affected.

2001 Another very good year across the board.
2000 Great year for both whites and, especially, reds.
1999 A very good year for both reds and whites.
1998 Great vintage of decent to very good wines.
1997 Good to excellent vintage, favourable to red wines for ageing.
1996 Ample harvest of mixed results; better for white wines than reds, which lack structure for long ageing.
1995 Small crop of medium to good wines; the whites can lack aroma.
Notes on earlier vintages: 1990, 1994.

Appellations

DOCG
RAMANDOLO *w sw vt*
Produced from late-harvest Verduzzo grapes left on the vine to raisin. Amber gold, shows good balance tannins, acidity, and alcohol, pleasantly aromatic, characterized by ripe apricots and chestnut honey. Limited production of 150,000 bottle per year.

DOC
CARSO *w r*
Rosso Terrano/Terrano del Carso, Cabernet Franc, Merlot, Cabernet Sauvignon, Refosco del Peduncolo Rosso, Chardonnay, Malvasia, Pinot Grigio, Sauvignon, Traminer Aromatico, Vitovska.

COLLI ORIENTALI DEL FRIULI
w p r sup ris sw
Picolit, Chardonnay, Malvasia Istriana, Merlot, Pignolo, Pinot Bianco, Pinot Grigio, Pinot Nero, Refosco dal Peduncolo Rosso, Ribolla Gialla, Riesling, Sauvignon Blanc, Schioppettino, Tazzelenghe, Tocai Friulano, Verduzzo Friulano, Traminer Aromatico, Cabernet Franc, Cabernet Sauvignon.
Sub-zones: Cialla, Rosazzo.

COLLIO GORIZIANO/COLLIO
w r ris sw
Cabernet Franc, Cabernet Sauvignon, Chardonnay, Picolit, Malvasia Istriana, Merlot, Müller-Thurgau, Pinot Bianco, Pinot Grigio, Pinot Nero, Ribolla Gialla, Riesling Italico, Riesling Renano, Schioppetto, Sauvignon Blanc, Tocai Friulano, Traminer Aromatico.

FRIULI ANNIA *w r p ris fz sp sw*
Cabernet Franc, Cabernet Sauvignon, Chardonnay, Malvasia Istriana, Merlot, Pinot Bianco, Pinot Grigio, Refosco dal Peduncolo Rosso, Sauvignon Blanc, Tocai Friulano, Traminer Aromatico, Verduzzo Friulano.

FRIULI AQUILEIA *w r nov sup ris sp fz*
Refosco dal Peduncolo Rosso, Cabernet Franc, Cabernet Sauvignon, Merlot, Müller-Thurgau, Malvasia, Sauvignon Blanc, Chardonnay, Pinot Bianco, Pinot Grigio, Riesling Renano, Tocai Friulano, Traminer Aromatico, Verduzzo Friulano.

FRIULI GRAVE *w p r sup ris fz sp*
Cabernet Franc, Cabernet Sauvignon, Chardonnay, Merlot, Pinot Bianco, Pinot Grigio, Pinot Nero, Refosco dal Penduncolo Rosso, Riesling Renano, Sauvignon Blanc, Tocai Friulano, Traminer Aromatico, Verduzzo.

FRIULI ISONZO *w p r fz vt sw m sp*
Cabernet Franc, Cabernet Sauvignon, Chardonnay, Franconia, Malvasia, Merlot, Moscato Giallo, Moscato Rosa, Pinot Bianco, Pinot

Grigio, Pinot Nero, Refosco dal Peduncolo Rosso, Riesling Renano, Riesling Italico, Sauvignon Blanc, Schioppettino, Tocai Friulano, Traminer Aromatico, Verduzzo Friulano.

FRIULI LATISANA *w r sup ris fz nov sp sw*

Cabernet Franc, Cabernet Sauvignon, Chardonnay, Franconia, Malvasia Istriana, Merlot, Pinot Bianco, Pinot Grigio, Pinot Nero, Refosco dal Peduncolo Rosso, Riesling Renano, Sauvignon Blanc, Tocai Friulano, Traminer Aromatico, Verduzzo.

LISON-PRAMAGGIORE *w p r ris fz sp sw*

See also Veneto

Chardonnay, Pinot Bianco, Pinot Grigio, Cabernet Sauvignon, Cabernet Franc, Merlot, Malbec, Refosco dal Peduncolo Rosso, Riesling Italico, Sauvignon, Tocai Italico, Verduzzo.

IGT
Alto Livenza
Delle Venezie
Venezia Giulia

Producers

The key provinces have been abbreviated as follows:
GO = Gorizia; PN = Pordenone;
TS = Trieste; UD = Udine.
"COF" stands for Colli Orientali del Friuli.

Attems, Lucinico (GO) *w* ☆→☆☆* 52ha, 350,000 bottles. Founded in 1506 by Count Douglas Attems, today the vines belong to the Marchesi de Frescobaldi estate and complete its holistic range with a crisp white wine from the north. The production is based on Collio: Bianco, Pinot Bianco, Pinot Grigio, Ribolla Gialla, Sauvignon, Tocai, and Chardonnay.

Bastianich, Premariacco, (UD) *w r* ☆☆→☆☆☆☆ 13ha, 80,000 bottles. Italian-American of Friulian origin Joe Bastianach's production (mainly based on COF wines) is already making headlines, with gutsy Pinot Grigio, Tocai, Vespa Bianco (Sauvignon/Chardonnay/Picolit), and more. Highlights include Tocai Plus, a 100% Tocai Friulano – amber, rich, and opulent with a slight late-harvest touch, fresh and balanced.

La Boatina, Cormòns (GO) *w r sw* ☆☆→☆☆☆ 78ha, 300,000 bottles. Loretto Pali's production includes a wide range of Collio varietal wines and excels in the Collio Rosso Picol Maggiore, a vibrant Merlot/Cabernet blend – upfront fruit, full-bodied, with a long, lingering finish. Also very good Pérle, a 100% late-harvest Verduzzo, and Collio Bianco Pertè (Chardonnay/Pinot Grigio/Sauvignon), barrel-fermented and left on the lees six months.

Borgo Conventi, Farra d'Isonzo (GO) *r w* ☆☆ 62ha, 350,000 bottles. Rapid change is afoot at this prime Isonzo estate following its purchase by Tuscany's Ruffino company. Highlights include Braida Nuova, a Cabernet/Merlot blend; and Collio: Chardonnay, Ribolla Gialla, Sauvignon, Pinot Grigio, and Tocai.

Borgo del Tiglio, Brazzano di Cormòns (GO) *w r* ☆☆→☆☆☆ 8ha, 27,400 bottles. Nicola Manferrari, pharmacist by profession and passionate winemaker, produces classy whites, including outstanding Collio Tocai Ronco della Chiesa – full, round, with ripe peaches, long finish; and excellent Chardonnay Selezione – complex, with floral hints, honey, and vanilla, full structure, rich and mineral, with persistence. Also good Malvasia, Tocai, and Collio Bianco and Rosso.

Borgo San Daniele, Cormòns (GO) *w r* ☆☆→☆☆☆ 16ha, 52,000 bottles. Alessandra and Mauro Mauri's production focuses on well-balanced, elegant, complex wines. In particular, stunning Friuli Isonzo Tocai Friulano – ripe, warm, and structured, aged partly in 20hl Slavonian barrels; Arbis Bianco – a four-grape blend white (including Tocai and Müller-Thurgau) non-filtered and aged in Slavonian barrel – rich, concentrated, with mineral character. Also superb Pinot Grigio and an excellent Arbis Rosso blend.

Rosa Bosco, Rosazzo-Manzano (UD) *r w* ☆☆☆ 11,000 bottles. The highlights of Rosa Bosco's small estate are COF Rosso Boscorosso, a great Merlot aged 22 months in barrique – fine layers of complexity and aromas; and barrique-fermented COF Sauvignon Blanc – elegant, with floral bouquet. The latter undergoes bâtonnage, but no racking or clarification, and is a wine of great personality.

Branko-Igor Erzetič, Cormòns (GO) *w r* ☆☆→☆☆☆ * 6ha, 40,000 bottles. A small estate producing top-notch, individual-style Pinot Grigio, Tocai, Sauvignon, and Chardonnay. Their Collio Pinot Grigio is 20% vinified in new barrique, the rest in steel – finesse and elegance, hints of pear, banana, and vanilla, crisp, full, long.

Buttrio, Buttrio (UD) *w r* ☆☆ Roberto Felluga's rapidly emerging project focuses on unique indigenous vines. Highlights: red Marburg from Refosco and Pignolo – sapid, fragrant, elegance and character; and good Chardonnay Ovestein – fresh, full, and round, with crisp uplifting finish.

Ca' Bolani, Cervignano del Friuli (UD) *w r* ☆☆ Zonin-owned Aquileia winery grouping wines from Ca' Vescovo and Molin di Ponte estates. Tamanis Gianni Zonin Vineyards (Sauvignon) and Alturio Gianni Zonin Vineyards (Refosco) lead the stalwart range. Also good Conte Bolani, a Refosco/Merlot/Cabernet blend showing structure and berry fruit.

Paolo Caccese, Pradis di Cormòns (GO) *w r* ☆☆ 6ha, 30,000 bottles. Caccese started winemaking as a hobby with a handful of hectares. He now has six, and wine has become a full-time passion. He focuses on quality wines with tipicity, covering the Collio range, including Traminer Aromatico and Müller-Thurgau, along with Tocai, Pinot Grigio, and Pinot Bianco.

Cantina Produttori di Cormòns, Cormòns (GO) *w r* ☆☆☆→☆☆☆ 420ha, 2,200,000 bottles. Most members of this large, quality-directed co-op cultivate vines organically. Sound Collio, Aquileia, and Isonzo, as well as unique Vino della Pace, made from more than 550 grape varieties, both red and white, coming from five different continents. Bottles are sent to all heads of state.

Ca' Ronesca, Dolegna del Collio (GO) *w r* ☆☆→☆☆☆ 52ha, 220,000 bottles. Sergio Comunello's production features a good range of COF whites and reds, including racy Pinot Grigio Podere San Giacomo – nutty, appley, and mineral in character. Collio Bianco Marnà is a blend of Pinot Bianco and Malvasia vinified and aged ten months in barrique – fine, complex aromas, buttery biscuits with toasted nuts, well-structured. Also good Chardonnay and Sauvignon.

La Castellada, Oslavia (GO) *w r* ☆☆☆→☆☆☆☆ * 10ha, 22,000 bottles. Giorgio and Nicola Bensa produce several admired oak-fermented Collio wines, led by Bianco della Castellada, a four-grape blend – flowery bouquet, dried fruit, full, round, balanced. Also good Ribolla Gialla – mineral and spicy; and Chardonnay – ripeness and exotic fruit.

Castello di Spessa, Spessa di Capriva (GO) *w r* ☆☆☆→☆☆☆☆ 30ha, 100,000 bottles. Historical 15th-century estate with a magnificent park and a bottle production of excellent Collio wines. Owner Loretto Pali also owns the renowned La Boatina estate in Cormòns. Highlights: Tocai, Pinot Bianco di Santarosa, and Sauvignon Segrè, as well as Collio Rosso Conte di Spessa.

Castelvecchio, Sagrado (GO) *w r* ☆☆→☆☆☆☆ 40ha, 250,000 bottles. Giovanni Bignucolo's vines, deeply rooted in the Carso's rock, overlook the Gulf of Trieste and are mainly planted to red varieties showing Carso's range of varietal wines. Highlights include Sagrado Rosso, a Cabernet Sauvignon/Franc blend aged 36 months in barrique – finesse, elegance, and structure; excellent Refosco dal Peduncolo Rosso; and Terrano.

Colle Duga, Cormòns (GO) *w r* ☆☆→☆☆☆☆ * 7ha, 30,000 bottles. Damina Princic's emerging, well-exposed estate has a fine production of Collio varietals, including well-priced wines that show structure, elegance, and balance. In particular, the property's Collio wines are noteworthy: Pinot Grigio, Tocai, Chardonnay, Merlot, and Bianco.

Conti D'Attimis Maniago, Buttrio (UD) *w r sw* ☆→☆☆☆☆ 84ha, 390,000 bottles. Historical estate dating back to 1585 with 84ha of vines, 40 of which are being replanted to COF varietals. Highlights include excellent Sauvignon, Tocai, and Chardonnay. Bianco Ronco Brolo is a blend of Pinot Bianco and Chardonnay aged in different types of wood – complex, evolved, and long. In the reds, good Cabernet, Refosco, and Pinot Noir.

Conti Formentini, San Floriano del Collio (GO) *w r* ☆→☆☆☆☆ 350,000 bottles. Medieval castle dating back to 1520 belonging to Gruppo Italiano Vini and producing fine reds and whites. Among the top labels feature good Furmint, Chardonnay, Tocai, and Pinot Bianco. Also good Collio Bianco Rylint, a Chardonnay/Pinot Grigio/Sauvignon blend, Collio Merlot Tajut, and Pinot Noir Torre di Borea.

Dario Coos, Ramandolo (UD) *w sw* ☆→☆☆☆☆ 7ha, 35,000 bottles. Small vineyard producing fine, elegant Ramandolo and COF Picolit. Highlights: Ramandolo Romandus, from Verduzzo – amber, rich, with aromas of orange peel, dates, and caramel, excellent persistence; and COF Picolit – yellow topaz, fine and complex, citrus and custard, fresh and long.

Girolamo Dorigo, Buttrio (UD) *w r* ☆☆☆→☆☆☆☆ 32ha, 150,000 bottles. Girolamo and Alessio Dorigo's estate is noted for its fine production of COF reds and whites. Highlights: Rosso Montsclapade – richly structured, powerful, berry, spices, and a touch of herbaceous character; and Chardonnay Ronc di Juri, left on the lees in barrel for 11 months – exotic fruit, vanilla, tobacco, rich and powerful. Also good Pignolo, aged 30 months in barrique – hints of marasca cherry, prunes, leather, and coffee.

Le Due Terre, Prepotto (UD) *w r*
☆☆☆→☆☆☆☆ * 4ha, 19,000 bottles.
Silvano Forte and Flavio Basilicata
have a handful of hectares of well-
tended vines and
a small production of boutique,
age-worthy COF wines, including
prized Merlot and Pinot Nero.
Their IGT Sacrisassi Rosso (a
Refosco/Schioppettino blend)
is aged 22 months in barrique –
structure, depth, and elegance.
Also very good Bianco Sacrisassi
(Tocai/Ribolla), aged 18 months
in barrique – voluptuous, exotic
fruit, spice, round and full; and
Picolit-based Implicito.

Ermarcora, Premariacco (UD) *w r sw*
☆☆→☆☆☆ 22ha, 150,000 bottles.
Estate producing COF reds and
whites. In the reds, the Pignolo
shows good complexity, with hints
of cherry, tobacco, and bitter
chocolate, with a long, fresh finish.
Also good Merlot – cherry and
herbaceous character. In the
whites, good Pinot Grigio, Pinot
Bianco, Sauvignon, Verduzzo,
and sweet Picolit.

Fantinel, Tauriano di Spilimbergo (UD)
w r sw ☆→☆☆☆ * 250ha, 2,500,000
bottles. Large family-run estate
with vineyards in Grave, Collio,
and COF producing some
premium wines under the
Sant'Helena and Santa Caterina
labels. Highlights include Refosco
dal Peduncolo Rosso Sant'Helena,
Sauvignon Sant'Helena, Bianco
Triology (a Tocai/Pinot Bianco/
Sauvignon blend), Barone Rosso
Platinum (Merlot/Cabernet Franc/
Refosco), and Cabernet Sauvignon
Sant'Helena.

Livio Felluga, Brazzano di Cormòns
(GO) *w r sw* ☆☆→☆☆☆☆ 135ha,
650,000 bottles. Family-run winery
with a production of widely
acclaimed COF from Rosazzo and
other vineyards. Highlights include

Bianco Terre Alte, a Tocai/Pinot
Bianco/Sauvignon blend – fresh,
intense, with complex notes,
balanced, persistent palate; and
good Pinot Bianco Illivio. Also good
Vertigo (an international Cabernet/
Merlot blend), Shàrjs (Chardonnay/
Ribolla Gialla), and Picolit Riserva.

Marco Felluga, Gradisca d'Isonzo (GO)
w p r ☆☆→☆☆☆☆ * 120ha, 610,000
bottles. The Fellugas produce
appealing Collio wines, including
alluring Bianco Molamatta (a Pinot
Bianco/Tocai/Ribolla blend; Tocai
and Ribolla are vinified in steel and
Pinot Bianco in barrique) – mineral,
fresh, and slightly *boisé*. Also stylish
varietals such as Chardonnay, Pinot
Grigio, and Moscato Rosa.

Fiegl, Oslavia (GO) *w r* ☆→☆☆☆ * 26ha,
120,000 bottles. Historic estate (est.
1782), where production of
attractive Collio wines, mostly
white, is based on two lines:
Standard and Leopold. Very good
Malvasia Leopold – fine aromatic
complexity, full and round, with
structure and persistence; and
Bianco Leopold Cuvée Blanc, a
four-grape blend – flavoursome
and fresh. Also good Collio: Tocai,
Pinot Grigio, and Ribolla Gialla.

Foffani, Trivignano Udinese (UD)
w r ☆☆ 10ha, 110,000 bottles.
Historic estate established in
1600 forming part of a medieval
hamlet in the Aquilea area. The
production includes some attractive
Friuli Aquileia: Pinot Grigio, Tocai,
Chardonnay, Sauvignon, Refosco
dal Peduncolo Rosso, and Merlot.

Adriano Gigante, Corno di Rosazzo
(UD) *w r* ☆☆→☆☆☆ * 20ha, 90,000
bottles. Gigante's production is
based on sound COF varieties.
His top-ranking Tocai from the
Vigneto Storico (historic vineyard)
produces an elegant, aromatic
wine with a floral and herby
bouquet, round and full, with a

bitter-almond finish. Also good COF: Schioppettino, Refosco, Sauvignon, and Chardonnay.

Gravner, Oslavia (GO) *w r* ☆☆☆☆ 20ha, 48,000 bottles. Josko Gravner, a dedicated cult winemaker with his own philosophy, is considered one of Friuli's top producers, with wines of unique character. His latest project involves ageing his wines in terracotta amphorae, as the ancient Romans and Greeks did – the wine is still to be tasted. Bianco Berg is a four-grape blend fermented in small open wooden vats for 12 days with no temperature control – amber, rich, herbal, berry notes, incredible structure and persistence. Also very good Ribolla and Rosso Gravner (Merlot/Cabernet).

Jermann, Villanova di Farra (GO) *w r* ☆☆☆☆→☆☆☆☆ 95ha, 650,000 bottles. Historic estate founded in 1881. Although in the Collio zone, Silvio Jermann eschews the DOC in his impeccable varietals and blends. Highlights: Vinnae (a Ribolla Gialla/Riesling/Malvasia blend); Capo Martino in Ruttaris (Pinot Bianco/Pinot Grigio/Tocai/ Picolit/Malvasia); and the singular Vintage Tunina, a wine that has long stood as one of Italy's whites of greatest stature. It comes from late-harvested Sauvignon and Chardonnay, with Ribolla Gialla, Malvasia, and a hint of Picolit.

Edi Kante, Duino Aurisina (TS) *w r* ☆☆☆ 11ha, 35,000 bottles. Small leading quality producer with vines plated to hard, rocky Carso terrain giving good, elegant wines. The production includes Carso: Terrano, Malvasia, Sauvignon, Chardonnay, and Vitovska. Highlights: Sauvignon Selezione – mineral character, racy, elegant, and very persistent; Malvasia Selezione – structured, with

attractive aromas, well-integrated oak; and Chardonnay Selezione – mineral, sapid, and complex.

Edi Keber, Zegla di Cormons (GO) *w r* ☆☆☆ * 10ha, 60,000 bottles. Estate producing fine Collio reds and whites. Highlights include Collio Rosso, a Merlot/Cabernet blend aged six months in barrique and tonneau – ripe, red fruit, smooth, fine tannins; Collio Bianco, a five-grape blend – fragrant, with flower and ripe fruit, balanced and long; and Collio Tocai – a dynamic wine with intense aromas and elegance.

Renato Keber, Zegla di Cormòns (GO) *w r* ☆☆☆ * Keber's full range of Collio whites with excellent price/quality ratio includes Tocai, Sauvignon Grici, Tocai Grici, Bianco Beli Grici, Sauvignon, Rosso, Merlot Grici, and Pinot Grigio.

Lis Neris, San Lorenzo Isontino (GO) *w r sw* ☆☆☆→☆☆☆☆ 50ha, 300,000 bottles. Alvaro Pecorari's production focuses on an impeccable range of Isonzo whites showing excellent aromatic profile. Highlights: Chardonnay Jurosa, aged in tonneau – complex aromas mingled with notes of tropical fruit and toasted almonds; and Pinot Grigio Gris, aged in tonneau – structured and full. Also good Sauvignon Picòl, Rosso Lis Neris, and IGT Bianco Lis Verduzzo Passito Tal Lùc.

Livon, Dolegnano (UD) *w r* ☆→☆☆☆☆ 92ha, 572,000 bottles. Family business with separate estates making up a large production, including a large range of Collio wines in three ranges: Classica, Cru, and Grand Cru. The latter includes the leading Braide Alte white blend (Chardonnay/ Sauvignon/Picolit/Moscato Giallo), Braide Mate Chardonnay, Tiare Blu (a Cabernet Sauvignon/ Cabernet Franc/Merlot blend),

Tiare Mate Merlot, and Picotis Schioppettino. Also some COF, plus easy-going Grave from the Villa Chiopris estate.

Masut da Rive, Mariano del Friuli (GO) *w r* ☆☆→☆☆☆ * 18ha, 85,000 bottles. Fabrizio and Marco Gallo's production represents a notable array of Isonzo whites, with a good quality/price ratio. Particularly appealing are Pinot Bianco, Pinot Grigio, Tocai, and Chardonnay.

Oscar Sturm, Cormòns (GO) *w r* ☆☆☆ 10ha, 52,000 bottles. Historic estate established in 1850 with well-exposed vines and a production focused on refined varietal Collio wines. Among the top labels is the Pinot Grigio, vinified in steel with 5% in oak – floral bouquet, citrus and apple, rich and silky, elegant balance. Also very good Sauvignon, Tocai, Ribolla Gialla, and Chardonnay, all showing good varietal character.

Petrucco, Buttrio (UD) *w r sw* ☆☆ 25ha, 95,000 bottles. Paolo Petrucco's vineyards are among the best-exposed in the Buttrio area and produce finely honed COF whites. Among the top labels are Chardonnay, Ribolla Gialla, and Pinot Grigio. Among the reds, Refosco, Cabernet Franc, and Merlot Vigna del Balbo excel. Also good Picolit.

Petrussa, Prepotto (UD) *w r* ☆☆☆ * 10ha, 55,000 bottles. Gianni and Paolo Petrussa produce COF varietals, including excellent Schioppettino, macerated for three months and aged 24 in barrique – berry fruit, spice, and tobacco, rich, velvety, full texture, slightly herbaceous on the finish. Also very good Verduzzo under the Pensiero label from late-harvest botrytized grapes picked in December. Both the Bianco and the Rosso Petrussa are also noteworthy.

Roberto Picech, Cormòns (GO) *w r ris* ☆☆→☆☆☆ 8ha, 25,000 bottles. Small estate producing exceptional Tocai, a wine with decisive personality – intense floral character, nuts, and herbal aromas, round and full, with a long, bitter-almond finish. Also very good Collio Malvasia and Collio Rosso (Cabernet Franc-based with some Cabernet Sauvignon).

Pierpaolo Pecorari, San Lorenzo Isontino (GO) *w r* ☆☆☆ 30ha, 130,000 bottles. An Isonzo estate focusing on wines from low yields, expressing terroir character. This can be seen with their selection of Sauvignon Kolaus, vinified and aged one year in barrique – complex aromatic profile, structured and rich. Also good Chardonnay Soris, *riserva* versions of Merlot, and Refosco dal Peduncolo Rosso Tao.

Dario Raccaro, Cormòns (GO) *w r* ☆☆☆ * 4.5ha, 20,000 bottles. Raccaro's low-yielding and highly selected grapes are vinified in steel – according to the estate's philosophy, in order to highlight the intense and complex sphere of aromas and fruitiness on the wines. Reds and whites are produced under the Collio banner with excellent varietal wines: Malvasia, Tocai, Bianco, Merlot, and Isonzo Rosso

Stanislao Radikon, Oslavia (GO) *w* ☆☆☆→☆☆☆☆ * "Stanko" Radikon's vineyards stretch over the Oslava hills near the Slavonian border. They produce powerful Collio wines with plenty of individuality, most notably Merlot, Ribolla Gialla, and Bianco Oslavje. The vineyards are certified biodynamic – hence no use of pesticides, herbicides, or fertilizers. Likewise, the winemaking is as natural a process as possible, which means no selected yeasts, no temperature control, and no filtration or clarification. The wines show depth, character, and persistence.

Rocca Bernarda, Ipplis di Premariacco (UD) *w r sw* ☆☆→☆☆☆ 55ha, 200,000 bottles. This historic medieval property, dating back to 1559 and still owned by the Sovereign Military Order of Malta, makes fine COF, especially Merlot (Centis) and top-notch Picolit, late-harvested and traditionally laid out on cane mats to dry for 32 days, then aged 15 months in barrique – excellent tipicity, with hints of orange peel, apricots, yellow bell pepper, and nuts, soft and full.

Paolo Rodaro, Spessa di Cividale (UD) *w r sw* ☆☆→☆☆☆ 40ha, 200,000 bottles. The Rodaro brothers' historic estate (established in 1846) is situated on the slopes of Spessa; with its COF wines, it ranks among Friuli's top estates. Highlights include a fine Picolit – sublime nectar; an intense, elegant, and persistent Schioppettino Romain; and a delectable, sweet, weighty Verduzzo. Also elegant Ronc Bianco (Pinot Bianco/ Chardonnay).

La Roncaia, Nimis (UD) *w r* ☆☆→☆☆☆ 22ha, 50,000 bottles. This small estate belonging to the Fantinel family produces some premium COF wines, including Ramandolo, Chardonnay, Refosco, and Bianco Eclisse. The winemaking was initially supervised by the late Tibor Gàl.

Il Roncat di Giovanni Dri, Ramandolo (UD) *w r sw* ☆☆☆ 8ha, 50,000 bottles. The leading producer of Ramandolo, Friuli's only DOCG, also makes COF Picolit, Refosco, Sauvignon, and Cabernet. Highlights include IGT Il Roncat Rosso, a four-grape blend including Refosco and Cabernet Sauvignon; Monte dei Carpini, a Schioppettino/Refosco blend; Ramandolo Il Roncat; and Ramandolo Uve Dicembrine.

Ronchi di Cialla, Cialla di Prepotto (UD) *w r sw* ☆☆☆ 20ha, 35,000 bottles. Rapuzzi's family-run estate, with four new hectares of Schioppettino planted to traditional medieval terraces, produces classy and personalized COF: Ciallabianco, a Ribolla/Verduzzo/Picolit blend; Refosco; Schioppettino; and Picolit. All are well-structured wines with excellent ageing potential.

Ronchi di Manzano, Manzano (UD) *w r* ☆☆→☆☆☆ 60ha, 300,000 bottles. Roberta Borghese's production covers a wide, reliable range of COF varietals, including some interesting, quality indigenous varietals such as Rosazzo, Pignolo, and Refosco. Highlights: oak-fermented Rosazzo Bianco, a four-grape blend; along with Refosco, Pinot Grigio, and Chardonnay.

Ronco dei Tassi, Cormòns (GO) *w r vt sw* ☆☆→☆☆☆ * 12ha, 70,000 bottles. Fabio Coser's production is labelled under Ronco dei Tassi and Vigna del Lauro. It includes a range of Collio varietals with an excellent quality/price ratio. In particular: Ronco dei Tassi Cjarandon Collio Rosso (Merlot/ Cabernet Sauvignon/Cabernet Franc), Collio Sauvignon, Tocai, Pinot Grigio, Chardonnay, Bianco Fosarin, and Vigna del Lauro Merlot.

Ronco del Gelso, Cormòns (GO) *w* ☆☆→☆☆☆ * 18ha, 150,000 bottles. Giorgio Badin's production covers a wide range of Isonzo varietals of enviable style and individuality, especially with Tocai, Sauvignon, Pinot Grigio, and Merlot, which are almost exclusively vinified in steel at low temperatures. They are vibrant, fresh wines with wide aromatic profile and persistence.

Ronco delle Betulle, Manzano (UD) *w r*
☆☆☆ * 13ha, 60,000 bottles.
Ivana Adami's vines are situated
near the historic abbey of Rosazzo.
Wine production, overseen by
consultant winemaker Donato
Lanati, includes fine COF Rosazzo,
notably Rosso Narciso, a Merlot/
Cabernet Sauvignon blend – fresh,
crushed berries, spice, pepper, and
coffee, compact, rich, and sapid,
with a long, elegant finish; and
Pinot Grigio – fine, floral bouquet,
elegant, and fleshy. Also good
Rosazzo Bianco Vanessa, a four-
grape blend, Ribolla Gialla,
Sauvignon, and Tocai.

Russiz Superiore, Capriva del Friuli,
(GO) *w r ris* ☆☆☆→☆☆☆☆
60ha, 200,000 bottles. The Felluga
family's production of fine Collio
wines, overseen by Roberto
Felluga, is rapidly rising to the
heights of Friuli's top wines.
Highlights include excellent
Riserva Degli Orzoni, a Bordeaux
blend (Cabernet Sauvignon/
Cabernet Franc/Merlot) showing
compact structure and age-worthy
potential. Also very good Pinot
Grigio, Sauvignon, and Bianco
Col Disôre, a four-grape blend
(Tocai/Ribolla Gialla/Pinot
Bianco/Sauvignon).

Mario Schiopetto, Spessa di Capriva
(GO) *w r* ☆☆☆☆ * 28ha, 200,000
bottles. The late Mario Schiopetto
is considered one of the pioneers
of structured whites showing
individual potential, finesse, and
precise aromatic character. His
Collio production shows wines
of immense stature, notably from
Pinot Bianco, Sauvignon, and
Tocai. There are also new IGT
blends, namely Mario Schiopetto
Bianco (Chardonnay/Tocai) and
Blumeri Rosso (Merlot/Cabernet
Sauvignon/Refosco).

Scubla, Premariacco (UD)
w r sw ☆☆→☆☆☆ 11ha, 60,000
bottles. Roberto Scubla's vines,
covering the hills of Rocca
Bernarda, produce fine COF wines
that are overseen by consultant
oenologist Gianni Menotti. The
distinctive range is led by late-
harvest Verduzzo Bianco Pomédes,
Verduzzo Friulano Cràtis, Rosso
ScuRo, Merlot, Cabernet Franc,
Pinot Bianco, and Tocai.

Franco Toros, Cormòns (GO) *w r*
☆☆→☆☆☆ 10ha, 70,000 bottles.
Franco Toros's turn-of-the-20th-
century estate has low-yielding
vines and a production that
includes some dazzling,
concentrated Collio whites.
The range is led by Pinot Bianco –
typical varietal aromas with
fresh apples, yeast, balanced
and intense, elegant, crisp finish.
Also excellent Merlot Selezione
from late-harvest grapes –
concentrated berry fruit, violets,
liquorice, silky, persistent; and
good Chardonnay, Tocai, and
Sauvignon.

La Tunella, Ipplis di Premariacco (UD)
w r ☆☆→☆☆☆ * 69ha, 400,000
bottles. The Zorzetting family
production includes a reliable
range of COF varietal wines with
an excellent quality/price ratio.
In particular: Pinot Grigio, Tocai,
Chardonnay, and Bianco Campo
Marzio, a fine Tocai/Pinot Bianco/
Ribolla blend.

Venica & Venica, Dolegna del Collio
(GO) *w r* ☆☆☆→☆☆☆☆ 34ha,
240,000 bottles. The Venica family
estate has vines mainly planted
to Collio whites and produces
fresh, aromatic wines, vinified in
steel, that are sapid and long in
character. Highlights include
starry Sauvignon Ronco delle
Mele, Tocai Ronco delle Cime,
Pinot Bianco, Ribolla Gialla,

Collio Malvasia, and Collio Merlot Perilla. There is also a fine white blend: Tre Vignis (Tocai/Chardonnay/Sauvignon).

Vie di Romans, Mariano del Friuli (GO) *w* ☆☆☆☆ * 40ha, 145,000 bottles. Gianfranco Gallo's Isonzo whites are among Friuli's top wines. They show masterful use of oak in fermentation and ageing, as can be seen in Sauvignon Pière and Sauvignon Vieris, Chardonnay Ciampagnis Vieris, Pinot Grigio Dessimis, and Bianco Flors di Uis (a Malvasia/Riesling/Tocai blend), as well as Bianco Dut'Un, from Chardonnay/Sauvignon Blanc.

Le Vigne di Zamò, Rosazzo di Manzano (UD) *w r* ☆☆☆ 60ha, 280,000 bottles. Pierluigi and Silvano Zamò's production is overseen by consultant oenologist Franco Bernabei. They make highly admired COF wines, most notably Merlot and Tocai, both from Vigne Cinquant'Anni (fifty-year-old vines) that produce sapid, full-bodied wines. Also very good Refosco Il Re Fosco – powerful, concentrated, tannic, and vibrant; and Rosazzo Ronco delle Acacie (a Chardonnay/Tocai/Pinot Bianco blend) – elegant, creamy, and floral.

Vigneti Pittaro, Rivolto di Codroipo (UD) *w p r sw sp* ☆☆ 85ha, 450,000 bottles. Pietro Pittaro's production of admired Grave varietals includes Rosso Agresto (a Cabernet Sauvignon/Merlot/Refosco blend), Valzer in Rosa (Moscato Rosa), Manzoni Bianco, and Picolit Ronco Vieri. Also unusual sweet Apicio (Manzoni/Sauvignon/Chardonnay) and sparkling brut Millesimato.

Vistorta, Sacile (PN) *r* ☆☆☆ Brandino Brandolini d'Adda's eminent Grave family estate dates back to 1850 and comprises 35has of vineyards and a magnificent 200ha park on the border between Friuli and Veneto. The estate produces excusively distinguished Merlot. The property also incorporates Villa Ronche, with 36ha of vines. Brandino has ties linking him to Bordeaux, including the two French oenologists who oversee his production, hence the wines' intrinsic Bordeaux style and character.

Volpe Pasini, Torreano (UD) *w r* ☆☆☆ 52ha, 285,000 bottles. Emilio Rotolo's historic 15th-century estate produces highly admired COF varietals and IGT wines, which are masterfully blended to international style by consultant oenologist Riccardo Cotarella. Highlights include Focus, a full-bodied, concentrated, warm Merlot – rich in ripeness and texture, with a long creamy finish. Also good Chardonnay, Pinot Bianco, and Refosco.

Zidarich, Duino Aurisina (TS) *w r* ☆☆☆ 12,000 bottles. Benjamino Zidarich's small eminent estate is situated in the Carso hills overlooking the Timavo River estuary. Production includes impressive Carso Terrano – sour cherry, crushed red fruit, spicy, concentrated. Also Vitovska; aromatic Malvasia; and Prulke, a Malvasia/Sauvignon/Vitovska blend.

Zuani, San Floriano del Collio (GO) *w* ☆☆☆ 10ha, 60,000 bottles. Patrizia Felluga's emerging estate in the Collio hills produces just two wines, both Collio Bianco, both Tocai/Pinot Grigio/Chardonnay/Sauvignon blends, and both excellent: the unoaked Zuani Vigne – fresh and lively; and the oaked Zuani.

Wine & Food

In Friuli-Venezia Giulia, East meets West around the *fogolar* (a cosy open hearth with a conical chimney). A melting pot of European cookery, the region gives its own touch to gulasch, dumplings, cabbage and bean soups, and Viennese pastries. But the tangs of Slovenia, Croatia, Bohemia, Austria, and Hungary are merely a bonus added to Friuli's own tasty peasant heritage of pork, beans, mutton, sausages, soups, blood puddings, polenta, turnips, game, and cheese. Venezia Giulia, the coastal strip of the region, gives fish to the menu, with soups, chowders, and refined risottos with prawns, squid, or scallops that reflect the influence of Venice. From the hill town of San Daniele comes a prosciutto that some consider to be the most exquisite made anywhere.

Boreto alla graisana Fish chowder (ideally turbot-based) cooked with oil, vinegar, and garlic; specialty of the port of Grado.

Brovada Turnips marinated in fresh wine pressings, then cut into strips and cooked with *muset*, a pork sausage.

Capriolo in salmì Venison in a rich wine sauce.

Frico Grated Montasio cheese, both fresh and aged, fried with onions in butter until crunchy.

Granzevola alla triestina Spider crab baked with breadcrumbs, garlic, and seasonings.

Jota Filling soup of pork, beans, cabbage, and cornmeal.

Paparot Cream soup including spinach and cornflour.

Palacinke Seasonal fruit tart.

Prosciutto di San Daniele Thin slices of air-cured ham.

Spetzli Small potato and flour dumplings (like gnocchi).

Strucolo Friuli's answer to strudel, made with ricotta cheese and apples, or other fruit.

Hotels

Castello di Spessa, Capriva del Friuli (GO) €€
This wine estate with magnificent grounds and century-old trees and vineyards offers princely accommodation in the castle. It is an ideal place to relax and enjoy a wine tour. Good parking.

Da Afro, Spilimbergo (UD) €
Traditional dwelling with eight cosy rooms, furnished with characteristic local rustic furniture. There are also excellent dining opportunities, with San Daniele hams, snails, soups, pasta, duck, chicken, veal, or roast pigeon. Good 350-label wine list.

Golf Hotel, San Floriano del Collio (GO) €€
A 16th-century villa belonging to the aristocratic Formentini family. Surrounded by a park and overlooking the town of Gorizia, the villa offers elegant rooms with all comforts. Other amenities include a restaurant and a pool.

Locanda Al Castello, Cividale del Friuli (UD) €–€€
This ancient castle overlooking Cividale was once a Jesuit monastery. A hotel since 1906, it has quiet, comfortable rooms, terraces, sitting rooms, a restaurant, and a parking area.

Terra & Vini, Cormòns (GO) €
Livio Felluga offers comfortable hospitality located among his vineyards. It is ideally located for

exploring the wine region. There is also an excellent *osteria* serving local cuisine and Felluga wines.

Venica & Venica, Dolegna del Collio (GO) **€**
Country dwelling amid the vineyards, with comfortable rooms and apartments, a pool, and tennis courts. Enjoy the location by biking and hiking through it.

Vinnaeria La Baita, Capriva del Friuli (GO) **€–€€**
Jermann estate offers a B&B with 12 comfortable rooms and apartments, plus fine dining and wine bar. Well situated for wine touring. Good parking.

Restaurants

Al Giardinetto, Cormòns **€–€€**
This 17th-century palazzo has a terrace and a garden for alfresco dining. The menu offers a cross-culture of dishes. Excellent food and wines; there are also five comfortable bedrooms.

Alla Luna, Gorizia (UD) **€**
Historic 1876 *osteria* in the centre of town, owned by the Pintar family. On the menu, typical fare from Gorizia; specialties include *jota*, gnocchi, herb omelettes, risotto, gulasch, *patacinke*.

Antica Trattoria La Primula, San Quirino (PN) **€€**
Established in 1875, this *trattoria* serves traditional dishes with a creative, contemporary twist. Specialties include snails, excellent meat dishes, and cheeses.

Castello di Buttrio, Buttrio (UD) **€**
Situated among the Collio vineyards on the Felluga estate, this restaurant offers excellent cured hams, gnocchi with game ragout, risotto with herbs, duck, wild boar in wine sauce, and much more.

Devetak, Savogna D'Isonzo (GO) **€€**
Set in the heart of the Carso area is this restaurant offering a cross-cultural cuisine. Excellent cheeses and home-made bread, *selinka* (a soup with pork and celery), *linci* (a vegetable or game sauce pasta baked in the oven), and a good selection of desserts. The excellent (and extensive) wine list comprises 600 labels.

Korsic, San Floriano del Collio (GO) **€**
Follow the flow of vineyards from Cormòns to Collio, and you will reach Korsic, near the Slovenian border. This restaurant set in a beautiful summer garden serves local pasta with duck sauce, *spetzli* with speck, gulasch, *lubijanska* (pork fried in batter with cheese filling), and more.

Kursaal, Sauris (UD) **€–€€**
Renowned restaurant serving well-prepared and well-researched dishes rooted in local tradition and ingredients supplied by local artisans and farms. Creative recipes and a good wine list.

L'Osteria di Tancredi, San Daniele del Friuli (UD) **€**
Modern wine bar and *trattoria* nestled in a 15th-century building serving excellent San Daniele cured ham, hearty soups, pasta, sausages, and meat loaf. Good 200-label wine list with more than 50 available by the glass.

Trattoria agli Amici, Godia di Udine (UD) **€€**
Emanuele Scarello's fifth-generation *trattoria* (originally established in 1887) has two dining rooms and an outdoor terrace. It serves good local fare and has a well-stocked cellar.

Emilia-Romagna *Emilia-Romagna*

Emilia and Romagna are northern Italy's cheerful oddities, making wines that have not much to do with those of their neighbours and little more to do with one another's. Emilia's gift to the world is red (or pink or even white) Lambrusco, the bubbles of which buoy the masses while inspiring the disdain of wine snobs. Romagna keeps the Adriatic's sun-worshippers content with its white Albana, and proudly claims the virtues of its (non-Tuscan) Sangiovese. What the wines of Emilia and Romagna do have in common is that they are usually affordable and cheeringly drinkable. In addition, to native palates at least, they provide an ideal complement to some of Italy's richest and most remarkable cooking.

These abundantly fertile twin provinces are watered by the River Po to the north and Apennine streams to the south. Emilia extends westwards through the cities of Modena, Reggio, Parma, and Piacenza, where wines take on similar styles to those produced in the adjacent Oltrepò Pavese, in Lombardy. The area is otherwise noted for lightish, bubbly, and often softly sweet wines from both plains and hills (although the Lambrusco admired locally is dry, with body and character), but even more renowned for its production of Parma ham and Parmigiano Reggiano cheese.

Romagna stretches eastwards, from Bologna (the regional capital) to the Adriatic, across Ferrara and Faenza to Ravenna, Forlì, Cesena, and Rimini. Here the emphasis is on still wines led by the popular Albana, Trebbiano, and Sangiovese. However, wine production in the Emilia-

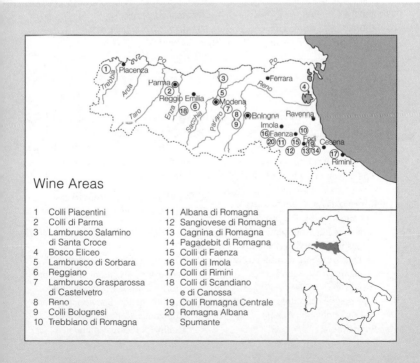

Wine Areas

1	Colli Piacentini	11	Albana di Romagna
2	Colli di Parma	12	Sangiovese di Romagna
3	Lambrusco Salamino di Santa Croce	13	Cagnina di Romagna
4	Bosco Eliceo	14	Pagadebit di Romagna
5	Lambrusco di Sorbara	15	Colli di Faenza
6	Reggiano	16	Colli di Imola
7	Lambrusco Grasparossa di Castelvetro	17	Colli di Rimini
8	Reno	18	Colli di Scandiano e di Canossa
9	Colli Bolognesi	19	Colli Romagna Centrale
10	Trebbiano di Romagna	20	Romagna Albana Spumante

Romagna region also takes in some local curiosities, especially close to the coast, and some international stars, particularly in the Colli Bolognesi zone. Emilia-Romagna ranks second only to the Veneto in volume of production in northern Italy. Besides its twenty DOCs and single DOCG (*passito* Albana di Romagna), there are several IGTs, of which Emilia is the most extensive.

Wine tourism is well developed in the region, most notably in Romagna, where wine taverns at Bertinoro (Ca' de B), Predappio Alto (Ca' de Sanzves), Ravenna (Ca' de Vin) offer a wide range of local wines both to taste and to buy. In Emilia, the scenic Colli Bolognesi are a treasure trove of little-known wines. In the Colli Piacentini, the *enoteca* at Castell'Arquato displays wines of the zone. Lambrusco admirers can quench their thirst in the lush plains around Modena and Reggio, specifically at the *enoteca* in the castle of Levizzano Rangone, near Castelvetro. The Enoteca Regionale Emilia-Romagna is housed in the Rocca Sforzesca at Dozza in Romagna. Good wine shops include Enoteca Fontana and Pedrelli in Parma and Enoteca Guinot in Modena.

Recent Vintages

Lambrusco and most white wines are for drinking young, but many Emilia-Romagna reds age well.

2004 Higher yields compared to 2003, but overall balanced wines.
2003 Drought and high temperatures brought early ripening, low acidity, and lower yields. Some areas fared well with concentrated wines.
2002 Summer rain meant quality was good only for carefully selected grapes.
2001 A very good year giving ripe, well-balanced wines.
2000 Excellent. Reds are concentrated, structured, and balanced.
Notes on earlier vintages: 1999, 98, 95, 94, and 93.

Appellations

DOCG
ALBANA DI ROMAGNA
w sw pas

The wines from this ancient Roman vine, which made Italy's first DOCG white back in 1987, are today often firm and elegant, whether dry or, less often, sweet. The *passito* version (made from semi-dried grapes with botrytis) is still the best type, though: it can be truly excellent.
Passito *98 00 03 04*
Age: *passito* 6 months.
See also Romagna Albana Spumante.

DOC
BOSCO ELICEO *w sw fz*
Trebbiano, Merlot, Malvasia Bianca di Candia, Fontana, Sauvignon Blanc.

CAGNINA DI ROMAGNA *r sw*
Refosco (known locally as Terrano).

COLLI BOLOGNESI *w r ris fz sup sp*
Albana, Trebbiano, Barbera, Cabernet Sauvignon, Chardonnay, Merlot, Pignoletto, Pinot Bianco, Riesling Italico, Sauvignon Blanc.
Sub-zones: Colline di Oliveto, Colline di Riosto, Colline

Marconiane, Monte San Pietro, Serravalle, Terre di Montebudello.

COLLI BOLOGNESI CLASSICO PIGNOLETTO *w*

Pignoletto, Pinot Bianco, Riesling Italico, Trebbiano Romagnolo.

COLLI DI FAENZA *w r ris sp*

Chardonnay, Pignoletto, Pinot Bianco, Trebbiano, Sauvignon Blanc, Cabernet Sauvignon, Ancellotta, Ciliegiolo, Merlot, Sangiovese.

COLLI D'IMOLA *w r sup fz ris nov*

Barbera, Cabernet Sauvignon, Chardonnay, Pignoletto, Sangiovese, Trebbiano.

COLLI DI PARMA *r ris fz sw*

Chardonnay, Barbera, Bonarda, Croatina, Cabernet Franc, Cabernet Sauvignon, Lambrusco, Malvasia, Merlot, Pinot Bianco, Pinot Grigio, Pinot Nero, Sauvignon Blanc.

COLLI DI RIMINI *w r ris pas*

Romagna Trebbiano, Biancame, Mostosa, Sangiovese, Cabernet Sauvignon, Barbera, Ancellotta, Ciliegiolo, Terrano, Rébola (local name for Pignoletto), Riesling Italico, Müller-Thurgau, Mostosa, Chardonnay, Merlot.

COLLI DI SCANDIANO E DI CANOSSA *w cl fz*

Sauvignon Blanc (known locally as Spergola), Cabernet Sauvignon, Chardonnay, Pinot Bianco, Pinot Grigio, Malvasia di Candia.

COLLI PIACENTINI *w p r fz sw cl sup ris sp nov vs*

Barbera, Bonarda, Cabernet Sauvignon, Chardonnay, Malvasia, Pinot Grigio, Pinot Nero, Sauvignon, Trebbiano, Croatina.
Sub-zones: Gutturnio (*classico*), Monterosso Val d'Arda, Trebbianino Val Trebbia, Val Nure, Vigoleno.

COLLI DELLA ROMAGNA CENTRALE *w r ris*

Chardonnay, Bombino, Sauvignon Blanc, Trebbiano, Pinot Bianco, Cabernet Sauvignon, Sangiovese, Barbera, Merlot, Montepulciano.

LAMBRUSCO DI SORBARA *r p sw*

Sorbara strain of Lambrusco.

LAMBRUSCO GRASPAROSSA DI CASTELVETRO *r p sw*

Grasparossa strain of Lambrusco.

LAMBRUSCO SALAMINO DI SANTA CROCE *r p sw*

Salamino strain of Lambrusco.

PAGADEBIT DI ROMAGNA *w sw fz*

Bombino Bianco and other local white varieties.

REGGIANO *w p r nov sp sw*

Lambrusco.

RENO *w fz sw*

Albana, Trebbiano, Montuni, Pignoletto.

ROMAGNA ALBANA SPUMANTE *w sp*

Albana.

SANGIOVESE DI ROMAGNA *r sup nov ris 95 97 98 99 00 01 04*

Sangiovese.

TREBBIANO DI ROMAGNA *w fz sp sw*

Trebbiano and other local white varieties.

IGT

Bianco di Castelfranco Emilia
Emilia/Dell'Emilia
Forlì
Fortana del Taro
Modena/Provincia di Modena
Ravenna
Rubicone
Sillaro/Bianco del Sillaro
Terre di Veleja
Val Tidone

Producers

The key provinces have been abbreviated as follows: BO = Bologna; FC = Forlì-Cesena; FE = Ferrara; MO = Modena; PC = Piacenza; PR = Parma; RA = Ravenna; RE = Reggio Emilia; RN = Rimini.
"Sangiovese" refers to Sangiovese di Romagna unless stated otherwise.

Agricola Reggiana, Borzano di Albinea (RE) *w r sw* ☆☆ * 67,000 bottles. Family-run estate with a production of good Lambrusco Reggiano: Vigna di Tedola and Vecchio Filare, from old vines. Also good Colli di Scandiano e Canossa: Lambrusco Grasparossa Tralcio Rosso and fine sweet Malvasia Dolce Vigna dei Gelsi, with local Malbo Gentile.

Francesco Bellei, Bomporto (MO) *w p r fz sp* ☆☆→☆☆☆ 8ha, 60,000 bottles. Giorgio Battilani and Christian Bellei's production is noted for its exceptional bottle-fermented Lambrusco di Sorbara Rosso Brut, from organic grapes. Since 1976 the estate has been producing a good range of sparklers from Pinot Noir and Chardonnay coming from vineyards in the Riccò di Serramazzoni hills.

La Berta, Brisighella (RA) *w r sw* ☆☆ 22ha, 85,000 bottles. Third-generation estate with a production overseen by Stefano Chioccioli. Fine Sangiovese Superiore Solana and Olmatello Riserva, good Colli di Faenza Rosso, and intriguing sweet Infavato from Malvasia.

Stefano Berti, Forlì (FC) *r* ☆☆ 7ha, 30,000 bottles. Berti's very low-yielding vines produce only two wines, reflecting a highly extolled Sangiovese. They are Superiore Calisto, aged for 12 months in barrique – rich in aromatic profile, with hints of vanilla, cherry, and cocoa, fresh and well weighted on the palate; and Superiore Ravaldo, which shows good quality/price value – less oak (it has been aged in steel), fresh, fruity appeal, finesse and good length.

Cantine Medici Ermete, Reggio Emilia (RE) *w r fz sw* ☆☆☆→☆☆☆☆ * 60ha, 800,000 bottles. Giorgio Medici's family estate has vines planted to high density, producing some 11 tons/ha. Highlights include *cru* Lambrusco Concerto – well-structured, concentrated, vibrant aromas; Colli Piacentini Campo Rosso Riserva, a Sangiovese aged 12 months in barrique – full-bodied, complex, and balsamic; and Gutturnu Sigillum Riserva – a Bonarda/Barbera blend. Also good sweet Malvasia Passito Soleste.

Castelli del Duca, Piacenza *w r ris fz* ☆☆ * Promising new Colli Piacentini estate with improving, good-value wines, including varietal Sauvignon Duchessa Vittoria and Bonarda Duca Ottavio. Highlights include Passito di Malvasia Soleste – sweet, oily, aromatic, with good persistence and balance; and Gutturnio Superiore Duca Alessandro and Gutturnio Riserva Sigillum – full-bodied, ripe, with fresh, balsamic notes and a long, velvety finish.

Castelluccio, Modigliana (FC) *w r* ☆☆☆→☆☆☆☆☆ 12ha, 90,000 bottles. This estate is especially renowned for a praised Sangiovese showing complexity and structure, made by Tuscan wine consultant Vittorio Fiore. Castelluccio is run by Fiore's son Claudio. Highlights include IGT red Ronco delle Ginestre and Ronco dei Ciliegi, both aged in tonneau. Also good Sangiovese Le More and white IGT Lunaria and Ronco del Re, both Sauvignon

– complexity, depth, exotic fruits, and staying power.

Cavicchioli, San Prospero (MO) *r fz* ☆→☆☆ 150ha, 15,000,000 bottles. Estate established in 1928 and owned by the Cavicchioli family, who have managed to maintain a distinctive character to their wines. They own about 150ha of vineyard and also buy in carefully selected grapes. They are the most widely distributed brand of Lambrusco in Italy. Like some other large producers, they turn out some top-range Lambruscos that are bottle-fermented. Vigna del Cristo is a pleasant, light Lambrusco Sorbara, rather austere but elegant. Col Sassoso is a traditional Lambrusco Grasparossa – dark, rich, and fruity, with plenty of body and character.

Celli, Bertinoro (FC) *w r ris sw sp* ☆☆→☆☆☆ * 29ha, 300,000 bottles. Estate run by the Sirri and Casadei families with a production offering a full range of Romagna varietals led by admirable Albana Passito Solara and Sangiovese Superiore Le Grillaie. Also worthy of mention are Bron e Ruseval, a Sangiovese/Cabernet blend; Bron e Ruseval Chardonnay; as well as good Albana Secco I Croppi and Spumante La Talandina.

Umberto Cesari, Castel San Pietro Terme (BO) *w r ris* ☆☆→☆☆☆ 100ha, 900,000 bottles. Large family winery that started off with 20ha in 1965 and today owns 100ha of vines spread over five estates. Highlights include Albana Colle del Re (both *secco* and *passito*); a structured Sangiovese Tauleto; Polvere di Stelle – a concentrated Sangiovese/Cabernet blend; Liano Riserva (also Sangiovese/Cabernet) – full-bodied; and IGT Malise Riserva (Pignoletto/Chardonnay).

Chiarli, Modena *w p fz* ☆→☆☆ This historic estate dates back to 1860.

It has a current production of 24 million bottles, of which a half are exported. In addition to their production agreements with cooperative wineries, they now make a top range coming from their own 100ha of vineyards. These *cru* Lambruscos carry the name of the founders, Chiarli Cleto e Figli: Vecchia Modena (a dry, old-style sparkler); Lambrusco Scuro Nivola – lively and fruity; and Lambrusco Grasparossa di Castelvetro Villa Cialdini.

Floriano Cinti, Sasso Marconi (BO) *w r fz sw* ☆☆→☆☆☆ * 17ha, 60,000 bottles. A Colli Bolognesi estate with a production focusing on quality: Classico Pignoletto and Chardonnay, as well as serious Cabernet Sauvignon, Merlot, and Barbera. Also good sweet Rubrum Cor Laetificans from partially dried Merlot, Pinot Noir, and Cabernet Sauvignon, aged 18 months in barrique.

Conte Otto Barattieri, Vigolzone (PC) *w r fz* ☆☆→☆☆☆ The Barattieri family estate in the Colli Piacentini produces excellent *vin santo* Albarola Val di Nure, characterized by dates and dried figs, dense and vibrant on the palate; and Il Faggio, from Brachetto Passito. Lively Gutturnio, Bonarda, and Ortrugo complete the range, along with fine Barbera and Sauvignon.

Corte Manzini, Castelvetro di Modena (MO) *r p fz* ☆☆→☆☆☆ A 30ha estate with an *agriturismo* and 10ha of vines planted on the slopes of Castelvetro, producing some 80,000 bottles of hand-crafted Lambrusco Grasparossa. Highlights include a range of Lambrusco Grasparossa di Castelvetro: L'Acino, Secco, and Amabile.

Drei Donà Tenuta La Palazza, Forlì (FC) *w r ris* ☆☆☆→☆☆☆☆ 27ha, 100,000 bottles. Claudio Drei Donà's production focuses on top-notch Sangiovese di Romagna Superiore Pruno Riserva – floral spicy notes mingled with balsamic and tobacco, elegant, vibrant, with fine tannic structure and length. Also very good IGT Cabernet Sauvignon Magnificat; Graf Noir, a four-grape blend (including Sangiovese and Cabernet Sauvignon); and Sangiovese Notturno.

Fattoria Paradiso, Bertinoro (FC) *w r sw* ☆☆→☆☆☆ 100ha, 500,000 bottles. Renowned estate producing a large range of individual, stylish wines with international appeal led by Mito, a red IGT Merlot/Cabernet Sauvignon/Syrah blend aged in barrique 24 months – concentrated ripe fruit with hints of plums, tobacco, liquorice, very long and persistent. Also very good Sangiovese Albana and Barbarossa – floral in character, structured, and round; and Passito Gradisca.

Stefano Ferrucci, Castelbolognese (RA) *w r ris sw* ☆☆→☆☆☆ 16ha, 95,000 bottles. Fourth-generation estate with a production of fine Albana Passito Domus Aurea from late-harvested grapes. Also excellent Sangiovese Superiore Domus Caia Riserva, made from partially raisined grapes and aged 14 months in tonneau – concentrated, full-bodied, with ample aromas and mineral character; and Sangiovese Superiore Centurione – fresh floral and berry character.

Vittorio Graziano, Castelvetro (MO) *r fz* ☆☆☆ 7ha, 30,000 bottles. Graziani's vineyard is planted at very high density and produces traditional Lambrusco. Highlights: bottle-fermented, organic Lambrusco Grasparossa di Castelvetro – intense ruby colour, elegant bouquet and rich in aromas on the nose, slightly vegetal and smoky. On the palate it is round and smooth, with slight perlage and good persistence.

Luretta, Gazzola (PC) *w r* ☆☆→☆☆☆☆ 57ha, 130,000 bottles. Lucio Salamini's organically farmed estate is situated near the Castle of Mormellaro in Val Luretta. He produces Colli Piacentini: Malvasia, Gutturno, Candida Aromatica, Barbera, Bonarda, Cabernet, and Chardonnay. Highlights: Malvasia Boccadirosa, Malvasia Le Rane, Cabernet Sauvignon Corbeau, Gutturnio Superiore L'Alba del Drago, and Pantera, a Bonarda/Barbera/Pinot Noir blend.

Gaetano Lusenti, Ziano Piacentino (PC) *w r* ☆☆→☆☆☆☆ * 17ha, 96,000 bottles. Up-and-coming estate with a production of Colli Piacentini wines. Highlights: Cabernet Sauvignon Villante; Bonarda La Picciona, Malvasia Bianca Regina, Pinot Grigio Fiocco di Rose, and Gutturnio Superiore Cresta al Sole, all showing good terroir expression and varietal character.

Giovanna Madonia, Bertinoro (FC) *w r ris sw* ☆☆☆ 11ha, 30,000 bottles. Madonia's vineyards, overseen by Attilio Pagli, are planted to a fairly high density with low yields. Highlights: Merlot Sterpigno – sapid, concentrated, and vibrant; Sangiovese Superiore Ombroso Riserva – fine aromas, depth and longevity; and a fine Albana Passito Chimera, from grapes harvested in November – fragrant and fresh.

Poderi Morini, Faenza (RA) *w p r sw* ☆☆→☆☆☆☆ * 35ha, 60,000 bottles. Alessandro Morini's production is based on local indigenous varieties. Highlights: Nadèl, a Sangiovese/Longanesi/Merlot/Sauvignon Rosso (aka Centesimino) blend, aged in tonneau 18 months – full, powerful, with fine tannins; Rubacuori – a sweet red from partly raisined Centesimino; and Traicolli, from Centesimino – power, spice, and length.

Moro, Sant'Ilario d'Enza (RE) *w r ris sw fz sp* ☆☆→☆☆☆ 15ha. Paola Rinaldini's 1884 farm with a small wine museum and old cellars produces unusual wines from low-yielding vines deriving from a clone of Lambrusco called Pjcol Ross. The wine is bottle-fermented and left in contact with the yeast for 18 to 24 months, followed by *dégorgement* without freezing. The resulting Lambrusco Vigna del Picchio is characterized by an intense and incisive bouquet; it is vivacious, round, full-bodied, with a fresh, fruity aftertaste. Also good Moro del Moro (Lambrusco/Ancellotta) showing impressive structure.

Il Poggiarello, Travo (PC) *w r ris sp fz* ☆☆→☆☆☆ 18ha, 110,000 bottles. Ferrari and Perrini's production of *frizzante* wines, *spumante*, and some excellent Colli Piacentini varietal labels includes Gutturnio Riserva La Barbona – structured, solid, with persistence; and oak-fermented Announo I Perinelli, from exemplary low-yielding Sémillon/Malvasia/Viognier.

San Patrignano, Coriano (RN) *w r ris* ☆☆☆→☆☆☆☆ * 100ha, 100,000 bottles. A rehabilitation community centre for ex-drug addicts producing quality wines from low-yielding vines. The production is overseen by consultant oenologist Riccardo Cotarella. Highlights: Sangiovese Avi Riserva – warm, full-bodied, round, with tight tannins, long and luscious; well-crafted Bordeaux-blend Montepirolo; and Colli di Rimini Rosso Noi, a Sangiovese/Cabernet Sauvignon/Merlot blend.

Santarosa, Monte San Pietro (BO) *w r* ☆☆→☆☆☆ 10ha, 40,000 bottles. Starry Colli Bolognesi wines led by two excellent, full-bodied reds: Merlot Giò Tondo and Cabernet Sauvignon Giò Rosso – ripeness, balance, and structure. Also good oak-fermented Chardonnay Giòcoliere, as well as a solid Colli Bolognesi Rosso and a fresh Bianco.

La Stoppa, Ancarano di Rivergaro (PC) *w r fz sw* ☆☆☆ 30ha, 150,000 bottles. Elena Pantaleoni's vines, some of them century-old, surround the medieval castle of Ancarano. The estate's fine Colli Piacentini wines are produced organically, using only natural yeast. Highlights: Buca delle Canne, a sweet Sémillon; Malvasia Passito Vigna del Volta; and IGT Ageno (Malvasia/Ortrugo/Trebbiano).

Tenuta Bonzara, Monte San Pietro (BO) *w r* ☆☆→☆☆☆ 16ha, 65,000 bottles. Francesco Lambertini's low-yielding, well-tended vines produce classy Colli Bolognesi wines, including the well-extracted, elegant, age-worthy Cabernet Sauvignon Bonzarone. Also very good Monte Severo, a Chardonnay/Sauvignon/Pignoletti blend, and Pignoletto Classico Vigna Antica, from old vines – excellent complexity and aromatic profile.

La Tosa, Vigolzone (PC) *w r sw* ☆☆→☆☆☆ 13ha, 110,000 bottles. Stefano and Ferruccio Pizzamiglio produce outstanding Colli Piacentini Gutturnio Vignamorello, expressing incisive varietal character. Also good Cabernet Sauvignon La Luna Selvatica – medium structure and very drinkable; and Malvasia Sorriso di Cielo – rich, aromatic, round, fresh, and characteristic bitter finish.

Tre Monti, Imola (BO) *w r ris sw fz* ☆☆☆ 60ha, 220,000 bottles. Vittorio Navacchia's production, overseen by consultant winemaker Donato Lanati, is known for its Trebbiano, Sangiovese, and Albana wines.

Highlights include the attractive Albana Passito and Dolce – persistent, intense aromas, balanced by a fresh, long finish. Also excellent Sangiovese Superiore Thea – powerful, with silky tannins, balsamic and persistent; and a reliable Colli di Imola range of varietal wines.

Treré, Faenza (RA) *w r ris sw* ☆☆→☆☆☆ * 35ha, 200,000 bottles. Top estate with low-yielding vines; production is overseen by consultant oenologist Attilio Pagli. Highlights include Sangiovese Amarcord d'un Ross – big, weighty wine with structure, round, with balanced acidity; excellent Sangiovese Renero – ripe fruit and floral aromas, medium body with soft tannins; and a convincing Albana Passito with good varietal character; as well as a range of Romagna and Faenza DOCs.

Vallona, Castello di Serravalle (BO) *w r* ☆☆→☆☆☆ * Fine Colli Bolognesi estate with two reds, Cabernet Sauvignon Selezione and Merlot Afederico, leading the range. Also very good Pignoletto Premartina – citrus, mineral, with tropical fruit. Among the highlights of the Colli Bolognesi range: Chardonnay, Sauvignon, Pignoletto, Cabernet Sauvignon, and Altr-Uve Passito, a Pignoletto/Albana/Sauvignon blend.

Venturini Baldini, Roncolo di Quattro Castella (RE) *w p r sp sw fz* ☆☆→☆☆☆ 50ha, 300,000 bottles. A 15th-century estate with a production of admirable Reggiano Lambrusco from organic grapes, including Tenuta di Roncolo, a sparkling red, and good Lambrusco Marani Rubino del Ducato Terzi. Good Spumante Rosa di Roncolo (a Pinot Grigio/Pinot Noir blend) and Colli di Scandiano e Canossa Il Grinto (Cabernet Sauvignon),

as well as Malvasia dell'Emilia Secca and Dolce.

Vigneto delle Terre Rosse, Zola Predosa (BO) *w r* ☆☆☆→☆☆☆ 20ha, 100,000 bottles. The Terre Rosse name (meaning "red earth") comes from the red clay soil, rich in iron that is the base of the vineyard. The estate philosophy is to vinify and age in steel, rather than use oak, in order to preserve the fresh, fruity appeal of the wine. Production is overseen by consultant winemaker Luca D'Attoma. Highlights include a Colli Bolognesi range of varietal wines: Chardonnay (including a Cuvée Giovanni Vallania), Sauvignon, Pinot Noir, Cabernet, and Merlot.

Villa di Corlo, Cavezzo (MO) *r* ☆☆→☆☆☆ * 30ha, 70,000 bottles. Emerging estate with a 17th-century villa belonging to the Giacobazzi family and a fine production of Lambrusco Grasparossa and Lambrusco Sorbara – both showing excellent varietal character, succulent fruit, and clean acidity. Corleto is a fuller Lambrusco, with finer aromas and weightier body. The family have now planted a few hectares of Pinot Noir at an altitude of 500m (1,640ft).

Zerbina, Marzeno di Faenza (RA) *w r ris sw* ☆☆☆→☆☆☆ * Maria Cristina Geminiani's leading Romagna estate produces an exemplary range of Sangiovese di Romagna wines and, in particular, Albana Passito Scacco Matto – rich, complex, and elegant, with ample aromas balanced with notes of botrytis. Also, impeccable Sangiovese Superiore Riserva Pietramora – vibrant, expressive, persistent; and superb Marzieno, a slightly herbaceous, elegant Sangiovese/Cabernet/Merlot blend.

Wine & Food

Pasta alone would elevate Emilia-Romagna's cooking to the divine. The making of tagliatelle, tortellini, agnolini, cappelletti, passatelli, and lasagne, to name a few, is a daily routine performed by the *sfogliatrice*, a living testimony to the regional conviction that pasta must be fresh and made by hand. But pasta is just the entrée of a culinary heritage as religiously adhered to as any of France. Bologna *la grassa* ("the fat"), with its mortadella and lasagne verdi and other delights, is the capital of regional gastronomy, but some provincial centres – especially Parma, Modena, Reggio, and Piacenza – can rival its battery of good things to eat. Foremost are Parmigiano Reggiano cheese and prosciutto di Parma, but Modena weighs in heftily with its *cotechino* and *zampone*. Modena is home to the true *aceto balsamico tradizionale* (balsamic vinegar made in the *solera* method – too glorious to be considered vinegar), though imitations abound. There is so much more to Emilia-Romagna's cornucopia that this list could only whet the appetite.

Anatra alla romagnola Duck cooked with bacon, wine, and seasonings. A Romagna specialty.

Cappelletti in brodo Hat-shaped pasta with meat filling served in broth.

Lasagne verdi al forno Green lasagne cooked with layers of meat ragout and béchamel sauce.

Parmigiano Reggiano This, the greatest of grating cheeses, is also eaten in chunks, sometimes topped with a drop of *aceto balsamico*.

Piadina Flat bread served with pecorino cheese or prosciutto.

Prosciutto e melone Parma ham with cantaloupe (or fresh figs).

Tortelli all'erbetta Large pasta envelopes filled with ricotta and *erbetta*, a chard-like green, served with melted butter and Parmesan.

Tortellini in brodo Small pasta envelopes with meat and cheese filling served in capon broth with grated Parmesan.

Zampone Pig's feet sausage from Modena, generally served with lentils or mashed potatoes.

Hotels

Canalgrande Hotel, Modena €€–€€€ This worldly hotel dates from the 16th century and was once the convent of the Holy Trinity. The recently renovated comfortable rooms offer relaxed charm and elegance. Quieter rooms overlook the garden at the back.

Charming Hotel De Prati, Ferrara € A characteristic hotel with 15 rooms, all featuring modern comforts. It is located in a quiet street at the end of the city's central pedestrian zone, close to Estense Castle and the Palazzo dei Diamanti.

Palace Maria Luigia, Parma €€–€€€ A centrally located hotel with 102 large, comfortable rooms and suites with modern facilities and comforts. The place to stay if you want to pay repeated visits to Parma's restaurants.

Palazzo Viviani, Montegridolfo (RN) €€–€€€ Luxury country house with eight suites, fireplaces, and reading rooms. It is located in a hamlet a few kilometres from the Adriatic coast. There are gardens for sunbathing, as well as a Jacuzzi and

a fitness centre. Elegant dining.
Agriturismo Torre Pratesi,
Brisighella (RA) €€ A 15th-century
tower with nine comfortable

rooms offering B&B or half/full
board. A pool, horse riding, and
hiking are available to guests. The
restaurant offers local cuisine.

Restaurants

Aldina, Modena € (lunch only)
An institution where genuine,
excellent-value home-made
fare is served with simplicity.
Buriani (BO) €€ Historic castle
at the gates of Bologna with three
dining rooms. Regional creative
fare – veal carpaccio with rocket
and porcini pesto, fresh fish, lamb,
duck, and rabbit. Superb wine list.
Ermes, Modena € Hole-in-the-
wall *osteria* run by Ermes and his
wife – with genuine traditional
dishes at ridiculously low prices.
Francescana, Modena €–€€
Massimo Bottura is a talented chef
of contemporary Italian cuisine. His
menu features reworked traditional
dishes crafted with chromatic and
aesthetic expertise. Good wine list.
La Frasca, Castrocaro Terme (FC)
€€–€€€ Arguably the region's
top restaurant, with first-class
traditional fare. Every detail, from
the home-made breads to the
desserts, is impeccable. Excellent
wine list.
Lido Lido, Cesenatico (FC) €€
Quality ingredients and creative
cooking feature in Vincenzo
Cammerucci's excellent fish-
orientated menu. Good wine list.
Locanda della Colonna,
Tossignano (BO) €€–€€€ Chef
Marina Garramone is creative
in restyling traditional dishes.
Specialties include meat salad with
Tropea onions, octopus stew, pasta
with goat's cheese, pheasant breast
wrapped in bacon, and lamb.
Mamma Rosa, San Polo d'Enza
(RE) € This restaurant specializes
in fish dishes: tuna carpaccio,

black tagliatelle in fish sauce,
and calamari soup with barley.
There is also a good cheese
selection, and home-made desserts
Osteria del Povero Diavolo,
Torriana (RN) €–€€ Ivan Brizzi
serves excellent traditional recipes
with top ingredients such as
truffles, local cheeses, ground
Saracen grain, wild asparagus,
lamb, and guinea fowl.
Osteria di Rubbiara, Rubbiara
(MO) € Italo Pedroni's country
trattoria is well worth a visit. Leave
your mobile phone in the lockers
as you enter – the emphasis here
is solely on eating and drinking.
Parizzi, Parma €€ Elegant dining
in a palazzo in the historic centre
with creative regional dishes –
pasta with rabbit sauce, guinea
fowl in a dried fruit crust, beef
stew *alla parmigiana*, and more,
plus a 500-label wine list.
Riva, Ponte dell'Olio (PC) €€
Traditional *osteria* attached to a
medieval castle offering traditional
fare in a light, cutting-edge style.
Excellent wine list.
San Domenico at Imola (BO)
€€–€€€ Elegant dining situated
in a 15th-century convent, with
garden and cloister. Excellent local
cuisine with an innovative touch,
and a well-stocked wine cellar.
**Il Sole Antica Locanda del
Trebbo,** Trebbo di Reno (BO) €€
Run by Marcello and Gianluca
Leoni, this restaurant combines
creative and traditional dishes.
Try the pigeon on aubergine
salad with herbs, or the pasta
with spicy calamari sauce.

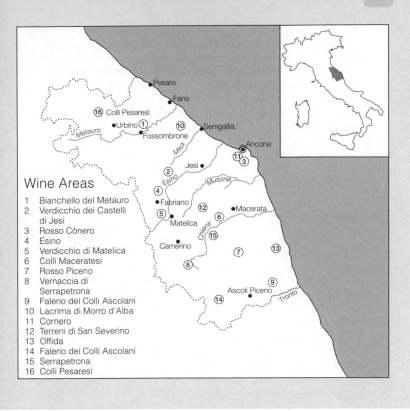

Wine Areas

1 Bianchello del Metauro
2 Verdicchio dei Castelli di Jesi
3 Rosso Cònero
4 Esino
5 Verdicchio di Matelica
6 Colli Maceratesi
7 Rosso Piceno
8 Vernaccia di Serrapetrona
9 Falerio dei Colli Ascolani
10 Lacrima di Morro d'Alba
11 Cornero
12 Terreni di San Severino
13 Offida
14 Falerio dei Colli Ascolani
15 Serrapetrona
16 Colli Pesaresi

Marche *Marche*

Verdicchio put the Marche on the wine map decades ago with its amphora-shaped bottle. But as the amphora slowly went out of style, Verdicchio grew beyond its role as a simple fish wine to become one of Italy's most multifaceted and dignified whites. Control of harvesting time and vinification method can produce a crisp, lively wine with a succulent heart, or a deep, rich, buttery one that develops slowly and ages with aplomb – or various stages in between. Oak can bring additional nuances, too, for those who wish to use it. Yet quality rises in the large Castelli di Jesi and small Matelica zones have generally outstripped price rises, so that Verdicchio remains a healthy cut above the general level of Italy's popular whites.

Verdicchio firmly dominates the Marche's wine production. Other whites in this region between the Apennines and the Adriatic Sea are mostly light and insubstantial, the main exception being Bianchello del Metauro, from the Marche's more northerly part, and Passerina and Pecorino, from Offida, in the Ascoli Piceno hills.

Reds are very much in second place for quantity, but production is often quality-led. Rosso Piceno, based on Sangiovese, can show class as one of the true bargains in aged red wines left in central Italy, with little exported outside the region. Rosso Conero, based on Montepulciano grown on the outskirts of Ancona, can reach even greater heights, but here too its local admirers somehow keep much of it for themselves. And much as wine aficionados may search out the weird and wonderful Lacrima di Morro d'Alba or the curious sparkling red DOCG Vernaccia di Serrapetrona, these wines remain primarily local.

Most tourists come here to bask on Adriatic beaches, but those who wander into the interior will find peaceful, relaxing scenery in the hills. Urbino is a renowned art centre, Loreto a religious shrine, and Ascoli Piceno one of many well-preserved medieval towns. There are two regional Enoteca dei Vini Marchigiani – one in Jesi, the other in Offida. For wine shops: Enoteca Kursaal in Ascoli Piceno; Enoteca Bulgari in San Benedetto del Tronto; Enopolis in Ancona; and Alma Bibe in Fano.

Recent Vintages

Most Marche whites are for drinking young, though Verdicchio from both Jesi and Matelica can develop impressively with three to five years of age, sometimes longer. Rosso Conero and Rosso Piceno may also sometimes be made to be drunk fairly young, but more frequently they age well for a decade or more.
2004 A good vintage with a twenty-five per cent increase in yields on 2003.
2003 Good quality, with some areas of excellence and an average fifteen per cent lower yields due to drought.
2002 Very good quality despite drastic yield reductions due to a rainy summer.
2001 Supreme (except in the Ascoli Piceno province).
Notes on earlier vintages: 2000, 1999, 1998, and 1997 were all very successful. Among older vintages, 1995 was very good and 1990 magnificent. Other good vintages are 1988, 87, 85, 83, and 82.

Appellations

DOCG
CONERO r
This dry, full-bodied red takes its name from Monte Conero, which overlooks the regional capital of Ancona. From at least 85% Montepulciano and up to 15% Sangiovese. Aged 2 years.

VERNACCIA DI SERRAPETRONA
r sw sp
Sparkling red wine based on dark Vernaccia grapes grown around Serrapetrona, near Macerata. Deep garnet-purple and fragrant, with some deliberate mouth-cleansing bitterness on the finish. It can be *secco*, *amabile*, or *dolce*.

DOC
BIANCHELLO DEL METAURO w
Biancame (aka Biancone).

COLLI MACERATESI w r ris pas sw nov
Maceratino (also known as Ribona), Trebbiano, Verdicchio, Sangiovese, Chardonnay, Sauvignon, Pecorino, Grechetto, Merlot, Montepulciano.

COLLI PESARESI w r ris
Trebbiano Toscano, Verdicchio, Biancame, Pinot Grigio, Pinot Nero, Riesling, Sangiovese, Cabernet Sauvignon, Merlot, Chardonnay.
Sub-zones: Focara and Roncaglia.

ESINO w r nov fz
Verdicchio, Sangiovese, Montepulciano, others.

FALERIO DEI COLLI ASCOLANI *w*
Trebbiano, Passerina, Pecorino.

LACRIMA DI MORRO D'ALBA
r sw pas
Lacrima, Montepulciano,
Verdicchio.

OFFIDA *w r vs sp pas sw*
Montepulciano, Cabernet
Sauvignon, Passerina, Pecorino.

ROSSO CONERO *r 90 95 97 98 99 00 01 02 03 04*
Montepulciano, Sangiovese.

ROSSO PICENO *nov ris 95 97 98 99 00 01 02 03 04*
Sangiovese, Montepulciano.

SERRAPETRONA *r*
Vernaccia Nera, others.

TERRENI DI SAN SEVERINO *r*
pas sup sw
Vernaccia, Montepulciano.

VERDICCHIO DEI CASTELLI DI JESI *w cl ris pass w sp 97 98 99 00 01 02 03 04*
Verdicchio.

VERDICCHIO DI MATELICA
w ris pas sw sp 97 98 99 00 01 02 03 04
Verdicchio.

IT
Marche

Producers

The key provinces have been abbreviated as follows: AN = Ancona; AP = Ascoli Piceno; MC = Macerata; PS = Pesaro e Urbino.

Accadia Angelo, Serra San Quirico (AN) *w r* ☆☆☆ 5ha, 30,000 bottles. Small estate with vineyards in the Sasso and Castellano areas, on the southeastern border of the DOC Verdicchio Classico zone. Two good Castelli di Jesi Classico Superiore: Cantori and Conscio. Also good Rosso Piceno Riverbero – deep cherry with evident tannins, vinous and mineral in character.

Aurora, Offida (AP) *w r* ☆☆→☆☆☆ * 50,000 bottles. Estate with a rigorously organic production of Barricadiero (Montepulciano/Cabernet/Merlot) – vibrant, austere, elegant, flinty, meaty. Also good Offida Pecorino Fiobbo, a structured, floral, round, elegant white; and very drinkable Rosso Piceno Superiore.

Bisci, Matelica (MC) *w r ris* ☆☆→☆☆☆ 19ha, 100,000 bottles. A historic estate producing fine, oak-fermented Verdicchio di Matelica

Vigneto Fogliano – structure, aromatic complexity, and length. Also good Sangiovese/Cabernet Villa Castiglioni – fruity with cherry, oak, and vanilla.

Boccadigabbia, Civitanova Marche (MC) *w p r* ☆☆→☆☆☆☆ 25ha, 100,000 bottles. Elvidio Alessandri's production is overseen by winemaker Fabrizio Ciufoli. Top labels: a Cabernet Sauvignon called Akronte – full berry fruit, balsamic, powerful, fresh, with a delicious, lengthy finish; Chardonnay Montalperti, aged five months in barrique – elegant floral character, structure; Sangiovese Saltabicchio, aged 15 months in barrique and containing prune, cherry aromas mingled with tobacco and cocoa. Good ageing potential. Also fine Rosso Piceno.

Brunori, Jesi (AN) *w r* ☆→☆☆ * 80,000 bottles. Mario and Giorgio Brunori have been producing traditional San Nicolò and Le Gemme Verdicchio di Jesi Classico selections for more than 50 years. Also good Lacrima di Morro, Rosso Conero, and Rosso Piceno.

Le Caniette, Ripatransone (AP) *w r sw* ☆☆☆ Giovanni Vagnoni's wines are concentrated and extracted, as in top labels Morellone and Nero di Vite. Also good *vin santo* – tropical fruit, herbs, mineral character, with a sapid, fresh, bitter-almond finish; and Sibilla Samia (100% Passerina), a late-harvest wine aged three years in a range of woods – ample aromas and complexity.

Cantine Belisario, Matelica (MC) *w r ris* ☆☆→☆☆☆ * 300ha, 800,000 bottles. Admirable 180-member co-op producing above-average Verdicchio di Matelica: Vigneti del Cerro, Vigneti Belisano, and Riserva Cambrugiano – citrus, clean mineral touch, vibrant, rich, with fresh acidity. Excellent quality/price ratio.

Casalfarneto, Serra de' Conti (AN) *w sw* ☆☆☆ * 25ha, 220,000 bottles. Danilo Solustri and Massimo Arcangeli's emerging estate produces several types of Verdicchio di Jesi Classico Superiore: Cimaio, Fontevecchia, and Gran Casale – the latter being classy, elegant, fresh in style; and the six-month oak-aged Cimaio, from late-harvest grapes, partially botrytized – complexity and finesse.

Cocci Grifoni, San Savino di Ripatransone (AP) *w r sp* ☆☆→☆☆☆☆ 40ha, 380,000 bottles. Leading family estate producing Piceno Superiore Il Grifone – classic elegance, sapid; Vigna Masseri (Montepulciano/ Sangiovese) – complex, spicy nose, rich palate, cassis and liquorice, minerality, supple tannins, long finish. Also good Pecorino Colle Vecchio, Falerio Vigneti San Basso, and Offida Passerina Brut.

Colonnara, Cupramontana (AN) *w r sp ris* ☆☆→☆☆☆☆ * 210ha, 1,500,000 bottles. Large co-op with a production overseen by Pierluigi Gagliardini. Reliable Verdicchio di Jesi Classico Tufico and Cuprese at attractive prices, as well as Rosso Piceno and Rosso Conero. Also a much-admired sparkling range: Ubaldo Rosi Brut Riserva and a brut *metodo classico millesimato*.

Fattoria Coroncino, Staffolo (AN) *w* ☆☆☆ * 9ha, 45,000 bottles. Lucio and Fiorella Canestrari's estate produces exquisite Verdicchio di Jesi Classico in two top labels: Gaiospino – structured, powerful, with vibrant fruit and aromatic complexity; and Il Coroncino – deep, powerful, warm, round, and full, with mineral character and length. Also a good Trebbiano Le Lame.

Fattoria Dezi, Servigliano (AP) *w r* ☆☆☆→☆☆☆☆ 18ha, 50,000 bottles. Brothers Romolo and Remo Dezi's monovarietal wines from a biodynamic estate include Solo Sangiovese – age-worthy, vibrant, with depth and structure; Regina Del Bosco (100% Merlot); Dezio (100% Montepulciano); and Le Solagne, a Verdicchio/Malvasia/ Pecorino blend.

Fazi-Battaglia, Castelplanio (AN) *w r sw* ☆☆→☆☆☆☆ 350ha, 3,800,000 bottles. This long-time market leader is back in the limelight with Verdicchio di Jesi Classico Superiore Titulus (in amphora), plus selections Le Moie, San Sisto, and Massaccio – wide aromatic profile, tenacious, with depth. Also Rosso Conero Passo del Lupo Riseva and a fine Muffi di San Sito from late-harvest grapes, aged in barrique – creamy, apricot, caramel, and tropical spice.

Garofoli, Loreto (AN) *w r ris sw* ☆☆☆→☆☆☆☆ * 50ha, 2,000,000 bottles. Family estate producing stylish and good-value wines, such as Verdicchio di Jesi Classico: Macrina, Serra Fiorese, and Podium; Rosso Conero: Piancarda and Grosso Agontano Riserva – rich and sapid with toasted notes. Also Spumante Metodo Classico Brut Riserva and Passito Le Brume.

Lanari, Ancona (AN) *r* ☆☆☆ * 12ha, 40,000 bottles. Luca Lanari produces refined, yet intense Rosso Conero from low-yielding vines and highly selected grapes. Both Rosso Conero and Rosso Conero Fibbio are richly extracted wines, structured with fine tannins, which show well with some bottle-ageing.

Malacari, Offagna (AN) *r* ☆☆☆ * 16ha, 40,000 bottles. At Alessandro Starabba's emerging estate, production is based on an elegant, age-worthy Rosso Conero Grigiano made from 100% Montepulciano – fine extraction and silky tannins.

Stefano Mancinelli, Morro d'Alba (AN) *w r sw* ☆☆→☆☆☆ * 22ha, 150,000 bottles. Stefano Mancinelli is a leading producer of Lacrima di Morro: Santa Maria del Fiore, Sensazioni di Frutto, San Michele, and Passito Re Sole. This rare indigenous grape is named Lacrima (meaning "tear") because when it is ripe the grape splits and sheds its tears. It is difficult to vinify, and praise goes to this estate for a fine example.

Marchetti, Ancona (AN) *w r sw* ☆☆→☆☆☆ 16ha, 60,000 bottles. This estate produces excellent Rosso Conero, such as Villa Bonomi (100% Montepulciano), aged in barrique for 18 months – varietal character with marasca, violet, and cloves, and high in alcohol. Also good Verdicchio dei Castelli di Jesi Classico Tenuta del Cavaliere.

Marotti Campi, Morro d'Alba (AN) *w r ris* ☆☆→☆☆☆ 52ha, 150,000 bottles. Marotti's family estate is focused on fruit-rich Lacrima di Morro: Rubico and Orgiolo – vinous, floral, fruity. Also stylish late-harvest Verdicchio dei Castelli di Jesi Classico Salmariano Riserva, 20% aged in barrique, the rest in steel, giving it extra freshness – melon, honey, savoury, with high alcohol and structure. Also good Passito Onyr.

La Monacesca, Matelica (MC) *w r ris* ☆☆☆ 27ha, 140,000 bottles. Casimiro Cifola's production is overseen by winemakers Fabrizio Ciufoli and Roberto Potentini. Top labels: classy Verdicchio di Matelica La Monacesca and Mirum Riserva, IGT Chardonnay Ecclesia, and Camerte Riserva, an age-worthy Sangiovese/Merlot blend.

Moncaro, Terre Cortesi, Montecarotto (AN) *w r ris sw* ☆☆→☆☆☆ * 1,600ha, 7,000,000 bottles. One of the Marche's largest co-ops. Top labels include Verdicchio Castelli di Jesi: Verde di Ca' Ruptae, Le Vele, and excellent Passito Tordiruta; Rosso Conero: Nerone Riserva and Vigneti del Parco Riserva; and Rosso Piceno Superiore: Campo delle Mura and Roccaviva.

Monte Schiavo, Maiolati Spontini (AN) *w r sw* ☆☆→☆☆☆ * 115ha, 1,800,000 bottles. The Pieralisi family's quality-orientated production includes starry Rosso Conero Adeodato. Also lively Verdicchio di Jesi Classico Superiore Nativo, Le Giuncare Riserva, Coste del Molino, Bando di San Settimio, Arché Passito, and late-harvested Pallio di San Floriano IGT Esio Rosso, a Montepulciano/Cabernet blend.

Alessandro Moroder, Ancona (AN) *p r sw* ☆☆→☆☆☆ 26ha, 120,000 bottles. Family estate founded in 1837 with a production overseen by Franco Bernabei. Admirable age-worthy Rosso Conero led by classy selection Dorico. Also good IGT Ankon (a Montepulciano/Cabernet/Merlot blend), which needs time in bottle to come round, but very expressive when it does; and Rosa di Montacuto (Alicante Nero).

Oasi degli Angeli, Cupra Marittima (AP) *r* ☆☆☆ 10ha, 5,500 bottles. Eleonora Rossi's old vines, planted to high density, are dedicated to just one wine: the famous, supremely

impressive Kurni, from 100%
Montepulciano, aged 22 months in
new barrique. It is a complex nectar
that opens up and evolves with time.

Saladini Pilastri, Spinetoli (AP) *w r*
☆☆→☆☆☆ 140ha, 600,000 bottles.
Well-established estate with a
production overseen by consultant
oenologist Alberto Antonini. Of
particular interest: single-vineyard
Rosso Piceno Superiore Vigna
Monteprandone – blackcurrant,
cherries, and prunes, liquorice
palate, firm tannins with lashings of
chewy fruit, and elegant, persistent
finish. Also very good Rosso Piceno
Vigna Montetinello, Falerio Vigna
Palazzi, and Vigna Piediprato.

San Giovanni, Offida (AP) *w r sw* ☆☆
35ha, 150,000 bottles. Emerging
estate with a production of
characterful Falerio and Rosso
Piceno. Highlights: Rosso Piceno
Superiore Axée – floral, marasca
cherry, spice, medium structured;
and Offida Passerina Passito,
showing good potential and charm.

San Savino, Ripatransone (AP) *w r* ☆☆
* 120,000 bottles. Simone Capecci's
production is based on IGT Fedus
Sangiovese, Ver Sacrum
Montepulciano, Piceno Superiore,
and Offida Pecorino Ciprea –
mineral character, structure, and
zesty acidity. A range with aplomb.

San Lorenzo, Montecarotto (AN) *w r ris*
☆☆☆ * 36ha, 100,000 bottles.
Natalino Crognaletti produces
full-bodied wines that express
terroir character, such as his
single-vineyard Rosso Piceno
(Montepulciano/Sangiovese/
Merlot) and IGT Vigneto Sellone
(100% Montepulciano). Also classy
Verdicchio dei Castelli di Jesi Vigna
delle Oche Riserva, from very low-
yielding vines – ripe and complex
aromas retaining a fresh, fruity
appeal after 16 months in steel.

Santa Barbara, Barbara (AN) *w r*
☆☆→☆☆☆ * 40ha, 500,000 bottles.
Stefano Antonucci's production
covers a good range of styles of
Verdicchio di Jesi Classico, Rosso
Piceno, and IGT Rosso, all with
excellent quality/price ratios. Top
labels: Rosso Piceno Il Maschio da
Monte (100% Montepulciano), and
Vigna San Bartolo (Montepulciano/
Cabernet). In the Verdicchio di Jesi
Classico Superiore, good Stefano
Antonucci, Nidastore, and Pignocco.

Sartarelli, Poggio San Marcello (AN)
w sw ☆☆☆ * 66ha, 320,000 bottles.
Donatella Sartarelli's Verdicchio dei
Castelli di Jesi is limited to three
labels and shows great character,
in particular in Tralivio and the
late-harvested Balciana, produced
only in top vintages – elegance,
finesse, and complexity.

Silvano Strologo, Camerano (AN) *r ris*
☆☆→☆☆☆ 10ha, 53,000 bottles.
Giancarlo Soverchia's production is
focused on Rosso Conero of great
class. Top wines: Decebalo Riserva,
Julius, and Traiano – rich herbal
fibre, ripeness, spice, and structure,
aged 12 months in barrique and
needing a fair amount of bottle-age
before being ready to drink.

Tenuta De Angelis, Castel de Lama (AP)
w r ☆☆→☆☆☆ * Fruit-forward
IGT Anghelos (Montepulciano/
Sangiovese/Cabernet Sauvignon)
leads the range – spicy, peppery
palate, velvety tannins, powerful,
impressive structure, seductive
finish. Also good Rosso Piceno.

Le Terrazze, Numana (AN) *r sp sw*
☆☆☆→☆☆☆☆ 20ha, 85,000 bottles.
Antonio Terni is passionate about
this 1884 estate, where the wines
are produced under the guidance
of Attilio Pagli. Highlights: Rosso
Conero Sassi Neri, Visions of J, IGT
Chaos, a Montepulciano/Merlot/
Syrah blend, and Le Cave
(Chardonnay). Powerful, yet

elegant wines from very low yields and highly selected grapes show good ageing potential. Also good pink Spumante Metodo Classico Donna Giulia (Montepulciano).

Umani Ronchi, Osimo (AN) *w r sw* ☆☆→☆☆☆☆ * 230ha, 4,400,000 bottles. Large estate with a quality-orientated production exported worldwide. Highlights: Verdicchio di Jesi Classico Superiore: Casal di Serra and Villa Bianchi; Rosso Conero: Cumaro and San Lorenzo; the full-bodied Pelago, a Cabernet/Merlot/Montepulciano blend, Le Busche (Chardonnay/Verdicchio), Maximo (botrytized Sauvignon), Bianchello del Metauro, and Montepulciano d'Abruzzo.

Vallerosa-Bonci, Cupramontana (AN) *w sw* ☆☆☆ Giuseppe Bonci's vineyards produce fine, aromatic wines showing complexity, structure, and elegance. Highlights: Verdicchio di Jesi Classico: Barré Riserva, Le Case, Pietrone, and San Michele, as well as Passito Royano.

Ercole Velenosi, Ascoli Piceno *w r* ☆☆☆→☆☆☆☆ 100ha, 800,000 bottles. This emerging estate produces fine Rosso Piceno Il Brecciarolo and Roggio del Filare, aged 18 months in barrique – full-bodied, generous, savoury. Also good IGT Ludi, a Montepulciano/Cabernet/Merlot blend – dark, impenetrable, with balsamic and liquorice hints, persistent. Also good Falerio Vigna Solaria, Velenosi Brut Metodo Classico, Chardonnay Rêve, and Sauvignon Linaigre.

Villa Bucci, Ostra Vetere (AN) *w r ris* ☆☆→☆☆☆☆ * 26ha, 100,000 bottles. This estate produces a supreme, long-lived Verdicchio di Jesi Classico and Riserva Villa Bucci, aged 24 months in oak barrels and possibly the area's finest, with plenty of complex, fine aromas. Also highly regarded Merlot/Sangiovese blend Rosso Piceno Tenuta Pongelli – fresh and fruity, to drink young. Giorgio Grai oversees the production.

Fratelli Zaccagnini, Staffolo (AN) *w r sw* ☆☆→☆☆☆ 42ha, 300,000 bottles. Livia Cerioni's production is noted for refined Verdicchio di Jesi Classico Superiore Salmàgina – acacia, peach, and apple aromas mingled with a mineral quality, rich and long. Also very good IGT Vigna Vescovi (Cabernet/Pinot Noir) – floral, wild cherry and tobacco, structured with medium body.

Wine & Food

The food of the Marche draws from both land and sea. Local chefs put the best of both on the table, often together. Roast pig (*porchetta*) is cooked with wild fennel, rosemary, garlic, and pepper, as are duck, rabbit, and even shellfish. Both fowl and fish may be cooked in *potacchio* (with tomato, rosemary, garlic, onion) and white wine.

Anatra in porchetta Duck with wild fennel, ham, and salt pork.

Brodetto Among the many fish soups bearing this name, Ancona's is the most famous, maybe because it includes at least 13 types of fish.

Faraona in potacchio Guinea fowl cooked with onion, garlic, rosemary, tomato, and wine.

Olive all'ascolana Hollowed giant green olives of Ascoli with a meat stuffing, fried in olive oil.

Stocco all'anconetana Salt cod cooked with a sauce of milk, tomatoes, carrots, garlic, rosemary.

Vincisgrassi An elaborate lasagna that includes butter, cream, prosciutto, and black truffles.

Hotel

Albergo San Domenico, Urbino
€€ A beautiful historic hotel built
in the 15th-century, centrally
located in Urbino, in front of the
magnificent Palazzo Ducale.

Ca' Andreana B&B, Frazione
Gadana, Urbino € Country bed &
breakfast 6km (3.7 miles) from the
centre of Urbino. It features six
charming bedrooms and excellent
à la carte dining, alfresco in the
summer. Good parking.

Il Castello di Montegiove, Fano
(PS) €€ This charming hotel is
located within a medieval castle
on the slopes of Monte Giove,
overlooking the sea and the
surrounding countryside.

Comfortable rooms, good
restaurant, and parking.

Hotel Giardino, San Lorenzo in
Campo (PS) € Small hotel with
20 well-furnished rooms. Good
pool and renowned restaurant
with excellent food.

Hotel Monteconero, Sirolo (AN)
€€ This beautifully restored
Romanesque Camaldolese abbey
is a great place to relax and enjoy
the countryside. Good parking.

Hotel Villa Amalia, Falconara
Marittima (AN) € Small hotel with
seven well-equipped rooms with
their own independent entrance
from the courtyard. Good parking,
and an excellent restaurant.

Restaurants

Chichibio, San Benedetto del
Tronto (AP) €€–€€€ Four different
set menus – fish, meat, vegetarian,
and a mix – comprise first-class
dishes blending creativity and
tradition. Good wine list.

La Madonnina del Pescatore,
Marzocca di Senigallia (AN) €€€
Moreno Cedroni's fish restaurant
with cutting-edge, creative
preparations is often voted one of
Italy's top fish restaurants. Prime
ingredients and a good wine list.

Oasi degli Angeli, Cupra
Marittima (AP) €€ Great emphasis
on light dishes that show the
excellence of the primary
ingredients. The restaurant also
serves good wines, home-made
salami, and *olive ascolane*. There is
a winery and lodgings attached.

Osteria dell'Arancia,
Grottammare (AP) €€ Renowned
for traditional dishes, this
restaurant also offers an excellent
tasting menu that will take you
through a real culinary journey.

Good cold meats and cheeses;
excellent wine list.

La Rocca, San Leo (PS) €–€€
Characteristic, rustic ambience
with a large fireplace. Genuine
local fare, cured meats, tortelloni,
strozzapreti (a type of pasta), and
a good selection of cheeses.
Accommodation is also available.

Lo Scudiero, Pesaro €€ Located
in a historic Renaissance building,
this 40-seat restaurant with a nice
ambience serves fine, local food.
Also good wine list.

Symposium, Cartoceto (PS)
€€–€€€ Lucio Pompili is a
passionate and talented chef who
prepares excellent regional fare
with home-grown vegetables,
herbs, fresh fish, and meat.
Excellent desserts and cellar.

Uliassi, Senigallia (AN) €€–€€€€
One of the Marche's top locations
serving good seafood. Specialties
include *fritto misto* (mixed fried
fish), seabass with shellfish sauce,
mussel kebab, and fab desserts.

Tuscany *Toscana*

Tuscans have evolved over a generation from downcast purveyors of flask Chianti into the nation's prime movers of premium wine. The renaissance, as it's called, began in Florence, when the influential house of Antinori revised a 600-year heritage with new styles in wines of international class. Others followed with wines that, rather than purely modern, might better be described as regenerated classics. The epicentre of this oenological revival was Chianti, the heart of Tuscany, but it spread into Montalcino and Montepulciano, and from there across the region and the rest of Italy, attracting a lot of money and talent into the country along the way.

Chianti remains the nucleus of Tuscan viniculture, still the most voluminous of Italy's classified wines and the most prominent expression of the noble Sangiovese vine that dominates the region's reds. But Chianti shares the stage with the majestic Brunello di Montalcino, the impressive Vino Nobile di Montepulciano, the rejuvenated Vernaccia di San Gimignano, the classy Bolgheri, and, increasingly, Morellino di Scansano. This once-minor wine, produced in the hills behind the coastlands of southern Tuscany, has seen unprecedented levels of interest in recent years, with many (mainly Tuscan) leading producers recognizing its potential and scrambling to buy land in the zone. As the results of these investments begin to emerge, Morellino's profile climbs ever higher. The coastal area of Tuscany, known as the Maremma (incorporating Bolgheri, Suvereto, Montescudaio, Val di Cornia, and others) is perhaps one of the most exciting new areas, with the potential to produce young, fruity wines, mingled with elegance, tradition, and a modern style of winemaking.

Chianti was also the original source of those controversial wines that became known as Super Tuscans, a rash of wines of unprecedented quality from producers that scorned DOC restrictions. They caused such intense comment worldwide – and such acute embarrassment internally, on a denomination system that could breed this rebellion – that eventually the entire DOC(G) regulations were overhauled. Now Tuscans are among the most DOC-conscious of Italians, and their denominations are regularly amended to expand their ambit and take improved production criteria into account. The Super Tuscans, the names of which remain well known and highly admired, have therefore either been accommodated back into these revised DOC(G)s or have slipped naturally into an IGT, most commonly Colli della Toscana Centrale or the all-embracing Toscana. Meanwhile many more IGT wines have been spawned, encompassing an unlimited range of grape varieties to the extent that it is practically *de rigueur* to produce at least one.

Modest yields on rugged contours bring volumes in Tuscany to eighth in rank among the twenty regions, but third after Veneto and Piedmont in the production of classified wines. It boasts six of the nation's thirty DOCGs (Brunello, Carmignano, Chianti, Chianti Classico, Vernaccia di San Gimignano, and Vino Nobile) and a further thirty-four DOCs. The elevation of the entire non-*classico* Chianti area (a vast ring around the *classico* heartland producing variable styles and qualities) to DOCG has long been recognized as a clamorous error but one that no longer causes much heartache as ever fewer wines are released under the denomination.

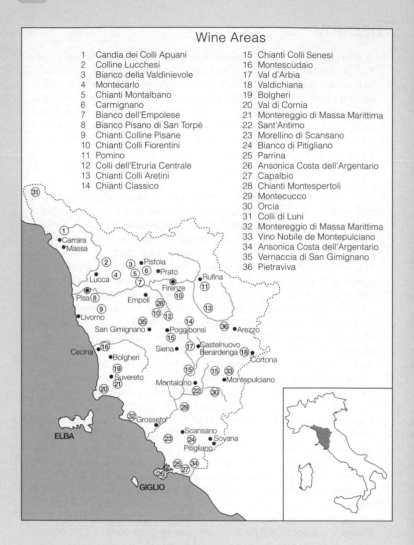

Wine Areas

1	Candia dei Colli Apuani	15	Chianti Colli Senesi
2	Colline Lucchesi	16	Montescudaio
3	Bianco della Valdinievole	17	Val d'Arbia
4	Montecarlo	18	Valdichiana
5	Chianti Montalbano	19	Bolgheri
6	Carmignano	20	Val di Cornia
7	Bianco dell'Empolese	21	Montereggio di Massa Marittima
8	Bianco Pisano di San Torpè	22	Sant'Antimo
9	Chianti Colline Pisane	23	Morellino di Scansano
10	Chianti Colli Fiorentini	24	Bianco di Pitigliano
11	Pomino	25	Parrina
12	Colli dell'Etruria Centrale	26	Ansonica Costa dell'Argentario
13	Chianti Colli Aretini	27	Capalbio
14	Chianti Classico	28	Chianti Montespertoli
		29	Montecucco
		30	Orcia
		31	Colli di Luni
		32	Montereggio di Massa Marittima
		33	Vino Nobile de Montepulciano
		34	Ansonica Costa dell'Argentario
		35	Vernaccia di San Gimignano
		36	Pietraviva

Despite exciting Cabernet/Sangiovese blends, fine reds from Cabernet, Merlot, Syrah, and Pinot Noir, and equally fine whites from Chardonnay, Sauvignon, Viognier, and the Pinots, it is Sangiovese that determines the intrinsic style and eminence of the region's output. Ever-greater concentration on the variety and ever-greater skills in drawing out and fine-tuning its supreme qualities are resulting in wines that grow in stature (and, sadly, price) year after year. Tuscany is less blessed with its native whites, but there have been some surprisingly impressive results from the uninspiring Trebbiano and Malvasia for those who dedicate enough effort to them, and Vernaccia, too, has much to offer the diligent winemaker.

Even non-wine-loving visitors who come to see Florence, Siena, Pisa, and San Gimignano will often tour the scenic vineyards that grace the hillsides, a rural civilization shaped over centuries into a landscape of extraordinary harmony and beauty. The most important wine route is the Chiantigiana, which winds its way through the heart of Tuscany between Florence and Siena (home of the Enoteca Italiana – the national wine library – in the Medici fortress). In Siena's province are the ancient hilltop villages of Montepulciano and Montalcino; the latter houses an *enoteca* for Brunello in the town fortress. Recommended specialist wine shops include Fiaschetteria de' Redi and La Torre di Gnicche in Arezzo, Montagnani in Gaiole in Chianti, Porciatti in Radda in Chianti, I Terzi and San Domenico in Siena, Enoteca Gallo Nero in Greve, Drogheria Franci in Montalcino, Oinochoe in Montepulciano, Enoteca Marsili in Lucca, Di Ghino in Pienza, and Enoteca Gambi and Bonatti in Florence.

Recent Vintages

Chianti Riserva, Vino Nobile, Carmignano, and many Super Tuscans approach their prime around four to seven years, though some vintages favour ageing of a decade or more. Brunello often needs six to ten years to open up, and great vintages can last for decades.

2004 Balanced weather throughout the year, long ripening with good temperature variations, and higher-than-average quantities producing good whites and reds.
2003 Very hot, dry weather throughout the summer, giving ripe wines of concentration, depending on exposition; some may lack elegance.
2002 Despite much thinning of grapes, a rainy summer took its toll. Attractive wines of good drinkability, but few long-livers and only a small number of *crus*.
2001 Another hot, dry summer, but a drop in temperature and some rain prior to harvest ensured impressively fine, balanced wines. A hard frost in spring reduced quantities in some parts.
2000 Very hot, dry weather in August gave full, ripe wines of concentration, although some, in the hottest locations, may lack finesse.
1999 An average harvest in terms of quantity, but of very good quality.
1998 Bumper crop of mixed results due mainly to rain during the harvest; some good to very good red wines were made nonetheless.
1997 Some rate this as the greatest modern vintage for red wines throughout Tuscany, though quantities were painfully limited and prices have risen.
1996 Rain took its toll. Wines often lack substance and strength for long ageing, though good medium-weight reds are available.
1995 Perfect weather in October turned doubts, after a damp summer, to delight in a small but memorable vintage for Brunello, Vino Nobile, and Chianti.
1994 Harvest rains did more harm in Chianti than parts of the south, where Brunello and Vino Nobile ranged from good to excellent.
1993 Rain interrupted picking, but many estates made wines that were very good or better.
1992 Damp and cool weather made this, with few exceptions, a year to forget.
1991 Disappointing after the great 1990, but certain Brunello, Vino Nobile, and Super Tuscans show class.

1990 Small crop considered the greatest of recent times for Chianti and most other reds, with structure to last and harmony evident from the start.
Notes on earlier vintages: 1985, 83, 82, 79, 78, 77, 75, 71, 70, 64, 62, 58, 55, 47, and 45.

Appellations

DOCG
BRUNELLO DI MONTALCINO
r ris 85 88 90 95 96 97 98 99 00 01

This majestic red from Sangiovese, grown in the community of Montalcino, south of Siena, ranks as one of Italy's most prized and most expensive wines. Powerfully structured, it matures in cask and bottle into a warm, amply flavoured wine of deep ruby to brick-red colour and richly complex bouquet. Brunello is capable of austere grandeur with great age. Vineyards and production have expanded dramatically in the last 30 years, from a handful of estates to over 220, and styles have become a little less uniform. Brunello produced on the high, north-facing slopes in the north of the zone tends to be more racy and elegant than the opulent, rich wines from the warm, south-facing vineyards. Oak-ageing is a minimum of two years, within an overall ageing requirement (cask and bottle) of five years, six for the *riserva*.

CARMIGNANO *r ris 85 88 90 92 95 97 98 99 00 01 04*

Recognized as one of Europe's first controlled wine zones by the Grand Duchy of Tuscany in 1716, Carmignano is noted for an aristocratic red. What sets it apart from Tuscany's other Sangiovese-based wines is the inclusion of Cabernet, planted here in the 18th century.

CHIANTI *r ris sup 99 00 01 04*

Produced in a vast hilly ring around the heartland denomination of Chianti Classico (*q.v.*) and covering much of central Tuscany. The zone extends from north of Florence to well south of Siena, and from the first coastal rises inland to the Apennines. Chianti is based on Sangiovese and Canaiolo, with optional small quantities of Cabernet and Merlot to give additional fruity roundness. Many producers make their best wines under other denominations that overlap the Chianti zone and deliberately keep their Chianti fresh and uncomplicated. Chianti is split into seven sub-zones, each with distinct terrains and microclimates.

Sub-zones: Chianti Colli Fiorentini, Chianti Colli Senesi, Chianti Colline Pisane, Chianti Colline Lucchesi, Chianti Montalbano, Chianti Montespertoli, and Chianti Rufina.

CHIANTI CLASSICO *r ris 88 90 93 96 97 98 99 00 01 04*

The Classico is Chianti's heartland, the historical area between Florence and Siena where the original Chianti League was formed in the 13th century. This is also where Barone Bettino Ricasoli devised the formula for Chianti production in the mid-1800s and where today, the "golden triangle" of Castellina, Radda, and Gaiole are considered the true Chianti core. A complex geological structure and microclimatic differences mean that there is considerable variability from commune to commune and, often, from estate to estate. Regular Chianti Classico can be drunk from two to seven years, although many of the leading *riserve* may improve for well beyond a decade from top vintages. Currently, Chianti Classico may come from 80–100% Sangiovese. The additional varieties may include the traditional Canaiolo or Colorino, for instance, or the international Cabernet or Merlot.

VERNACCIA DI SAN GIMIGNANO *w ris 99 00 01 04*

Tuscany's most famous white comes from the ancient Vernaccia vine grown around the medieval town of San Gimignano. At its best, it can show characterful, classy elegance. Diversification has also crept in with many producers making several versions: straight (100% Vernaccia); Vernaccia with Chardonnay (exploiting the 10% of other varieties permitted under DOCG); and *riserva* (often oak-fermented). Age: *riserva* 16 months.

VINO NOBILE DI MONTEPULCIANO *r ris 95 96 97 98 99 00 01 04*

The hill town of Montepulciano in southeast Tuscany is the home of Vino Nobile, which bears family resemblances to both Chianti Classico and Brunello, since its mainstay is Prugnolo Gentile, a variant of Sangiovese. But Vino Nobile di Montepulciano stands in a class of its own, due to the special conditions of soil and climate on the slopes facing the Chiana Valley and the presence in the blend of Canaiolo, which softens Prugnolo's inherent vigour, and Mammolo, which lends a telling bouquet of violets. Normal Vino Nobile does not need as long as Brunello to reach its peak: usually four to seven years, a little longer for the *riserva*. Some producers aim to exalt its elegance, others try for all-out power. Age: 2 years, *riserva* 3 years.

DOC
ANSONICA COSTA DELL'ARGENTARIO *w*

Ansonica and other local varieties.

BIANCO DELLA VALDINIEVOLE *w sw vs*

Trebbiano, Malvasia del Chianti, Canaiolo Bianco, Vermentino, and other local white varieties.

BIANCO DELL'EMPOLESE *w sw vs*

Trebbiano and other local white varieties.

BIANCO DI PITIGLIANO *w sup sp*

Trebbiano, Greco, Malvasia del Chianti Bianca, Verdello, Grechetto, Chardonnay, Pinot Bianco, Sauvignon Blanc.

BIANCO PISANO DI SAN TORPÈ *w sw vs ris*

Trebbiano and other local white varieties.

BOLGHERI & BOLGHERI SASSICAIA *w p r sup sw vs*

Trebbiano, Vermentino, Sauvignon, Cabernet Sauvignon, Cabernet Franc, Merlot, Sangiovese.

CANDIA DEI COLLI APUANI *w fz vs sw*

Vermentino, Albarola, Trebbiano, Malvasia del Chianti.

CAPALBIO *w p r ris vs sw*

Trebbiano, Vermentino, Sangiovese, Cabernet Sauvignon, and other local non-aromatic whites and reds.

CARMIGNANO ROSÉ/BARCO REALE DI CARMIGNANO *r p ris sw vs*

Sangiovese, Canaiolo, Cabernet Franc, Cabernet Sauvignon, Trebbiano, Malvasia del Chianti.

COLLI DELL'ETRURIA CENTRALE *w p r ris sw vs*

Trebbiano, Malvasia del Chianti, Vernaccia, Pinot Bianco, Pinot Grigio, Pinot Nero, Chardonnay,

Sauvignon, Sangiovese, Cabernet Sauvignon, Cabernet Franc, Merlot, Canaiolo.

COLLI DI LUNI *w r ris*
Vermentino, Trebbiano, Canaiolo, Sangiovese, Ciliegiolo.
See also Liguria.

COLLINE LUCCHESI *w r ris vs sw*
Trebbiano, Greco, Grechetto, Vermentino, Malvasia del Chianti, Chardonnay, Sauvignon, Merlot, Sangiovese, Canaiolo, Ciliegiolo.

CORTONA *w p r vs ris*
Chardonnay, Grechetto, Pinot Bianco, Pinot Grigio, Riesling Italico, Sauvignon, Cabernet Sauvignon, Gamay, Merlot, Canaiolo, Sangiovese, Syrah.

ELBA *w p r sw pas sp m ris vs sw*
Trebbiano, Sangiovese, Ansonica, Aleatico, Moscato.

MONTECARLO *w r ris vs sw*
Trebbiano, Sémillon, Pinot Grigio, Pinot Bianco, Vermentino, Sauvignon, Sangiovese, Roussanne, Canaiolo, Ciliegiolo, Colorino, Malvasia del Chianti Nera, Cabernet Franc, Cabernet Sauvignon, Syrah.

MONTECUCCO *w r ris*
Sangiovese, Trebbiano, Vermentino, plus other local non-aromatic red varieties and white varieties.

MONTEREGIO DI MASSA MARITTIMA *w p r nov ris vs sw*
Trebbiano, Vermentino, Malvasia del Chianti, Ansonica, Sangiovese, and other local white and red varieties.

MONTESCUDAIO *w r ris vs sw*
Trebbiano, Chardonnay, Sauvignon, Vermentino, Cabernet, Sangiovese, Merlot.

MORELLINO DI SCANSANO *r ris*
Morellino (a local Sangiovese clone)

MOSCADELLO DI MONTALCINO *w sw vt fz*
Moscato Bianco.

ORCIA *w r nov sw vs*
Sangiovese, Trebbiano Toscano, and other local non-aromatic red and white varieties.

PARRINA *w p r ris*
Sangiovese, Trebbiano, Ansonica, Chardonnay.

PIETRAVIVA *w p r ris sup vs sw*
Merlot, Cabernet Sauvignon, Chardonnay, Sangiovese, Canaiolo, Ciliegiolo, Malvasia del Chianti.

POMINO *w r ris sw*
Pinot Bianco, Chardonnay, Trebbiano, Sangiovese, Canaiolo, Cabernet Sauvignon, Cabernet Franc, Merlot.

ROSSO DI MONTALCINO *r*
Sangiovese.

ROSSO DI MONTEPULCIANO *r*
Sangiovese (locally known as Prugnolo Gentile), Canaiolo, Malvasia del Chianti.

SAN GIMIGNANO *w r ris nov vs sw*
Vernaccia, Trebbiano, Malvasia del Chianti, Sangiovese.

SANT'ANTIMO *w r nov vs ris sw*
Cabernet Sauvignon, Chardonnay, Merlot, Pinot Grigio, Pinot Nero, Sauvignon.

SOVANA *r p sup sw ris*
Sangiovese, Aleatico, Cabernet Sauvignon, Merlot, and other local non-aromatic red varieties.

VAL D'ARBIA *w sw vs*
Trebbiano, Malvasia del Chianti, Chardonnay.

VAL DI CORNIA *w p r pas sw sup ris*
Trebbiano, Vermentino, Sangiovese, Ciliegiolo, Cabernet Sauvignon, Merlot, Aleatico.

VALDICHIANA *w p r fz sp vs ris*
Trebbiano, Chardonnay, Pinot
Grigio, Pinot Bianco, Grechetto,
Malvasia Bianca, Sangiovese,
Cabernet, Merlot, Syrah.

VIN SANTO DEL CHIANTI
w r sw ris
Trebbiano, Malvasia del Chianti,
Sangiovese.

**VIN SANTO DEL CHIANTI
CLASSICO** *w r ris sw*
Trebbiano, Malvasia del Chianti,
Sangiovese.

**VIN SANTO DI
MONTEPULCIANO** *w r ris sw*
Trebbiano, Malvasia del Chianti,
Grechetto, Sangiovese.

IGT
Alta Valle della Greve
Colli della Toscana Centrale
Maremma Toscana
Toscana/Toscano
Val di Magra

Producers

*The key provinces have been
abbreviated as follows:
AR = Arezzo; FI = Firenze;
GR = Grosseto; LI = Livorno;
LU = Lucca; PI = Pisa; SI = Siena.*

Altesino, Montalcino (SI) *r w ris sw*
☆☆→☆☆☆ *90 95 97 98 99 01 03 04*
27ha, 200,000 bottles. Established
in 1970 and housed in the 14th-
century Palazzo Altesi. Highlights:
Brunello di Montalcino Montosoli
– hints of pepper, prunes, mingled
with undergrowth; and Alte
d'Altesi IGT, a rich, full-flavoured
Merlot/Cabernet/Sangiovese blend
aged 14 months in barrique – hints
of tobacco and red berry fruit, fine
persistence. Also excellent Palazzo
Altesi and Rosso di Altesino, both
Sangiovese-based.

Antinori, Florence *r w p ris sw sp*
☆→☆☆☆☆ * *90 93 95 96 97 98 99
01 03 04* (Solaia *also 92 94 02*) One
of Italy's largest and most
prestigious family estates,
renowned globally for a wide
range of quality wines. Its
winemaking history reaches back
to 1385. Today Antinori owns a
total of 1,800ha (more than 1,300 in
Tuscany alone, including in the
Chianti Classico area and the
Bolgheri coastal area), and its 18
million bottle production is
managed by Renzo Cotarella. Top
labels: Tignanello, primarily from
Sangiovese, originally created in
1971 (Italy's first Super Tuscan)
and upgraded by Giacomo Tachis
in 1975 to include 20% Cabernet
Sauvignon; classy Solaia (Cabernet
Sauvignon/Sangiovese/Cabernet
Franc); Guado al Tasso (Cabernet
Sauvignon/Merlot/Syrah). The
wines are aged for 14 months
in barrique, acquiring further
complexity with bottle-ageing.
The Antinori range also includes
Badia a Passignano, a well-reputed
Chianti Classico; Cortona
Bramasole La Braccesca, a 100%
Syrah; Pian delle Vigne Brunello;
La Braccesca Vino Nobile di
Montepulciano; and the good-value
Santa Cristina (Merlot/Sangiovese).

Argiano, Montalcino (SI) *r ris* ☆☆☆ *90
95 97 99 03 04* (Solengo *95 96 97 00
01)* 50ha, 300,000 bottles. With its
15th-century tower, this fabulous
property purchased by Contessa
Noemi Marone Cinzano in 1992
dominates the Orcia Valley, south
of Montalcino. Three top wines
are made under the guidance of
winemakers Giacomo Tachis and
Hans Winding Diers: Brunello di
Montalcino – earthy, with very ripe

solid fruit; IGT Solengo – an extracted, stylish Cabernet/Merlot/Syrah blend, considered one of the top Super Tuscan labels; and the new IGT Suolo, made from 100% Sangiovese and a superb wine, solid, with a firm tannic structure, complex and age-worthy.

Avignonesi, Valiano di Montepulciano (SI) *r w ris sw* ☆☆→☆☆☆☆ *90 93 97 99 03* 116ha, 700,000 bottles. The Falvo brothers' production derives from four small estates focusing on Vino Nobile. Highlights include the Grandi Annate label (Merlot/Cabernet Sauvignon), produced only in top vintages. Avignonesi's praised premium wine, Vin Santo Occhio di Pernice (from Prugnolo Gentile) spends its autumn and winter in the *vinsantaia* until it loses about 70% of its original must juice. It is aged in small casks for about ten years, giving a luscious, richly textured *vin santo,* with layers of depth, complexity, and length.

Badia a Coltibuono, Gaiole in Chianti (SI) *r w p ris sw* ☆→☆☆☆☆ * 70ha, 300,000 bottles, plus 700,000 bottles under négociant operation Coltibuono. This 11th-century Benedictine monastery is among the most scenic wine estates in Tuscany. The property (est. 1846) belongs to the Stucchi Prinetti family, whose wide range includes Chianti Classico wines, Coltus Boni, Chianti Classico Riserva, Selezione RS, and a top Sangiovese labelled as Sangioveto. Coltibuono produces a reliable well-priced range of Chianti and Syrah, as well as Trebbiano, Chardonnay, and Sauvignon under the Cetamura and Cancelli labels. Try the Coltibuono restaurant for alfresco eating with plenty of ambience, excellent service, and good food.

Badia di Maronna, Terricciola (PI) *w r* ☆☆ * 75ha, 180,000 bottles. Filippo Alberti's 1939 estate, where production is overseen by Giorgio Marone, is currently looking to expand its vineyard potential. The top label N'Antia is a well-crafted Sangiovese/Cabernet/Merlot blend – red berries, rich, sapid, and elegant, with a long finish.

Banfi, Montalcino (SI) *r w ris sw sp* ☆→☆☆☆☆ * *90 95 97 99 01 04* 850ha, 10,500,000 bottles. This American-owned estate founded in 1978 by the Mariani family is the largest and the most modern winery in Montalcino. However, above the industrial-scale winery, on top of a hill, sits the emblematic medieval *castello* with a famous glass museum, a wine bar/shop of cathedral proportions, and a *taverna* serving a set Tuscan lunch with five Banfi wines. Highlights: age-worthy Brunello di Montalcino Poggio alle Mura, made only in top vintages; Sant'Antimo Excelsus, a Cabernet/Merlot blend; and Sant'Antimo Summus (Sangiovese/Cabernet/Syrah). All are full-bodied, sturdy reds. Also good value Rosso Cum Laude and Centine.

Biondi-Santi, Montalcino (SI) *r ris* ☆☆→☆☆☆☆ *90 95 97 99 (Schidione 93 95 97 98 00)* Much credit for Montalcino's success should be attributed to the Biondi-Santi family, in particular to Ferruccio Biondi-Santi, who invented Brunello in 1888, after much experimentation. Today Biondi-Santi owns three estates. Il Greppo, from where the unique clone originated, produces their age-worthy top Brunello label, which has maintained its aristocratic status (and relative price) over the years. Villa Poggio Salvis Brunello is more accessible in price and needs less ageing before being ready to drink. The third property is the spectacular Castello di Montepò at

Pancole, near Scansano, producing Morellino and an elegant Schidione Castello di Montepò (Sangiovese/ Merlot/ Cabernet), produced in 2000 as a collector's item.

Il Borro, San Giustino Valdarno (AR) r ☆→☆☆ 40ha, 120,000 bottles. The vineyards of fashion guru Salvatore Ferragamo's family form part of the larger country estate Il Borro, in the Valdarno. Production is overseen by consultant oenologist Niccolò D'Afflitto. Top label Il Borro is a Merlot/Cabernet Sauvignon/ Syrah blend – round, elegant, with fine tannins. Also good Polissena (100% Sangiovese) and Pian di Nova (Sangiovese/Syrah).

Boscarelli, Montepulciano (SI) r ris sw ☆→☆☆☆☆ 90 95 97 99 01 03 2.5ha, 77,000 bottles. Podcri Boscarelli has been with the Genoese Marchesi De Ferrari Corradi family since 1962. Today it is managed by the two sons, Luca and Nicolò, along with winemaker Maurizio Castelli. They produce some of the region's finest Nobile di Montepulciano – elegant, age-worthy. Single-vineyard Nocio dei Boscarelli, aged two years in oak, is a full-bodied, well-structured wine, marked by typical Sangiovese hints of cherry and violet, and a noble, restrained elegance.

Ca' Marcanda, Castagneto Carducci (LI) r w ☆☆→☆☆☆ 60ha, 150,000 bottles. Angelo Gaja's Tuscan estate, founded in 1996 in the Bolgheri DOC, produces fine Mediterranean-style wines, marked by a ripe, fruity warmth. Top labels: international blends Bolgheri Camarcanda and Magari (Merlot/ Cabernet Sauvignon/Cabernet Franc), and Promis, which has some Sangiovese in the blend. The wines are very drinkable at an early age and develop well over a period of eight to ten years.

Cantine Vittorio Innocenti, Montepulciano (SI) r ris sw ☆→☆☆☆ 32ha, 12,000 bottles. This family estate lies between Montepulciano and Montefollonico. Among the highlights: Chianti Colli Senesi, an unfiltered, unfined Sangiovese/Canaiolo blend showing genuine character; and Nobile di Montepulciano, produced with the same traditional philosophy. In addition, the absence of temperature control, the 20 days of maceration, and frequent racking yield a very grapey, intense, yet fresh, quality to the wine, which needs time to open. Outstanding, small production of vin santo.

Carobbio, Greve in Chianti (FI) r ris ☆☆→☆☆☆ 9ha, 45,000 bottles. Monica Pierleoni's vineyard in Panzano makes reliable Chianti Classico wines showing individual character, structure, balance, and longevity. Highlights: Leone, a classy Sangiovese; and Pietraforte, a fruity, full-bodied Cabernet.

Casanova di Neri, Montalcino (SI) r ris ☆☆☆→☆☆☆☆ 90 95 97 99 00 01 03 04 45ha, 175,000 bottles. Giacomo Neri has brought Brunello di Montalcino to the forefront of premium-quality production. His wine comes from very low yields of selected grapes giving a concentrated Sangiovese that is aged in oak without overpowering or interfering with the delicate aromas. Brunello di Montalcino Tenuta Nuova is the estate's top label, followed by Brunello di Montalcino and Rosso di Montalcino. The Sant'Antimo Pietradonice is Cabernet-based with 10% Sangiovese – elegance, structure, balance, and longevity.

Castellare di Castellina, Castellina in Chianti (SI) r w ris sw ☆☆→☆☆☆☆ 90 93 95 97 98 99 00 26ha, 200,000 bottles. Paolo Panerai's is one of

Chianti Classico's top estates. The grapes are organically farmed, yielding elegant Sangiovese. Top labels: I Sodi di San Niccolò (Sangiovese/Malvasia Nera) – great personality, vivacity, persistence, and balance; Chianti Classico Riserva Il Poggiale; and Poggio ai Merli (100% Merlot) – rich, ripe, round, with great length. The *vin santo* also rates high.

Castello di Ama, Gaiole in Chianti (SI) *r w p sw ris* ☆☆☆→☆☆☆☆ *90 93 95 97 99 01 04* (Apparita *90 92 93 94 95 97 98 99 00 01 04*) 82ha, 360,000 bottles. One of Tuscany's top estates. Managed by winemaker Marco Pallanti and his wife Lorenza Sebasti, Ama also features a collection of artistic works carried out in situ by some of the world's top contemporary artists. Ama's wines are renowned for their terroir character, elegance, depth, and longevity. Highlights include Chianti Classico: Castello di Ama and two Sangiovese-based single-vineyards Vigneto Bellavista and Vigneto la Casuccia, produced only in top vintages in limited numbers. Also excellent Rosso di Toscana Vigna L'Apparita (single-vineyard Merlot), classified as one of Tuscany's first premium Merlots.

Castello di Bossi, Castelnuovo Berardenga (SI) *r ris* ☆☆ 124ha, 340,000 bottles. Since the Bacci brothers founded the estate in 1973, they have acquired two other Tuscan properties: Ranieri and Terre di Talamo in the Scansano and Montalcino areas. Highlights: Chianti Classico Berardo Riserva (mellowed by an additional 15% Merlot); Corbaia IGT (a Sangiovese-based wine with some Cabernet Sauvignon); and Girolamo, an opulent 100% Merlot – raspberries, blueberries, chocolate, and mocha.

Castello di Brolio, Gaiole in Chianti (SI) (Barone Ricasoli) *r w ris sw* ☆☆→☆☆☆☆ * *97 99 01 03* 230ha, 2,000,000 bottles. Since the 12th century, Brolio's magnificent castle has towered above the vineyards and olive groves that embrace the medieval town of Gaiole in Chianti. The 18th-century Barone Bettino Ricasoli, twice prime minister of Italy, was responsible for developing the statute of the original Chianti Classico appellation, based on Sangiovese, Canaiolo, and Colorino. The property buys in additional grapes and production is today managed by Barone Francesco Ricasoli. Highlights include Chianti Classico: Castello di Brolio and Rocca Guicciarda Riserva; Campo Ceni (a 100% Sangiovese); and Super Tuscan Casalferro.

Castello dei Rampolla, Panzano in Chianti (FI) *r ris* ☆☆→☆☆☆☆ *90 95 97 99 01 04* 42ha, 90,000 bottles. The splendid Castello dei Rampolla in Panzano's Conca d'Oro, a valley formed by the Pesa stream beneath the town of Panzano, is where some of the finest Chianti Classico originates. The Di Napoli Rampolla family's production, overseen by consultant oenologist Giacomo Tachis, includes fine Chianti Classico and two noble Super Tuscans: Cabernet Sauvignon-based Sammarco and Vigna d'Alceo, which has an additional 15% Petit Verdot – the vine cuttings originate from Château Lafite in Bordeaux.

Castello del Terriccio, Castellina Marittima (PI) *w r* ☆☆→☆☆☆☆ *95 97 00 01* 50ha, 250,000 bottles. Gian Annibale Rossi di Medelana's vines, looked after by wine consultant Carlo Ferrini, produce international- and Mediterranean-style IGT wines. Top labels: Lupicaia, a Cabernet-based wine with 10% Merlot – ripe berries, spice, tobacco, liquorice, depth and persistence; Castello del Terriccio (Syrah/Mourvèdre/Petit Verdot) – hints of prunes, nutmeg, and balsamic notes, round, generous, fleshy on the palate; Con Vento (100% Sauvignon Blanc) – fresh and savoury, with a mineral finish; and Rondinaia (Chardonnay) – fruity, enticing aromatic appeal and good acidity.

Castello di Cacchiano, Monti in Chianti (SI) *r ris sw* ☆☆ 160,000 bottles. Baron Giovanni Firidolfi Ricasoli's formidable 12th-century castle is set in the Chianti hills. Production focuses on a traditional, slightly austere, aristocratic Chianti Classico – elegant and restrained, with depth. Cacchiano also produces an excellent *vin santo* marked by harmony and balance.

Castello di Querceto, Greve in Chianti (FI) *r* ☆☆ 90ha, 800,000 bottles. A traditional Chianti Classico estate producing some classic wines with personality and good ageing capability. Highlights: Riserva Il Picchio, a robust, powerful Sangiovese; and La Corte, a fresher-style Sangiovese. The Chianti Classico wines are produced with indigenous varieties: Sangiovese, Colorino, Malvasia, and Canaiolo.

Castello di Verrazzano, Greve in Chianti (SI) *r ris sw* ☆→☆☆ It was on this magnificent property that Giovanni da Verrazzano, who later sailed to the New World and discovered the bay of New York, was born. The estate's ancient tradition of winemaking is documented as far back as 1170. It is well worth visiting the estate and sampling their Chianti Classico and Super Tuscan Bottiglia Particolare.

Castello di Volpaia, Radda in Chianti (SI) *r ris sw* ☆☆→☆☆☆ *90 95 97 99 00 01 03* 45ha, 290,000 bottles. Castello di Volpaia was one of the founder members of the Consorzio del Chianti Classico, established in 1924. Its 14th-century hamlet and castle were built to guard the fertile valley with its precious olive groves and vineyards. Today production is overseen by consultant oenologist Riccardo Cotarella and includes good Chianti Classico Coltassala Riserva, aged 18 months in barrique – cherry aromas, spice and floral scents; Super Tuscan Balifico, a Sangiovese/Cabernet blend; and a delectable v*in santo.*

Castello Ginori di Querceto, Ponteginori (PI) *w r* ☆☆ * 16ha, 50,000 bottles. Marchesi Ginori Lisci's vines planted to Merlot, Sangiovese, and Cabernet Sauvignon surround the 16th-century castle. This emerging estate started bottling its wines in 2002 under the supervision of consultant oenologist Niccolò d'Afflitto. Today the production includes two fine labels: Castello Ginori, a Merlot/Cabernet Sauvignon blend, and Campordigno (Merlot/Sangiovese).

Cecchi, Castellina in Chianti (SI) *r w ris sw* ☆→☆☆ * The Cecchi family have been active Tuscan wine producers since 1893. Today the 260ha of vines incorporate two estates in Tuscany and one in Umbria, producing a total of seven million bottles. Cecchi combines a traditional style with an innovative technique. This is well reflected in Chianti Classico Villa Cerna Riserva and IGT Spargolo (100% Sangiovese), both discreet and elegant in style. Morellino di Scansano Val delle Rose Riserva is produced at the Maremma estate; Vernaccia di San Gimignano Castello di Montauto, a vibrant white, is produced at the Montauto estate; and Sagrantino Tenuta

Alzatura originates from the Umbrian winery at Montefalco.

Cennatoio, Panzano in Chianti (FI) *r ris* ☆☆→☆☆☆ 16ha, 90,000 bottles. Situated at 600m (1,950ft), Cennatoio dominates the surrounding countryside, with magnificent views over the Conca d'Oro. Founded in 1971 by the Alessi family, this organically grown estate enjoys some of Chianti Classico's best exposures, producing premium wines of great complexity. In addition to Chianti Classico and the Cennatoio Oro Riserva, the Super Tuscan labels are represented by Mammolo (100% Merlot) and Arcibaldo (an elegant Cabernet/ Sangiovese blend aged 18 months in barrique), characterized by structure and length. Also good Etrusco, a superb 100% Sangiovese Grosso.

Cesani, Pancole, San Gimignano (SI) *w r* ☆☆ * 15ha, 85,000 bottles. Letizia and Marialuisa Cesani's estate is one of San Gimignano's emerging lights with two well-made Vernaccias. The Cesani label is vinified in steel – zesty mineral quality, fruit appeal, and medium length; Sanice is partially barrel-fermented.

Chiappini Giovanni (Podere Feliciano), Bolgheri (LI) *r ris* ☆☆ 6ha, 35,000 bottles. Rising star Giovanni Chiappini's estate was converted to vineyards only a few years ago (he started bottling in 1999) and now competes successfully alongside Bolgheri's big names. Highlights: Guado de' Gemoli, a concentrated, extracted Cabernet/Merlot blend; and Bolgheri Rosso Feliciano – a well-crafted Sangiovese/Cabernet/ Merlot blend.

Ciacci Piccolomini d'Aragona, Montalcino (SI) *r ris* ☆☆☆ *90 95 97 98 99 01 04* 40ha, 150,000 bottles. This 17th-century palazzo, now the property of the Bianchini family, is situated in Castelnuovo dell'Abate, south of Montalcino. Production is overseen by consultant oenologist Paolo Vagaggini. The Brunello is traditional and elegant in style, not overly concentrated, but shows depth and good ageing capacity – ripe fruit, gamey, cedar notes, round, balanced, with length. The top Brunello Vigna di Pianrosso is aged three years in Slavonian oak followed by eight months in bottle. Other labels include a Rosso, a Montecucco, and a Sant'Antimo.

Colognole, Rùfina (FI) *r ris* ☆→☆☆ *90 95 97 99 01* 27ha, 100,000 bottles. Mario Coda Nunziante's vines have good exposition and they dominate the valley, at an altitude between 250m and 450m (820ft–1,500ft). The Chianti Rùfina and Riserva show good ripeness and structure.

Il Colombaio di Cencio, Gaiole in Chianti (SI) *r ris* ☆☆→☆☆☆ 30ha, 100,000 bottles. An estate overseen by consultant oenologist Paolo Vagaggini. Top labels: Chianti Classico I Massi – full, round, and expressive in character; Il Futuro, a Sangiovese/Cabernet/ Merlot blend – dark, dense, and rich in berry fruit, elegant, with good minerality and persistence; and Sassobianco, a Chardonnay/Malvasia/Trebbiano/ Sauvignon blend.

Donatella Cinelli Colombini, Montalcino (SI) *r ris* ☆☆→☆☆☆ * *99 01 03 04* An all-female estate (with the exception of consultant oenologist Carlo Ferrini) producing fine Brunello based on Sangiovese Grosso – character and elegance, with depth. Orcia Cenerentola is based on Sangiovese and the unusual varietal Foglia Tonda, an almost extinct local grape that Donatella has revived. The wine, aged 12 months in barrique, has a delicate fruity quality and expresses medium structure and length.

Daviddi, Montepulciano (SI) *r ris sw* ☆☆ *
15ha, 65,000 bottles. Aldimaro
Daviddi is a small emerging
producer with vines cultivated on
clayey, stony grounds at Gracciano,
Valiano, Abbadia, and Acquaviva.
He makes traditional Nobile made
from Prugnolo Gentile, Mammolo,
and Canaiolo – excellent tipicity
and individual character.

Dei, Montepulciano (SI) *r ris sw*
☆☆→☆☆☆ *90 93 95 97 99 01*
(Sancta Catharina also 98 00) 42ha,
140,000 bottles. Maria Caterina
Dei's estate is divided between the
factions of Bossona, Martiera, La
Ciarlana, and La Pioggia. Production
is overseen by consultant oenologist
Niccolò D'Afflitto. Highlights:
Sancta Catharina, the estate's
premium wine, a Prugnolo Gentile/
Cabernet/Syrah blend; and Bossona
Riserva, a traditional, full-bodied
well-extracted Nobile di
Montepulciano – concentration
and fine balance.

Duca, Riparbella (PI) *r* ☆☆ * 6ha. Elena
Celli and Luca D'Attoma's emerging
biodynamic vines of Cabernet
Franc, Merlot, and Syrah are
planted to high density in the
dense, clay-filled, stony-rocky soils
of the Maremma. The wines, aged
12–15 months in barrique, are
elegant, mineral, persistent. Top
labels: Duemani (Cabernet Franc/
Merlot) and Suisassi (100% Syrah).
The estate was granted the official
biodynamic Demeter seal in 2004.

Fattoria dei Barbi, Montalcino (SI)
r w ris ☆→☆☆☆ * *90 95 97 98 03*
90ha, 800,000 bottles. One of
Montalcino's historic estates,
owned by Stefano Cinelli
Colombini, Fattoria dei Barbi now
also boasts a museum based on
Montalcino's arts, crafts, and
rural/wine history. Barbi's wines
focus on a traditional style of
Brunello. Highlights: Brunello di
Montalcino, Rosso di Montalcino,
and Brusco dei Barbi – all 100%
Sangiovese. Also good Morellino
di Scansano Vivaio dei Barbi and
IGT Birbone – a blend with an
international character. The *fattoria*
produces some excellent aged
pecorino cheese and wild boar
salame, both of which can be
sampled at their *taverna*.

Fattori del Cerro, Montepulciano (SI) *r
w ris sw* ☆☆→☆☆☆ 167ha, 790,000
bottles. This large estate belongs
to one of Italy's main insurance
companies, which has invested
in both vineyard management and
technology. Consultant oenologist
Lorenzo Landi oversees the
production of the Vino Nobile di
Montepulciano Vigneto Antica
Chiusina – depth and balance. Also:
Vino Nobile di Montepulciano and
the Rosso di Montepulciano. Corte
D'Oro Vendemmia Tardiva
(Sauvignon Blanc/Moscadello),
an interesting late-harvest.

Fattoria di Petroio, Castelnuovo
Berardenga (SI) *r ris* ☆☆→☆☆☆
95 97 99 01 13ha Gian Luigi and
Pamela Lenzi's estate is planted
to Sangiovese, Malvasia Nera,
Canaiolo, and Ciliegiolo producing
authentic, classic Chianti Classico
characterized by a vivacious,
ripe cherry quality, full-bodied
with structure. The Riserva is
sapid, fruity, with a good undertone
of acidity and silky tannins that
balance well on the palate. Age-
worthy with length and elegance.

Fattoria di Petrolo, Mercatale Valdarno
(AR) *r* ☆☆→☆☆☆ *90 94 95 97 99
00 01 03 04* 31ha, 53,000 bottles.
A well-established Colli Aretini
estate managed by Luca Sanjust,
with production overseen by
consultant oenologist Carlo Ferrini.
The two reds are monovarietal
wines: Galatrona is an elegant,
well-structured Merlot – dark,

pulpy, concentrated, wooded, berries and spice, showing good length; while Il Torrione is a Sangiovese representing a fine expression of the terroir's potential. Their good *vin santo* shows fine balanced elegance and a complex aromatic bouquet.

Felsina, Castelnuovo Berardenga (SI) *r w ris sw* ☆☆☆→☆☆☆☆ *90 93 95 97 99 00 01* 122ha, 450,000 bottles. Felsina's Sangiovese wines are among Tuscany's most respected labels, with worldwide exports. Established in 1966 by the Poggiali family, it wasn't until 1982, when Giuseppe Mazzacolin stepped in with consultant oenologist Franco Bernabei, that Felsina managed to show the true potential of its excellent exposition and terroir. Highlights: Chianti Classico Rancia Riserva, 100% Sangiovese aged 16–18 months in oak and a further 6–12 in bottle; and Fontalloro, an elegant 100% Sangiovese that is aged a little longer in barrique – full-bodied, silky texture, with spicy, peppery notes and a long finish. Both show good ageing potential.

Folonari, Florence (Tenute di Ambrogio & Giovanni Folonari) *r w ris* ☆☆→☆☆☆ 310ha, 876,000 bottles. After the Rufino split in 2000, Ambrogio Folonari and his son Giovanni took over the management of the following estates: in Greve, Tenute del Cabreo, producing Super Tuscan wines, and Tenuta di Nozzole, producing Chianti Classico DOCG; in Montepulciano, Fattoria Gracciano Svetoni, producing Nobile DOCG; in Montalcino, Tenuta La Fuga, producing Brunello; in Chianti Rufina DOCG, Conti Spalletti; and in the Colli Orientali del Friuli, Tenuta di Novacuzzo, producing Pinot Grigio. Each estate has its own individual character with an overall good to high average quality wines. Of particular note: Cabreo Il Borgo, a Super Tuscan; Nozzole Chianti Classico Riserva La Forra; Il Pareto, a 100% Cabernet Sauvignon; and a classy Brunello from La Fuga estate.

Castello di Fonterutoli, Castellina in Chianti (SI) *r ris sw* ☆☆→☆☆☆☆ *90 93 95 97 99 01 03 04* 72ha, 600,000 bottles. The Marchesi Mazzei's magnificent 14th-century castle is one of Tuscany's leading estates. Production is overseen by consultant oenologist Carlo Ferrini. Fonterutoli's Chianti Classico, produced from a noble Sangiovese, is exported worldwide – sapid, with fine, silky tannins, balanced, elegant, persistent. Super Tuscan Poggio Alla Badiola is a Sangiovese-based blend with Merlot and Cabernet, while Siepi (Merlot/ Sangiovese) shows good ageing potential. The 30ha Belguardo estate in Maremma produces fine, fruit-forward Morellino.

Fontodi, Panzano in Chianti (FI) *r ris sw* ☆☆☆→☆☆☆☆ *90 93 95 97 99 01 04* 70ha, 300,000 bottles. Founded in 1981, managed and owned by Giovanni Manetti, this classic estate lies in prime wine country, in the Conca D'Oro. Production is overseen by consultant oenologist Franco Bernabei. Top wines: Flacianello della Piave, a 100% Sangiovese aged 18 months in barrique – extreme elegance, fine tannins, spices, tobacco, leather, and undergrowth, with round ripe fruit; and Vigna del Sorbo Riserva Chianti Classico (Sangiovese with 10% Cabernet), a richly textured wine that rivals the elegance and balance of Flacianello.

Eredi Fuligni, Montepulciano (SI) *r ris* ☆☆→☆☆☆☆ *90 93 95 97 99 01 03 04* 12ha, 45,000 bottles. Roberto Guerrini's production represents one of the most authentic expressions of Brunello, bringing together balance and elegance characterized by fine tannins, depth, and freshness, with good ageing potential.

La Gerla, Montalcino (SI) *r ris* ☆☆☆ *90 93 95 97 99 01 04* 11ha, 80,000 bottles. A small estate with a production overseen by consultant oenologist Vittorio Fiore. Highlights: earthy, elegant Brunello from Sangiovese Grosso – gamey, leather, and cedar notes, with underlying ripe fruit; and a good Super Tuscan IGT Birba, from 100% Sangiovese – ripeness and balsamic notes.

Tenuta di Ghizzano, Ghizzano de Peccioli (PI) *r w ris* ☆☆☆→☆☆☆ 18ha, 50,000 bottles. Rising star Ginevra Venerosi Pesciolini's vineyards are located in the Colline Pisane. Production, overseen by consultant winemaker Carlo Ferrini, focuses on IGT blends and includes international varieties well suited to the soil, climate, and intensity of light. Top labels: Tenuta di Ghizzano Veneroso, a Sangiovese/Cabernet Sauvignon blend – rich in texture, elegant, and fine in style; Nambrot, a Merlot-based wine with Cabernet Sauvignon and some Petit Verdot – concentrated, rich, and balsamic, with dark, ripe fruit, good structure, balance, length, and elegance.

I Giusti e Zanza Vigneti, Fauglia (PI) *w r* ☆☆ 14ha, 65,000 bottles. The production at Paolo Giusti's emerging estate (founded in 1995) is supervised by skilled consultant winemaker Stefano Chioccioli. Two wines stand out: Dulcamara, a modern, concentrated Cabernet Sauvignon-based blend with Merlot – soft, fruity, with a velvety, long finish; and Belcore, Sangiovese-based with Merlot – lighter, fresh, fruity, a pleasure to drink.

Grattamacco, Castagneto Carducci (LI) *w r* ☆☆☆ *90 93 95 98 99 01* 11ha, 45,000 bottles. Founded in 1977 by Piermario e Paola Meletti Cavallari, this is one of the most respected names on the Tuscan coast. The property has recently been rented out to Claudio Tipo (of Colle Massari in the Grosseto province). Grattamacco Rosso is an artful Cabernet/Merlot/Sangiovese blend – fine, silky tannins, ripeness, mineral and balsamic notes; Grattamacco Bianco is a 100% Vermentino – fresh with an aromatic profile of acacia and exotic fruit, with a very long and characteristic bitter-almond finish.

Gualdo del Re, Suvereto (LI) *r* ☆☆ *00 01* 20ha, 90,000 bottles. Suvereto, in the Maremma, is a fairly new area of production. Its rising fame is partly due to Nico Rossi of Gualdo del Re, a passionate, hard-working *vignaiolo* with emerging national and international acclaim. Top labels: Gualdo del Re (100% Sangiovese), Federico I (100% Cabernet), and I Rennero (100% Merlot) – elegant, earthy, full-bodied with vibrant fruit, velvety tannins, and a fine, long finish.

Isole e Olena, Barberino Val d'Elsa (SI) *w r ris sw* ☆☆☆→☆☆☆☆ *90 93 96 97 99 01 03 04* 50ha, 210,000 bottles. Paolo De Marchi takes no short cuts when it comes to vineyard management of his renowned estate. Production focuses on an aristocratic Ceparello (100% Sangiovese) – age-worthy, elegant, structured, with depth. Also excellent 100% Syrah bottled under the label Syrah Collezione De Marchi, and an elegant Cabernet Sauvignon/Cabernet Franc blend aged for 18 months in barrique – excellent complexity and sound ageing capacity. His *vin santo* is characterized by wonderful complex aromas of nuts, toasted almonds, dates, and dried apricots.

Cantine Leonardo da Vinci, Vinci (FI) *r ris* ☆→☆☆ * 3,000,000 bottles. Quality-conscious Tuscan co-op (est. 1961), with 500 members. It is especially commendable for good prices in relation to the quality of wine produced, in particular the Chianti Leonardo and Chianti Riserva Leonardo labels, which are reliable, straightforward Chianti Classico wines. San Zio is a more structured 100% Sangiovese – rich spicy character with hints of cedar and tobacco. Merlot degli Artisti is a 100% Merlot, and Santo Ippolito a Merlot/Syrah blend.

Lisini, Montalcino (SI) *r ris* ☆☆☆→☆☆☆☆ *90 95 97 99* 18ha, 80,000 bottles. This top Brunello estate between Sant'Angelo in Colle and Castelnuovo dell'Abate produces Brunello and Rosso di Montalcino, overseen by consultant oenologist Franco Bernabei. The estate boasts a half-hectare vineyard of pre-phylloxera Sangiovese vines dating back to the mid-1800s. These produce 280 bottles a year of Prefillossero – age-worthy, complex, powerful, with a fine aromatic bouquet. Also excellent single-vineyard Brunello Ugolaia – powerful, mellow, with plum confit, leather, cedar, and moss aromas, balance and persistence.

Le Macchiole, Castagneto Carducci (LI) *r* ☆☆☆→☆☆☆☆ *95 97 98 99 01* 21ha, 90,000 bottles. One of Bolgheri's top estates, headed by Cinzia Merli Campolmi and consultant oenologist Luca D'Attoma. Four very good wines originate: top label Paleo Rosso, 100% Cabernet Sauvignon – bold structure and a spicy, warm, Mediterranean character; Scrio, 100% Syrah – peppery, balsamic character; Messorio, 100% Merlot – solid

fruit, round, full, with aromatic herbs, spices, and chocolate; and Macchiole, the only blended wine. Aged 18 months in barrique and then 24 in bottle, the wines show excellent ageing potential.

Malenchini Diletta, Grassina (FI) *r w sw* ☆☆ * 18ha. Former 11th-century royal hunting lodge producing two main labels: Bruzzico, an intense, well-developed Cabernet Sauvignon/Sangiovese blend – hints of plums, spicy vanilla, and small berry fruit, balanced and persistent; and Chianti Colli Fiorentini, a Sangiovese/Canaiolo Nero blend – cherry and spicy tobacco. Also good *vin santo*.

Mannucci Droandi, Mercatale Valdarno, (AR) *r ris* ☆→☆☆ * Serious producer and emerging estate with 26ha of well-managed vineyards in the Colli Aretini and 6ha in the Chianti Classico. The 55,000-bottle production (aiming to increase to 80,000) includes well-crafted Chianti Colli Aretini DOCG; Ceppeto Chianti Classico; and Campolucci IGT Toscana (an excellent 100% Sangiovese).

Marchesi de' Frescobaldi, Florence *r w ris sw* ☆→☆☆☆☆ * *90 93 95 97 99 00 01 03 04* 1,000ha, 6,700,000 bottles. Founded in 1300, one of Tuscany's most prestigious estates now owns leading Tenuta dell'Ornellaia (*see* separate entry), Castelgiocondo in Montalcino, Castello di Nipozzano in Rufina, and Castello di Pomino in Pomino. Top labels: Lamaione Castelgiocondo (a Mondavi-Frescobaldi joint venture), an international-style Merlot aged 24 months in barrique – smoky, tobacco, and vanilla aromas; Chianti Rufina Riserva Nipozzano; and Mormoreto Castello di Nipozzano (Cabernet Sauvignon/Merlot/Cabernet Franc) – opulent in character, with incredible structure, concentrated, with underlying ripe fruit and hints of liquorice and leather. A crisp Chardonnay-based white comes from the high vineyards at Pomino, along with a classic 100% Chardonnay aged 12 months in barrique.

La Massa, Panzano in Chianti (FI) *r ris* ☆☆☆ *95 97 99 00 01 03 04* 27ha, 100,000 bottles. La Massa has been producing wine since the 1400s. Neapolitan-born Giampaolo Motta's southeast- and southwest-facing vines are situated in some of Chianti's most privileged sites and create some of Chianti Classico's most sought-after wines. Modern in style, his production reflects the potential of the terroir and Carlo Ferrini's fine winemaking. Motta has opted to produce Super Chianti Classico wines, rather than Super Tuscans. He blends some Merlot in with the prevalent Sangiovese, both picked at peaks of ripeness. The top label is Giorgio I, Sangiovese-based with a little Merlot – elegant, polished, with good fruit ripening and concentration; La Massa, with a slightly higher percentage of Merlot, is the second label and follows in style.

Mastrojanni, Montalcino (SI) *r ris* ☆☆☆ *90 93 95 97 99 01 04* 24ha, 80,000 bottles. Mastrojanni's vines are situated in Castelnuovo dell'Abate and produce elegant Brunello wines under the guidance of consultant oenologist Maurizio Castelli. Both the Brunello di Montalcino and the Riserva are noteworthy for their classic style. The Schiena d'Asino, produced only in top vintages, is an age-worthy, powerful, complex wine. Also good *passito* Botrytis made with Candia and Sauvignon.

Il Molino di Grace, Panzano in Chianti (FI) *r ris* ☆→☆☆ 30ha, 130,000 bottles. US business magnate Frank Grace's scenic estate, founded in 1999, is managed by Gerhard Himer, with the assistance of consultant oenologist Franco Bernabei. The production shows good potential for Sangiovese-based wines. Top labels: straight Chianti Classico and Chianti Classico Il Margone Riserva – ripe cherries and plums, deep warmth, and a long, balanced, fine finish. The Gratius label is a more complex 100% Sangiovese, made from very selected grapes – concentrated and powerful, it promises to age well.

Montenidoli, San Gimignano (SI) *w r* ☆☆→☆☆☆ 20ha, 130,000 bottles. Elisabetta Fagiuoli's organic estate overlooks the hills of San Gimignano and produces Vernaccia and Chianti Colli Senesi. The Vernaccia labels include: Vernaccia Tradizionale, Vernaccia Fiore, and top label Vernaccia Carato, aged 12 months in oak – structured and elegant, long and sapid. The reds range from Chianti Colli Senesi to Il Garrulo (Sangiovese/Canaiolo). Top red Sono Montenidoli is from selected Sangiovese grapes, vinified separately and aged in barrique. Both the whites and the reds are food-friendly wines, with individual personality and longevity.

Monsanto, Barberino Val d'Elsa (SI) *r w* ☆☆→☆☆☆ *90 95 97 99 00 01 03 04* 70ha, 400,000 bottles. Fabrizio Bianchi's estate (founded in 1961) is managed by his daughter Laura. The wines, which age in an impressive vaulted cellar, include excellent Chianti Classico Riserva Il Poggio (Sangiovese with some Canaiolo and Colorino) – robust, fragrant in ripe, fruity aromas, good depth and persistence. Other labels include well-made, full-bodied Chardonnay Fabrizio Bianchi and ripe, full-bodied, round, mineral Cabernet Nemo Vigneto il Mulino.

Montepeloso, Suvereto (LI) *r* ☆☆☆ *97 99 00 02* 7.5ha. Small leading estate with vines in DOC Val di Cornia producing individual, quality-driven wines. Highlights: Nardo, a Sangiovese/Montepulciano/Cabernet blend – concentrated, earthy, full-bodied, densely textured; and Gabbro (Cabernet Sauvignon/Cabernet Franc) – good mineral character, full-bodied, vigorous, and vibrant. Also two monovarietal wines (a Syrah and a Sangiovese) showing the potential of the Maremma's coastal lands.

Montevertine, Radda in Chianti (SI) *w r ris* ☆☆→☆☆☆ *90 95 99 01* 13ha, 55,000 bottles. This estate was founded in 1967 by Sergio Manetti, who was instrumental in the renaissance of Tuscan wines and one of Chianti's legendary personalities. Today his son Martino and Klaus Reimitz, with consultant oenologist Giulio Gambelli, manage the estate, which comprises a production of wines aged in traditional Slavonian oak barrels. Top, age-worthy wines include Le Pergole Torte, a 100% Sangiovese – elegant complexity, full-bodied, balanced, with hints of ripe cherries, tobacco, and cedar; and Montevertine, a classic Sangiovese – vibrant and dynamic in character.

Moris Farms, Massa Marittima (GR) *r ris* ☆→☆☆☆ * 70ha, 400,000 bottles. Adolfo Parenti's production, overseen by consultant oenologist Attilio Pagli, includes Morellino di Scansano, an earthy, ripe, everyday Sangiovese that together with the Riserva represents excellent quality at a reasonable price. Top label Avvoltore is a powerful structured Sangiovese (with some Cabernet and Syrah) – soft, warm notes of ripeness mingled with balsamic, spices, silky tannins, persistent.

Pacenti Siro, Montalcino (SI) *r ris* ☆☆→☆☆☆☆ *90 95 97 99 04* 20ha, 50,000 bottles. Each year Giancarlo Pacenti's production of Brunello is reconfirmed among Montalcino's top labels. Since 1971, the Pacenti family, assisted by Bordeaux consultant oenologist Yves Glorie, have gained worldwide acclaim for a highly personalized style of Brunello produced from very low yielding vines that demand careful management. Both the Brunello di Montalcino and the Riserva are characterized by their rich aromatic profile – hints of ripe plums and almonds, full, with fine grain, tight tannins, very deep and persistent, with good complexity that reveals its true character with ageing.

Il Palagione, San Gimignano (SI) *w r* ☆☆→☆☆☆ * 10ha, 35,000 bottles. Giorgio Comotti's production includes top label Hydra, a 100% Vernaccia left on the lees until March and vinified in steel – good fruit, structure, and a long, fresh focus. Also good Antajir, a Sangiovese/Cabernet/Merlot blend – full-bodied, with a brambly quality, well-balanced between fruit, acidity, and length.

Il Palazzino, Gaiole in Chianti (SI) *r ris* ☆☆☆ *90 91 95 97 98 00 01* 12ha, 60,000 bottles. A small estate in Monti in Chianti where production includes fine Chianti Classico from Sangiovese Grosso (labelled under Argenina and La Pieve). Casina Girasole IGT, a fine, fruity, fresh bottling of Sangiovese, Malvasia Nera and Canaiolo, highlights the potential of Tuscany's native grapes.

Panizzi Giovanni, San Gimignano (SI) *w r* ☆☆→☆☆☆ 30ha, 200,000 bottles. Established in 1989 with a production of Colli Senesi reds and white Vernaccia di San Gimignano. Highlights include Vernaccia di San Gimignano Vigna

Santa Margherita – balance and elegance, delicate floral aromas, full on the palate, crisp, with a persistent mineral finish.

Petra, Suvereto (LI) *r* ☆☆→☆☆☆ * 93ha, 200,000 bottles. Vittorio Moretti's estate (founded in 1997) is a rising star in the Maremma, with a state-of-the-art winery inaugurated in 2003. Oenologist Francesca Moretti produces an elegant blend of Merlot and Cabernet Sauvignon under the top label Petra. It is a powerful, structured wine, characterized by fine tannins, excellent balance, and length. Other labels include a 100% Merlot and other international blends.

Podere Le Bonce, Castelnuovo Berardenga (SI) *r* ☆☆☆ 3ha, 13,000 bottles. Giovanna Morganti's bush-trained vines include Sangiovese, Colorino, Mammolo, and Foglia Tonda. It is precisely these local varietals, the well-managed vines, and the lack of cellar technology that produce authentic Chianti Classico Le Trame, reflecting true terroir expression. The production is personally overseen by Morganti.

Podere Uccelliera, Montalcino (SI) *r ris* ☆☆→☆☆☆ 6ha, 30,000 bottles. Paolo Cortonesi's production expresses true terroir character. His Brunello di Montalcino is marked by vigorous structure, a ripe aromatic profile of prunes, tobacco, leather, and spice, balanced by acidity, full on the palate, with mineral notes, rustic elegance, and a long, savoury finish. IGT Rapace, a Sangiovese with 20% Merlot and 10% Cabernet, is an inky, full, soft, round wine, characterized by berry fruit and undergrowth.

Poliziano, Montepulciano (SI) *r* ☆☆→☆☆☆ *90 93 95 97 99 00 01 03 04* 140ha, 600,000 bottles. Federico Carletti's leading Nobile estate, with a production overseen by winemaker Carlo Ferrini, focuses on polished, modern Nobile planted to high density and select Sangiovese aged in barrique. Top labels include single-vineyard Vino Nobile di Montepulciano Asinone – vibrant aromatic profile, firm, full-bodied, with a good structure and a smooth, long finish; Le Stanze del Poliziano (Cabernet/Merlot/Sangiovese), international in style – elegance, depth, with balsamic character; and Mandorle del Lhosa, a juicy, ripe Sangiovese and Ciliegiolo from the Morellino estate.

Le Pupille, Piagge del Maiano (GR) *r w* ☆☆→☆☆☆ * 74ha, 600,000 bottles. Elisabetta Geppetti and Stefano Rizzi's Maremma estate is known for top-quality concentrated ripe wines, starting with Saffredi, the estate's top label, a Merlot/Cabernet/Alicante label – extremely sapid in character, with ripe, concentrated fruit, balsamic and round, with balanced elegance. Also good Morellino Poggio Valenete and late-harvest Solalto (Sauvignon/Sémillon/Traminer).

Querciabella, Greve in Chianti (FI) *w r ris* ☆☆→☆☆☆ (Chianti Classico *97 99 00 01 02*; Batàr *97 98 00 01 03*; Camartina *90 95 97 99 00 01*) 60ha, 200,000 bottles. Giuseppe Castiglioni's vineyards have been biodynamically farmed since 2000. Production is overseen by consultant oenologist Giacomo Tachis and includes Chianti Classico and Riserva, plus Super Tuscans: Camartina (Sangiovese/Cabernet/Syrah), aged 18–24 months in barrique, can age 15–20 years – rich, persistent bouquet of morello cherries, hints of tobacco and spice; Palafreno (Merlot/Sangiovese) – intense, concentrated berries and prunes, elegant in style; and Batàr (Chardonnay/Pinot Bianco) – fine, fresh, and balanced.

La Regola, Riparbella (PI) *w r* ☆☆ 13ha, 40,000 bottles. At Luca Nuti's emerging Montescudaio estate, the emphasis is depth rather than width. Influenced by the River Cecina, which creates a good temperature range, the wines are characterized by distinct aromas, elegance, and fresh acidity. Top labels: La Regola, a concentrated, fruity Sangiovese/Cabernet Sauvignon/Merlot blend; and Vallino Delle Conche (Sangiovese-based with Cabernet Sauvignon). Also good Steccaia, a zesty Vermentino/Sauvignon blend, and Passito Sondrete.

Riecine, Gaiole in Chianti (SI) *r ris* ☆☆→☆☆☆☆ *90 95 97 98 99 01 04* 40,000 bottles. Renowned Chianti Classico estate producing Chianti Classico, Riserva, and La Gioia IGT Toscana (100% Sangiovese). Sean O'Callaghan ably manages both the estate and the winemaking. The wines are characterized by fresh vibrant fruit, structure, elegance, and balance, with well-integrated use of oak and a persistent finish. They tend to show good ageing capability.

Rocca delle Macie, Castellina in Chianti (SI) *w r ris* ☆☆→☆☆☆☆ * 250ha, 5,000,000 bottles. The Zingarelli family's estate, including Riserva di Fizzano, Tenuta Sant'Alfonso, and holdings in Maremma, rates as one of the largest Chianti Classico wineries. Top labels include Chianti Classico Riserva di Fizzano and Chianti Classico Tenuta Sant'Alfonso – both excellent Sangiovese; Roccato, a Cabernet/Sangiovese Grosso blend; and Ser Gioveto (Sangiovese/Cabernet/Merlot).

Rocca di Castagnoli, Gaiole in Chianti (SI) *r ris sw* ☆☆→☆☆☆☆ 130ha, 200,000 bottles. Emerging Chianti Classico estate. The Chianti Classico Riserva Capraia and Riserva Poggio à Frati wines are well-structured, showing elegance and balance. Super Tuscan labels include La Pratola, an elegant, silky Merlot; Burlano, a full-bodied, concentrated Cabernet, with hints of spice; and Stielle, a Sangiovese/Cabernet blend with mineral character and complexity showing the potential of the terroir. The wines are aged for about 15 months in barrique, except the *vin santo*, which is aged 72 months in small casks.

Rocca di Montegrossi, Gaiole in Chianti (SI) *r ris sw* ☆☆→☆☆☆☆ *90 93 95 98 99 01 03 04* 18ha, 70,000 bottles. Marco Ricasoli Firidolfi's is one of Chianti Classico's most inspiring estates, producing wines that express individual personality and genuine terroir appeal. Vigneto San Marcellino Riserva is a 100% Sangiovese from a single vineyard, produced only in top vintages – elegant, vibrant in acidity, dynamic structure and mineral complexity as it evolves slowly. Geremia, also produced only in top vintages, was born a pure Sangiovese but has evolved to a blend of Cabernet and Merlot. The *vin santo* (particularly 1977) is classic, with great length and complexity.

Massimo Romeo, Montepulciano (SI) *r ris sw* ☆☆☆ Romeo is one of Nobile's most coherent producers, never wavering to fads or market trends. His purist winemaking philosophy is reflected in some excellent wines. His classic, authentic Nobile is a fine expression of the power and character of Montepulciano. Top label single-vineyard Riserva dei Mandorli, produced from Sangiovese and Mammolo, is sapid with silky tannins and vibrant acidity – complex notes of tobacco and liquorice, floral and ripe cherries, long and elegant.

Ruffino, Pontassieve (FI) *w r ris* ☆→☆☆☆ 600ha, 14,000,000 bottles. In 2000 the Folonari family, owners of Ruffino, split up their assets, and the new generation, Adolfo and Luigi Folonari, took the helm with enthusiasm and desire for change, continuing the production of wines with a keen focus on quality. The estates comprise: La Solatia near Monteriggioni, producing white wines; Lodola Nuova Estate in Montepulciano, for the production of Vino Nobile; and Greppone Mazzi in Montalcino, for Brunello wines. Pontassieve remains the headquarters where the three Chianti Classico estates (Gretole, Montemasso, and Santedame) are vinified. The Murlo estate, purchased in 2001 is managed by Carlo Ferrini, who oversees the vineyards, vinification, and ageing. The first harvest is to be released in 2005. Ruffino's classic Chianti Classico Riserva Ducale, first produced in 1927, was one of the first ambassadors of quality Chianti Classico wines.

Russo, Suvereto (LI) Podere Metocchina, *r w* ☆☆→☆☆☆ 5ha, 45,000 bottles. Maremma's rising star Michele Russo has vines producing well-structured, generous wines, such as Barbicone, a Sangiovese/Ciliegiolo blend – concentrated, ripe, fruity, aromatic complexity and freshness; Sasso Bucato (Merlot/Cabernet) – generous and balanced with persistence; and Pietrasca (Chardonnay/Vermentino) – well-structured, with lengthy tropical bouquet.

Salustri, Poggi del Sasso (GR) *w r* ☆☆→☆☆☆ * 15ha, 60,000 bottles. Marco Salustri's estate in the Montecucco DOC boasts a growing production overseen by competent consultant oenologist Maurizio Castelli. Farmed organically, with good management and the utmost respect for the environment, his vineyards produce three fine Sangiovese-based reds from low-yielding vines: Marlero, Santa Maria, and Grotte Rosse. All are basically 100% Sangiovese, expressing individual character and showing solid, sapid fruit, elegance, and persistence. The reds are fermented in tonneau, with a long 180-day maceration of the lees. Also good, vibrant, aromatic Narà Vermentino.

San Felice, Castelnuovo Berardenga (SI) *w r ris* ☆☆→☆☆☆☆ *90 95 97 99 01 04* 180ha, 1,100,000 bottles. This small medieval hamlet incorporates Relais and country lodging, with vines set in the Val d'Arbia. Top labels: elegant Chianti Classico Il Grigio Riserva; and Super Tuscan Vigorello, a Sangiovese/Cabernet Sauvignon/Merlot blend aged 20 months in barrique – full-bodied, with impressive structure. San Felice also owns the small Brunello di Montalcino Campogiovanni estate, producing some excellent, age-worthy, traditional Brunello and Riserva wines.

San Giusto a Rentennano, Gaiole in Chianti (SI) *r ris sw* ☆☆→☆☆☆☆ *90 93 95 97 99 01 03 04* 30ha, 85,000 bottles. Brothers Francesco and Luca Martini di Cigala's production includes some of the top Sangiovese wines in the area. Top label Percarlo (100% Sangiovese) is a bold wine showing terroir character, aged 22 months in barrique – crushed cherries, spice, and tobacco, persistent and age-worthy. Also noteworthy are Chianti Classico Le Broncole and La Ricolma, an elegant Merlot –

herbaceous quality, round and very long on the palate. The Vin Santo San Giusto 1997 is exquisitely complex and very long.

San Guido, Bolgheri (LI) *r* ☆☆→☆☆☆☆ 90ha, 390 bottles. Marchesi Incisa della Rocchetta's premium estate (founded in 1940) is an emblem of excellence in Italian winemaking, especially since Mario Incisa della Rocchetta and winemaker Giacomo Tachis blended the first Sassicaia here in 1968. A fine, aristocratic blend of Cabernet Sauvignon (85%) and Cabernet Franc (15%) aged 24 months in barrique, Sassicaia is one of the first Super Tuscans. Today it represents 50% of the estate's production; the rest is split between the fairly recent Guidalberto label (a Cabernet Sauvignon/Merlot/Sangiovese blend), and the latest label Le Difese, a more accessible Sangiovese with 15% Cabernet Sauvignon – ripe blackberry and spice with a fresh, balanced finish.

San Luciano, Monte San Savino (AR) *w r* ☆☆ 63ha, 120,000 bottles. The production at this emerging Valdichiana estate includes two Trebbiano-based whites with Chardonnay/Grechetto/Vermentino, and three reds: Colle Carpito, Sangiovese-based with Montepulciano; Boschi Salviati, same blend, with an addition of Cabernet; and top label age-worthy D'Ovidio IGT Toscana, a Sangiovese/Montepulciano/Merlot/Cabernet Sauvignon blend aged 18 months in Allier – fine complexity, depth, and individual personality.

Enrico Santini, Castagneto Carducci (LI) *w r* ☆☆ * Enrico Santini's emerging garage winery, situated under the medieval village of Castagneto Carducci, produces two Bolgheri DOC reds: Poggio Al Moro, a Cabernet Sauvignon/Sangiovese/Merlot/Syrah blend – full-bodied, dark, and rich; and Montepergoli, made from a selection of international varieties vinified separately. His Bianco Campo alla Casa is a Vermentino with hints of tropical fruit.

Michele Satta, Castagneto Carducci (LI) *w p r* ☆☆→☆☆☆ 30ha, 170,000 bottles. One of the coast's top estates, producing wines with a good quality/price ratio. Its reliable track record goes back to 1984. Satta's wines are based on balance and elegance, in particular his Sangiovese Toscana Rosso IGT Cavaliere and Bolgheri Rosso DOC Piastraia. Good Toscana Bianco IGT Costa di Giulia (Vermentino/Sauvignon) and elegant IGT Giovin Re, a new addition from 100% Viognier, plus refreshing Bolgheri Rosato DOC.

Selvapiana, Pontassieve (FI) *r ris sw* ☆☆→☆☆☆ 60ha, 180,000 bottles. Francesco Giuntini's Rufina wines show a pedigree of their own. The leading label is a single-vineyard wine, Chianti Rufina Riserva Vigneto Bucerchiale – deep garnet red, with a concentrated ripe cherry bouquet mingled with spice and floral scents, firm structure, depth, and ample acidity, with a long, fine finish. Aged 15 months in Slavonian oak casks, the wine can age for about 12–15 years. The production is overseen by Franco Bernabei.

Sesti, Montalcino (SI) *r ris* ☆☆→☆☆☆ * 8ha, 55,000 bottles. The splendid Castello di Argiano, owned by astronomer Giuseppe Sesti, produces a biodynamic Brunello full of persuasive personality. The Brunellos and the Riservas are traditional in style, with hints of liquorice, leather, tar, and sweet aromatic tobacco, balanced by freshness and persistence. The estate also produces Sant'Antimo, a rich and round blend of Merlot and Cabernet, and Grangiovese (100% Sangiovese).

Le Sorgenti, Bagno a Ripoli (FI) *w r sw* ☆☆ * 12ha, 40,000 bottles. Elisabetta and Gabriele Ferrari's production includes well-priced Chianti Respiro, made to drink young; and Scrius, the top label, a low-yielding Merlot/Cabernet Sauvignon blend – full-bodied, with a rich texture, ripe fruit, long, balanced, and elegant. The new label Gaiaccia is a promising Sangiovese/Merlot blend.

Tenimenti Luigi d'Alessandro, Cortona (AR) *w r* ☆☆→☆☆☆ 45ha, 150,000 bottles. The d'Alessandro brothers' estate is among Tuscany's rising stars. Assisted by consultant oenologist Stefano Chioccioli, the brothers produce, among other wines, DOC Cortona Syrah, a monovarietal wine – juicy, ripe fruit, fleshy, with pulp, round, rich in aromatic complexity, with fine, silky tannins and a long, elegant finish balanced with acidity; and Fontarca IGT, a Chardonnay/Viognier blend – rich, exotic, elegant, and crisp.

Tenuta dell'Ornellaia, Bolgheri (LI) *r* ☆☆→☆☆☆☆ 90 95 97 98 99 01 91ha, 600,000 bottles. Founded in 1981 by Ludovico Antinori, Ornellaia, a flagship of Italian premium production, was recently bought out by Marchesi de' Frescobaldi. Production focuses on Bordeaux-style wines, including Bolgheri Superiore Ornellaia, a full-bodied, seductive Cabernet Sauvignon/Merlot/Cabernet Franc blend, aged 18 months in barrique – blackberries, liquorice with Mediterranean warmth, depth. Its younger brothers, Le Volte and Le Serre Nuove, are equally suave reds, and more approachable at an earlier age. The top label Masseto, an age-

worthy 100% Merlot, reflects terroir character – fine, silky tannins, fresh, fruit-forward appeal, and elegance.

Tenuta di Capezzana, Carmignano (PI) *r p w ris sw* ☆→☆☆☆ 90 95 99 00 01 106ha, 600,000 bottles. Capezzana, founded by the Contini Bonacossi family, is by far one of the most aristocratic and historic estates in Carmignano. In 1960 Count Ugo Contini Bonacossi brought back Cabernet Sauvignon cuttings from Château Lafite in Bordeaux, which he planted and consequently blended to Sangiovese. Today the production is fine-tuned by Tuscany's consultant oenologist Stefano Chioccioli. Highlights include an excellent Carmignano DOCG and a well-crafted Super Tuscan Ghiaie delle Furba. The *vin santo* is also top notch, aged five years in *caratelli*. Both the estate and *vinsantaia* are well worth visiting.

Tenuta di Trinoro, Sarteano (SI) *r* ☆☆☆ 99 01 03 28ha, 81,000 bottles. Andrea Franchetti's vines, planted to a density of 10,000 plants per hectare, produce some international-style cult wines, including Le Cupole, a Cabernet Franc/Merlot/Cabernet Sauvignon blend showing instant appeal – sweet tannins, round and fleshy, with crushed cherries. Tenuta di Trinoro (Cabernet Franc/Merlot/Cabernet Sauvignon/Petit Verdot) is a weighty, full-bodied wine, fresh, with ripe fruit and spice.

Tenuta il Poggione, Montalcino (SI) *r ris* ☆☆☆ 90 95 97 99 113ha, 500,000 bottles. Historic Montalcino estate founded in 1800 at Sant'Angelo in Colle with a production of fine Brunello di Montalcino and Riserva. Both wines are well-structured and elegant, showing ripeness, minerality, and complexity. They will age with grace and elegance.

Tenuta Sette Ponti, San Giustino Valdarno (AR) *r* ☆☆→☆☆☆☆ 75ha, 166,000 bottles. Antonio Moretti is among the area's rising stars. Assisted by consultant oenologist Carlo Ferrini, he produces wines that are well structured and elegant in style. Highlights include IGT: Crognolo, a polished Sangiovese-based wine, and Oreno, a Sangiovese/Cabernet blend. Moretti's Maremma estate Poggio al Lupo produces an interesting IGT blend of Cabernet Sauvignon, Alicante, and Petit Verdot – rich, elegant, and vibrant.

Tenuta di Valgiano, Valgiano (LU) *w r* ☆☆→☆☆☆☆ * *95 97 99 01 03 04* 16ha, 45,000 bottles. Moreno Petrini's production of commendable DOC Colline Lucchesi is driven by terroir character and quality. Highlights include Tenuta di Valgiano, a Sangiovese-based wine with 20% Syrah, aged 18 months in barrique – concentrated, complex, and structured; Scasso Lucchesi, a 100% Sangiovese aged 18 months in barrique and 12 in bottle – savoury bouquet of ripe cherries, plums, and chocolate, sustained by vibrant acidity; Palistorti, a well-priced, less complex Sangiovese with Syrah and Merlot; and Giallo dei Muri, a crisp Vermentino/Trebbiano/ Malvasia blend – hints of broom, cedar, and grapefruit.

Terradonna, Suvereto (LI) *w r* ☆☆ * 5ha, 15,000 bottles. Nedi Collaveri's emerging estate was established in 2002 with vines planted to a high density on the slopes of the Val di Cornia DOC. Production is overseen by consultant oenologist Luca d'Attoma. Highlights include Prasio, a Sangiovese/Cabernet blend; Kalsi, a vibrant 100% Vermentino; and the top label

Okenio (Cabernet/Merlot), aged 12 months in barrique.

Tua Rita, Suvereto (LI) *w r* ☆☆→☆☆☆ This Maremma estate produces full-bodied, fruit-forward reds made from international varieties planted to a high density with low yields. Redigaffi is an expensive Merlot – impressive on the nose, with rich, concentrated jammy fruit and warm balsamic notes. Giusto dei Notri, produced from a Cabernet Sauvignon/Merlot/ Cabernet Franc blend, is similar in style – opulent and weighty.

Vecchie Terre di Montefili, Greve in Chianti (FI) *w r* ☆☆→☆☆☆ *90 93 95 97 98 99 00 01* 13ha, 65,000 bottles. Roccaldo Acuti's production of quality-driven Super Tuscan and Chianti Classico wines is assisted by consultant winemaker Vittorio Fiore. Highlights: Anfiteatro, 100% Sangiovese – structured, complex, fine tannins, spice, with a long finish; Bruno di Rocca, an elegant Cabernet/Sangiovese blend – ripe, fruity bouquet, balanced and fresh; and Vigna Regis (Chardonnay/Sauvignon/ Gewürztraminer) – full, aromatic, and fresh, with a mineral finish.

Vicchiomaggio, Greve in Chianti (FI) *r ris* ☆☆→☆☆☆ 33ha. John Matta's vines produce some fine reds, including IGT Ripa delle More (Sangiovese/Cabernet/ Merlot); and Chianti Classico La Prima Riserva, 100% Sangiovese usually harvested in October – ripeness, complexity with depth. Also very good Chianti Classico San Jacopo Vicchiomaggio.

Vignamaggio, Greve in Chianti (FI) *r ris sw* ☆☆ 40ha, 240,000 bottles. Giovanni Battista Nunziante, assisted by oenologist Giorgio Marrone, owns one of Tuscany's legendary Renaissance properties, surrounded by an elegant garden.

This prestigious property claims fame from Leonardo da Vinci's Mona Lisa, said to have been born at Vignamaggio in 1479. The production includes Chianti Classico, as well as an elegant Cabernet Franc – depth and length. Wine Obsession, a Merlot/Syrah/ Cabernet Sauvignon blend, is a concentrated, international-style, fruit-forward wine.

Villa Cafaggio, Panzano in Chianti (FI)
 r ris ☆☆→☆☆☆ *95 97 99 01 03*
 31ha, 400,000 bottles. Renowned

estate with a production that includes top label San Martino, a 100% Sangiovese – rich, ripe, fleshy, with a powerful structure, showing depth, elegance, and persistence. Cortaccio is 100% Cabernet aged for 18 months – rich in colour and texture, savoury, with balsamic notes, silky, and elegant. Both wines together with the Chianti Classico Riserva are potentially age-worthy.

Wine & Food

Tuscan food is a triumph of nature; simplified country cooking, it lacks imagination, but expresses an almost mystical symbiosis between a people and their land. The elaborations exported to France by the Medici are long gone and mostly forgotten. Also vanishing, sadly, are the inspired dishes that used to take the Tuscan *massaia* (housewife) all morning to create. But the basics are still there: country bread baked in wood-fired ovens and the emerald-green extra virgin olive oil that combine so well in *bruschetta* and *pane unto*; exquisite vegetables and greens that make a *minestrone* easy (Tuscans have always been more resourceful with hearty thick soups than pasta); the rosemary, garlic, onion, sage, basil, bay leaves that heighten flavour; and, of course, the bean, so adored that when detractors couldn't think of anything worse they called Tuscans *mangiafagioli* (bean eaters). Tuscans are also big meat eaters and Tuscan food is greatly characterized by grilled or roasted meats: chicken, pork, duck, pigeon, and Florence's legendary *bistecca alla fiorentina*, a hefty slab of Chianina beef (a genuine *fiorentina* weighs about 1kg with bone and all).

Boar and game birds are also prized in this most wooded Italian region. Some of Italy's tastiest pecorino cheese comes from sheep grazing in the stark hills around Siena.

Acquacotta Vegetable soup
Arista Pork loin roasted with rosemary and garlic.
Cacciucco alla livornese Piquant fish soup with garlic toast.
Cinghiale in agrodolce Wild boar in a sweet and sour sauce.
Cinta senese Cured ham/lard/salami/ pork from a special Sienese breed.
Crostini di fegatini Breadcrusts with chicken-liver pâté.
Panzanella Stale bread soaked with water and crumbled with chopped tomatoes, onions, basil, oil, and vinegar in a sort of salad.
Pappa al pomodoro Tomato and bred soup.
Pappardelle alla lepre Flat wide tagliatelle with a rich hare sauce.
Pici Home-made pasta, thicker than spaghetti, usually served with a rich meat sauce.
Ribollita Hearty soup with beans, black cabbage, and other vegetables, thickened with bread.
Tordi allo spiedo Spit-roasted wood thrush.

Hotels

La Collegiata, San Gimignano (SI) €€€ At this ex-Franciscan convent, commissioned in 1587 by San Gimignano's citizens, tapestries and frescoes evocative of Siena's Renaissance create a fine atmosphere. There is also a good restaurant serving eclectic food and a patio for alfresco dining.

Il Falconiere, Cortona (AR) €€–€€€
A 17th-century villa situated amid the vineyards and olive groves at the foothills of Cortona, offering wonderful views. Hospitable service, an exclusive pool, comfortable suites, and an excellent restaurant make this one of Tuscany's top places to stay. Owner Riccardo Baracchi also makes his own Super Tuscan wines.

JK Place Florence, Florence €€€
A trendy townhouse with 20 rooms squeezed between the palazzi that form the contour of one of Florence's most beautiful historic squares, that of Santa Maria Novella. Centrally located, JK is ideal for shopping and soaking up the city's atmosphere in style and comfort.

La Forra, Montegonzi (AR) €–€€
Well-run country lodging with a number of outbuildings converted into comfortable, self-contained apartments, situated among the olive groves above the small hamlet of Montegonzi. Spectacular views over the Valdarno. Good pool, restaurant, riding stable/horses, tennis courts.

Locanda dell'Amorosa, Sinalunga (SI) €€€ This ancient convent with 20 rooms is located between the wine towns of Montepulciano and Montalcino, just outside Sinalunga. Great atmosphere and good food/wines.

Pensione Bencistà, Fiesole (FI) €€–€€€ A 14th-century villa nestled in the foothills with a bird's-eye view of Florence. Lots of character: the jumble of sitting rooms, bars, and parlours is furnished with antique furniture. The bedrooms vary in size. Reservations should be made well in advance, especially for a room with a view over Florence.

Terre di Nano, Monticchiello-Montepulciano (SI) €–€€€ A charming 18th-century country house set between Montepulciano and Pienza, with spectacular view across Val di Chiana and Val d'Orcia. This is an hospitable, well-run, reasonably priced, ideal location for sightseeing and wine touring. They offer apartments for eight, four, or two people as well as double rooms. Good pool.

Restaurants

Acquamatta at Capolona, Arezzo €€
Located in a 14th-century hamlet on the banks of the Arno, and run by three young chefs, Andrea, Leonardo, and Paolo, who offer tasty, creative local dishes.

Albergaccio di Castellina, Castellina in Chianti €€€
According to Francesco Cacciatori, a good kitchen needs a good cellar, above all one with good wines! Here you'll also find excellent revisited Tuscan cuisine.

Arnolfo, Colle di Val d'Elsa €€€
Gaetano Trovato is an outstanding chef with a special feel for food and ingredients, which he

prepares with a light touch focusing on flavours and textures. His dishes originate from traditional Tuscan cuisine. The excellent wine list features more than 700 labels.

Badia a Coltibuono, Gaiole in Chianti €€–€€€
Paolo Stucchi's restaurant is in the heart of Chianti and part of the scenic 11th-century Benedictine monastery: it is ideal for alfresco lunches and serves traditional Tuscan food with a creative flair and a touch of fusion here and there. B&B accommodation is also available.

Il Canto del Maggio, Terranuova Bracciolini €€
Characteristic restaurant with a beautiful garden for alfresco eating. It is tucked away in the little hamlet of Penna Alta. Chef/owner Mauro Quirini focuses on traditional medieval Tuscan recipes and simple, country-style dishes. Excellent pasta, superb desserts, and a reliable wine list. Country lodging is also available.

Da Caino, Montemerano €€€
Valeria Piccini and her husband Maurizio run this top Tuscan restaurant serving traditional dishes that stem from well-known staples of the local cuisine, such as *tortelli cacio e pere* (pasta with cheese and pears) and *acquacotta*. Excellent cellar.

Da Ugo, Castagneto Carducci €€
Old-fashioned *trattoria* run by Pasquino Malenotti and his family, serving typical Maremma dishes including *tagliatelle al sugo di cinghiale* (pasta with a wild boar ragout). There is also an excellent *enoteca*.

Gambero Rosso, San Vincenzo €€€
Fulvio Pierangelini's Gambero Rosso is located facing the harbour of the small seaside town of San Vincenzo, in close proximity to Italy's prime wine-producing area of Bolgheri. Gambero Rosso is known for its excellent seafood and encyclopedic wine list.

La Grotta, Montepulciano €€
Just off the beaten track, with good parking by the church of San Biagio, La Grotta is by far the most authentic Tuscan restaurant in Montepulciano, serving traditional local dishes. Very good wine list.

Osteria del Vecchio Castello, Montalcino €€
Susanna Fumi's *osteria* in the Pieve of San Sigismondo is praised for her simple, fresh enticing style of cooking, prepared with local seasonal ingredients.

Osteria Le Logge, Siena €€–€€€
Laura and Gianni Brunelli's Le Logge (also a Brunello producer) is the place to eat when in Siena. Creative Tuscan dishes include special Cinta Senese suckling pig baked in a Parmesan crust, home-made *pici* with bacon, pecorino, and onion sauce. Excellent wine list.

Osteria San Regolo, Gaiole in Chianti €
Authentic Tuscan trattoria near Castello di Brolio at San Regolo, where the day's special might include *crostini*, *tagliatelle alla lepre*, *ribollita*, *bistecca*, *arrosto*, and other hearty Tuscan specials.

La Pineta, Marina di Bibbona €€–€€€
Luciano Zazzeri's La Pineta enjoys the perfect beachfront setting on Maremma's wild coastline, away from the busy crowds and everyday rush. The chef's style is Mediterranean seafood: no heavy sauces, just fresh, light ingredients that exalt the individual flavours.

Umbria *Umbria*

The breadth of Umbrian wines is not as widely appreciated as it might be. Indeed, Umbria is usually considered a one-wine region: at one time, the only wine that stood out was Orvieto, from the town where the Etruscans mastered oenological techniques two millennia before its golden sweet wines inspired Renaissance artists. Then, the sole name attracting interest was Torgiano, which was eventually replaced by Montefalco as the single area worthy of consideration. Now attention has turned to Colli del Trasimeno. Yet Umbria embraces all these wines and more. After a lapse, Orvieto has bounced back as one of Italy's most exported whites. Torgiano Rosso Riserva has claimed DOCG status, as has Montefalco Sagrantino, one of Italy's most potent and age-worthy reds. And Colli del Trasimeno, the current centre of attention, is surrounded by several other areas where winemakers are turning out a treasure trove of wines, some with distinct international style, others highlighting the tipicity of the varieties. There are still oddities and examples of hit-or-miss winemaking, but these are now outweighed by proficient, consistent styles that range from simple to inspired.

Wine Areas

1	Colli Altotiberini	6	Colli Martani
2	Colli del Trasimeno	7	Orvieto
3	Colli Perugini	8	Colli Amerini
4	Torgiano	9	Montefalco Sagrantino
5	Montefalco	10	Lago di Corbara

Most of Umbria's eleven DOCs are toward the west of this land-locked hilly region, often straddling its river valleys (Colli Altotiberini, Orvieto, Rosso Orvietano, Colli Amerini) or its lakes (Colli del Trasimeno, Lago di Corbara). There are also six IGTs, of which the region-wide Umbria is the most commonly used. The array of vines grown in the region include central Italy's standard Sangiovese, Canaiolo, Trebbiano, and Malvasia, but there is also the ancient and highly esteemed Grechetto and international varieties, such as Chardonnay, Cabernet, and Merlot.

Discovering Umbria's wines can be as rewarding as exploring its ancient hilltop towns. The region mixes art and history with the bucolic attractions of a countryside known as "the green heart of Italy". Oenophiles should not miss Lungarotti's Museo del Vino and Museo dell'Olio in Torgiano, or the Enoteca Provinciale in Perugia. Well-stocked shops include Enoteca Properzio Due in Spello, Enoteca Piazza Onofri in Bevagna, and La Loggia in Orvieto.

Recent Vintages

Umbria has a favourable climate for both reds and whites. 2001, 2000, 1999, 1997, and 1995 were superb; 2004, 1998, 1996, 1994, and 1993 good to very good; 2003, 2002, 1992, and 1991 fair; 1990 and 1988 outstanding; and 1985 first-rate, especially for reds. Earlier vintages of note are mentioned with entries of wines for ageing.

Appellations

DOCG
MONTEFALCO SAGRANTINO
r sw pas ris 88 90 93 94 95 96 97 98 99 00 01 04

A niche wine with cult status. Despite its popularity, there's not much of it (constituting a mere 5% of Umbria's total production). Sagrantino is a tough, small-berried grape with large pips and a thick skin giving it its tannic structure. As a late-ripening grape it needs to reach perfect phenolic ripeness, or its harsh, untamed tannins can make it undrinkable. Its average 14% alcohol makes this wine potentially age-worthy. Good vintages can age well up to 25 years and longer.

Sagrantino di Montefalco Passito *88 90 93 94 95 96 97 98 99 00 01 04* A rich, red *passito* made from semi-dried grapes (minimum 14.5% alcohol) with a light tannic bite. It becomes smoother and more complex with age. Age: 30 months.

TORGIANO ROSSO RISERVA
r 95 96 97 98 99 00 01 04

The first Umbrian wine to be awarded a DOC (1968). Sangiovese, Canaiolo, Montepulciano, Ciliegiolo, Trebbiano. Age: 3 years.

DOC
ASSISI *w p r nov*
Trebbiano, Grechetto, Sangiovese, Merlot.

COLLI ALTOTIBERINI *w p r*
Trebbiano, Malvasia del Chianti, Sangiovese, Merlot.

COLLI AMERINI *w p r nov ris sup*
Trebbiano, Grechetto, Garganega, Verdello, Malvasia, Sangiovese, Canaiolo, Montepulciano, Barbera, Ciliegiolo, Merlot.

COLLI DEL TRASIMENO *w p r ris fz sp nov sw vs*
Grechetto, Chardonnay, Pinot Bianco, Pinot Grigio, Trebbiano, Sangiovese, Ciliegiolo, Gamay, Merlot, Cabernet Sauvignon.

COLLI MARTANI *w r ris*

Grechetto, Malvasia Bianca del
Chianti, Garganega, Trebbiano,
Verdicchio, Sangiovese, Canaiolo,
Ciliegiolo, Barbera, Merlot,
Montepulciano.

COLLI PERUGINI *w r vs sw*

Trebbiano, Grechetto, Chardonnay,
Pinot Bianco, Pinot Nero, Pinot
Grigio, Sangiovese.

LAGO DI CORBARA *r*

Sangiovese, Cabernet Sauvignon,
Cabernet Franc, Merlot, Pinot
Nero, Aleatico, Canaiolo,
Cesanese, Ciliegiolo, Colorino,
Dolcetto, Montepulciano.

MONTEFALCO *w r ris*

Grechetto, Trebbiano, Sangiovese,
Sagrantino.

ORVIETO *w sup cl sw*

Trebbiano, Verdello, Grechetto,
Canaiolo Bianco, Malvasia Toscana

ROSSO ORVIETANO/ ORVIETANO ROSSO *r sw*

Aleatico, Cabernet Franc,
Cabernet Sauvignon, Canaiolo,
Ciliegiolo, Merlot, Montepulciano,
Pinot Nero, Sangiovese.

TORGIANO *w p r sp*

Trebbiano, Grechetto, Sangiovese,
Canaiolo, Cabernet Sauvignon,
Chardonnay, Pinot Grigio, Pinot
Nero, Riesling Italico.

VIN SANTO

Grechetto, Malvasia, Trebbiano,
and other grapes.

IGT

Allerona
Bettona
Cannara
Narni
Spello
Umbria

Producers

*The key provinces have been
abbreviated as follows: PG =
Perugia; TR = Terni.
"Sangrantino" implies Montefalco
Sagrantino.*

Antonelli, San Marco, Montefalco (PG)
w r ris sw ☆☆☆☆→☆☆☆☆☆ *90 93 95
97 98 99 00 01 03 04* 30ha, 200,000
bottles. At Filippo Antonelli's 1886
estate, production focuses on
impeccable Sagrantino – elegant
and balanced, plums, red berry
aromas, cedar and leather, fresh and
persistent. Also very good *passito*,
Montefalco Rosso (also *riserva*),
and Colli Martani Grechetto.

Arquata-Fratelli Adanti, Bevagna (PG)
w r ris sw ☆☆→☆☆☆☆ *90 94 95 97 98
99 00 01 03* 30ha, 130,000 bottles.
Despite its ups and downs, this
family-run estate is now back with
mighty but mellow Sagrantino,

both dry and sweet; Montefalco
Rosso and Bianco; Colli Martani
Grechetto; and IGT Rosso d'Arquata,
a Cabernet Sauvignon/Barbera/
Merlot blend– sapid and powerful.

Barberani-Vallesanta, Baschi (TR) *w r
sw* ☆☆ 50ha, 350,000 bottles. Estate
with vines in the hills around Lake
Corbara and a production overseen
by consultant winemaker Maurizio
Castelli. Highlights include Orvieto
Classico: Castagnolo (dry),
Pulicchio (medium-sweet), and
Calcaia Muffa Nobile (late-harvest);
Lago di Corbara Foresco Villa
Monticelli, a Sangiovese/Cabernet
Sauvignon/Merlot blend; and
Moscato Passito Villa Monticelli.

Bea Paolo, Montefalco (PG) *w r ris sw*
☆☆☆→☆☆☆☆ 7ha, 50,000 bottles.
Giampiero Bea's vines produce
Sagrantino *passito* and Montefalco
Rosso (also *riserva*). This passionate
winemaker defines his production
as *vini veri* (true wines), made in

the most natural way possible: they are remarkable in quality and individual in character, fine examples of genuine terroir expression.

Bigi, Orvieto (TR) *w r sw* ☆→☆☆ * 250ha, 4,000,000 bottles. Large winery of the Gruppo Italiano Vini producing a range of Orvieto wines, from Classico Torricella and *amabile* Orzalume to IGT Marrano (Chardonnay/Grechetto), Umbria Grechetto, Umbria Sangiovese, and Sartiano, a Sangiovese-based wine with Merlot and Pinot Noir.

Cantina Colli Amerini, Fornole di Amelia (TR) *w r sw* ☆☆ * 400ha, 1,000,000 bottles. Model co-op with production overseen by consultant oenologist Riccardo Cotarella. Their wines provide outstanding value in Colli Amerini Rosso: Carbio, a four-grape blend, and Olmeto Merlot; as well as Bianco Terre Arnolfe (Trebbiano/Grechetto/Malvasia), and more.

Cantina Monrubio, Castel Viscardo (TR) *w r* ☆☆ * 650ha, 1,300,000 bottles. Proficient co-op with 300 members producing Orvieto Classico: Soana, Salceto, and Roana – minerality, fresh, zesty; good-value IGT Monrubio (Sangiovese/Ciliegiolo/Montepulciano/Merlot); and IGT Nociano (Cabernet).

Arnaldo Caprai-Val di Maggio, Montefalco (PG) *w r sw* ☆☆→☆☆☆☆ *90 93 95 97 98 00 01 03* 150ha, 750,000 bottles. Over the years, Marco Caprai has invested in clonal research, contributing to the high quality of his Sagrantino. Highlights: prestigious Sagrantino 25 Anni and Colle Piano, both intense, powerful, age-worthy wines. Also good Montefalco Rosso and Colli Martani Grechetto, plus Grecante Villa Belvedere.

Cardeto, Orvieto (TR) *w r sw* ☆→☆☆ * 1,000ha, 4,500,000 bottles. Large co-op with a production overseen by consultant winemaker Maurilio Chioccia. They make a reliable and well-priced range of Orvieto Classico Superiore: L'Armida and Febeo; as well as excellent IGT Umbria Arciato (Merlot/Cabernet Sauvignon/Sangiovese), and Nero della Greca (Sangiovese/Merlot).

La Carraia, Orvieto (TR) *w r* ☆☆→☆☆☆☆ * 119ha, 600,000 bottles. The Cotarella and Gialetti joint family estate produces fine Orvieto Classico Poggio Calvelli – ripe tropical fruit, toasted almonds, finesse and persistence. Also good IGT red Fobiano, a structured Merlot/Cabernet blend; Tizzonero (Montepulciano), and IGT Sangiovese, plus other well-priced, quality-focused wines.

Castello della Sala, Ficulle (TR) *w r* ☆☆→☆☆☆☆ * Antinori's Umbrian estate makes estimable Orvieto Classico DOC Campogrande and an array of IGT Umbria, led by Cervaro della Sala, an refined, oak-fermented Chardonnay/Grechetto. Good sweet Muffato della Sala (Sauvignon/Grechetto/Riesling/Gewürztraminer) with noble rot; Conte della Vipera Sauvignon; and Pinot Nero Vigneto Consola.

Castello delle Regine, Amelia (TR) *w r* ☆☆→☆☆☆ 75ha, 220,000 bottles. Up-and-coming farming estate where highlights include four exciting reds: two from Sangiovese (including oak-aged Podernovo), a Merlot, and a Cabernet Sauvignon/Merlot/Sangiovese blend, Princeps – terroir character, vibrance, and minerality. Also good white Bianco delle Regine (Sauvignon/Riesling Renano/Pinot Grigio/Chardonnay) – floral, citrussy, and zesty.

Colpetrone, Gualdo Cattaneo (PG) *r sw* ☆☆☆ In 1994 Saiagricola started off with 4ha of Sagrantino, making an excellent *passito*. Today the

Colpetrone estate comprises 140ha, with 46ha of Montefalco DOC producing good Sagrantino and fine *passito*. A recent investment includes a massive winery with a 1,000-barrique capacity.

Le Crete, Giove (TR) *w r* ☆☆ 5ha, 40,000 bottles. Giuliano Castellani's emerging estate uses organically farmed vines and produces a few well-made labels, including Petra Nera, an interesting Sangiovese-based wine with Merlot and Barbera; and Cima del Giglio (Malvasia), both gaining renown.

Decugnano dei Barbi, Orvieto (TR) *w r sw sp* ☆☆→☆☆☆ 39ha, 170,000 bottles. Claudio Barbi's production includes sparkling brut Metodo Champenoise (Chardonnay/ Verdello/Procanico), aged in an excavated cellar dating back to the Etruscans. Other highlights: fine Orvieto Classico IL – subtle fruit, minerality, full and persistent; acclaimed IGT Umbria Rosso IL; and Lago di Corbara, a Sangiovese/ Montepulciano/Canaiolo blend.

Fanini, Castiglione del Lago (PG) *w r* ☆☆ * 12ha. The emerging estate of Marco Fornaciari, professor of agriculture, focuses on Colli del Trasimeno: Rosso Morello del Lago and Bianco Albello del Lago; plus IGT varietals including Merlo+T, Chardonnay Robbiano, and Sangiovese Vigna La Pieve, which contains well-balanced, subtle, fresh fruit.

Fattoria Colleallodole, Montefalco (PG) *r sw* ☆☆☆* 10ha, 30,000 bottles. Francesco Antano's production focuses on fine Sagrantino, *passito*, and Rosso di Montefalco. The top label is a single-vineyard Sagrantino Colleallodole with great depth, structure, and an individual, slightly austere character.

Fattoria Le Poggette, Montecastrilli (TR) *w r* ☆☆→☆☆☆ 18ha, 70,000 bottles.

Emerging estate producing Colli Amerini Rosso and IGT varietals of impressive dimension. The highlight is the Montepulciano, aged in Allier tonneau for two years, acquiring a soft, round quality with power and structure. Also good Canaiolo and Grechetto – fresh, grapey, floral.

Goretti, Perugia *w r* ☆☆ 60ha, 400,000 bottles. Confident range of Colli Perugini: highly admired Rosso L'Arrignatore (Sangiovese/Merlot/ Ciliegiolo) – prune, cherry, and tobacco aromas, balsamic finish; Bianco Torre del Pino (Chardonnay/ Grechetto/Malvasia); and varietal Chardonnay and Grechetto. Also well-made Sagrantino and Montefalco Rosso Le Mure Saracene.

Lamborghini La Fiorita, Panicale (PG) ☆☆→☆☆☆☆ * 32ha, 157,000 bottles. Renowned estate founded by car magnate Ferruccio Lamborghini and revived by his daughter Patrizia. Highlights: IGT Campoleone (Merlot/Sangiovese) – upfront fruit, prunes, cassis, balsamic notes, and silky tannins; and admirable Trescone (Sangiovese/Ciliegiolo/ Merlot) – floral with red berry fruit, mineral and persistent.

Lungarotti, Torgiano (PG) *w p r ris sw sp* ☆☆→☆☆☆☆ 90 92 97 00 01 03 04 290ha, 3,000,000 bottles. This estate is an important emblem of Umbrian viticulture. The Lungarotti sisters are back on form with an extensive range of Torgiano (white, red, rosé, and sparkling) and a supporting range of IGTs and *vin santo*. The trademark Rubesco applies to Torgiano Rosso and Rosso Riserva. Top label San Giorgio is a complex Sangiovese/Cabernet blend.

La Palazzola, Stroncone (TR) *w r sw sp* ☆☆→☆☆☆☆ 36ha, 150,000 bottles. Stefano Grilli's estate (est. 1920) produces admirable *vin santo* –

robust, with fine aromas of caramel, nougat, nuts, and spice, underlying dried fruit. Also fine Vendemmia Tardiva (Sauvignon/Traminer), IGT Merlot and Rubino (Cabernet Sauvignon/Merlot), Riesling, and Pinot Nero (dry, sweet, sparkling).

Palazzone, Orvieto (TR) *w r sw* ☆☆☆→☆☆☆☆ *90 91 93 95 97 98 01 04* 25ha, 130,000 bottles. Giovanni and Ludovico Dubini produce classy, age-worthy Orvieto Classico: Terre Vineate and Campo del Guardiano, from selected grapes aged 18 months in bottle with an ageing potential of ten years – vitality, freshness, structure, and complexity. Dubini favours indigenous varieties that are fermented in stainless steel, with the exception of L'Ultima Spiaggia, a 100% Viognier, fermented and aged five months in barrique. Also good Muffa Nobile (Sauvignon) and well-balanced varietal Sangiovese.

Perticaia Montefalco (PG) *r* ☆☆☆ One of Umbria's rising estates. Guido Guardigli has 14ha of vines, with currently 50% in production making 30,000 bottles. Highlights: well-crafted Montefalco Rosso, Sagrantino, and *passito*. The wines show structure and elegance.

Pieve del Vescovo, Corciano (PG) *r* ☆☆ 22ha, 75,000 bottles. Production at this up-and-coming estate in the Colli del Trasimeno area is overseen by Riccardo Cotarella. The range includes stylish wines Piovano and Lucciao, Sangiovese-based with Merlot and Cabernet.

Poggio Bertaio, Castiglione del Lago (PG) *r* ☆☆☆ 20ha, 48,000 bottles. Consultant oenologist Fabrizio Ciufoli and his family produce some admired Sangiovese-based reds. Top labels: IGT Cimbolo (Sangiovese) – solid black berry fruit, sapid, with spice and leather, smooth and persistent; and

Crovello (Merlot/Cabernet) – meaty, with crushed berries and musk, firm structure and an elegant finish.

Rocca di Fabbri, Montefalco (PG) *w r sw* ☆☆→☆☆☆ * *90 95 97 00 01 03* Assisted by consultant winemaker Giorgio Marrone, the Vitali family have not succumbed to the allure of new oak. Their Sagrantino is aged in larger Slavonian oak barrels, producing food-friendly wines such as Sagrantino, *passito*, IGT Faroaldo (Sagrantino/Cabernet Sauvignon), and Grechetto.

Scacciadiavoli, Montefalco (PG) *r sw* ☆☆☆ * 28ha, 80,000 bottles. Amilcare Pambuffetti's is one of Montefalco's historic estates (est. 1884). Production is overseen by Stefano Chioccioli and focuses on good, well-priced Sagrantino, *passito*, and Montefalco Rosso.

Fratelli Sportoletti, Spello (PG) *w r* ☆☆→☆☆☆ * 30ha, 240,000 bottles. Ernesto and Remo Sportoletti's is one of Assisi's leading estates. Its production is overseen by Riccardo Cotarella, and highlights include admirable, well-priced Grechetto, Rosso, Bianco, and IGT Fedelia Rosso (Merlot/Cabernet Sauvignon/Cabernet Franc) and Bianco (Grechetto/Chardonnay).

Tabarrini, Montefalco (PG) *w r sw* ☆☆☆ 8ha, 45,000 bottles. Dynamic fourth-generation winemaker Giampaolo Tabarrini's estate is rapidly emerging. His Sagrantino is well-structured, fruit-forward, full, round, and persistent. Also good Rosso – sapid, ripe, and juicy; and *passito* – individual character and class.

Tenuta Alzatura, Montefalco (PG) *r* ☆☆ 20ha, 30,000 bottles. New estate owned by Tuscany's Cecchi family producing well-crafted Sagrantino Uno di Uno and Rosso di Montefalco. The Cecchis also own Palazzo Paulucci, a historic house in Montefalco that will be used as a hospitality and tasting centre.

Tenuta Corini, Montegabbione (TR) *w r*
☆☆ 8ha, 21,500 bottles. Fausto
Corini's up-and-coming estate
produces IGT varietal wines under
the guidance of Riccardo Cotarella.
Top labels are Cameriti Pinot Noir,
Casteldifiori Sauvignon, and
Frabusco, a blend of local and
international: Sangiovese, Merlot,
and Montepulciano.

Tenuta Le Velette, Orvieto (TR) *w r* ☆☆
104ha, 390,000 bottles. Historic
estate (est. 1860) with a production
of much-admired Orvieto Classico.
Rosso Orvietano Rosso di Spicca is
Sangiovese-based with a dash of
Canaiolo. Also good IGT Gaudio
Merlot and Traluce Sauvignon.

Terre de' Trinci, Foligno (PG) *w r* ☆☆→
☆☆☆ *93, 97, 01, 03* 350ha, 550,000
bottles. Emerging Sagrantino co-
op managed by Ludovico Mattoni
producing good Montefalco Rosso
and single-vineyard Sagrantino
Ugolino – marasca cherry, pepper,
spice. Also IGT Cajo, a blend of
Sagrantino/Merlot/Cabernet.

Il Toppello, Mantignana (PG) *r* ☆☆☆
7ha, 40,000 bottles. The production
at Lorenzo Bizzarri's emerging
estate is overseen by consultant
winemaker Fabrizio Ciufoli, and
focuses on two high-quality
wines: Selciaio (100% Sangiovese)
– intense, with balanced acidity
and long finish, good ageing
potential; and Rocceto,
Sangiovese-based with some
Merlot added.

Wine & Food

Umbrians humbly relate that they
eat only what their good earth
provides. Granted, menus are
spare, repetitive, and orthodox –
in other words, highly selective.
There are few secrets to Umbrian
cooking, which is based on home-
grown produce and recipes that
have barely changed since the
Middle Ages. Oil is so good that
it's called Umbria's "liquid gold".
There are thick soups and exquisite
pastas, including home-made
tagliatelle mixed with a ragout that
often contains chicken livers. Meat
and game – Perugina beef, poultry,
wood pigeon, and lamb – are
common in this landlocked region.
Pork is so artfully prepared in the
town of Norcia that pork-butcher
shops throughout Italy are known
as *norcinerie*. Among things that
grow, a special place is reserved for
cardoons, the artichoke-like thistles
known here as *gobbi*. But the most
delicious irony of this region's
"modest" cuisine is the truffle.

Whether black or white, it is so
prolific that Umbria has become
the nation's leading supplier.

Anguille alla brace Grilled eels.

Cipollata Onion soup with tomato,
salt pork, basil, and Parmesan.

Gobbi alla perugina Fried
cardoons with meat ragout.

Mazzafegati Spicy pork-liver
sausages, served around Christmas.

Minestra di farro Soup of spelt
cooked with tomatoes and onions,
in broth of a prosciutto bone.

Palombacci alla ghiotta Spit-
roasted wood pigeons with a sauce
of wine, vinegar, ham, and livers.

Porchetta alla perugina Whole
young pig roasted in a wood oven
with fennel, rosemary, and garlic.

Spaghetti alla norcina Pasta with
a sauce of sausages with onions in
cream. It may be topped with
grated cheese or white truffles.

Stringozzi Short noodles with
garlic, oil, and sometimes tomatoes.

Torcolo Sponge cake to be dipped
in *vin santo*.

Hotels

Park Hotel Cappuccini, Gubbio €€–€€€ Beautifully restored 17th-century monastery located a stone's throw from the historic centre.

Sauro, Tuoro sul Trasimeno, Isola Maggiore € Take a ferry ride to this picturesque island in the middle of Lake Castiglione, visit the 12th-century churches of San Salvatore and San Michele Arcangelo, and lodge at Sauro's, where you will find excellent cuisine based on lake fish.

Le Tre Vaselle, Torgiano €€ Owned by the Lungarotti family, this hotels offers refined elegance, large rooms, and a good restaurant. It is well located for touring. Don't miss the Lungarotti Wine Museum and the Olive Oil Museum, which is only a couple of doorsteps away from the hotel.

Agriturismo Tuoro sul Trasimeno, Lake Trasimeno € Attractive country lodge ideal for a few days' relaxation, with pool.

Villa Pambuffetti, Montefalco €€–€€€ Charming historic villa with 15 guest rooms, set in a park surrounded by majestic trees. Views look on to the surrounding Umbrian towns of Assisi and Spello, as well as Mount Subasio. Pool and good parking.

Hotel Villa Roncalli, Foligno € A 17th-century villa with ten rooms and an excellent restaurant (€€) based on Umbria's local flavours and ingredients. Specials include chicken broth with white truffles, polenta and lentils from Castelluccio, and duck stuffed with chestnuts and set in aspic.

Restaurants

Trattoria del Borgo, Perugia € *Trattoria* in the historic centre with authentic atmosphere: wooden tables and chairs. Excellent home-made regional fare that changes according to the season. *Alfresco* dining in the garden in summer.

Enoteca di Piazza Onofri, Bevagna €–€€ In this picturesque medieval hamlet you can snack in what used to be an old mill. Thick soups, pasta, and meat dishes, plus an excellent assortment of local cheeses. Good 600-label wine list.

Pane e Vino, Todi €–€€ *Osteria* in the historic centre of Todi, by the Basilica di San Fortunato. Excellent antipasti, salami, cheeses, thick soups, pasta with truffles, rich meat dishes, and well-assorted wine list.

Postale di Marco e Barbara, Città di Castello €€ Originally a coach house, now a trendy loft serving top-notch food including creative, locally inspired fare, such as dried cod in a ricotta and marjoram sauce, roast pigeon stuffed with seasonal vegetables, fig terrine with vanilla cream and Sagrantino *passito* sauce. Good wine list.

I Sette Consoli, Orvieto €€ Bang in the historic centre of Orvieto, in what was once the sacristy of Sant'Angelo, chef Rita Simoncini will serve you some of the region's top dishes while sommelier Mauro Stoppini leads you through the wines. Good alfresco eating in the garden.

Vissani, Baschi €€€ Vissani ranks among Italy's top restaurants, excellent cuisine, with genuine regional recipes finely crafted using prime ingredients. Excellent wine list.

Lazio *Lazio*

Lazio's wines are, mainly, Rome's wines. The Castelli Romani, a green-clad ring of spent volcanoes not far from the Italian capital, harbour seven of Lazio's twenty-six DOC zones and lie within view of eight others. Their star player is Frascati, one of Italy's most famous whites and one of its most quaffed. Est! Est!! Est!!! di Montefiascone is Lazio's other resounding name, but this white comes from vineyards around the crater lake of Bolsena, in the north of the region, well distant from Rome. Another well-known name, Orvieto, although mostly situated in Umbria, extends into Lazio, too. Yet, despite the renowned names, most wines from this prolific region had been stuck with a somewhat everyday image, mostly because all the traditional whites (and ninety per cent of DOC output is white) come from the often-unexciting Malvasia or Trebbiano, or combinations of the two.

In the old days, the lush vineyards of the Castelli Romani produced soft, fleshy wines the full flavours of which matched the pungently spicy fare of the *cucina romana*. But those wines were so unstable that they often failed to survive the short trip into Rome. Modern winemaking has rendered pale, balanced, pure whites that can be shipped anywhere with confidence.

Wine Areas

1 Colli Etruschi Viterbesi
2 Vignanello
3 Frascati
4 Genazzano
5 Castelli Romani
6 Colli Albani
7 Colli Lanuvini
8 Circeo
9 Colli della Sabina
10 Atina
11 Orvieto
12 Bianco Capena
13 Nettuno
14 Cesanese di Affile
15 Cesanese del Piglio

Perversely, many of Lazio's most esteemed wines are red. As usual, there are several IGTs to embrace those that are not covered by a DOC, and the region-wide Lazio is easily the most commonly used.

The prime wine trip from Rome is a circuit of the Castelli Romani, taking in Frascati, Marino, Colli Albani, Colli Lanuvini, Montecompatri Colonna, and Velletri. An extended trip includes Zagarolo and the three DOC zones producing wine from the red Cesanese. The best shops are the Enoteca-Wine Bar Trimani, Cavour, Piero Costantini, Al Parlamento, Ferrara, and Anacleto Gleve, all in Rome; and the Enoteca Frascati in Frascati.

Recent Vintages

For red wines and the few whites that may be kept for more than a couple of years, recommended vintages appear with each entry.

Appellations

DOC
ALEATICO DI GRADOLI *r sw liq*
00 01 02 03 04
Aleatico.

APRILIA *w r*
Merlot, Sangiovese, Trebbiano.

ATINA *r ris 00 01 02 03 04*
Cabernet Sauvignon, Syrah, Merlot, Cabernet Franc.

BIANCO CAPENA *w*
Malvasia, Trebbiano, Bellone, Bombino.

CASTELLI ROMANI *w p r sw fz nov*
Trebbiano, Malvasia, Cesanese, Merlot, Montepulciano, Sangiovese, Nero Buono.

CERVETERI *w p r sw nov fz 00 01 02 03 04*
Trebbiano, Malvasia, Sangiovese, Montepulciano, Cesanese.

CESANESE DEL PIGLIO/PIGLIO
r sw fz sp 99 00 01 02 03 04
Cesanese Affile, Cesanese, Sangiovese, Montepulciano, Barbera, Trebbiano, Bombino.

CESANESE AFFILE/AFFILE & CESANESE DI OLEVANO ROMANO/OLEVANO ROMANO
r fz sp sw
Cesanese Affile, Cesanese,

Montepulciano, Barbera, Trebbiano, Sangiovese, Bombino.

CIRCEO *w p r fz sw nov*
Trebbiano Toscano, Malvasia di Candia, Merlot, Sangiovese.

COLLI ALBANI *w sup nov sp sw*
Trebbiano, Malvasia del Lazio, Malvasia di Candia.

COLLI DELLA SABINA *w p r fz nov sp*
Trebbiano, Sangiovese, Montepulciano.

COLLI ETRUSCHI VITERBESI
w p r fz sw pas
Malvasia, Trebbiano, Sangiovese, Montepulciano, Canaiolo, Grechetto, Grechetto Rosso, Merlot, Moscatello, Procanico, Rossetto, Violone.

COLLI LANUVINI *w sup*
Malvasia, Trebbiano.

CORI *w r 00 01 02 03 04*
Malvasia, Trebbiano, Montepulciano, Cesanese.

EST! EST!! EST!!! DI MONTEFIASCONE *w sp sw*
Trebbiano, Malvasia Bianco, Greco.

FRASCATI *w nov sup sp sw*
Malvasia di Candia, Malvasia

del Lazio, Greco, Trebbiano.

GENAZZANO *w r nov*
Malvasia di Candia, Bellone,
Bombino, Sangiovese, Cesanese.

MARINO *w sw sup sp*
Malvasia di Candia, Malvasia
del Lazio, Trebbiano.

MONTECOMPATRI COLONNA
w sup fz sw
Malvasia, Trebbiano, Bellone.

NETTUNO *w p r fz nov*
Bellone, Trebbiano, Sangiovese,
Merlot, Cacchione.

ORVIETO
Part of this Umbrian DOC zone
extends into Lazio. *See* Umbria.

TARQUINIA *w p r fz sw nov*
Trebbiano, Malvasia, Sangiovese,

Montepulciano, Cesanese.

VELLETRI *w r sup sp ris sw 00 01 02 03 04*
Trebbiano, Malvasia, Bellone,
Bonvino, Montepulciano, Merlot,
Sangiovese, Cesanese, Ciliegiolo.

VIGNANELLO *w p r sup sp ris nov 00 01 02 03 04*
Trebbiano, Malvasia, Sangiovese,
Ciliegiolo, Greco.

ZAGAROLO *w sup*
Malvasia, Trebbiano, Bellone.

IGT
Civitella d'Agliano
Colli Cimini
Frusinate/del Frusinate
Lazio
Nettuno

Producers

The key provinces have been abbreviated as follows: FR = Frosinone; LT = Latina; RI = Rieti; RM = Roma; VT = Viterbo.

Cantina Cerveteri, Cerveteri (RM) *w r* ☆☆→☆☆☆ * 1,300ha, 3,700,000 bottles. Large co-op with a production overseen by Riccardo Cotarella. Good Cerveteri Rosso and Bianco in the Fontana Morella and, especially, Vigna Grande lines. Top labels: Rosso Vigna Grande, a Merlot/Montepulciano/Sangiovese blend – tight, compact, and balanced, cherry, tobacco, liquorice; Tertium (Montepulciano/Sangiovese); and Novae (Malvasia).

Cantina Colacicchi, Anagni (FR) *w r* ☆☆☆ 6ha, 25,000 bottles. Marco Trimani's production is noted for Torre Ercolana, a Cabernet/Merlot/Cesanese blend aged 12 months in barrique and 24 in bottle – elegant and powerful. Also good IGT Schiaffo ("slap") (Cabernet/Merlot), and Romagnano Bianco and Rosso.

Cantina Conte Zandotti, Roma *w r* ☆☆☆ Enrico Zandotti's 40ha of vines between Montecompatri and Frascati are renowned for their whites, in particular Malvasia del Lazio Rumon – flowery bouquet with white-peach aromas, round, soft, with bitter-almond finish. Also very good Frascati Superiore and Frascati Cannellino.

Cantina Oliveto, Santa Severa (RM) *w r* ☆☆ * 44ha, 20,000 bottles. Gianfranco Spinelli's estate is rapidly emerging with well-priced, easy-drinking varietal IGT wines, such as Cabernet Monte Grande, Rosato Pian Sultano (Cabernet), Merlot Monterosso, and Chardonnay Pirgy.

Casale del Giglio, Borgo Montello (LT) *w r sw* ☆☆☆→☆☆☆☆ 138ha, 600,000 bottles. Antonio Santarelli is a leader in quality production with worldwide exports. Winemaking is overseen by Paolo Tiefenthaler. Highlights: varietal IGT

Chardonnay, Sauvignon, Cabernet, Merlot, Petit Verdot, and Shiraz (Syrah), and blends Mater Matuta (Syrah/Petit Verdot), Antinoo (Chardonnay/Viognier), Madreselva (Merlot/Cabernet), and Aphrodisium (various nobly rotted grapes).

Casale della Ioria, Acuto (FR) w r ☆☆→☆☆☆ 24ha, 40,000 bottles. Paolo Perinelli's estate produces elegant Cesanese del Piglio – notes of cherry, spice, tobacco, vibrant structure, evident tannins, full, long finish; good IGT Colle Bianco Passerina del Frusinate; and Cesanese del Piglio Torre del Piano.

Castel de Paolis, Grottaferrata (RM) w p r sw ☆☆→☆☆☆ 13ha, 70,000 bottles. Adriana Croce Santarelli's production, overseen by Franco Bernabei, is a breath of fresh air in the Castelli, with acclaimed Frascati: Vigna Adriana, Campo Vecchio, and Cannellino; IGT Selve Vecchie (Sauvignon/Chardonnay); Quattro Mori (Syrah/Merlot/Cabernet/Petit Verdot); and sweet Muffa Nobile (Sauvignon/Sémillon).

Casale Marchese, Frascati (RM) w r ☆☆→☆☆☆ 40ha, 200,000 bottles. Historic estate (est. 1713) producing individual Frascati – sweet-scented, herbaceous and mineral, with fine, fresh finish. Also good IGT Cortesia, oak-fermented from late-harvest grapes (Bombino/Trebbiano/ Malvasia) and Vigna del Cavaliere (Cabernet Sauvignon/Cabernet Franc/Merlot/Montepulciano).

Coletti Conti, Anagni (FR) r ☆☆ 16ha, 12,000 bottles. Emerging estate producing fine Cesanese del Piglio, aged 12 months in Vosgi oak – balsamic notes, delicate violet, marasca, and strawberry, high in glycerine, powerful structure, very persistent. Also excellent four-grape red Bordeaux blend IGT Cosmato – elegant nose, complexity, sound balance, and a long, classy finish.

Colle Picchioni-Paola di Mauro, Frattocchie di Marino (RM) w r ☆☆☆ * 13ha, 130,000 bottles. Di Mauro's production is overseen by Riccardo Cotarella. Top labels: Bordeaux blend Vigna del Vassallo – vibrant, fruit-forward, underlying minerality, complex, and fine, silky tannins; Marino Selezione Oro, a Malvasia-based blend – aromatic, full, and round, with a slightly bitter finish; and Colle Picchioni Rosso (Merlot/Sangiovese/Cabernet) – warm, balsamic, balanced.

Falesco, Montefiascone (VT) w p r sw ☆☆☆→☆☆☆☆ * Renowned oenologists Renzo and Riccardo Cotarella make excellent Est! Est!! Est!!! Poggio dei Gelsi, both dry and *vendemmia tardiva*; as well as IGT wines: Vitiano (Cabernet/ Merlot/Sangiovese) – velvety, fresh, grippy tannins, capsicum finish; Marciliano (Cabernet Sauvignon/ Cabernet Franc) – full-bodied, round and structured, with well-extracted tannins, a little austere; and Montiano, a sapid Merlot.

Fontana Candida, Frascati (RM) ☆☆→☆☆☆ * 7,500,000 bottles. Large winery owned by Gruppo Italiano Vini and managed by Francesco Bardi. It buys in most of its grapes in order to produce wines of consistent quality. Top labels: single-vineyard Santa Teresa; Merlot-based Kron – aromatic, silky, with depth and a classy finish; and Malvasia Terre dei Grifi – aromatic, round, and fresh.

Mazziotti, Bolsena (VT) w r ☆☆→☆☆☆ 29ha, 160,000 bottles. Historic estate (est. 1900) producing fine Est! Est!! Est!!!, but veering to more complex IGT wines, notably Chardonnay Canuleio and Volgente (Merlot/Sangiovese/Montepulciano) – fruit-forward, concentrated, with floral aromas, weighty on the palate, with balanced acidity.

Sergio Mottura, Civitella d'Agliano (VT) *w r sw* ☆☆☆ 40ha, 100,000 bottles. Organic estate praised for its fine structured whites. Highlights: Latour Civitella (Grechetto) – yellow peaches, cedar, resin, and vanilla; Orvieto Vigna Tragugnano (Procanica/Grechetto/Verdello) – yeasty, with herbal notes, mineral, structured, with fine balance and length; and botrytized Il Muffo.

L'Olivella, Frascati (RM) *w r* ☆☆→☆☆☆ * 12ha, 80,000 bottles. This estate produces well-priced wines, such as Frascati Superiore Racemo, a four-grape blend – sapid, citrussy, and exotic, with almonds, zesty finish; Racemo Rosso (Sangiovese/ Cesanese); and Concento (Cesanese/Syrah) – ripe berries, leather, tobacco, mineral character.

Giovanni Palombo, Atina (FR) *w r ris* ☆☆☆ 10ha, 59,000 bottles. The Palombo family focus on red international-style IGTs. Top labels: Bordeaux blend Atina Cabernet Duca Cantelmi Riserva – black cherries, cocoa, coffee, vanilla, silky tannins, well-balanced, long finish; classy Capralitt (Cabernet/ Merlot); and Atina Cabernet.

Pietra Pinta – Colle San Lorenzo, Cori (LT) *w r* ☆☆→☆☆☆ 100ha, 800,000 bottles. Francesco and Cesare Ferretti produce admired IGTs as well as international-style varietals, including Chardonnay and Merlot. Highlights: Colle Amato (Cabernet Sauvignon/Syrah) – blackberries and spice, long, full, round finish; and Bianco and Rosso La Pietraia.

Poggio Le Volpi, Monteporzio Catone (RM) *w r sw* ☆☆→☆☆☆ 30ha, 71,000 bottles. Quality production by Felice Megrè, overseen by Maurilio Chioccia, is rapidly gaining acclaim. Highlights: Baccarossa (Merlot/ Montepulciano) – ripe fruit, hints of tobacco and spice; Donnaluce, a partly oak-aged Chardonnay; and Frascati Superiore People.

Principe Pallavicini, Colonna (RM) *w r sw* ☆☆☆ 80ha, 1,000,000 bottles. Maria Camilla Pallavicini produces fine Cesanese, along with whites of Frascati. Top labels: sweet Malvasia Puntinata; fine, elegant Moroello (Sangiovese/Merlot); and Frascati Superiore Poggio Verde – fresh aromatic character.

San Marco, Frascati (RM) *w r sp* ☆☆→☆☆☆ 60ha, 1,800,000 bottles. Well-managed estate where top labels include IGT varietal wines SoloShiraz and SoloMalvasia; Meraco Rosso (Sangiovese/Cesanese/ Cabernet) – earthy and complex; Frascati Superiore De Notari; and unusual Frascati Spumante.

Tenuta Le Quinte, Montecompatri (RM) *w r* ☆☆☆ 15ha, 100,000 bottles. Elio Papi is one of the most innovative producers of the Castelli Romani. His production focuses on whites: Montecompatri Superiore Virtù Romane (Malvasia Puntinata/ Bonvino/Bellone/Trebbiano Giallo) – exotic fruit, floral, almonds, and mineral notes; and Canestraro (Grechetto/Malvasia Puntinata).

Terra Delle Ginestre, Spigno Saturnia (LT) *w r sw* ☆☆→☆☆☆ 3ha, 9,500 bottles. Small estate belonging to six friends with a passion for wine. Highlights: Lentisco (Bellone), aged six months in chestnut barrels – amber, ripe peaches, nuts, spice, and powerful; and Il Generale (Metolano/Primitivo/Aglianico) – sapid, with dark marasca cherries, tobacco, and berries, and high acidity. Also good Passito Promessa.

Trappolini, Castiglione in Teverina (VT) *w r sw* ☆☆→☆☆☆ * 24ha, 150,000 bottles. Roberto and Paolo Trappolini's range is led by a tannic, powerful IGT Sangiovese Parterno, aged in barrique for 24 months; and Breccetto, an oak-fermented Chardonnay. Also good Orvieto, Est! Est!! Est!!!, and Cenereto

(Sangiovese/Montepulciano).

Christine Vaselli, Castiglione in Teverina (VT) *r* ☆☆→☆☆ 19ha, 120,000 bottles. Production is overseen by Riccardo Cotarella and includes an ambitious Cabernet Sauvignon/Merlot IGT Le Poggere, aged 12 months in barrique and then bottle-aged. Also good Supreme Rosso

Orvietano Torre Sant'Andrea.

Villa Simone, Monteporzio Catone (RM) *w r* ☆☆☆ * 27ha, 300,000 bottles. Piero Costantini produces well-structured and elegant Frascati: single-vineyard Vigneto Filonardi, Cannellino, and Vigna dei Preti. Also good IGT Ferro e Seta (Sangiovese/Cesanese), with ageing potential.

Wine & Food

Contemporary Roman cooking is a monument to miscellany. Its foundations – the recipes of the ancient Romans and the bourgeoisie of ensuing epochs – have all but crumbled away. What remains has been patched together by the poor and propped up by what could be borrowed from other places. Yet, for all the salt cod, salt pork, brains, entrails, feet, tails, mussels, anchovies, beans, chickpeas, and pecorino romano, Rome lays one of the tastiest and most coloured tables of Italy. But what really enriches the Roman diet are the vegetables that arrive fresh daily from the region's gardens – a visit to Rome's or the region's colourful markets is a visual must.

Abbacchio alla cacciatora Baby lamb cooked with rosemary, garlic, anchovies, and vinegar.

Bucatini all'amatriciana Pasta with *guanciale* (meat from the pig's cheek), red peppers (sometimes tomatoes), and pecorino.

Carciofi alla giudia Deep-fried whole artichokes, a specialty of Rome's Jewish quarter.

Carciofi alla romana Artichokes sautéed in oil, garlic, and mint.

Coda alla vaccinara Oxtail stewed with onion, tomatoes, celery, and wine.

Fettuccine al burro Pasta dressed with butter, cream, and Parmesan.

Pasta e ceci Soup of chickpeas with garlic, rosemary, and pasta.

Saltimbocca alla romana Veal filets with prosciutto and sage.

Spaghetti alla carbonara Pasta with a sauce of guanciale, grated Parmesan, pecorino, and raw eggs, which curdle and adhere to the strands

Hotels

Benito al Bosco, Velletri €–€€ Situated in the Castelli Romani, surrounded by pine forests and gardens, this pleasant 60-room hotel with pool makes a good escape from the soaring summer heat of Rome.

Country Hotel Rinaldone, Viterbo €–€€ Country lodging located on a large farm near Viterbo, with tennis courts, pool, mountain bikes, and a good restaurant. It is well located for

visiting Cerveteri, Tarquinia, Vulci, Castel d'Asso, and Tuscania, all rich in Etruscan remains.

Hotel Lancelot, Rome €–€€ A charming, friendly hotel in a residential area offering attentive personal service. Excellent value and well located for sightseeing being a short stroll from the Colosseum and the Roman Forum.

Villa Acquaviva, Frascati €€€ A 16th-century villa with 58 rooms, impressive frescoed halls, and

spectacular views. In-house dining offers an ample choice of typical Roman and Mediterranean dishes.
Villa Borbone, Frascati € Built in 1564, this 96-room hotel offers historical character and modern comfort. The restaurant offers fine views of Rome and the

neighbouring hills.
Villa del Monte, Rome €–€€
A former monastery with 97 spacious rooms surrounded by a large garden in Monte Mario, a short distance from the Vatican. Good in-house bar and restaurant.

Restaurants

Agata e Romeo, Rome €€
Romeo Caraccio and his wife Agata specialize in typical Roman cuisine: pasta with broccoli; rabbit croquettes; tuna coated with sesame seeds served in a sweet and sour sauce. Don't miss Agata's *millefoglie*, sweet puff pastry stuffed with almonds. Good wine list.
Antico Ristorante Pagnanelli, Castel Gandolfo €€ Located in a 19th-century building overlooking Lake Albano, this restaurant has a terrace for alfresco dining. The cuisine mixes tradition and innovation in seasonal recipes created using the products from the family farm. Excellent cellar worth plundering.
Antonello Colonna, Labico €€–€€€ One of Italy's top restaurants (est. 1874). The cuisine is traditional Roman, adapted to meet present tastes. Specialties include: escalope of foie gras with pizza bread and figs; ravioli with pecorino and tripe; pigeon on salt crust with bay leaf and pork fat.
Cantina Colonna, Marino €–€€
Hospitable *trattoria* serving rustic fare including *pasta e fagioli* (bean soup) *spaghetti all'amatriciana*, *abbacchio* (kid), roast pork, and grilled porcini mushrooms.
Le Colline Ciociare, Acuto €€
Good local specialties here include white truffles (in season), oxtail with spices and cannellini beans, and desserts such as honey ice cream with ginger in a chocolate sauce.

Da Armando al Pantheon, Rome €–€€ The Gargioli family have been serving local dishes since the 1960s, including *fettucine cacio e pepe* (pecorino cheese and pepper) *spaghetti all'amatriciana*, tripe, cutlets, and more.
Enoteca Anacleto Bleve, Rome €€ One of Rome's best wine bars, centrally located in the ghetto area. There is also a well-stocked *enoteca* where you can buy wines from all over Italy, taste by the glass, and sit and enjoy excellent snacks, cheeses, and more.
Enoteca Ferrara, Rome €–€€
Good wine bar in Trastevere with an excellent range of wines from all over Italy and a good selection of cheeses, plus a good range of dishes from the menu.
Ristorante-Enoteca La Torre, Viterbo €–€€ Excellent creative cooking based on traditional fare, plus a range of tasting menus with interesting combinations. Good wine list with more than 50 different kinds by the glass.
La Vecchia Osteria, Anzio €€
Excellent fresh seafood based on home recipes. Specialties include *risotto di scampi*, spaghetti with black squid ink, mixed fried or grilled fish, and more
Vino e Camino, Bracciano €–€€
Traditional *osteria*, overlooking the majestic Castello Odescalchi. Specialties include potato gateau, roast kid stuffed with artichokes, and local cheeses. Good wine list.

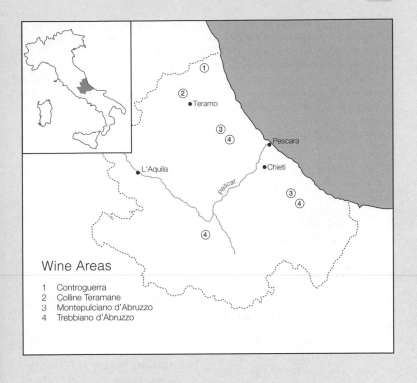

Wine Areas

1   Controguerra
2   Colline Teramane
3   Montepulciano d'Abruzzo
4   Trebbiano d'Abruzzo

Abruzzo *Abruzzo*

Until recently, Abruzzo had just two DOC denominations: Montepulciano d'Abruzzo for reds and Trebbiano d'Abruzzo for whites. Both covered practically all but the highest, least tractable lands in this Adriatic region that stretches from the Apennines through tumbling foothills down to the coast. Then, producers in the northerly province of Teramo, where wines are more stylish than the ones further south, sought recognition of their superiority, and in the mid-1990s Colline Teramane emerged as a Montepulciano d'Abruzzo sub-zone. This was swiftly followed by a new DOC, the small zone of Controguerra, with wines reflecting the more innovative scene in the region's far north, where Abruzzo borders the Marche. Now Montepulciano d'Abruzzo Colline Teramane has emerged with DOCG status in its own right.

The Montepulciano variety (not to be confused with Tuscany's Vino Nobile di Montepulciano) combines power with suppleness. Even its cherry-pink version (Cerasuolo) can be impressive. Trebbiano d'Abruzzo refers to the rather classy local sub-variety of Trebbiano, more often called Bombino, as well as the denomination. Yet the DOC, somewhat perversely, also allows for Trebbiano Toscano – and it is this that dominates white production.

Abruzzo boasts Italy's fifth-largest output at around three million hectolitres. The refinement of Teramo and the power of Chieti are balanced by wines from the intervening province of Pescara and counterpoised by the elegance of those from upland L'Aquila, where Cerasuolo is prevalent. Indeed, if you pick your spot carefully, you can find conditions suited to nearly every type of wine in this Adriatic region.

Wine tourism has not been explicitly developed in the area, but the coastal hills between Teramo and Chieti have numerous wineries and inns where local wines can be tasted. Enobar in Aquila and Enoteca Centrale in Teramo provide a good choice of wines from both Abruzzo and other regions.

Recent Vintages

Montepulciano improves with age, usually three to six years, sometimes much longer. Trebbiano is generally for drinking young, although some may be aged – in some cases, for five years or more. Among recent vintages, 2004, 2001, 2000, 1999, 1998, and 1997 were the most successful. 1996 was disappointing, but 2003, 2002, 1995, 1994, and 1993 were good; 1992 and 1991 were better for whites than for reds; 1990 and 1988 were generally superb for reds. Earlier good vintages for reds were 1987, 85, 83, 82, 79, 78, and 77.

Appellations

DOCG
MONTEPULCIANO D'ABRUZZO
COLLINE TERAMANE *r ris*

The comparatively cool hills around Teramo produce some excellent Montepulciano. This DOCG sets the grape's presence at 90% minimum, any remainder being made up with Sangiovese, to make a structured, firm, yet well-fruited wine of at least 12% alcohol. Age: 2 years, at least one in wood; *riserva*: 3 years.

DOC
CONTROGUERRA *w r fz sp sw nov ris*

Trebbiano Toscano, Montepulciano, Passerina, Cabernet Sauvignon, Merlot, Chardonnay, Ciliegiolo, Malvasia, Moscato Amabile, Pinot Nero, Riesling, Verdicchio, Pecorino

MONTEPULCIANO D'ABRUZZO
w r ris fz

Montepulciano d'Abruzzo, Bombino, Trebbiano, Cerasuolo.

TREBBIANO D'ABRUZZO *w fz*

Bombino (known here as Trebbiano d'Abruzzo or Trebbiano Toscano).

IGT
Alto Tirino
Colli Aprutini
Colli del Sangro
Colline Frentane
Colline Pescaresi
Colline Teatine
Del Vastese/Historium
Terre di Chieti
Valle Peligna

Producers

The key provinces have been abbreviated as follows:
AQ = L'Aquila; CH = Chieti;
PE = Pescara; TE = Teramo.

Agriverde, Ortona (CH) *w r*
☆☆→☆☆☆ 75ha, 600,000 bottles.

Giannicola di Carlo's vines are organically farmed and his production is mainly focused on Montepulciano. Top labels include Plateo and Solarea, as well as good Trebbiano, Pecorino, and Chardonnay. The estate is also one of the few in Abruzzo that offer *vinoterapia* – wine therapy treatments.

Barba, Scerne di Pineto (TE) *w r* ☆☆→☆☆☆ * 65ha, 200,000 bottles. Emerging estate with a production concentrating on Montepulciano characterized by dense black berry fruit and silky tannins. Top labels: Vigna Franca, aged 18 months in barrique on the lees, and Colle Morino, a well-priced, approachable wine. Also good Trebbiano Colle Morino.

Barone Cornacchia, Torano Nuovo (TE) *w r m sw ris* ☆☆ * 42ha, 312,000 bottles. Historic estate owned by Piero Cornacchia, whose family descends from 15th-century feudal landowners. His Montepulciano: Poggio Varano and Vigna Le Coste show good varietal typicity. Also good Controguerra Cabernet Villa Torri.

Cantina Tollo, Tollo (CH) *w p r* ☆☆→☆☆☆ * 3,500ha, 16,000,000 bottles. With more than 1,000 grape-growers, this co-op is by far the largest producer in the region. Highlights include Montepulciano: Aldiano, Cagiòlo, Colle Secco, Colle Cavalieri; and Cerasuolo Hedòs. Also good IGT Cagiòlo Bianco Chardonnay.

Casal Thaulero, Roseto degli Abruzzi (TE) *w r* ☆☆→☆☆☆ * 2,300,000 bottles. Quality-conscious co-op making reliably good ranges of Montepulciano, Cerasuolo, and Trebbiano. In particular Trebbiano Borgo Thaulero – full, aromatic, and very persistent, an excellent-value wine; and Montepulciano: Duca Thaulero and Borgo Thaulero.

Cataldi Madonna, Ofena (AQ) *w p r* ☆☆→☆☆☆ * 33ha, 230,000 bottles. One of Abruzzo's top estates producing some elegant, structured wines. Montepulciano Toni shows distinction and class; Cerasulo Piè

delle Vigne is a rosé with a fruity-cherry bouquet; IGT Malandrino (Montepulciano/Cabernet) is vinified in 35hl barrels on the lees for three months.

Ciccio Zaccagnini, Bolognano (PE) *w p r sw* ☆☆☆ 78ha, 500,000 bottles. Marcello Zaccagnini's reliably fine Montepulciano Abbazia San Clemente from highly selected grapes has fruit-forward appeal, sweet tannins, and a round, long finish. Also good IGT Capisco Rosso (Cabernet Franc) – intense, berry fruit aromas, warm, soft, with a bitter-chocolate finish; and San Clemente Chardonnay.

Farnese, Ortona (CH) *w p r ris sw* ☆☆☆ 150ha (plus bought-in grapes), 10,000,000 bottles. Huge winery producing good Montepulciano and Edizione Cinque Autoctoni from Montepulciano, Primitivo, Sangiovese, Negroamaro, and Malvasia Nera – modern, elegant, powerful, fruit-forward. Also good Opis Riserva, Montepulciano from the Colline Termane.

Fattoria La Valentina, Spoltore (PE) *w p r* ☆☆→☆☆☆ * 31ha, 265,000 bottles. Sabatino Di Properzio's production ranks high for its Montepulciano, in particular the Bellovedere label – intense sour cherry notes and spice, rich and velvety, high in alcohol. Aged in barrique for two years, it also needs to gain some bottle-age. Also good Binomio and Trebbiano Vigneto Spilla.

Il Feuduccio, Orsogna (CH) *w r* ☆☆☆ 56ha, 80,000 bottles. Gaetano Lamaletto's production, overseen by consultant oenologist Franco Bernabei, includes fine Montepulciano at three levels: top label Margae is an ambitious, age-worthy wine, aged 16 months in barrique and one year in bottle; Ursonia is aged partly in large barrel and partly in barrique;

Il Feuduccio is aged in large barrels, making it a very drinkable, enjoyable Montepulciano.

Lorenzo Filomusi Guelfi, Tocco di Casauria (PE) *w p r* ☆☆ 10ha, 69,000 bottles. Small estate belonging to the descendants of the 14th-century feudal Filomusi Guelfi family. It produces impressive Montepulciano Fonte Dei and Cerasuolo, as well as new release Sauvignon Perlei.

Dino Illuminati, Controguerra (TE) *w r ris* ☆☆☆→☆☆☆☆ 112ha, 1,000,000 bottles. Large property producing Montepulciano, Cerasuolo, and Controguerra. Top labels include three fine, elegant, age-worthy *riservas*: Montepulciano Zanna – warm, rich, sour cherry notes, smoky, tar finish; Montepulciano Pieluni; and Lumen Controguerra, a Montepulciano/Cabernet blend.

Marramiero, Rosciano (PE) *w p r* ☆☆☆→☆☆☆☆ 40ha, 412,000 bottles. Estate producing impressive Montepulciano, good Cerasuolo, and Trebbiano. Top label Montepulciano Dante Marramiero is elegant and evolved – dark cherry, tobacco, leather, and floral notes, powerful, structured, yet balanced, with a long finish. Also good Trebbiano Altare and Montepulciano Inferi.

Masciarelli, San Martino sulla Marrucina (CH) *w p r* ☆☆→☆☆☆☆ 140ha, 1,100,000 bottles. Gianni Masciarelli produces reliable Montepulciano, Cerasuolo, and Trebbiano. Top labels: Montepulciano Villa Gemma and Trebbiano Marina Cvetic, aged 22 months in barrique and showing well-integrated oak; and Cerasuolo Villa Gemma. International-style IGTs Chardonnay and Cabernet Sauvignon (both labelled Marina Cvetic) round out a supreme range.

Camillo Montori, Controguerra (TE) *w r ris* ☆☆→☆☆☆☆ * 55ha, 600,000 bottles. This estate produces wines with personality and individual character, including a new range under the Coste Tronto label. Highlights: Montepulciano Colline Teramane Fonte Cupa Riserva, Cerasuolo, and Trebbiano Fonte Cupa.

Bruno Nicodemi, Notaresco (TE) *w p r ris* ☆☆→☆☆☆ * 30ha, 190,000 bottles. Production at this estate is overseen by consultant oenologist Paolo Caciorgna and is prized for consistently good Montepulciano, Cerasuolo, and Trebbiano. One of the highlights is Montepulciano Colline Teramane Neromoro Riserva, from highly selected grapes from old pergola vines – age-worthy, elegant, silky, balanced.

Franco Pasetti, Francavilla al Mare (CH) *w p r* ☆☆ * 28ha, 160,000 bottles. Emerging estate producing admirable Montepulciano d'Abruzzo Testarossa and Trebbiano Zarachè, as well as excellent Pecorino.

Valentini, Loreto Aprutino (PE) *w p r* ☆☆☆→☆☆☆☆ 64ha. Edoardo Valentini is a great individualist, shunning trade fairs, journalists, trends, and barriques. He produces three wines: a wonderful Cerasuolo; a voluptuous Montepulciano that ages superbly; and the only Trebbiano anywhere to deserve the epithet "great" – complex aromas and a zesty mineral quality.

Wine & Food

The Abruzzesi enjoy strongly flavoured food, and lots of it. The maximum expression of their gourmand lifestyle was the *panarda*, a meal of 30 to 40 courses eaten through a day, an extravaganza no longer in vogue. Though the Adriatic is full of fish, even coastal dwellers look to the land for sustenance – lamb and mutton are favoured meats. Ewe's milk is the source of pecorino cheese, and the Apennine uplands produce outstanding artichokes, cardoons, lentils, potatoes, and beans, as well as Italy's main supply of saffron, used along with hot chilli pepper.

Brodetto Fish soup cooked with green peppers.

Cicoria, cacio e uova Soup of chicory and other vegetables with salt pork in chicken broth thickened with eggs and grated pecorino.

Indocca Pungent stew of pork ribs, feet, ears, and rind with rosemary, bay leaf, peppers and vinegar.

Maccheroni alla chitarra Pasta served with a lamb ragout stewed in wine and olive oil, with tomatoes, garlic, bay leaf, and peppers.

Scrippelle 'nfuss (or 'mbusse) Crêpes served in chicken broth.

Virtù or le sette virtù Legendary soup of Teramo, with pork, beans, peas, greens, herbs, carrots, garlic, onions, tomato and pasta.

Zuppa di cardi Soup of cardoons with tomatoes and salt pork.

Hotels

Locanda La Corte, Acciano (AQ) € This 16th-century villa set in the regional park of Sirente-Velino has 25 rooms and an excellent restaurant serving traditional Abruzzese cuisine.

Villa Fiore, Torano Nuovo (TE) € A welcoming *agriturismo* set in the Torano countryside with five rooms and two apartments. The restaurant offers genuine local specialties.

Villa Majella, Guardiagrele (CH) € Right under Mount Majella, Angela and Peppino's well-run hotel has 14 comfortable rooms and a renowned restaurant serving a fascinating range of traditional recipes.

Restaurants

L'Angolo d'Abruzzo, Carsoli (AQ) €€ Good meat dishes, with a range of cured meats (including mules testicles), pasta with lamb ragout, risotto with black truffle, braised wild boar, rabbit with truffle and Abruzzese desserts. Excellent wine cellar with encyclopaedic listings.

Antiche Mura, Aquila € Traditional *trattoria* in the centre of town offering a rich choice of traditional local dishes, featuring lentil soup, rabbit cooked in saffron and peppers, and meat balls with herbs. Simple but good wine list.

La Bandiera, Civitella Casanova (PE) €€ One of Abruzzo's top restaurants, offering fine ambience with tasting menu or à la carte from a worthy selection of local delicacies. Excellent wine list.

Barilotto Trattoria, Campotosto (AQ) € A simple *trattoria* in the Laga chain of mountains that divides the Marche, Lazio, and Abruzzo. On the menu: *mortadella di Campotosto*, *lasagnette* with mushrooms, and roast meats. Rooms are also available.

Circolo della Vela at Pescara €€ Benito will be happy to prepare some of his finest fish dishes including *brodetto* and *guazzetti di pesce* (another fish soup), freshly marinated calamari, lobster tails in Tabasco sauce and more. Good Abruzzese white wines.

Molise *Molise*

Molise, long an appendix of neighbouring Abruzzo, is still sometimes regarded as an afterthought. References to the region's wines date back to Roman times, though little of special regard seems to have emerged from this region's vineyards since.

Through the ages, the hill people kept their rustic wines to themselves. The advent of DOCs Biferno and Pentro added official status in the 1980s, a step up from total obscurity. But wines from Pentro are notable by their absence, and there are just two producers of note in Biferno. Additionally, a newer DOC, called Molise, now covers all of Biferno's DOC and the heartland of Pentro DOC.

The most inviting thing about Molise is that few people go there, possibly because few people know where it is. It has a narrow strip of Adriatic coast (at Termoli) and extensive uplands to explore, and it offers rustically tasty wine and food at bargain prices in the local *trattorie*.

Recent Vintages

Recommended vintages are given with individual wines.

Appellations

DOC
BIFERNO *w p r ris*
Bombino, Malvasia, Montepulciano, Aglianico, Trebbiano Toscano.

MOLISE/DEL MOLISE *w r ris fz sp pas nov*
Montepulciano, Aglianico, Cabernet Sauvignon, Chardonnay, Falanghina, Greco Bianco, Moscato Bianco, Pinot Bianco, Sangiovese, Sauvignon, Trebbiano, and Tintilia (the local name for Bovale).

PENTRO DI ISERNIA/ PENTRO *w p r*
Trebbiano Toscano, Bombino Bianco, Montepulciano, Sangiovese

IGT
Osco/Terre degli Osci.
Rotae

Producers

The key provinces have been abbreviated as follows: CB = Campobasso; IS = Isernia.

Borgo di Colloredo, Campomarino (CB) *w p r* ☆☆ 70ha, 300,000 bottles. Production at Enrico and Pasquale Di Giulio's emerging estate focuses on Biferno, white and rosé, plus varietals from Montepulciano, Aglianico, Falanghina, Trebbiano, and Sangiovese.

Masseria Di Majo Norante, Campomarino (CB) *w r* ☆☆→☆☆☆☆ * 85ha, 800,000 bottles. Despite this estate being located on hot plains once considered unsuitable for vines, its production, overseen by Riccardo Cotarella, is rarely matched for class, even in more prodigious neighbouring terrains. Highlights: varietals from Aglianico Contado, Tintilia, Prignolo, Falanghina, Greco, and an excellent Moscato Apinae.

Masserie Flocco, Portocannone (CB)
w r ☆☆☆ * 158ha, 200,000 bottles.
With vines planted close to the
coast, the production at the
Flocco family's emerging estate
is focused on quality IGT wines,

including Podere dei Castelli
(Merlot); Podere del Canneto
(Chardonnay); Sirifarà?, a blend
of local varieties; along with
Bosco delle Guardie Rosso,
a Merlot/Cabernet blend.

Wine & Food

Molise doesn't have a cuisine
all its own, but instead it shares
recipes with its northerly
neighbour Abruzzo, while picking
up occasional ideas from other
adjacent regions, such as Puglia,
Campania, or Lazio. The cooking
is rustic and authentically good.
Lamb and kid are stalwarts in the
hill country, where pecorino cheese
is eaten in chunks or grated over
pasta, and pork is preserved as
prosciutto and salame. Mountain
streams provide freshwater trout
and crayfish. Along the coast,
simply prepared fish from the
Adriatic is widely consumed.
Calcioni di ricotta Circular pasta
shells containing ricotta and

provolone cheese, prosciutto, and
eggs, and then deep-fried in oil.
Lepre a ciffe e ciaffe Hare cooked
in a marinade of herbs, vinegar,
and wine.
Mazzarelle d'agnello Lamb's
lung and intestines wrapped in
beet greens and cooked in oil
and white wine.
Polenta maritata d'Isernia
Polenta fried with garlic, layered
with red beans and chillis, and
baked in the oven.
Tacconi Quadrangular pasta
often served with a meat sauce.
Zuppa di ortiche Soup of nettle
sprouts, tomato, bacon, and onion.

Hotels

Vecchio Granaio, Vastogirardi €
Country house with four rooms
located by the estuary of the
Trigno River. The owners also
breed horses and Saint Bernard

dogs. Excellent food is on offer
at the in-house restaurant, with
a wide range of cheeses, ravioli
filled with cheese and mushrooms,
and grilled meats.

Restaurants

Ribo, Guglionese €€
Founded over 100 years ago, this
place still retains the same charm
and tradition as always. It serves
an assortment of rustic dishes:
pasta with lamb ragout, polenta,
and aubergine escalopes. Whatever
you order, you can't go wrong here.

Vecchia Trattoria Tonino,
Campobasso €€ In the centre
of Campobasso, this traditional
trattoria in existence since 1954
offers Molise's top dishes. Excellent
baccalà mantecato all'olio (cod) and
olive pâté with smoked herring on
a bed of citrus orange salad.

Puglia *Puglia*

Puglia's fortunes have changed more dramatically in the past decade than anywhere else in Italy. The once-ignominious title of "Europe's wine cellar", earned for its high exports of blending wines, now has a more positive ring. Producers have learned to harness the fruit and vigour of their wines while eliminating the rough edges and taming their tendency to develop prodigious amounts of alcohol. This, along with the comparatively low costs of production, has made Puglia a prime source of the mouth-filling, moreish, good-value wines, reds in particular, that European markets crave. This is particularly so in the southernmost Salento peninsula, the sun-drenched "heel" of Italy, where the Negroamaro, Malvasia Nera, Primitivo, and, more recently, the revived Sussumaniello and Ottavianello varieties dominate. Negroamaro is the powerhouse, but bush-trained Primitivo (the variety that became Zinfandel in California) thrives on the hot plains to produce a rich, strong wine of great character. Central and northern Puglia are more the domain of red Uva di Troia, Montepulciano, and Bombino Nero. Rosés here show style rarely equalled elsewhere. Made by the *lacrima* (teardrop) system using only about half the juice of uncrushed grapes, they are delicately dry, and may be pale roseate in colour – comparable to what Americans call "blush" – or more deeply pink. The climate is warm and dry along the coast, becoming cooler in the interior, and reds may even have the delicately perfumed qualities of northerly wines. And, naturally, international varieties, white Chardonnay and Sauvignon in particular, have made inroads.

All this is amply covered by Puglia's twenty-five DOCs (although most of those in the Salento have similar criteria and are distinguished only by the geographical area they cover). Wines falling outside these criteria will come under one of six IGTs, of which Puglia and Salento are the most prevalent.

As Italy's perennial gateway to Greece, Puglia has remnants of Hellas, plus reminders of innumerable other peoples. The octagonal Swabian structure of Castel del Monte is well worth a visit, as is the Salento Peninsula, with its ancient Greek cities of Lecce, now a marvel of baroque, and Gallipoli. Select Puglian wines are on display at the Enoteca Vinarius De Pasquale in Bari, and Nel Regno di Bacco in Taranto.

Recent Vintages

Many Apulian reds are noted for their longevity, as are certain rosés of Salento, although, as a rule, the region's pink and white wines should be drunk young. The hot Salento Peninsula tends to have more consistent harvests than the more temperate hilly zones. Recommended vintages are shown with each entry.

Appellations

DOC

ALEATICO DI PUGLIA *r sw liq ris 99 00 01 03 04*

Aleatico, Negroamaro, Malvasia.

ALEZIO *p r ris 99 00 01 03 04*

Negroamaro, Malvasia Nera, Sangiovese, Montepulciano.

BRINDISI *p r ria 97 98 99 00 01 03 04*

Negroamaro, Malvasia, Sangiovese, Montepulciano, Sussumaniello.

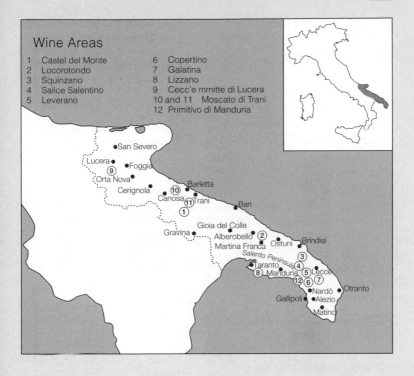

Wine Areas

1 Castel del Monte
2 Locorotondo
3 Squinzano
4 Salice Salentino
5 Leverano
6 Copertino
7 Galatina
8 Lizzano
9 Cecc'e mmitte di Lucera
10 and 11   Moscato di Trani
12 Primitivo di Manduria

CACC'E MMITTE DI LUCERA *r*
Uva di Troia, Montepulciano, Sangiovese, Malvasia, Trebbiano, Bombino, others.

CASTEL DEL MONTE *w r p ris fz*
Aglianico, Bombino Bianco, Bombino Nero, Cabernet Sauvignon, Cabernet Franc, Chardonnay, Pinot Bianco, Pinot Nero, Sauvignon, Uva di Troia.

COPERTINO *p r ris 99 00 01 03 04*
Negroamaro, Malvasia, Montepulciano, Sangiovese.

GALATINA *w p r ris fz nov 99 00 01 03 04*
Negroamaro, Chardonnay.

GIOIA DEL COLLE *w p r sw liq ris*
Trebbiano Toscano, Primitivo, Montepulciano, Negroamaro, Sangiovese, Malvasia Nera, Aleatico

GRAVINA *w sw sp*
Malvasia, Greco di Tufo, Bianco d'Alessano, Bombino, Trebbiano, Verdeca.

LEVERANO *w p r sw pas vt nov ris 99 00 01 03 04*
Malvasia Bianca, Bombino Bianco, Negroamaro, Malvasia Nera, Montepulciano, Sangiovese.

LIZZANO *w p r sup nov fz sp*
Trebbiano, Chardonnay, Pinot Bianco, Sauvignon, Negroamaro, Montepulciano, Sangiovese, Malvasia, Bombino.

LOCOROTONDO *w sp*
Verdeca, Bianco d'Alessano.

MARTINA FRANCA/MARTINA *w sp*
Verdeca, Bianco d'Alessano, Fiano, Bombino, Malvasia.

MATINO *p r 99 00 01 03 04*
Negroamaro, Malvasia, Sangiovese.

MOSCATO DI TRANI *w sw liq 99 00 01 02 03 04*
Moscato Bianco.

NARDÒ *p r ris 99 00 01 03 04*
Negroamaro, Malvasia Nera.

ORTA NOVA *p r*
Sangiovese, Uva di Troia, Lambrusco Maestri, Montepulciano, Trebbiano.

OSTUNI *w r*
Impigno, Francavilla, Bianco d'Alessano, Verdeca, Ottavianello, Negroamaro, Malvasia Nera, Notar Domenico, Sussumaniello.

PRIMITIVO DI MANDURIA *r sw liq 96 97 98 99 00 01 03 04*
Primitivo.

ROSSO BARLETTA *r 01 02 04*
Uva di Troia, Sangiovese, Montepulciano, Malbec.

ROSSO CANOSA/CANUSIUM *r ris 99 00 01 03 04*
Uva di Troia, Montepulciano, Sangiovese.

ROSSO DI CERIGNOLA *r ris*
Uva di Troia, Negroamaro, Sangiovese, Barbera, Malbec, Montepulciano, Trebbiano.

SALICE SALENTINO *w p r liq sw sp nov ris 90 93 94 95 96 97 98 99 00 01 03 04*
Chardonnay, Negroamaro, Malvasia Nera, Aleatico, Pinot Bianco.

SAN SEVERO *w p r sp*
Bombino Bianco, Trebbiano Toscano, Malvasia, Montepulciano, Sangiovese.

SQUINZANO *p r ris 99 00 01 03 04*
Negroamaro, Malvasia Nera, Sangiovese.

IGT
Daunia
Murgia
Puglia
Salento
Tarantino
Valle d'Itria

Producers

The key provinces have been abbreviated as follows: BA = Bari; BR = Brindisi; FG = Foggia; LE = Lecce; TA = Taranto.

Accademia dei Racemi, Manduria (TA) *r ☆☆→☆☆☆ ** 120ha, 1,200,000 bottles. A group of small, quality-focused estates (including Pervini, Accademia, and Casale Bevagna) working mainly with indigenous vines. Top labels: Primitivo di Manduria Zinfandel Sinfarosa; Primitivo: Portile Masseria Pepe and Giravolta Tenuta Pozzopalo; Alberello Felline (Negroamaro/Primitivo); and Sum Torre Guaceto (Sussumaniello) – silky tannins, fruity, hints of leather and graphite.

Agricole Vallone, Lecce *w r sw ☆☆☆ ** 170ha, 620,000 bottles. Vallone's production ranks high in Salice Salentino of classic style. Top labels: Brindisi Vigna Flaminio; Salice Salentino Rosso Vereto (Negroamaro/Malvasia Nera); rich IGT Graticciaia (Negroamaro); and two variations on Sauvignon: Corte Valesio and dessert wine Passo de le Viscarde.

Antica Masseria del Sigillo, Guagnano (LE) *w r ☆☆* 34ha, 200,000 bottles. Emerging estate with premium international-style labels, such as Chardonnay Sigillo Primo and Terre del Guiscardo, a Primitivo/Merlot/Cabernet Sauvignon blend – austere, with complex spice, tobacco, and ripe berry notes. Also good Primitivo Sigillo Primo.

Apollonio, Monteroni di Lecce (LE) *w p r ris* ☆☆→☆☆☆ * 100ha, 1,200,000 bottles. Historic estate (est. 1870) in the heart of Salento. Top labels: Salice Salentino – ripe, smooth, with juicy fruit and a long finish; Copertino Rosso Divoto Riserva – warm, round, soft, sapid, and elegant; and Terragnolo (Primitivo).

Botromagno, Gravina in Puglia (BA) *w r sw* ☆☆☆ 145ha, 500,000 bottles. Beniamino d'Agostino's production is led by an excellent Gravina (Greco/Malvasia) – good mineral character; and Pier delle Vigne (Aglianico/Montepulciano), aged 24 months in barrique – complex, spicy, balsamic notes, fresh acidity, and persistence. Also good Primitivo and sweet Gravisano Malvasia Passita.

Francesco Candido, San Donaci (BR) *w p r sw* ☆☆→☆☆☆ 160ha, 2,000,000 bottles. The production, overseen by Donato Lanati, focuses on stylish Salice Salentino red and white, as well as fine, rare Aleatico. Highlights: Cappello di Prete (Negroamaro), Duca d'Aragona (Negroamaro/Montepulciano), Immensum (Negroamaro/Cabernet Sauvignon), Casina Cucci (Chardonnay), and sweet Paule Calle (Chardonnay/Malvasia).

Cantele, Lecce *w p r* ☆☆☆ * 80ha, 2,000,000 bottles. Dynamic family estate producing a well-honed quality range with global exports. Top labels include Salice Salentino (Primitivo) and Teresa Manara: Rosso (Negroamaro/Aglianico) and Bianco (Chardonnay). Also a fine Amativo, a supple, fruit-forward Primitivo/Negroamaro blend.

Cantine Due Palme, Cellino San Marco (BR) *w r ris* ☆☆→☆☆☆ 900ha, 2,800,000 bottles. Go-ahead co-op with 400 members and a production overseen by Angelo Maci. Top labels: Salice Salentino Rosso Selvarossa, Brindisi Rosso, Ettamiano IGT Primitivo, and Tinaia IGT Chardonnay.

Castel di Salve, Tricase (LE) *w p r* ☆☆→☆☆☆ 40ha, 130,000 bottles. The descendant of the Duke of Salve Antonio Winspeare, Francesco Winspcare has carried on the family tradition of winemaking. Highlights: Il Volo di Alessandro (Sangiovese), Lama del Tenente (Primitivo/Montepulciano/Malvasia), Priante (Negroamaro/Montepulciano), Armecolo (Negroamaro/Malvasia), and other Salento IGTs.

Castello Monaci, Salice Salentino (LE) *w p r* ☆☆ 110ha, 2,300,000 bottles. Historic castle (part of the Gruppo Italiano Vini) producing good Salice Salentino, Primitivo, Keros (Negroamaro/Malvasia Nera), and Artas (Primitivo/Negroamaro) – terroir character, fruit-forward appeal, with ripe, spicy notes and a balanced, long finish.

Conti Zecca, Leverano (LE) *p r ris* ☆☆☆→☆☆☆☆ * 320ha, 1,800,000 bottles. Large family estate with a production covering ranges of Leverano. Highlights: Nero (Negroamaro/Cabernet) – cassis, leather, cigar aromas mingle with cherry, spice, and chocolate, silky, fine tannins and a fresh, long finish; Primitivo Donna Marzia; and well-priced Donna Marzia Rosato (Negroamaro/Malvasia Nera).

D'Alfonso del Sordo, San Severo (FG) *w p r* ☆☆→☆☆☆ * 90ha, 350,000 bottles. Renowned estate producing fine San Severo and IGT varietals from Bombino Bianco, Uva di Troia, Merlot, and Cabernet Sauvignon. Top label: IGT Cava del Re (Cabernet), aged in barrique 12 months – fruit-forward, prune and cherry compote, spice, tobacco, structured, with a long finish.

Felline, Manduria (TA) *p r* ☆☆☆ * 45ha. Gregory Perrucci's vines produce some rich, powerful, trend-setting Primitivo di Manduria. Also prized IGT Vigna del Feudo (Primitivo/Malvasia Nera/Ottavianello), and Salento Rosso Albarello (Primitivo/Negroamaro), all showing a good quality/price ratio.

Leone De Castris, Salice Salentino (LE) *w p r ris* ☆☆☆ * 250ha, 2,700,000 bottles. Renowned family estate producing Salice Salentino Rosso Riserva Donna Lisa, IGT Illemos (a four-grape Primitivo-based blend), IGT Messere Andrea (Negroamaro/Cabernet), and the legendary Five Roses, one of Italy's first bottled rosés, plus more well-priced wines.

Marco Maci, Cellino San Marco (BR) *w p r* ☆☆☆ 100ha, 1,000,000 bottles. Large winery with a huge range led by IGT Sire (Negroamaro), Bella Mojgan (Negroamaro/Malvasia), Dragonero (Merlot/Negroamaro), and Vita (Negroamaro/Cabernet). Also fine varietal whites: Sauvignon, Pinot Bianco, and Chardonnay.

Masseria Monaci, Copertino (LE) *w r* ☆☆ 36ha, 620,000 bottles. The production at consultant winemaker Severino Garofano's family estate is led by IGT Le Braci Negroamaro – rich, fruity nose, balanced and elegant on the palate; stylish Copertino Rosso Eloquenzia, (Negroamaro) – great value; and fine IGT I Censi (Negroamaro/Primitivo).

Mille Una, Lizzano (TA) *w r* ☆☆→☆☆☆ 30ha, 70,000 bottles. Emerging estate with a large range of labels, including Montenero (Negroamaro) – powerful, warm, and round, with structure, firm tannins, and a long finish; Maviglia (Viognier) – tropical, aromatic, sapid, and fresh; and Ori di Taranto (Primitivo).

Rivera, Andria (BA) *w p r* ☆☆☆→☆☆☆☆ * 85ha, 1,500,000 bottles. Leading winery with a range of Castel del Monte wines, led by Puer Apuliae (Nero di Troia), aged 14 months in barrique – concentrated, with balanced acidity, persistent. Also good Rosso Rupicolo, Il Falcone Riserva, Bianco Fedora; varietals: Chardonnay, Aglianico, Pinot Bianco, and Sauvignon; and Moscato di Trani Piani di Tufara.

Rosa del Golfo, Alezio (LE) *w p r* ☆☆→☆☆☆ * 40ha, 250,000 bottles. The late Mino Calò, creator of the acclaimed Rosa del Golfo, was known as Italy's "prince of rosé". His son Damiano has carried forward the tradition with an oak-fermented rosé – bright cherry-pink, flowery scent, and a dry, harmonious, exquisite flavour. Also good IGT Salento: Primitivo, Portulano, Scaliere; white Bolina; and red Quarantale.

Cosimo Taurino, Guagnano (LE) *w p r* ☆☆☆→☆☆☆☆ 150ha, 1,200,000 bottles. Leading estate producing long-living, late-harvested Brindisi Patriglione – tobacco, cocoa, tar, and ripe fruit aromas, silky tannins, fresh, long finish; superb Salento Notarpanaro; Scaloti (Negroamaro); I Sierri (Chardonnay); and others.

Tenute Rubino, Brindisi *w r* ☆☆☆ * 200ha, 700,000 bottles. With his superb Salento (white and red), Luigi Rubino ranks among Puglia's finest producers. Top labels: Torre Testa (100% Susumaniello) – age-worthy, with depth, elegance, and balance; Visellio (Primitivo); Sedna (Malvasia Bianca); and Brindisi Rosso Jaddico (Negroamaro).

Tormaresca, San Pietro Vernotico (BR) *w r* ☆☆☆→☆☆☆☆ * 350ha, 1,000,000 bottles. The wines from Tuscan giant Antinori's investment in Puglia show the expected class. Highlights: Masseria Maime (Negroamaro), Castel del Monte Rosso Bocca di Lupo (Aglianico/Cabernet Sauvignon), Pietra Bianca

Chardonnay, and Tormaresca: Rosso (Negroamaro/Cabernet Sauvignon) and Chardonnay.

Torre Quarto, Cerignola (FG) w r ☆☆ * 40ha, 400,000 bottles. Revived by Stefano Cirillo, this long-standing estate producing principally Uva di Troia-based reds, Primitivo, and others is noted for its excellent-value wines. Top labels: Tarabuso (Primitivo), Bottaccia (Uva di Troia), and Claire (Chardonnay).

Torrevento, Corato (BA) p r ☆☆→☆☆☆ * 400ha, 2,000,000 bottles. A large winery housed in a 17th-century ex-monastery and producing well-priced Castel del Monte and other wines. Top labels: Kebir (Nero di Troia/Cabernet Sauvignon) – age-worthy, concentrated, and highly extracted, complex aromas, persistent finish; Castel di Monte: Bianco (Bombino Bianco/Pampanuto) and Rosato (Bombino Nero/Montepulciano).

Valle dell'Asso, Galatina (LE) w p r sw ☆☆ 60ha, 200,000 bottles. Gino Vallone's well-established estate has been producing wine in this sunny land since the 1860s. The range includes IGT Primàfo (Negroamaro), Salice Salentino Rosso, and Il Macaro (sweet Aleatico) – good terroir character.

Vigne & Vini, Leporano (TA) w r ☆☆☆ 155ha, 500,000 bottles. Maria Teresa Basile's estate focuses primarily on stylish Primitivo di Manduria. Top labels include Primitivo di Manduria: Chicca and Papale – fruit-forward, spicy, sapid, tenacious, persistent; and Zinfandel. Also good international-style oak-fermented Chardonnay Primadonna.

Vinicola Savese, Sava (TA) w r ☆☆ * 21ha, 200,000 bottles. The Pichierri family estate produces good traditional Primitivo di Manduria, especially Tradizione del Nonno, made from late-harvest grapes – good varietal character, ample aromas, powerful, full, round, with a fresh, elegant finish. Also good Manduria Dolce, a sweet "meditation" wine from 50-year-old vines and low yields.

Wine & Food

Balance seems built into the Puglian diet, probably because the region, if not perennially rich, has certainly never lacked for nutritive elements. The northern plains provide grain for pasta and bread; the plateaux lamb, sausages, and cheese; the Adriatic and Ionian seas plentiful fish. Everywhere there are fruit, olive oil (Puglia produces more than any other region), and wine, not to mention the abundance of fresh produce: broad beans, artichokes, chicory, aubergines, peppers, and more.

Agnello al cartoccio Lamb chops baked in paper with green olives and *lampasciuoli,* a bitter-tasting bulb similar to onion.

Burrata Soft, buttery mozzarella from the town of Andria.

Cavatieddi con la ruca Conch-shaped pasta served with rocket, tomato sauce, and pecorino.

Frisedde Hard rolls softened with water and served with fresh tomato, oregano, and olive oil.

Gniumerieddi Lamb innards flavoured with pecorino, lard, lemon, and parsley, rolled, skewered, and cooked over coals.

'Ncapriata Dried broad beans boiled, peeled, and mashed with chicory, pimento, onion, tomato, and lots of olive oil.

Orecchiette con cime di rapa Tiny, ear-shaped pasta with boiled turnip greens and chilli.

Hotels

Hotel Covo dei Saraceni, Polignano a Mare (BA) €€ Close to Alberobello and Ostuni, on the coast, this 36-room hotel features four tastefully refined suites.

Masseria Mosca, Gallipoli (LE) €€ A restored 17th-century olive mill converted into comfortable mini apartments set in beautiful grounds with a pool.

Masseria Parco di Castro, Fasano (BR) € This 17th-century restored rural farm with two large, stylish rooms is a good stopover after sampling the excellent local dishes at the in-house restaurant, renowned for its genuine dishes.

Masseria San Domenico, Savelletri di Fasano (BR) € A refined rural dwelling converted into a hotel. Located a few minutes' walk from the beach, it also boasts a pool, tennis courts, and a good restaurant.

Hotel Patria Palace, Lecce €€–€€€ An 18th-century aristocratic building in the centre of Lecce, facing the splendid baroque Basilica di Santa Croce and ideally located for sightseeing. It has 67 comfortable rooms.

Villa Masseria Puglia, Santa Caterina (LE) €–€€ A rural building on a hill surrounded by a park with secular olive trees and sea views (it is only 1km/ 0.6 miles from some of Salento's most beautiful beaches).

Restaurants

Antichi Sapori, Andria (BA) €–€€ Pietro Zito's *trattoria* offers dishes from Alta Murgia's cuisine, such as baked onions, snails with wild mint, aubergine cooked in terracotta, *cime di rapa*, and more.

Centro Storico, Locorotondo (BA) €–€€ Small *trattoria* in the historic centre serving good salami, fried meat balls, *orecchiette* with tomato and basil, *cavatelli* with meat sauce, lamb escalopes, and local wines.

Chacaito L'Osteria di Zio Aldo, Foggia €€ Aldo and Letizia run one of Foggia's top eateries for local character. Situated next to the fruit market, it serves seafood and meat as well as a good assortment of vegetable-based dishes.

Cibus, Ceglie Messapica (BR) €€ A traditional *osteria* located in the cellar of a 14th-century Dominican monastery. Excellent local specialties and a good wine list.

Cucina Casareccia, Lecce € One of the best addresses to sample Lecce's local fare. On the menu, excellent soups, *orecchiette*, local vegetable dishes, and more. Limited wine selection.

Osteria delle Travi, Bari € Simple, rustic local cuisine with good vegetarian dishes, seafood such as *cozze arraganate* (mussels with garlic), and lots more.

Il Poeta Contadino, Alberobello (BA) €€–€€€ This is the place for a real gastronomic treat. Elegant and refined, this place serves traditional dishes with a creative touch, including creamy cheese with wild chicory, pasta with *cime di rape* and baby tomatoes, and beef fillet with olive pâté. Excellent wine list.

La Puritate, Gallipoli (LE) €€ Situated in a traditional building facing the sea, in the old "oriental" centre of Gallipoli, which is definitely worth a visit. Paolo Fedele's menu is strictly fish-based with a fairly good selection of local wines.

Campania *Campania*

The ancients knew that vines thrived in the volcanic soil of Campania. The Greeks introduced the varieties now known as Aglianico, Falanghina, and Greco; while the Romans celebrated the wines of Falernum and the Campi Flegrei, Vesuvius, and Avellino. The wines of the Kingdom of Naples were raved about by chroniclers from the Renaissance to the Risorgimento. In modern times viticulture declined in the region; however, over a span of a few years, Campania has come bounding back with a new generation of winemakers producing stylish wines that reflect positively on the wisdom of the ancients. Falernian has re-emerged with great class as Falerno, Vesuvius has regained respectability, and ancient lustre has been restored to the wines of Avellino with Taurasi, Fiano di Avellino, and Greco di Tufo (all elevated to DOCG). Wines from the Campi Flegrei, the Amalfi Coast, the Sorrento Peninsula, the islands of Capri and Ischia, and even the more remote southern Cilento uplands are steadily rebuilding fine reputations, often based on traditional local varieties. The wooded hills and high mountains of Irpinia and Sannio are responsible for the beneficial cooler temperatures at night, a thermic variation that brings freshness and aromatic complexity to the grapes.

Today, rather than the small handful of estates that existed less than twenty years ago, there are over sixty estates with vines planted to some

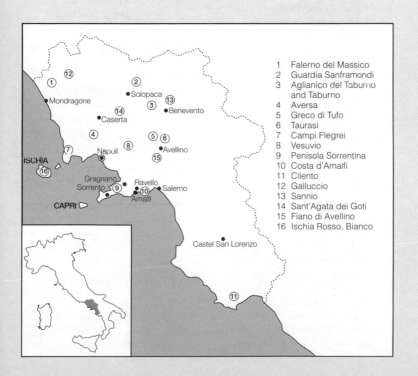

1 Falerno del Massico
2 Guardia Sanframondi
3 Aglianico del Taburno and Taburno
4 Aversa
5 Greco di Tufo
6 Taurasi
7 Campi Flegrei
8 Vesuvio
9 Penisola Sorrentina
10 Costa d'Amalfi
11 Cilento
12 Galluccio
13 Sannio
14 Sant'Agata dei Goti
15 Fiano di Avellino
16 Ischia Rosso, Bianco

7,000 hectares, with a quarter of these in the DOCG zones. In addition to the DOCGs, there are nineteen DOCs and eight IGTs, of which Irpinia, the ancient name for the Avellino area, is most prevalent. In addition to the better-known varieties, a recent rediscovery of indigenous Sciascinoso, Montonico, and Mangiaguerra – along with Asprinio, Forastera, and Roviello – has opened new horizons on the region.

Visiting wine-lovers, who should enjoy the spectacular Amalfi Coast and the islands of Capri and Ischia (best off season) and the ancient cities of Paestum and Pompeii, might also be intrigued by the vineyards around Avellino and Benevento. Recommended wine shops include Enoteca La Botte in Caserta, and Vinarium and Enoteca Partenopea in Naples.

Recent Vintages

Among Campania's wines, Taurasi is the best known for longevity, though reds from Solopaca, Taburno, and Falerno del Massico also age well, as do whites Fiano d'Avellino and Greco di Tufo. Recommended vintages for ageing are listed with each entry.

Appellations

Vintage years by the DOC apply to red wines unless otherwise specified.

DOCG

FIANO DI AVELLINO *w 01 02 03 04*
This wine can sometimes age well for three to six years or more, gaining depth and complexity, though most producers aim for fresher, fruitier wines for earlier consumption. Labels may mention the Roman name "Apianum" – a reference to its appeal to *api* (bees).

GRECO DI TUFO *w sp 01 02 03 04*
This is usually most impressive inside two to three years. On rare occasions, a *spumante* version may be seen locally.

TAURASI *r ris 88 90 91 93 94 95 96 97 98 99 00 01 03 04*
From Aglianico grown in the hills northeast of Avellino, centred in the village of Taurasi. Campania's most admired red is noted for long ageing thanks to the ample structure and tannins from late-ripening grapes. Youthful ruby turns mahogany with age as it develops remarkable depth of bouquet and flavour. Other red varieties may be included at up to 15%, but leading producers stick to pure Aglianico and age the wine in large casks before bottling it.
Age: 3 years (one in wood), *riserva* 4 years (1.5 in wood).

DOC

AGLIANICO DEL TABURNO *p r ris 95 96 97 98 99 00 01 03 04*
Aglianico (the variety that grows on the slopes of Mount Taburno, near Benevento).

AVERSA *w sp*
Asprinio or Asprino.

CAMPI FLEGREI *w r sp nov pas w ris 99 00 01 03 04*
Biancolella, Coda di Volpe, Piedirosso, Aglianico, Sciascinoso, Falanghina *00 01 02 03 04*

CAPRI *w r 99 00 01 02 03 04*
Falanghina, Greco, Biancolella, Piedirosso.

CASTEL SAN LORENZO *w p r ris sw m sp 99 00 01 02 03 04*

Trebbiano, Malvasia, Sangiovese,
Barbera.

CILENTO *w p r 99 00 01 03 04*
Fiano, Trebbiano, Greco Bianco,
Malvasia, Barbera, Piedirosso,
Primitivo, Aglianico.

COSTA D'AMALFI *w p r ris 99 00 01 03 04*
Falanghina, Biancolella, Piedirosso,
Sciascinoso, Aglianico.
Sub-zones: Furore, Ravello,
Tramonti.

FALERNO DEL MASSICO
w r ris 95 96 97 98 99 00 01 02 03 04
Falanghina, Aglianico, Piedirosso,
Barbera, Primitivo.

GALLUCCIO *w p r ris*
Falanghina, Aglianico.

GUARDIA SANFRAMONDI/ GUARDIOLO *w p r ris sp nov 99 00 01 03 04*
Malvasia, Falanghina, Sangiovese,
Aglianico.

ISCHIA *w r sup pas 99 00 01 03 04*
Biancolella, Forastera, Guarnaccia,
Piedirosso.

PENISOLA SORRENTINA *w r fz*
Falanghina, Biancolella, Greco,
Piedirosso, Sciascinoso, Aglianico.
Sub-zones: Gragnano, Lettere,
Sorrento.

SANNIO *w p r sp sw pas fz m nov mc*
Trebbiano, Sangiovese, Aglianico,
Barbera, Coda di Volpe, Greco,
Falanghina, Moscato, Piedirosso,
Sciascinoso.

SANT'AGATA DEI GOTI *w p r sw pas ris nov 95 96 97 98 99 00 01 03 04*
Falanghina, Greco, Aglianico,
Piedirosso.

SOLOPACA *w p r cl sup ris sp 98 99 00 01 03 04*
Greco, Piedirosso, Sciascinoso,
Aglianico, Falanghina.

TABURNO *w r sp nov*
Trebbiano, Falanghina, Sangiovese,
Aglianico, Coda di Volpe, Greco,
Piedirosso.

VESUVIO *w p r sw liq sp 99 00 01 03 04*
Verdeca, Coda di Volpe, Greco
Falanghina, Piedirosso, Aglianico,
Sciascinoso.

IGT
Beneventano
Campania
Colli di Salerno
Dugenta
Epomeo
Irpinia
Paestum
Pompeiano
Roccamonfina
Terre del Volturno

Producers

The key provinces have been abbreviated as follows: AV= Avellino; BN = Benevento; CE = Caserta; NA = Napoli; SA = Salerno.

Antica Masseria Venditti, Castelvenere
(BN) *w r* ✫✫✫ 11ha, 90,000 bottles.
Wine has been made from this
estate's organically farmed vines
since the 15th century. Today's
production includes finely crafted

ranges of Sannio and Solopaca,
some coming from 50-year-old
vines, containing little-known
local varieties such as Olivella,
Crieco, and Ceretto, and local
clones of the more common
varieties, vinified in steel to
capture the wine's pure character.
I Borboni, Lusciano (CE) *w r sp sw*
✫✫→✫✫✫ * 13ha, 130,000 bottles.
Carlo Numeroso is one of the top

(and few) producers of Asprinio, a traditional vine that grows some 15m (49ft) in heights and produces a zesty grape with high acidity. Top labels: Vite Maritata (Asprinio d'Aversa) – mineral, zesty, citrussy, spicy, with a rich, long finish; good Spumante I Borboni (Asprinio); Coda di Volpe; and Aglianico.

Antonio Caggiano, Taurasi (AV) *w r* ☆☆→☆☆☆☆ *94 97 99 01* 15ha, 120,000 bottles. Caggiano is a passionate winemaker and photographer with vines planted in the heart of the DOCG zone. He produces excellent Taurasi Vigna Macchia dei Goti, aged 18 months in barrique plus 20 months in bottle – rich, full, structured, spicy, with grippy tannins and a long, sapid finish. Also good Béchar (Fiano di Avellino), and Greco/Fiano blends from IGT Irpinia.

Cantina del Taburno, Foglianise (BN) *w r* ☆☆→☆☆☆ * 500ha, 1,500,000 bottles. Dynamic co-op producing reliable, well-priced Aglianico del Taburno: Albarosa and Fidelis; Taburno Amineo Coda di Volpe; Falanghina; and Greco. Top labels include two well-crafted Aglianico wines: Delius and the acclaimed, concentrated IGT Beneventano Bue Apis.

Cantine Caputo, Carinaro (CE) *w r sp* ☆☆→☆☆☆ * 46ha, 1,100,000 bottles. Estate founded in 1890 with a production including most of Campania's DOCs. In particular Aglianico: Taurasi and Zicorrà; Casavecchia; Asprino di Aversa (also in the sparkling version); Falanghina; and Greco.

D'Ambra Vini d'Ischia, Forio d'Ischia (NA) *w r ris* ☆☆☆ 12ha, 550,000 bottles. At Andrea D'Ambra's 1888 estate, vines are planted to steep terraces reached by a monorail cart. His inspiring wines are led

by Ischia: Frassitelli (Biancolella), Euopsia (Forastera); Rosso Riserva Mario d'Ambra; and Kime, from varieties from Greek Khalkis.

De Conciliis, Prignano Cilento (SA) *w p r sw* ☆☆→☆☆☆☆ *97 99 00 01 03* 24ha, 150,000 bottles. Family-run estate with a production of finely honed, stylish IGT reds, including Naima (Aglianico) – highly structured, concentrated, with fine tannins and a long, sapid finish; and Donnaluna Aglianico. Also good Donnaluna Fiano and late-harvest sweet Ka! , a Moscato/Malvasia blend, and Ra! (Aglianico/Barbera).

Di Meo, Salza Irpina (AV) *w r ris* ☆☆☆ 30ha, 500,000 bottles. Sound Taurasi, Greco di Tufo, Fiano di Avellino, Sannio Falanghina, and IGT Coda di Volpe. Top labels: Don Generoso, an Aglianico/Piedirosso blend – age-worthy, generous, full, with a long, elegant finish; and Taurasi Riserva – personality, depth, and structure. Also age-worthy Colle Dei Cerri (Fiano).

Benito Ferrara, Tufo (AV) *w r* ☆☆→☆☆☆ 8ha, 36,600 bottles. Gabriella Ferrara's production, assisted by consultant oenologist Paolo Caciorgna, is noted for finely crafted Greco di Tufo: Vigna Cicogna – ample fruit aromas, mineral, balanced, and persistent. Also good Fiano di Avellino and Irpinia Aglianico.

Feudi di San Gregorio, Sorbo Serpico (AV) *w r ris sw* ☆☆→☆☆☆☆ * *97 99 00 01 03* 300ha, 3,500,000 bottles. Dynamic estate with a production managed by Enzo Ercolino and Riccardo Cotarella, focusing on international-style wines. Top labels: Taurasi Piano di Montevergine Riserva; Fiano di Avellino Pietracalda; Greco di Tufo Cutizzi; IGTs Campanaro (Fiano) and Serpico (Aglianico); as well as

Patrimo, a generous Merlot, and the delicious, sweet Fiano Privilegio.

Fontanavecchia, Torrecuso (BN) *w p r ris* ☆☆☆ 8ha, 100,000 bottles. Libero Rillo's small estate is noted for its production of Aglianico del Taburno, in particular Vigna Cataratte Riserva – concentrated fruit, spice, liquorice, leather, big structure, ample, round, persistent. Also good Taburno Falanghina, Facetus, and IGT Orazio, an Aglianico/Cabernet blend, as well as good Rosato.

Furore, Furore (SA) *w r ris* ☆☆☆ 70,000 bottles. Gran Furor Divina Costiera has been an accepted market brand since 1942. Bought by Marisa Cuomo in 1980, today this leading estate with steep terraced vines above the Amalfi coast produces fine Bianco and Rosso from sub-zones Furore and Ravello, including white Furore Fior d'Uva from the local Fenile and Ginestra varieties.

Galardi, Sessa Aurunca (CE) *r* ☆☆☆☆ *94 95 99 00 01 03* 10ha, 15,000 bottles. Arturo Celentani's small estate produces just one wine fine-tuned by Riccardo Cotarella: Terre di Lavoro, a well-crafted Aglianico/Piedirosso with almost cult status – modern, powerful, intense, complex, with ageing potential.

Grotta del Sole, Quarto (NA) *w r* ☆☆→☆☆☆ * The Martusciello family are pioneers of quality production with local varietals such as Campi Flegrei, Falanghina, Asprinio, and Piedirosso. Their large but well-made range is led by Penisola Sorrentina: Gragnano and Lettere. Also good Campi Flegrei Piedirosso Montegauro Riserva (Piedirosso), Quartodisole (Piedirosso/Aglianico), Quartodiluna (Falanghina/Capretonne), and the irrepressible Asprinio di Aversa.

Luigi Maffini, Castellabate (SA) *w r sw* ☆☆☆ * 8ha, 70,000 bottles. A rising star in the Cilento, producing IGT oak-fermented Pietraincatenata; IGT Cenito; and two less structured, but very drinkable, good-value quality wines: Kléos, an Aglianico/Piedirosso/Sangiovese blend, and Kràtos (Fiano).

Mastroberardino, Atripalda (AV) *w r* ☆☆→☆☆☆☆ * *90 93 96 97 98 99 00 01 03 04* 400ha, 2,300,000 bottles. Historic 1878 premium estate headed by Piero Mastroberardino producing quality-driven wines. Top labels: Taurasi Radici; Naturalis Historia (Aglianico/Piedirosso); Fiano d'Avellino Radici; More Maiorum Fiano; Greco di Tufo Novaserra; plus Vesuvio Lacryma Christi Irpinia; and more.

Michele Moio, Mondragone (CE) *w r* ☆☆☆ * 13ha, 100,000 bottles. Winemaker consultant Luigi Moio heads his father's small estate with a production focusing on excellent Primitivo. Top label: Falerno Maiatico, a 100% Primitivo – earthy, sapid, powerful, yet elegant and complex, with a long finish. Also good Moio 57, Falerno del Massico, and Gaurano – all 100% Primitivo, as well as Falanghina.

Mollettieri, Montemarano (AV) *r ris* ☆☆☆→☆☆☆☆ 11ha, 39,000 bottles. Salvatore Molettieri's rising small estate focuses on impressive Taurasi, in particular age-worthy Vigna Cinque Querce Riserva – powerful and complex, with a fine balance between fruit and spice, and a long finish. Also very good Taurasi Cinque Querce, Ischia Piana Rossa, and Aglianico Cinque Querce.

Montevetrano, San Cipriano Picentino (SA) *r* ☆☆☆☆ *92 93 94 95 96 97 98 99 00 01 02* 6ha, 28,000 bottles. Silvia Imparato's production, assisted by consultant oenologist Riccardo

Cotarella, focuses on one great cult wine: IGT Montevetrano (Cabernet/Merlot/Aglianico) – fruit-forward quality, wide aromatic spectrum, spicy and balsamic, balanced, with an elegant, long finish. This is perhaps the top expression of an Aglianico blend.

Mustilli, Sant'Agata dei Goti (BN) *w r* ☆☆→☆☆☆ 35ha, 180,000 bottles. Mustilli's estate produces admirable Sant'Agata dei Goti Aglianico Cesco di Nece, vinified in wooden vats and then aged 18 months in steel and six in bottle – ripe, balsamic, elegant, and fresh. Also very good Conte Artus, an Aglianico/Piedirosso blend, Greco, and Falanghina.

Ocone, Ponte (BN) *w r sw* ☆☆ * 36ha, 240,000 bottles. Under Mount Taburno, Domenico Ocone's organic vines have been making Aglianico since the 1920s. Top labels: Aglianico del Taburno Diomede, aged 18 months in steel and then bottle-aged, in order to respect the intrinsic character of the wine; Taburno Piedirosso; Falanghina; Greco; and Coda di Volpe; *crus* Pezza la Corte (Aglianico) and Vigne del Monaco (Falanghina); plus Calidonio, a Piedirosso/Aglianico blend.

Pietratorcia, Forio d'Ischia (NA) *w r* ☆☆→☆☆☆ 8ha, 130,000 bottles. Small estate from the island of Ischia making indigenous and international wines of distinct personality. Highlights: Bianco Superiore Vigne del Cuotto, a Biancolella/Forastera/Greco blend, Rosso Vigne di Janno Piro (Piedirosso/Guarnaccia/Aglianico), and Mediatum (Viognier/Malvasia di Candia).

La Rivolta, Benevento *w r ris* ☆☆→☆☆☆ 25ha, 100,000 bottles. Rising star with a production of fine Aglianico del Taburno,

particularly Terra di Rivolta Riserva – fine tipicity, class, and longevity; Taburno Falanghina; Coda di Volpe; and Piedirosso. Also good oak-fermented IGT Sogno di Rivolta (Falanghina/Fiano/Greco).

Giovanni Struzziero, Venticano (AV) *w r ris* ☆☆→☆☆☆ 90 95 97 98 99 00 01 04 Struzziero has been producing traditional Taurasi since 1972; it is characterized by a slow 3–4 years' ageing in 25hl and 10hl barrels (no barrique), a process that allows the aromas and colour to develop with layers of complexity and freshness. Top Aglianico labels: Taurasi Campoceraso Riserva and Foscaro. Also fine Fiano di Avellino Rosato.

Telaro, Galluccio (CE) *w r sw* ☆☆ 70ha, 550,000 bottles. A major mover in the little-known Galluccio zone, with a production of good Aglianico, Fiano, Greco, and others. Top labels: Galluccio Ara Mundi, Passito delle Cinque Pietre, and fine Falanghina Vendemmia Tardiva.

Terredora, Montefusco (AV) *w r sw* ☆☆→☆☆☆ * 95 97 99 00 01 03 150ha, 950,000 bottles. Walter Mastroberardino's production of stylish Taurasi includes elegant Campore Riserva and age-worthy Fatica Contadina. Also very good Fiano di Avellino: Campore Riserva and Terre di Dora; Greco di Tufo: Loggia della Serra and Terre degli Angeli; in addition to a good range of IGTs from Aglianico, Falanghina, and Coda di Volpe, including a fine Fiano *passito*.

Vestini Campagnano, Caiazzo (CE) *w p r* ☆☆→☆☆☆ At this emerging high-quality estate production is overseen by consultant oenologist Paolo Caciorgna, who works with the almost extinct red and white Pallagrello and red Casavecchia varieties – to great effect. Top

labels: Connubio, a Casavecchia/
Pallagrello Nero blend, and Le
Ortole (Pallagrello Bianco).
Villa Matilde, Cellole (CE) *w r sw*
☆☆→☆☆☆ * *90 91 92 93 95 96
97 98 99 00 01 04* 130ha, 700,000
bottles. Francesco Avallone's estate
is divided between three estates in
the areas of Caserta, Benevento
and Avellino, producing reliable
ranges of wines from indigenous
grapes. Highlights: classy, refined
Falerno del Massico Bianco Vigna
Caracci; impeccable Rosso Vigna
Camarato; excellent Cecubo, an

Abbuoto/Piedirosso blend;
delightful Rosato Terre Cerase;
and more.
Villa Raiano, Serino (AV) *w r* ☆☆☆→☆☆☆☆
10ha, 130,000 bottles. Promising,
emerging Avellino estate with a
production of Aglianico, Fiano,
Greco, and Falanghina. The wines
are modern in style. Particularly
recommended is the Taurasi
Aglianico, aged 18 months in
barrique – spicy, austere, with
balsamic notes and evident oak
that should go with bottle-ageing.
Also good, crisp, structured whites.

Wine & Food

It is hard to imagine that Naples
was once a gastronomic capital –
first under the Romans, and again
under various monarchs between
the late Middle Ages and Italy's
unification in the 19th century.
Nowadays culinary improvisations
perfume the alleyways of the city:
pizza baking in wood-fired ovens;
onions, garlic, and herbs stewing
with tomatoes for *pommarola*
sauce; sweet pastries frying in
hot oil; steaming espresso; and
lots of fresh fish and seafood.
The fact that many of this region's
specialties can be eaten standing
up should not detract from their
inherent worth.
Baccalà alla napoletana Salt
cod with tomato, black olives,
raisins, pine nuts, capers, garlic.

Capretto in agrodolce Sweet
and sour kid, a specialty of Irpinia.
Lamb is also prepared this way.
Mozzarella in carrozza
Mozzarella sandwiches coated with
batter and deep-fried in olive oil.
'Mpepata di cozze Mussels
served in their shells with lemon,
parsley, and pepper.
Parmigiana di melanzane A local
specialty. Aubergine baked with
tomato sauce, mozzarella, and
Parmesan.
Pizza margherita With mozzarella
and grated pecorino.
Pizza napoletana marinara With
tomatoes, oregano, and fresh basil.
Spaghetti alla puttanesca
"Strumpet's spaghetti", dressed
with tomato, pepper, capers, olives,
and anchovies, a specialty of Ischia.

Hotels

Corbella, Cicerale (SA) €
Country lodging with ten elegant
rooms plus a cosy sitting room.
The in-house restaurant serves
good home-made pasta, farm-
produced cheese, meat, and
organic vegetables – all prepared
with creative flair.

Le Favate, Ascea (SA) €
An elegant restructured farm
situated on a large olive estate
with comfortable, well-furnished
rooms and a reading room with
an open fire. There is also a
museum in the old olive mill and
a pool. Excellent local cooking.

La Locanda del Fiume, Pisciotta (SA) €

A short drive from Palinuro is this converted 17th-century mill in a country setting with 12 gracious rooms. The restaurant serves excellent *cucina cilentana* prepared with organic produce, including lasagne, *cavitelli*, wholesome soups, grilled meats, and home-baked cakes.

Mustilli, Sant'Agata dei Goti (BN) €

This wine estate located in the medieval hamlet of Sant'Agata with six comfortable rooms makes for a fine, relaxing stay with the opportunity of visiting the working winery. There is also a good wine bar and an excellent restaurant with home-based cooking.

Torre Gaia, Dugenta (BN) €

A wine estate with 113ha of organic vines, offering fine hospitality in restored rural buildings. The in-house restaurant serves fine local specialties.

Villa Divina, Vietri sul Mare (SA) €

A lemon farm on the Amalfi coast, this elegant family villa has ten rooms, four suites, and a good terrace with views onto Vietri and the sea. An independent villa is also available, as is a pool. Meals and boat excursions on request.

Restaurants

La Caravella, Amalfi (NA) €€–€€€

Another Michelin-starred restaurant. Located in an elegant, historic palazzo, it offers seafood and meat dishes based on Amalfi recipes in a modern key. Good 15,000-bottle cellar.

Don Alfonso 1890, Sant'Agata sui Due Golfi (NA) €€€

Southern Italy's best restaurant boasts two Michelin stars; it also provides fine hotel accommodation (€€). The modern Mediterranean cuisine uses prime local ingredients and features oysters, caviar, linguine with clams and courgettes, marinated baby octopus, lobster salad, fish casserole, and more. Excellent and well-stocked cellar.

Oasis, Vallesaccarda (AV) €€

Refined ambience with three good tasting menus as well as à la carte. Very good fresh vegetables, legumes and pasta, meat, cheeses and home-made desserts. Also good selection of wines.

Quattro Passi, Nerano (NA) €€–€€€

Located between Capri and Positano, in the magnificent countryside of Marina del Cantone, close to the sea, Quattro Passi serves excellent freshly caught scampi on a bed of artichokes, crayfish salad, red mullet, freshly caught fried fish and *pezzogna*, fish parcels with curly *scarola* salad. The well-stocked wine cellar is dug out of the tufacious rock. Cookery lessons can be organized upon request.

Taverna del Capitano, Marina del Cantone (NA) €€–€€€

Excellent Mediterranean cuisine focusing mainly on fish, with wonderful prawns and sushi-style fish served on a panoramic terrace. Good wine list. There are also two suites available with a private terrace overlooking the sea.

La Torre del Saracino, Vico Equense (NA) €€–€€€

Small, elegant restaurant serving almost exclusively seafood. The good tasting menu includes stuffed calamari, swordfish ravioli, fish risotto, *paccheri* with fresh tomato, and more. Ample wine list.

Basilicata Basilicata

Basilicata, also known as Lucania, is one of Italy's least-known regions. It can boast neither fashionable beaches nor important Greek or Roman monuments – this is a strictly farming area that still preserves a wealth of biodiversity built on small-scale crops handed down by generations of hardy farming types. Today Basilicata is slowly changing, opening up to restrained tourism with hotels, restaurants, and wine bars.

There are more than fifty small producers in Basilicata, and most of its vine plantings are in the north of the province, on Mount Vulture – an extinct volcano with thin top soils, dry in the summer and bitterly cold in the winter, with barely enough rainfall for the vines to survive. Aglianico del Vulture, one of Italy's finest reds, shows depth, elegance, structure, fine tannins, acidity, and longevity. It is said that the vine was brought to Basilicata in the sixth or seventh century BC by the Greeks, which accounts for its name, a corruption of Hellenico. The few other varieties of note include Malvasia and Moscato, also grown around Monte Vulture, usually for sweet wine.

Basilicata is hardly a tourist paradise, but the ancient city of Matera is charming, and the Roman ruins at Venosa, home to the Latin poet Horace, are also well worth a visit. Enoteca Perbacco, Diciannovesima Buca, and Spirito Di Vino, all in Matera, carry a good selection of wines.

Recent Vintages

Aglianico del Vulture has had fine recent harvests, notably 2003, 2001, 2000, 1999, 1998, 1997, 1996, 1994, and 1993, following the excellent harvests of 1990, 1988, and 1985. Some good wines were also made in 2004, 2002, 1995, 1992, 1991, 1987, and 1986. Earlier notable vintages for Aglianico were 1982, 81, 79, 77, 75, and 73.

Appellations

DOC
AGLIANICO DEL VULTURE *r ris*
sp 88 90 93 94 97 98 99 00 01 02 03

From Aglianico grapes grown on the eastern slopes of Monte Vulture and hills to the southeast past Venosa and Genzano. Though it may be sold after a year as a dry or, occasionally, an off-dry wine (or even as *spumante*), it is the aged Aglianico that stands in the front rank of southern Italian wines. Its colour is deep ruby to garnet, taking on orange reflections with age in barrel and bottle; its bouquet heightens as it becomes richly smooth with an unusual firmness and depth of flavours. The better grapes come from volcanic soil high up around Rionero and Barile, where microclimates are similar to those in the northern regions, and where *riserve* are complex, age-worthy premium wines.
Age: 1 year, *vecchio* 3 years (2 in wood), *riserva* 5 years (2 in wood).

TERRE DELL'ALTA VAL D'AGRI
p r ris

Merlot, Cabernet Sauvignon, Malvasia

IGT
Basilicata
Grottino di Roccanova

oducers

he key provinces have been abbreviated as follows: MT = Matera; PZ = Potenza.

Agricola Eubea Famiglia Sasso, Potenza r ✩✩✩ 97 00 01 02 03 13ha, 50,000 bottles. Eugenia Sasso's production includes an extracted Aglianico del Vulture Ròinos, which reaches 16% alcohol – dark berry fruit, spice, coffee, and liquorice. Also admirable Aglianico: Covo dei Briganti, and Eubea.

Basilisco, Rionero in Vulture (PZ) r ✩✩✩ * 97 98 99 00 01 02 8ha, 20,000 bottles. Nunzia Calabrese produces just one admired DOC Aglianico: Aglianico del Vulture Basilisco. Overseen by consultant oenologist Lorenzo Landi, it has an austere, powerful structure, with ripe black berry fruit and mineral notes, warm, full, round on the palate, balanced by fresh acidity.

Cantina del Notaio, Rionero in Vulture (PZ) w r sw ✩✩✩ 22ha, 80,000 bottles. Gerardo Giuratrabocchetti, a solicitor ("notaio") by profession, is Vulture's rising star. His production is overseen by consultant oenologist Luigi Moio. Il Repertorio and La Firma are vibrant, polished Aglianicos, with great concentration, complexity, and the potential to age well.

Cantina di Venosa, Venosa (PZ) w p r ✩✩→✩✩✩✩ * 500,000 bottles. A co-op with 500 members and 1,000ha of Vulture DOC vines planted mostly to Aglianico. Cantina di Venosa presently sells 40% of its wine in bulk. The production is divided into four Aglianico DOC labels, a red and a rosé IGT, dry and sweet Moscato, and dry Malvasia, all of good flavour and style.

D'Angelo, Rionero in Vulture (PZ) w r ✩✩✩→✩✩✩✩ * 93 95 97 98 00 01 03 04 40ha, 350,000 bottles. Benchmark estate for Aglianico DOC producing age-worthy, single-vineyard Vigna Caselle – fresh minerality and depth; and IGT Canneto, aged in small oak barrels. Also good Aglianico del Vulture Donato D'Angelo, IGT Serre delle Querce (Aglianico/Merlot), and IGT Vigna dei Pini (Chardonnay/Pinot Bianco/Incrocio Manzoni).

Azienda Agricola Macarico, Barile (PZ) r ✩✩✩ 5ha, 20,000 bottles. Rino Botte and his brother-in-law Vito Paternoster have invested in low-yielding old vines planted to high-density Aglianico. They produce a single, classy Aglianico del Vulture DOC – complex, spicy, tobacco, ripe cherry notes, fresh and silky, with a long, elegant finish.

Armando Martino, Rionero in Vulture (PZ) p r ✩✩✩ 16ha, 100,000 bottles. Reliable Aglianico in numerous styles. Highlights include Aglianico del Vulture: Oraziano, Bel Poggio, and Rosé Donna Lidia.

Paternoster, Barile (PZ) w r ris sw ✩✩→✩✩✩✩ 90 93 95 97 98 99 00 01 03 04 20ha, 150,000 bottles. Anselmo Paternoster began this cellar in 1925. The top wine, named Don Anselmo after the winery's founder, is a classic Aglianico, made from 40-year-old vines and only in years where ripeness reaches its optimum. Its structure and potential for ageing allow it to reveal its true nature with time. Also superb DOC Aglianico Rotondo and Synthesi.

Tenuta del Portale, Barile (PZ) r ris ✩✩ * 15ha, 100,000 bottles. Donato D'Angelo's new estate is managed by Filena Ruppi. The style follows the classic, austere elegance of D'Angelo wines, each wine with a distinct terroir character. Highlights include delicious Aglianico del Vulture Riserva and Le Vigne a Campanno.

Tenuta Le Querce, Barile (PZ) *r*
☆☆→☆☆☆ *00 01* 135ha, 350,000
bottles. Wine production at this
family estate covers an impressive
range of DOC Aglianico led by
Vigna della Corona and Rosso di
Costanzo. Also good an indigenous
100% Tamurro Nero.

Terre degli Svevi, Venosa (PZ) *w r*
☆☆☆ 95ha, 180,000 bottles.
This Gruppo Italiano Vini-owned
estate produces excellent DOC
Aglianico Re Manfredi. Also
intriguing Müller-Thurgau and
Traminer Aromatico under the
label Re Manfredi Bianco.

Wine & Food

The cooking of Basilicata may be as
spare as the landscape, but it has a
warmth that comes directly from
the summer sun. Appetites are
satisfied with ample servings of
beans, pasta, soups, potatoes, and
bread. Vegetables play a key role in
stews cooked with olive oil, plenty
of herbs, and spices. Pimento
(known as *diavolicchio*) goes into a
sauce called *piccante*, fiery enough
to live up to its name and more. In
the old days, meat was used thriftily
in, for example, preserved pork
products: *soppressata*, *coppa*, or a
spicy sausage known as *luganiga*.

Cazmarr Stew of lamb's innards,
prosciutto, cheese, and wine.
Ciammotta Fried aubergine,
peppers, and potatoes stewed in
tomatoes.
Cotechinata Pork rind rolled
around a filling of salt pork,
garlic, and peppers, and stewed
in tomato sauce.
Focaccia a brazzudí Flatbread
with pork crackling, lard, and
oregano.
Pignata Lamb marinated with
vegetables, hot peppers, cheese,
and wine in an earthenware pot
(*pignata*) and left to simmer.

Hotels

Hotel Farese, Melfi (PZ) € Hotel
in the countryside near the volcanic
lakes of Monticchio. Also restaurant.
Agriturismo La Maddalena,
Venosa (PZ) € Family farm offering
typically southern hospitality.
Comfortable large rooms with air
con and heating. Good restaurant
with local produce and home
cooking. Pool and horse trekking.
Locanda del Palazzo, Barile (PZ)
€ Stylish 15th-century palazzo

with comfortable rooms in the
picturesque town of Barile. Excellent
restaurant with local dishes.
L'Oraziano, Venosa (PZ) €
A 15th-century family villa with lots
of character situated between the
main cathedral and the former
house belonging to Horace
Villa Cheta, Acquafredda (MT) €
Handsome Art Nouveau-style hotel
with a garden overlooking the
Tyrrhenian coast.

Restaurants

Le Botteghe, Matera €–€€ Set
in a house dug out of the tufa rock.
Wild chicory and aubergine meat
balls, pasta with chickpeas, roast
lamb, and wonderful sour cherry
tart. Good range of Aglianicos.

Il Giardino di Epicuro, Maratea
(PZ) €–€€ Truly a garden of
Epicure. Local salami, pappardelle
with mushrooms, grilled meats,
fish soup, and own-made desserts.
Good wine list.

Calabria *Calabria*

This region was once a garden of the Greeks, who favoured its wines. Local athletes returning in triumph from early Olympiads were welcomed with Krimisa, if not the world's oldest wine, then among the earliest in Europe. Krimisa was made where Cirò is made today, on the Ionian coast.

Calabria neglected its vinicultural splendour for many years. Today signs of progress are beginning to emerge from this ruggedly handsome land. Cirò is the paragon of Calabrian wines, and one of the better-known names among the twelve regional DOCs and thirteen IGTs. Its red and rosé derive from Gaglioppo, as do most Calabrian reds. White Cirò comes from Greco, a lively relic with sub-varieties capable of making both modern dry whites and luxuriant dessert wines. The revival by enlightened producers of the indigenous Magliocco grape, an age-worthy elegant red with Mediterranean aromas and soft tannis, has brought new excitement to Calabria's wines.

The toe of the Italian boot is largely mountainous, and its tourist attractions are mostly natural. The Sila Massif dominates the north around Cosenza and Catanzaro (the region's capital), while the Aspromonte range dominates the south, overlooking Reggio Calabria and, across the strait, Sicily's Mount Etna.

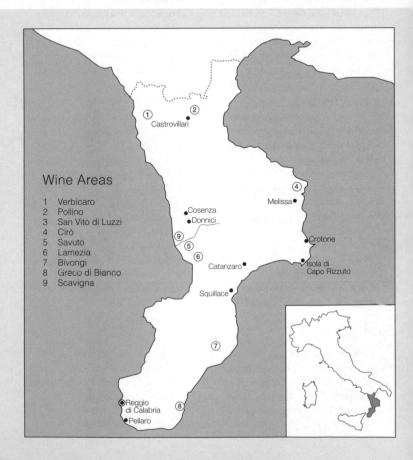

Wine Areas

1 Verbicaro
2 Pollino
3 San Vito di Luzzi
4 Cirò
5 Savuto
6 Lamezia
7 Bivongi
8 Greco di Bianco
9 Scavigna

Remnants of the Greeks are evident along the coasts, the most scenic of which is the Calabrian Riviera, between Reggio and Gioia Tauro. Wine tourism hasn't been developed, but there are many inviting beaches and charming ancient towns nestled into the arid hills. Oasi in Vibo Valentia and Enoteca La Cascina in Catanzaro Lido are well-stocked wine shops.

Recent Vintages

Among Calabrian reds, Cirò and Savuto are the best suited to ageing. Vintages from 1993 to 1998 were rated as very good to excellent, as was 1990, with 1992 and 1991 not far behind. The vintage years apply to *rosso* and *riserva* wines, unless otherwise indicated.

Appellations

DOC

BIVONGI *w p r nov ris 99 00 01 03 04*
Greco Bianco, Greco Nero, Montonico, Guardavalle, Ansonica, Malvasia Bianca, Gaglioppo, Nocera, Nero d'Avola, Castiglione

CIRÒ *w p r cl sup ris 97 99 00 01 02 03 04*
Greco Bianco, Gaglioppo, Trebbiano

DONNICI *w p r nov ris 99 00 01 03 04*
Montonico Bianco, Greco Bianco, Pecorello, Malvasia Bianca, Gaglioppo, Greco Nero.

GRECO DI BIANCO *w sw 93 94 95 96 97 98 99 00 01 02 03 04*
Greco Bianco.

LAMEZIA *w p r nov ris 96 97 98 99 00 01 03 04*
Malvasia Bianca, Greco Bianco, Trebbiano, Nerello Mascalese, Greco Nero, Marsigliana, Gaglioppo.

MELISSA *w r sup 00 01 03 04*
Greco Bianco, Gaglioppo, Malvasia Bianca, Greco Nero, Trebbiano.

POLLINO *r sup*
Gaglioppo, Greco Nero, Malvasia Bianca, Montonico, Guernaccia.

SAN VITO DI LUZZI *w p r 00 01 03 04*
Malvasia Bianca, Greco Nero, Gaglioppo, Sangiovese, Malvasia Bianca, Greco Bianco, and others.

SANT'ANNA DI ISOLA CAPO RIZZUTO
Gaglioppo, Nerello, Malvasia Nera, Nocera, Malvasia Bianca, Greco Bianco.

SAVUTO *p 95 96 97 98 99 00 01 03 04*
Gaglioppo, Greco Nero, Nerello Cappuccio, Malvasia Bianca, Magliocco, Sangiovese, Pecorino.

SCAVIGNA *w p r 97 98 99 00 01 03 04*
Gaglioppo, Nerello, Trebbiano, Chardonnay, Greco Bianco, Malvasia.

VERBICARO *w p r ris 98 99 00 01 03 04*
Gaglioppo, Greco Nero, Greco Bianco, Malvasia Bianca, Guarnaccia Bianca.

IGT

Arghillà
Calabria
Condoleo
Costa Viola
Esaro
Lipuda
Locride
Palizzi
Pellaro
Scilla
Val di Neto
Valdamato
Valle del Crati

Producers

The key provinces have been abbreviated as follows:
CZ = Catanzaro; CS = Cosenza; KR = Crotone; RG = Reggio di Calabria.

Caparra & Siciliani, Cirò Marina (KR) *w p r ris* ☆☆→☆☆☆ 213ha, 900,000 bottles. A new generation of winemakers from the Caparra and Siciliani families brings a breath of fresh air to the wines from these respected producers of Cirò, with both indigenous vines and new plantings of international varietals. Highlights: Cirò Rosso Classico Superiore, Volvito Riserva, and Rosato Le Formelle.

Cantine Lento, Lamezia Terme (CZ) *w r ris* ☆☆ * 100ha, 650,000 bottles. Salvatore Lento's vines are divided between the Tenuta Romeo and the lower-lying Tenuta Villa Caracciolo, producing a fine range of Lamezia, most notably Lamezia Riserva Dragone Rosso, Lamezia Greco, and the admired IGT Federico II (Cabernet Sauvignon), showing good varietal character and silky tannins, full, warm, and balanced in structure, with good length.

Cerraudo Roberto, Marina di Strongoli (KR) *w p r* ☆→☆☆ 20ha, 60,000 bottles. Emerging passionate producer with local and international vines, assisted by consultant oenologist Fabrizio Ciufoli. Highlights include Petraro, a Gaglioppo/Cabernet blend, aged 24 months in barrique – full, round, and long; Imyr, an oak-fermented Chardonnay; Grayasusi Etichetta Argento, a fine rosè from Gaglioppo.

Enotria, Cirò Marina (KR) *w p r* ☆☆ * 170ha, 1,000,000 bottles. Large, reliable co-op with a production of sound Cirò Bianco, Rosso, and Rosato from Greco and Gaglioppo grapes, harvested in September, soft-pressed, and accurately controlled during fermentation to ensure top quality.

Fattoria San Francesco, Cirò (KR) *w p r sw* ☆☆☆ 40ha, 300,000 bottles. Francesco Siciliani is a progressive, quality-conscious winemaker with a production of admired Cirò: Rosso Classico Superiore Donna Madda and rosé Ronco dei Quattroventi; along with modern-leaning Bianco Pernicolò (Greco/Chardonnay) and sweet IGT Passito Brisi.

Vincenzo Ippolito, Cirò Marina (KR) *w p r ris* ☆☆ 106ha, 1,000,000 bottles. Historic estate established in 1845. Since 2001, wine production has been overseen by consultant oenologist Franco Bernabei, who is responsible for reviving the winery's tradition of indigenous varietal wines. Top labels include Cirò Rosso Classico Superiore: Colli del Mancuso Riserva and Liber Pater, both excellent; along with Cirò Bianco Res Dei.

Librandi, Cirò Marina (KR) *w p r ris sw* ☆☆→☆☆☆ 230ha, 2,100,000 bottles. One of the most dynamic wineries in southern Italy, with a production overseen by consultant oenologist Donato Lanati and viticulturalist Attilio Scienza. The range of Cirò, topped by the red Duca Sanfelice Riserva, is impeccable, as is the elegant, age-worthy IGT Magno Megonio, from 100% Magliocco. The vineyards at Stringoli produce the award-winning Gravello, a Gaglioppo/Cabernet blend; light white Critone; rosé Terre Lontane; and the sweet *passito* Le Passule. New vineyards in Melissa make reds and whites of great promise.

Luigi Vivacqua, Luzzi (CS) *w p r* ☆☆→☆☆☆ 35ha, 100,000 bottles. Rising star of San Vito di Luzzi, with a production of indigenous and international varieties overseen by Tuscan consultant oenologist Luca D'Attoma, who is responsible for the fine, elegant Donna Aurelia, a Chardonnay from low-yielding vines. Also good red Marinò, a four-grape blend including Gaglioppo and Merlot, aged 24 months in pristine barrique and showing good ageing potential; and San Vito di Luzzi Rosso and Bianco.

Odoardi, Nocera Tirinese (CZ) *w r* ☆☆☆ * 95ha, 300,000 bottles. Gregorio and Giovanbattista Odoardi's production of powerful modern wines – concentrated and highly extracted in style – is overseen by Tuscan consultant oenologist Stefano Chioccioli. Highlights include the ripe, meaty Scavigna Vigna Garrone, a five-grape blend (including Merlot, Cabernet Sauvignon, and Franc), and the refined, vibrant red Savuto Vigna Mortilla, another five-grape blend (Gaglioppo/Sangiovese/Magliocco Canino/Nerello Cappuccio/Greco Nero). Also good Scavigna Bianco Pian della Corte.

Serracavallo, Cosenza *w r* ☆☆→☆☆☆ * 18ha, 30,000 bottles. Demetrio Stancati's vines are situated at 600m (1950ft) altitude, with a production of admired blends of indigenous and international grapes under Valle del Crati IGT. Highlights include two Magliocco/Cabernet Sauvignon blends: Terraccia and Sette Chiese; and Besidiae (Pecorello/Sauvignon Blanc/Riesling).

Statti, Lamezia Terme (CZ) *w r sw* ☆☆☆ 500ha, 250,000 bottles. Statti's estate is situated in the centre of Calabria, in the Due Mari denomination, producing good Lamezia Rosso and Bianco; IGT Cauro, a Gaglioppo/Magliocco/Cabernet blend; white IGT Ligeia (Chardonnay/Sauvignon Blanc); Lamezia Greco Bianco; and IGT passito Nòsside.

Vintripodi, Reggio Calabria *w r sw* ☆☆☆ * 14ha, 60,000 bottles. Ignazio Tripodi's historic estate is known for the finely crafted sweet Mantonico di Bianco and IGT reds from Nerello with Alicante: Arghillà and Magna Grecia Rosso; along with fine whites from Greco, Inzolia, and Cataratto.

Wine & Food

Calabrians, behind their mountain barriers, have always lived in isolation. Their cooking, although drawing on standard southern Italian ingredients, expresses this independence. Pork is so important that the pig has been called Calabria's "sacred cow". The great country tradition (which survives in home kitchens, if rarely in restaurants) relies on soups, pastas, and vast arrays of vegetables. When not in season, peppers, courgettes, artichokes, aubergines, and mushrooms are preserved in olive oil, of which the region is a

major producer. Besides the usual range of shellfish, Tyrrhenian waters also provide swordfish and tuna. Calabrians adore sweets, which are often based on citrus and other fruit, candied or dried, such as chocolate-covered figs.

Alalunga in agrodolce Young tuna cooked in a sweet and sour sauce of onion and vinegar.

Ciambotta Stew of aubergine, peppers, potatoes, onions, and tomatoes eaten hot or cold.

Licurdia Onion soup thickened with bread and grated pecorino, and laced with hot pepper.

Mursiellu Stew of tripe and pork innards cooked with tomato, peppers, and wine.

Mÿstica Baby anchovies preserved in olive oil, also known as "Calabrian caviar".

Pescespada Swordfish, a specialty of Bagnara on the Calabrian Riviera, cooked with peppers, lemon, garlic, capers, and herbs.

Pitta chicculiata Calabrian pizza, filled with tuna, tomato, anchovies, black olives, and capers.

Sagne chine Festive lasagne baked with as many ingredients as possible, usually pork, peas, artichokes, hard-boiled eggs, mozzarella, and mushrooms.

Sarde a scapece Fried sardines rolled in breadcrumbs and doused with a mixture of hot oil, vinegar, garlic, and mint

Hotels

Hotel Aquila & Edelweiss, Camigliatello Silano (CS) € Friendly family-run hotel located near the Sila National Park, with 40 comfortable and well-decorated rooms. The good restaurant offers local Calabrian specialties.

Antico Frantoio Oleario Bardari, Curinga (CZ) € This restored oil mill is set in beautiful surroundings with sea views. They still produce olive oil and wine, which feature, respectively, in the hotel's restaurant and wine list.

Restaurants

La Locanda D'Alìa, Castrovillari (CS) €–€€
Good decor, excellent food, lovely wine, and friendly service are the key elements of this *locanda*, which has a few rooms for those wishing to stay after a big meal. Specialties include tart of anchovies served with potatoes and baby cardoons; ravioli filled with broccoli and almonds in a sauce of anchovies, spices, black olives and walnuts; swordfish with a *caponata* of red Tropea onions, raisins, and pine nuts; and pear pralines. There is also an excellent wine list.

Max, Cirò Marina (KR) €
Situated in one of the region's most prominent wine zones, this restaurant offers simple fresh fish dishes from genuine local recipes. Wonderful *bianchetti* (white bait) when in season, *mpepata di cozze*, smoked swordfish, pizza, cheeses, and good desserts, as well as a good selection of local wines.

Osteria del Pescatore, Tropea, (Vibo Valentia) €
Typical *trattoria* in the historical centre of Tropea serving the daily catch made into tasty local fish-based recipes. Be sure to try the *mostaccioli* (a typical cookie) with a glass of sweet Zibibbo. Good wine list.

Il Setaccio Osteria,
Rende (CS) € Rustic country house owned by Domenico Zicarelli, who will proudly talk you through a menu offering genuine Calabrian fare. Excellent home-made pasta dishes with meat sauces, roast suckling lamb. Good local wines.

La Tavernetta, Spezzano della Sila (CZ) €€
A panoramic spot at the foothills of the Sila mountains by Lake Cecita. Enjoy local dishes such as potato gateaux with cheese and truffles, chestnut lasagne with mushrooms, roast suckling pig, and more. Good wine list.

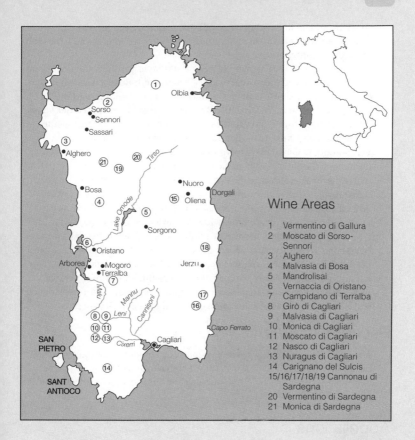

Wine Areas

1 Vermentino di Gallura
2 Moscato di Sorso-
   Sennori
3 Alghero
4 Malvasia di Bosa
5 Mandrolisai
6 Vernaccia di Oristano
7 Campidano di Terralba
8 Girò di Cagliari
9 Malvasia di Cagliari
10 Monica di Cagliari
11 Moscato di Cagliari
12 Nasco di Cagliari
13 Nuragus di Cagliari
14 Carignano del Sulcis
15/16/17/18/19 Cannonau di
   Sardegna
20 Vermentino di Sardegna
21 Monica di Sardegna

Sardinia *Sardegna*

The second-largest island in the Mediterranean, Sardinia is one of Europe's most desirable holiday destinations, with more than 1,800 kilometres (1,100 miles) of dramatic coastline contoured by rugged cliffs, hidden coves, and glorious sandy beaches, most notably those of the Costa Smeralda. Sardinia's history can be traced back thousands of years to the primaeval era; the region is rich in archaeological sites, such as its dolmen stone relics and *nuraghe*, squat round stone towers believed to be ancient forts.

Wine was made on these shores long before the Romans arrived in 238BC. Several of the region's grape varieties were brought by the Phoenicians, Carthaginians, Romans, and Spaniards. By the sixteenth century the region was known as *insuli vini*, and by the twentieth it was exporting its powerful wines to France to boost the weaker northern wines, including those produced on the "continent" – which is how the Sardinians refer to Italy.

Though the island remains a source of strong blending wines, recently there has been a greater desire among producers to look further than its coastline and, in line with the rest of Italy, maximize the potential of native grapes. A diverse range of more concentrated, more interesting wines is therefore beginning to emerge.

Of the nineteen DOCs, many represent old-style Sardinia and are strong in constitution, whether sweet or dry – Malvasia di Bosa, Nasco, and Girò di Cagliari, the rich Moscato di Cagliari and Sorso-Sennori, and the sherry-like Vernaccia di Oristano. But these are made in limited quantities. It is the island's four main varieties – red Cannonau and Monica, white Vermentino and Nuragus – that dominate production. The star is Vermentino, which, when grown in Gallura in the northeast, is DOCG. Cannonau, Sardinia's emblematic red, is at its best in the heights of the easterly province of Nuoro. Nuragus, introduced by the Phoenicians and possibly named after the *nuraghe*, the island's prehistoric stone towers, flourishes on the extensive Campidano plains north of Cagliari – as do most of the wines with a region-wide (di Sardegna) or province-wide (di Cagliari) denomination. Monica is a light, cheerful red. A further bright point comes from Torbato, grown mostly around Alghero, and Carignano del Sulcis, which makes for an elegant red. Most of Sardinia's DOCs cater for single varietals. For blends, producers use fifteen IGT designations.

The Antica Enoteca Cagliaritana and Bonu in Cagliari and Tore Monaco and Enosarda in Sassari sell a wide choice of the island's wines.

Recent Vintages

There are few Sardinian wines that require any amount of substantial ageing, but among the ones that do, Vernaccia di Oristano and other strong dessert or apéritif-style wines can last for some years. The recommended vintages for wines appear with each entry.

Appellations

DOCG
VERMENTINO DI GALLURA
w sup

A vine of Spanish origin, Vermentino apparently arrived via Corsica, but it rates native status in the wooded hills of the Gallura, where it is DOCG. The lively, fleshy roundness rarely disappoints. With careful handling, it can develop into a richly flavoured white of great character.

DOC
ALGHERO *w p r sp fz nov liq ris*
Cabernet Sauvignon, Cabernet Franc, Carmenère, Cagnulari, Chardonnay, Sangiovese, Sauvignon, Torbato, Trebbiano, Vermentino.

ARBOREA *w p r fz*
Sangiovese, Trebbiano.

CAMPIDANO DI TERRALBA/ TERRALBA *r*
Bovale, Pascale, Greco, Monica.

CANNONAU DI SARDEGNA
r sw li qris 97 98 99 00 01 02 03 04
Cannonau.

CARIGNANO DEL SULCIS *p r fz*
nov sup ris pas sw 95 96 97 98 99 00 01 02 03 04
Carignano.

GIRÒ DI CAGLIARI *r sw ris liq*
Girò.

MALVASIA DI BOSA *w sw liq 95 96 97 98 99 00 01 02 03 04*
Malvasia di Sardegna.

MALVASIA DI CAGLIARI *w sw liq*
95 96 97 98 99 00 01 02 03 04
Malvasia di Sardegna.

MANDROLISAI *p r sup 00 01 02 03 04*
Bovale Sardo, Cannonau, Monica..

MONICA DI CAGLIARI *r sw liq*
Monica.

MONICA DI SARDEGNA *r sup fz*
Monica.

MOSCATO DI CAGLIARI *r sw liq ris m*
Moscato Bianco.

MOSCATO DI SARDEGNA *w sp sw m*
Moscato Bianco.

MOSCATO DI SORSO-SENNORI *w sw liq m*
Moscato Bianco.

NASCO DI CAGLIARI *w sw liq ris*
Nasco.

NURAGUS DI CAGLIARI *w fz sw*
Nuragus.

SEMIDANO SARDEGNA *w s sup sw*
Semidano.

VERMENTINO DI SARDEGNA *w sp sw*
Vermentino.

VERNACCIA DI ORISTANO *w sup ris liq 71 80 85 88 90 91 93 94 96 97 98 99 00 01 02 03 04*
Unique vine trained low in the Tirso River flatlands, where grapes soak up the heat from the sandy soil, acquiring strength and flavour. Once very ripe, they are made into a wine of high natural alcohol, aged in small barrels in brick buildings with apertures to let in sunlight and air. The barrels are never full, so a veil of yeast (*flor*) forms over the wine, influencing development of bouquet and flavour. The same technique is used to produce sherry, so it is not surprising that there is a sherry-like character to Vernaccia, though differences in grapes and climate give it its own style. Truest to type are the unfortified versions, particularly the long wood-aged *superiore* and *riserva* of 15.5% alcohol, with nuances of toasted nuts, spices, and faded flowers that heighten with ageing as the sharp, bitter edges disappear. *Liquoroso* types, whether dry or sweet, are richer but less distinctive.
Age: 29 months; *superiore* 41 months in wood; *riserva* 48 months.

IGT
Barbagia
Colli del Limbara
Isola dei Nuraghi
Marmilla
Nurra
Ogliastra
Parteolla
Planargia
Provincia di Nuoro
Romangia
Sibiola
Tharros
Trexenta
Valle del Tirso
Valli di Porto Pino

Producers

The key provinces have been abbreviated as follows:
CA = Cagliari; NU = Nuoro;
OR = Oristano; SS = Sassari.

Antichi Poderi di Jerzu, Jerzu (NU) *w p r ris* ☆☆ →☆☆☆ 2,000,000 bottles.
This 800-member co-op has seen improved cellar management and better grape selections. Its main focus is Cannonau, with the top production coming from bush-trained vines. Very good Riserva Josto Miglior and Riserva Chuèrra.

Argiolas, Serdiana (CA) *w p r sw*
☆☆→☆☆☆☆ * 300ha, 2,500,000
bottles. One of southern Italy's most
dynamic family-run estates. Top
labels: Turriga, a Cannonau-based
blend – powerful, full-bodied; fine
Korem, a Bovale/Carignano/
Cannonau blend – silky, with firm
structure and a long, focused finish;
sweet Angialis (Nasco/Malvasia) –
ripe peaches, apricots, and almonds;
and oak-fermented Cerdeña –
pungent, aromatic, spicy, and long.

CS Gallura, Tempio Pausania (SS) *w p
r sp* ☆☆→☆☆☆☆ * 360ha, 1,130,000
bottles. This 110-member co-op run
by Dino Addis is known for its well-
priced quality wines. Highlights
include Vermentino: Piras, Canayli,
and Gemellae; and sweet Moscato
di Tempio Pausania.

CS Il Nuraghe, Mogoro (OR) *w p r sp*
☆☆ 450ha, 600,000 bottles.
A 650-member co-op producing
Cannonau, Vermentino, Monica,
and the rare – and often overlooked
– Semidano grape.

CS di Santadi, Santadi (CA) *w p r ris
sw* ☆☆→☆☆☆☆ * 600ha, 2,000,000
bottles. A 220-member co-op with a
production overseen by Giacomo
Tachis. Top labels include
Carignano del Sulcis: Rocca Rubia
and Terre Brune – intense berry
fruit, cedar notes, soft tannins; late-
harvest Latinia (Nasco); IGT Araja, a
Carignano/Sangiovese blend; Villa
di Chiesa (Vermentino/Chardonnay);
Cala Silente (Vermentino); Antigua
(Monica); and Pedraia (Nuragus).

CS del Vermentino, Monti (SS) *w r sp
sw* ☆☆ * 420ha, 2,600,000 bottles.
A quality-driven co-op noted for
Vermentino di Gallura: Aghiloia,
Funtanaliras, and S'Eleme,
including sparkling and *passito*,
and a range of IGT blends.

Capichera, Arzachena (SS) *w r*
☆☆☆→☆☆☆☆☆ 350,000 bottles. The
Ragnedda family estate has 60ha

of vines, plus 45ha being planted to
Vermentino and Carignano. They
produce elegant, balanced wines
with a mineral finish. Top labels:
Vermentino: Capichera and Vigna
'Ngena; and Carignano: Assajè and
Mantènghja, aged 18 months in
barrique – powerful, age-worthy.

Giovanni Maria Cherchi, Usini (SS)
w p r ☆☆☆ * 30ha, 170,000 bottles.
A family estate with 7ha of the
indigenous red Cagnulari, they also
produce Vermentino di Sardegna:
Vigna Tuvaoes and Boghes, both
partly fermented and aged in oak;
fresh, Vermentino Pigalva; and
long-lived IGT Luzzana
(Cagnulari/Cannonau). Production
is overseen by Piero Cella.

Attilio Contini, Cabras (OR) *w r ris sw*
☆☆→☆☆☆☆ 80ha, 600,000 bottles.
Assisted by Piero Cella, Paolo
Contini is the leading producer of
Vernaccia di Oristano, with *riserve*
dating back to the 1970s and a
blend of vintages called Antico
Gregori. Also strong, scented IGTs
from red Nieddera. The Nieddera
under the label Barrile is aged 12
months in barrique.

Ferruccio Deiana, Settimo San Pietro
(CA) *w r* ☆☆→☆☆☆ 50ha, 243,000
bottles. Emerging estate producing a
range of DOC and IGT wines. Top
labels: Cannonau Sileno; Vermentino
Arvali; international-style, oak-
fermented Pluminus, a Vermentino/
Chardonnay blend; and Ajana
(Cannonau/Carignano/ Cabernet),
aged 18 months in barrique.

Giuseppe Gabbas, Nuoro (NU) *r*
☆☆→☆☆☆☆ * 14ha, 70,000 bottles.
Small estate producing Arbeskia,
a well-crafted Cannonau/Cabernet
blend, as well as Cannonau DOC
Dule Riserva and Lillové.

Alberto Loi, Cardedu (NU) *w p r ris sw*
☆☆→☆☆☆☆ 65ha, 260,000 bottles.
One of the first estates to export
Jerzu Cannonau in bottle back in

the 1950s. Top labels: Alberto Loi Riserva – marasca cherries and plums, warm, full-bodied, excellent length; fine Cannonau Sa Mola; and interesting Leila Vendemmia Tardiva, a white Cannonau.

Piero Mancini, Olbia (SS) *w p r* ☆☆ 100ha, 1,400,000 bottles. This family estate produces admirable Vermentino: Cucaione and Saraina; as well as DOC Cannonau and IGTs using international/indigenous blends, including a particularly fine Antiche Cussòrgie (Cabernet/Merlot/Cannonau).

Pala, Serdiana (CA) *w r* ☆☆→☆☆☆ 58ha, 300,000 bottles. Up-and-coming estate with a production of DOC Vermentino, Nuragus, Monica, and Cannonau. Also good IGT S'Arai (Cannonau/Carignano/ Bovale).

Pedra Majore, Monti (SS) *w r* ☆☆→☆☆☆ 60ha, 190,000 bottles. The Isoni brothers' organic production is noted for a Vermentino with sapid minerality. Top labels: Vermentino di Gallura Hysony and I Graniti; Murighessa (Cannonau/Bovale).

Josto Puddu, San Vero Milis (OR) *w p r ris sp* ☆☆ 42ha, 300,000 bottles. A new generation has brought changes and improvements to this family winery producing good Vernaccia di Oristano Riserva and wines from Monica, Cannonau, and Nieddera. Also Vernaccia Brut.

Giuseppe Sedilesu, Mamoiada (NU) *w r ris sw* ☆☆→☆☆☆ * Salvatore and Francesco Sedilesu produce a terroir expression of Cannonau from 60-year-old bush-trained vines under the Carnevale and Mamuthone labels. The high alcohol content comes from long macerations (up to 25 days), no selected yeast, and hardly any filtration.

Sella & Mosca, Alghero (SS) *w p r* ☆→☆☆☆ 650ha, 7,000,000 bottles. The vast I Piani estate north of Alghero turns out an admirable commercial range of wines, led by Alghero Cabernet Marchese di Villamarina, Rosso Tanca Farrà (a Cannonau/Cabernet blend), and the *liquoroso* Anghelu Ruju, along with Bianco Le Arenarie (Sauvignon), rosé Oleandro, and admired Torbato Terre Bianche.

Tenute Dettori, Sennori (SS) *w r* ☆☆☆ 30ha, 40,000 bottles. Alessandro Dettori's estate is noted for robust, traditional Cannonau. Top labels: Dettori Rosso and Tuderi, both 100% Cannonau – high in alcohol, reaching up to 17.5%, from almost overripe grapes yielding a port-like wine, vinified without temperature control, selected yeast, and with hardly any filtration.

Wine & Food

Despite being surrounded by the sea, Sardinia's "real" cooking is that of the back country: pork, lamb, kid, soups of broad beans and barley, piquant pecorino cheese, and, most of all, the breads. It is said that every Sardinian village has a bread of its own. The most sung about is *pane carasau*, also known as "music paper", because, unleavened, it is that thin. Fish is a relatively recent exploitation of a source that has always been there in the deep

waters off the island's coasts. Most Mediterranean species can be savoured, sometimes together, as in the lavish fish soup *cassòla*.

Agnello con finocchietti Lamb stewed with onion, tomato, and wild fennel.

Aragosta alla griglia Grilled rock lobster.

Bottarga Dried mullet eggs sliced thin, eaten as a carpaccio or shaven over pasta.

Burrida Chowder usually based

on shark meat, though recipes vary from port to port.

Favata Stew of broad beans and pork.

Porceddu Suckling pig spit-roasted slowly on an open fire.

Sebadas or seadas Pastry with cheese and bitter honey.

Su farru Soup of spelt with mint.

Hotels

Arbatasar Hotel/Ristorante, Arbatax (NU) €–€€ Friendly, stylish hotel well located for discovering the east coast. Some of the comfortable rooms look out to sea. There is a small pool and an excellent restaurant with superb seafood and a good wine list.

Agriturismo Badu Orgolesu, Mamoiada (NU) € Small, rural farm set in the countryside just at the entrance of Mamoiada. Simple rooms. The owners will be happy to cook local fare on request.

Hotel Cala di Volpe, Porto Cervo (SS) €€€ Sardinia's top hotel is set in a natural reserve with pristine sandy beaches, glittering sea and breathtaking views of unspoiled natural surroundings. Impeccable rooms, service, and fine dining.

Hotel Mediterraneo, Cagliari €–€€ This 1950s-style hotel on the seafront is a functional good base for exploring Cagliari.

Hotel Villa Canu, Cabras (OR) € Friendly, well-run B&B in a typical island house with a pretty inner courtyard. The 23 well-furnished rooms have en-suite bathrooms and all mod cons. Guests get a special deal at the nearby restaurant Il Caminetto, which serves home-made specialties.

Villa Las Tronas Hotel/ Restaurant, Alghero (SS) €€–€€€€ The 19th-century former summer residence of the Italian king is set in a park with superb sea views. Elegant rooms and a good restaurant with a superb wine list.

Restaurants

L'Antica Hosteria, Sassari €–€€ Typical, friendly *trattoria* with excellent local fare, creative cuisine, and a well-stocked cellar.

Antica Locanda Rosella, Giba (CA) € Friendly *locanda* with rooms near Santadi. Great traditional food, including ravioli filled with pecorino and wild asparagus (when in season). Good choice of wines.

Da Gesuino, Olbia (SS) €–€€ Hotel and restaurant offering traditional recipes, cooked on a daily basis, including *canolicchi*, octopus *alla marinara*, ravioli filled with fish, or ricotta, and excellent fish soup.

Ristorante Dal Corsaro, Cagliari €€–€€€ Elegant ambience with first-class food (mainly fish) served with creative flair. Good wine list with more than 400 labels.

Gastronomia Belvedere, Cala di Volpe (SS) € A simple eatery with some of the island's freshest fish served on paper plates.

S'Apposentu, Cagliari €€–€€€ Renowned restaurant with superb local fare, served with style. Menu changes according to seasonal ingredients. Very good tasting menu and ample wine list.

Sa Pischedda, Bosa (NU) €–€€ Excellent seafood served, including *zuppa di pesce alla bosana* and *bottarga di muggine*. From a selection of unusual wines, try the local Malvasia di Bosa with dessert.

Wine Areas

1	Faro	11 and 12	Cerasuolo di Vittoria
2	Contea di Sclafani	13	Moscato di Siracusa
3	Menfi	14	Moscato di Noto
4	Santa Margherita di Belice	15	Riesi
5	Contessa Entellina	16	Delia Nivolelli
6	Regaleali	17	Contea di Sclafani
7	Sambuca di Sicilia	18	Erice
8	Eloro	19 and 20	Mamertino di Milazzo
9	Delia Nivolelli	21	Marsala
10	Sciacca		

Sicily *Sicilia*

Vines have flourished on the Mediterranean's largest island since the
dawn of history, yet Sicily's millennial aptitude for wine has been more
industriously exploited for quantity than quality. And although there is
now a noticeable shift in the other direction and the field of admirable
premium wines is growing, DOC production still represents only about
ten per cent of the total. Overall, Sicily's wines are the most reliable of
Italy's south, and it is generally acknowledged that there is still huge
potential for greatness that has only just begun to be tapped. Indeed, wine
companies from the north are keen to invest in a region whose natural
attributes, first among them sunshine, are a virtual guarantee of fine quality.

Perhaps the most significant development in Sicily has been the revival
of marsala, the once-famous fortified wine that was left behind during the
rush for the light and bright. Yet while critics smeared it, in Sicily's soul
it remained its pride and joy. On a smaller scale, the sweet and *passito*
wines made on Pantelleria from Moscato, and on the Aeolian islands from
Malvasia, have reinspired interest in this once-unfashionable category.

Although the island boasts twenty-one DOCs, several of which have
been approved or modified quite recently and many of which appear to
give ample span to the creative ingenuity of producers, DOC is frequently
ignored in favour of IGT, be it the region-wide Sicilia or one of six others.

Sicily bears the stamp of Greeks, Arabs, Normans, Spaniards, and many others. Major Greek ruins are at Siracusa (Syracuse), Agrigento, Segesta, and Erice – all near wine zones. Palermo, the capital, and nearby Monreale, have the Alcamo and Contessa Entellina zones at their heels, while the volcano of Mount Etna has Etna DOC curving round its lower slopes. The volcanic Lipari, or Aeolian, Islands are justifiably noted for sweet Malvasia. At Marsala, Florio's vast cellars and wine museum are worth visiting for wine-lovers. Good wine shops are Enoteca Per Bacco in Trapani, La Bottega dei Sapori in Erice, La Maison du Vin in Marsala, and Manfrè in Alcamo.

Recent Vintages

Sicily's temperate to torrid climate permits fairly consistent harvests, although drought can be a problem in non-irrigated areas. High-altitude vineyards have climatic conditions similar to northern regions, with the advantage of more sunlight. Recommended vintages appear with each entry.

Appellations

Vintage years by the DOC apply to red wines unless otherwise specified.

DOCG
CERASUOLO DI VITTORIA
98 99 00 01 02 03 04

A dark cherry-red wine from Nero d'Avola and Frappato grown around Vittoria, in southeast Sicily.

DOC
ALCAMO *w p r sp cl ris nov 99 00 01 02 03 04*

Frappato, Sangiovese, Perricone, Cabernet Sauvignon, Merlot, Syrah Catarratto, Inzolia, Ansonica, Grillo, Grecanico, Chardonnay, Müller-Thurgau, Sauvignon, Nero d'Avola, Calabrese.

CONTEA DI SCLAFANI *w p r vt sp nov ris sw 99 00 01 02 03 04*

Catarratto, Inzolia, Grecanico, Nerello Mascalese, Nero d'Avola, Perricone, Cabernet Sauvignon, Calabrese, Chardonnay, Syrah, Damaschino, Grillo, Inzolia, Merlot, Müller-Thurgau, Pinot Nero, Sangiovese, Sauvignon.

CONTESSA ENTELLINA *w p r ris sw vt 99 00 01 02 03 04*

Inzolia, Catarratto, Grecanico, Chardonnay, Sauvignon, Nero d'Avola, Syrah, Merlot, Cabernet Sauvignon, Pinot Nero.

DELIA NIVOLELLI *w p r ris sp 00 01 02 03 04*

Grecanico, Chardonnay, Inzolia, Damaschino, Grillo, Cabernet Sauvignon, Müller-Thurgau, Merlot, Nero d'Avola, Perricone, Sangiovese, Syrah.

ELORO *w p r ris 99 00 01 02 03 04*

Frappato, Pignatello, Nero d'Avola, Pachino.

ERICE *w r ris sp pas m vt sw*

Ansonica, Catarratto, Cabernet Sauvignon, Chardonnay, Grillo, Grecanico, Frappato, Merlot, Müller-Thurgau, Nero d'Avola, Syrah.

ETNA *w p r sup 98 99 00 01 02 03 04*

Carricante, Catarratto, Nerello Mascalese, Nerello Cappuccio.

FARO *r 96 97 98 99 00 01 02 03 04*

Nerello Mascalese, Nerello Cappuccio, Nocera, Nero d'Avola, Gaglioppo, Sangiovese.

MALVASIA DELLE LIPARI *w sw pas liq 95 96 97 98 99 00 01 02 03 04*

Malvasia.

MAMERTINO DI MILAZZO/ MAMERTINO *w r ris*
Grillo, Inzolia, Calabrese, Nero d'Avola.

MARSALA *w r sw ris sup vt sp*
Marsala is one of the world's four great fortified wines, alongside sherry, port, and madeira. It is based on four elements: colour, sugar, alcohol content, and length of ageing. It is made principally from Catarratto, Inzolia, and Grillo grapes, but can also contain red varieties. The base wine is sweetened and fortified with concentrated must or *cotto*, plus grape alcohol before ageing in large wooden barrels.

Fine, *oro*, or *ambra*:
17% alcohol, aged 1 year
Superiore, *oro*, or *ambra*:
18% alcohol, aged 2 years
Superiore/riserva:
18% alcohol, aged 4 years
Vergine soleras:
18% alcohol, aged 5 years
Vergine riserva or *stravecchio*:
18% alcohol, aged 10 years

Marsala *vergine*, or *soleras*, is the most prestigious. Dry to bone-dry, it is blended from wines aged in barrels for different lengths of time – often by the *solera* system of topping up the old with younger vintages.

MENFI *w r ris sw vt*
Catarratto, Chardonnay, Grecanico, Inzolia, Nero d'Avola, Sangiovese, Merlot, Cabernet Sauvignon, Syrah.
Sub-zones: Bonera, Feudo dei Fiori.

MONREALE *w p r sup ris nov nt sw*
Nero d'Avola, Catarratto, Ansonica, Perricone, Chardonnay, Cabernet Sauvignon, Merlot, Grillo, Pinot Bianco, Pinot Nero, Sangiovese, Syrah.

MOSCATO DI NOTO *w sw sp liq m*
Moscato Bianco.

MOSCATO DI PANTELLERIA *w sw liq sp pas m*
Zibibbo (Moscato d'Alessandria).

MOSCATO DI SIRACUSA *w sw m*
Moscato Bianco.

MOSCATO PASSITO DI PANTELLERIA *w sw liq 90 91 92 93 94 95 96 97 98 99 00 01 02 03 04*
Zibibbo.

RIESI *w p r sp ris nov vt*
Inzolia, Chardonnay, Nero d'Avola, Nerello Mascalese, Cabernet Sauvignon.

SAMBUCA DI SICILIA *w p r ris pas sw*
Inzolia, Grillo, Nero d'Avola, Syrah, Cabernet Sauvignon, Chardonnay, Sauvignon, Merlot, Sangiovese.

SANTA MARGHERITA DI BELICE *w r*
Catarratto, Grecanico, Inzolia, Sangiovese, Cabernet Sauvignon, Nero d'Avola.

SCIACCA *w r ris*
Inzolia, Catarratto, Grecanico, Chardonnay, other non-aromatic whites, Merlot, Sangiovese Cabernet Sauvignon, Nero d'Avola.

IGT
Camarro
Colli Ericini
Fontanarossa di Cerda
Salemi
Salina
Sicilia
Valle Belice

Producers

The key provinces have been abbreviated as follows: AG = Agrigento; CL = Caltanissetta; CT = Catania; EN = Enna; ME = Messina; PA = Palermo; RG = Ragusa; SR = Siracusa; TP = Trapani.

Abbazia Sant'Anastasia, Castelbuono (PA) *w r* ☆→☆☆ 70ha, 850,000 bottles. Francesco Lena's vines are planted on the slopes of a 12th-century Benedictine monastery estate, now converted into a spectacular hotel run by the Lena family. The accomplished, modern-styled production, overseen by Riccardo Cotarella, includes Litra (Cabernet Sauvignon); Montenero, a Nero d'Avola/Cabernet/Merlot blend; Gemelli and Baccante (both Chardonnay); and Passomaggio (Nero d'Avola/Merlot).

Abraxas, Fraz Bukkuram, Pantelleria *w sw* ☆☆→☆☆☆ 59,000 bottles. Excellent Passito di Pantelleria as well as good Moscato Kuddia del Gallo and white Bianco Kuddia delle Ginestre.

Baglio Hopps, Marsala (TP) *w r sw* ☆☆ 105ha, 450,000 bottles. Founded by John Hopps & Sons, producers of marsala, this historic estate dates back to 1811. Today the production still includes some very good marsala, but it is mainly concentrated on dry white Grillo, the traditional grape for marsala. The two ranges of production come under Selezione Baglio Hopps and the more economic Abadir.

Barone La Lumia, Licata (AG) *w r sw* ☆☆→☆☆☆ 40ha, 250,000 bottles. Historic estate (est. 1873) producing excellent Halikàs (Inzolia) – hints of ripe peach and melon, velvety, full and structured, long. Also highly admired Don Totò, Torreforte, Signorio, and Cadetto Rosso – all Nero d'Avola; and good Cadetto Bianco (Inzolia).

Barone Scammacca del Murgo, Santa Venerina (CT) *w p r sp* ☆☆ 25ha. This historic Etna estate has been making wine for the past 150 years. It was restructured in the 1980s, when the bush-trained vines were replanted to modern Guyot vines. Good Cabernet Tenuta San Michele; also Etna Bianco and Rosso, and a refreshing Spumante Brut Murgo.

Barone di Villagrande, Milo (CT) *w r sw* ☆☆ 100,000 bottles. Some stylish wines from Etna, including a minerally Bianco Superiore Fiore from Carricante and Etna Rosso from Nerello Mascalese and Cappuccio; as well as delicious Malvasia delle Lipari.

Benanti, Viagrande (CT) *w r* ☆☆☆→☆☆☆☆ * 39ha, 180,000 bottles. Benanti's bush-trained vines are located in a range of Etna's DOC production areas. Etna wines show real terroir appeal and are long-lived and elegant. The vineyard management and production is overseen by Salvo Foti, Sicily's most competent consultant oenologist. Top labels include Etna Rosso: Serre della Contessa and Rovittello, both Nerello Mascalese/Nerello Cappuccio blends. Also very good white Bianco Superiore Pietramarina (Carricante).

Buffa, Marsala (TP) *sw ris* ☆☆ * Emerging marsala producer with reliable, good wines showing individual character, in particular Marsala Superiore Oltre Due Anni, which is also well-priced. Good Vigne Oltre Cinque Anni and Marsala Superiore Riserva Oltre Quattro Anni.

Calatrasi-Accademia del Sole, San Cipirello (PA) *w r* ☆☆→☆☆☆ * Large winery with almost 2,000ha of vines (mostly rented) and a production of 8 million bottles split into four ranges: the Terre di Ginestra wines show class in Catarratto and Nero d'Avola; the D'Istinto range gives lively indigenous/international blends; Accademia del Sole are single-estate wines from Tunisia and Puglia as well as Sicily; and the Terrale varietals are simpler. High standards throughout.

CS di Trapani, Trapani *w p r* ☆☆→☆☆☆☆ * 458ha, 600,000 bottles. Well-managed co-op with a reliable production split into two main ranges: Forti Terre di Sicilia, which includes the cream of the production, with fruit-rich varietals; and Drepanum, noted for good quality/price ratios.

Ceuso, Alcamo (TP) *r* ☆☆☆ 50ha, 120,000 bottles. The Melia brothers' emerging estate is located on the slopes of the temple of Segesta and guided by consultant oenologist Giacomo Tachis. Ceuso produces two wines that embrace the ripeness and elegance of Sicily: an age-worthy Ceuso, a Nero d'Avola/Cabernet/Merlot blend; and Scurati, a new release from Sicily's flagship monovarietal Nero d'Avola.

COS, Vittoria (RG) *w r* ☆☆☆ * 28ha, 130,000 bottles. Giambattista Cilia and Giusto Occhipinti's production features some classy Cerasuolo di Vittoria, especially Pythos and Vastunca. Also superb single-site IGT Nero d'Avola Contrada Labirinto, Pojo di Lupo Nero d'Avola, and Rami (Inzolia/Grecanico).

Cottanera, Castiglione di Sicilia (CT) *w r* ☆☆→☆☆☆☆ * 50ha, 210,000 bottles. Modern-directed estate on Etna with vines planted to international and indigenous vines at 700m (2,300ft) altitude. Top labels: IGT Sole di Sesta (Syrah),

Grammonte (Merlot), and L'Ardenza (Mondeuse), as well as more typical Barbazzale Bianco (Inzolia) and Rosso (Nerello Mascalese/Nero d'Avola).

Cusumano, Partinico (PA) *w r* ☆☆ * 400ha, 1,700,000 bottles. Emerging estate focusing on international and indigenous blends and single-varietal wines. Top labels: Noà, a Nero d'Avola/Merlot/Cabernet Sauvignon blend; Sagana, a highly extracted Nero d'Avola; Agimbé (Inzolia/ Chardonnay); and Jalé (Chardonnay).

De Bartoli, Marsala (TP) *w sw ris* ☆☆→☆☆☆☆ With outspoken, passionate, and controversial decisions, De Bartoli has earned a reputation for bringing the quality of marsala to international acclaim. Top labels: Marsala Superiore Oro Vigna La Miccia and Riserva 20 Anni; Passito di Pantelleria Bukkuram and Pantelleria Pietranera (a dry Zibibbo); Vecchio Samperi 20 Anni; and more unique, enthralling wines.

Donnafugata, Marsala (TP) *w r sw* ☆☆☆ 300ha, 2,600,000 bottles. The Rallo family estate is headed by Giacomo Rallo, who is assisted by consultant oenologist Carlo Ferrini. The production is attuned to Sicily's climate and aided by modern technology. Top labels: white Contessa Entellina Vigna di Gabri (Inzolia); Contessa Entellina Tancredi, a Nero d'Avola/Cabernet blend; and Mille e una Notte, from Nero d'Avola and other native varieties. Also Passito di Pantelleria Ben Ryé – aromatic, dried fruits, round, well balanced, long finish.

Duca di Salaparuta, Casteldaccia (PA) *w p r* ☆☆→☆☆☆☆ * 104ha, 10,000,000 bottles. The house founded by the Duke of Salaparuta in 1824, and owned by the Ente

Siciliano per la Promozione Industriale until 2001, is now the property of the wine and spirits group Illva-Saronno (Como). Under the guidance of MD winemaker Carlo Casavecchia, it is regaining its position as the region's standard-bearer. Wines, nearly all IGT, come from grapes selected in various parts of Sicily. The simplest fall under the famous trademark Corvo. The range now houses Colomba Platino, an Inzolia/ Grecanico blend; Terre d'Agala (Nerello Mascalese); Triskelé (Nero d'Avola/ Cabernet Sauvignon/ Merlot); Passo delle Mule and Duca Enrico (both Nero d'Avola); Kados (Grillo); Megara (Frappato/Syrah), and the leading Bianca di Valguarnera (Inzolia).

Fatascià, Palermo *w r sw* ☆☆ * 30ha, 350,000 bottles. Stefania and Gianfranco Lena's estate produces an interesting range of IGTs from international varieties and Sicily's leading Nero d'Avola. Top labels: L'Insolente, a Merlot/Cabernet blend; Rosso del Presidente (Nero d'Avola/Cabernet Franc); and Almanera (Nero d'Avola).

Fazio Wines, Erice (TP) *w r sp* ☆☆ * 600ha, 650,000 bottles. Dynamic estate with a reliable production of indigenous and international varieties, including sapid Müller-Thurgau, good Chardonnay-based Spumante Petali Brut, and well-crafted blends such as Montélimo (Nero d'Avola/Merlot). Indigenous varietals include well-priced Inzolia, Catarratto, and Grillo.

Ferrandes, Pantelleria *sw* ☆☆☆☆ 1.6ha, 6,000 bottles. Salvatore Ferrandes has a micro-production of certified organic traditional Passito di Pantelleria. This sublime nectar is aged in steel and bottle to retain the character and secondary aromas of the raisined fruit, without adding extra aromas from ageing in wood.

Feudo Maccari, Pachino, Noto (SR) *r* ☆☆ 60ha, 60,000 bottles. Antonio Moretti's emerging Sicilian estate produces excellent Nero d'Avola under the Saia label – bold elegance and good, balanced fruit. Also good Renoto Nero d'Avola. Production is overseen by consultant oenologist Carlo Ferrini.

Feudo Principi di Butera, Butera (CL) *w r* ☆☆→☆☆☆ 180ha, 500,000 bottles. Zonin's Sicilian estate comprises vines in one of the leading Nero d'Avola zones. Highlights: IGT Deliella (Nero d'Avola), San Rocco (Cabernet Sauvignon), Calat (Merlot), and more.

Firriato, Paceco (TP) *w r* ☆☆→☆☆☆ * At this estate, an international winemaking team brings a sheen of class to a large range led by Camelot, a Cabernet/Merlot international-style blend – powerful, highly extracted; Harmonium (Nero d'Avola); and Santagostino Bianco (Catarratto/Chardonnay) and Rosso (Nero d'Avola/Syrah).

Florio, Marsala (TP) *w sw* ☆☆→☆☆☆☆ 3,500,000 bottles. This firm, founded in 1833 by Vincenzo Florio and now owned by Illva-Saronno, is the largest producer of marsala and a leader in its revival, with Baglio Florio, Terre Arse Superiore Riserva, Targa 1840, and Vecchioflorio. Also good IGT Morsi di Luce (Moscato).

Gulfi, Chiaramonte (RG) *w r* ☆☆☆→☆☆☆☆ * 35ha, 150,000 bottles. Rising star with vines near Pachino, famous for its bush-trained Nero d'Avola. Production, overseen by consultant oenologist Salvo Foti, focuses on individual-style wines, in particular three single-vineyard Nero d'Avolas: Nerosanlorenzj, Nerobufaleffj, and Nerobaronj. Also good white Carjcanti (Carricante) and Valcanzjria, a Chardonnay/Carricante/Albanello blend.

Carlo Hauner, Salina (ME) *w r sw* ☆☆☆
38ha, 80,000 bottles. The heirs of the
late Carlo Hauner continue to make
Malvasia delle Lipari, including
Passito Selezione Carlo Hauner, and
IGT Salina Bianco and Rosso.

Milazzo, Licata (AG) *w r ris sp*
☆☆→☆☆☆ * 52ha. Giuseppe
Milazzo's estate produces fine,
elegant wines and was one of the
first to produce good Chardonnay
sparkling wines by using the
méthode champenoise. Experiments
with different varieties have yielded
elegant reds, privileging Nerello
Cappuccio, Barbera, and Nero
d'Avola, as best suited to the terroir.
Top labels: Duca di Montalbo IGT
Selezione di Famiglia, a *cuvée* of
five different varieties; Terre della
Baronia Rosso, a Nero Cappuccio/
Nero d'Avola/Barbera blend;
Castello Svevo (Nero d'Avola/Nero
Cappuccio); and Maria Costanza
(Nero d'Avola).

Morgante, Grotte (AG) *r* ☆☆☆ 50ha,
285,000 bottles. Supremely classy
Don Antonio, a Nero d'Avola that
won acclaim worldwide for its
elegance, structure, and balance.
Also good basic Nero d'Avola.

Salvatore Murana, Pantelleria (PA) *w r
sw* ☆☆☆→☆☆☆☆ 20ha, 100,000
bottles. Murana produces the most
eclectic Moscato and Passito di
Pantelleria under the Mueggen,
Khamma, and Martingana labels.
Also good red Nero Nostrale
aged in barrique.

Palari, Messina (ME) *r* ☆☆☆ 7ha,
50,000 bottles. Salvatore Geraci's
production is based on indigenous
varieties, including some rare ones:
Acitana, Tignolino, Calabrese,
Nocera, Galatina, and others. The
top label is the excellent Faro, a
Nerello Mascalese/Cappuccio/
Nocera/Calabrese blend. Also
very good Rosso del Soprano
with the same varieties.

Carlo Pellegrino, Marsala (TP) *w r sw*
☆→☆☆☆ 350ha, 7,000,000 bottles.
Large winery with vineyards in
Sicily and on Pantelleria with a
production of marsala *superiore*
and *soleras*, Passito di Pantelleria,
and a proficient range of IGTs and
DOCs from all over Sicily.

Planeta, Menfi (AG) *w r* ☆☆☆→☆☆☆☆ *
350ha, 1,800,000 bottles. Gold-star
quality throughout the range of
wines from four estates. IGTs La
Segrela Bianco (a five-grape blend)
and Rosso (Nero d'Avola/Merlot/
Syrah) have stormed the world, as
have top varietal labels Cometa
(Fiano) and Planeta: Chardonnay,
Syrah, and Merlot; along with Santa
Cecilia (Nero d'Avola). Also delicious
Cerasuolo; Alastro (Grecanico/
Chardonnay); and Burdese, a
Cabernet Sauvignon/ Franc blend.
Planeta also owns the leading co-op
Settesoli in Menfi, with a huge
output of good-quality and excellent-
value IGT varietals and blends under
the Mandrarossa line.

Pupillo, Siracusa (SR) *w r sw* ☆☆☆
18ha, 80,000 bottles. Antonio
Pupillo is the leading producer
of the rare Moscato di Siracusa
Vigna di Mela – delicate, floral, and
fragrant, with hints of apricot. Also
very good Moscato di Siracusa
Solacium – powerful and intense,
hints of melon and ripe peaches.

Rapitalà, Camporeale (PA) *w r sw*
☆☆→☆☆☆ 180ha, 3,000,000 bottles.
Hugo De La Gatinais's historic
estate, recently acquired
by Gruppo Italiano Vini, makes fine
DOC Alcamo. Top labels: Hugonis,
a powerful Cabernet Sauvignon/
Nero d'Avola blend; Solinero, a
fragrant Syrah; and Grand Cru,
an oak-fermented Chardonnay.

Regaleali-Tasca d'Almerita, Vallelunga
Pratameno (CL) *w p r sp sw*
☆☆☆→☆☆☆☆ * 400ha, 3,000,000
bottles. Leading estate (est. 1830)

in the south, with an inspired range of IGT wines sold under the brand Regaleali. Top labels come under the Contea di Scafani label, with excellent Cabernet Sauvignon, Chardonnay, and Rosso del Conte Nero d'Avola. Also fine Almerita Brut (Chardonnay) and sweet Diamante D'Almerita, a Moscato/Traminer Aromatico blend.

Spadafora, Monreale (PA) w r ☆☆☆ 95ha, 220,000 bottles. Francesco Spadafora's production is based on quality international varieties, which do exceptionally well in Sicily. Top labels: the Schietto range, with Cabernet Sauvignon, Syrah, and Chardonnay. Also very good Sole dei Padri (Syrah); and Don Pietro Rosso (Cabernet/Merlot/Nero d'Avola) and Bianco (Inzolia/Catarratto/Grillo).

Valle dell'Acate, Acate (RG) w r ☆☆→☆☆☆ * 100ha, 387,000 bottles. The emerging Jacono family estate is headed by Gaetana Jacono, with a production of lively, fruit-packed IGT Frappato and Cerasuolo di Vittoria. Highlights: oak-fermented Bidis, a Chardonnay/Inzolia blend – elegance, balance, and length; and Il Moro (Nero d'Avola), vinified and aged in steel – excellent fruit, and fresh berry and cherry aromas.

Wine & Food

Sicily is the alleged birthplace of all sorts of good things to eat. The island's natural endowments of sunshine and fertile volcanic soil combined with a multitude of ethnic influences mean that Sicily boasts an unrivalled heritage of foods, such as couscous from North Africa. The modern diet relies on grains, vegetables, herbs and spices, olives and olive oil, fruit, nuts, cheese, and seafood – in particular tuna and swordfish. But recipes reveal a miscellany of local tastes. Sicily is also the capital of Italian sweets – sun-dried, candied fruits and almonds are a small part of the encyclopaedic array that culminates in *cassata*.

Beccaficu Sardines, either stuffed and baked or breaded and fried.
Pescespada Swordfish.
Caponata Aubergine and other vegetables in a rich stew.
Cùscusu Of Arab origin, couscous-style fish stew with semolina.
Farsumagru Braised veal roll stuffed with meat, cheese, and vegetables.
Pasta con le sarde Palermo's classic pasta flavoured with sardines and wild fennel.
Peperonata Peppers stewed with tomato, onion, and green olives.
Tonno alla siciliana Fresh tuna cooked with white wine, fried anchovies, herbs, and spices.

Hotels

Il Carrubo, Contrada Bosco, near Acate (RG) € Typical 19th-century *masseria* with 50ha of land offering comfortable, personal hospitality. As well as their own horses for pony-trekking, they have a good restaurant serving Sicilian dishes.
Eremo Della Giubiliana, Contrada Giubiliana (RG) €€

A 17th-century monastery situated 9km (5.5 miles) from Ragusa, with nine elegant, comfortable rooms overlooking the garden and a sea-facing restaurant. It even has its own private airport and plane offering sightseeing flights to Sicily's small islands, such as Pantelleria.

Grand Hotel Villa Igea, Palermo
€€–€€€ A splendid 18th-century
Art Nouveau villa with 110 rooms,
60 of which overlook the Bay of
Palermo. Tastefully set amid
terraced gardens leading to the sea,
it also offers alfresco dining.
Regaleali Estate, Vallelunga €–€€
Enjoy the countryside and get to
know Sicilian traditions at this
B&B on a 200-year-old estate.
Set amid luxuriant green vines,
it is the ideal base for a relaxing
break. Cooking courses are
available on request.

Relais Santa Anastasia,
Castelbuono (PA) €€ A restored
12th-century Benedictine monastery
and wine estate set in the hills above
the village of Cefalù. Two in-house
restaurants offer traditional dishes
based on local recipes and home-
grown ingredients.
Villa Palocla, Sciacca (AG) €–€€
Elegant 18th-century rural
residence with eight individually
styled rooms surrounded by a
fragrant orchard. The restaurant
opens onto an inside courtyard
for alfresco eating. Good pool.

Restaurants

Cantina Siciliana, Trapani €–€€
Located in Trapani's historic
centre, this restaurant specializes
in fish dishes. Excellent *sardine*
fish balls, swordfish roulade,
caponata, parmigiana, and fried
tuma (pecorino cheese). Don't miss
the *cassatelle.* Good wine selection.
La Conchiglia, Contrada
Khamma Conitro, Pantelleria €
Reliable family-run *trattoria* with
magnificent sea views offering
simple fish and island recipes,
including ravioli with ricotta and
mint, and spaghetti with *bottarga.*
Duomo, Ragusa Ibla (RG) €€–€€€
Set in the historic centre, a
UNICEF World Heritage Site.
Creative, self-taught chef Ciccio
Sultano upholds tradition using
only good, local ingredients, which
he sources from small farms,
artisans, and fishermen. Excellent
tasting menu and wine list.
Hosteria del Vicolo, Sciacca (AG)
€€
Nino Bentivenga's *osteria* serves
a rich selection of traditional fare
with a creative twist. Excellent
calamari salad, fish-filled ravioli,
fish roulade, and more. Good wine
list and wines by the glass.

Leon D'Oro, Agrigento €–€€
Nice restaurant offering traditional
fare with excellent antipasti,
caponata di melanzane, pasta
with red mullet sauce, swordfish
with pachino tomatoes, and real
cassata. Good wine list.
Metrò, Catania €–€€
The Baroque façade of this
building opens onto cosy dining
rooms serving an excellent
selection of cheese and salami,
plus assorted fish and pasta, and
excellent desserts. Ample wine
list, with many wines by the glass.
Monte San Giuliano, Erice (TP) €€
Typical house in the historic centre
with several dining rooms and a
garden with a spectacular view.
Good cheese antipasti, fish
couscous, *pasta alle sarde* and
more. Excellent lemon *granita.*
Il Mulinazzo, Villafrati (PA)
€€–€€€
Excellent local fare prepared in a
creative style, including tuna in
all variations, wonderful seafood
risotto, exquisite main courses,
and delightful desserts. The tasting
menu is a good way of trying
several dishes in one sitting. Ample
cellar with world-class wines.

Index

Wine-growing areas and wines named after them are indexed together;
similarly grape varieties and varietal wines are indexed together.
The following abbreviations are used in the index: Coop. Cooperativa;
CS Cantina Sociale; K Keller, Kellereigenossenschaft; Prod. Produttori.
Page numbers in italic refer to maps.